D0075604

The Fiction of Relationship

ARNOLD WEINSTEIN

The Fiction of Relationship

ILLUSTRATIONS BY DAN REED

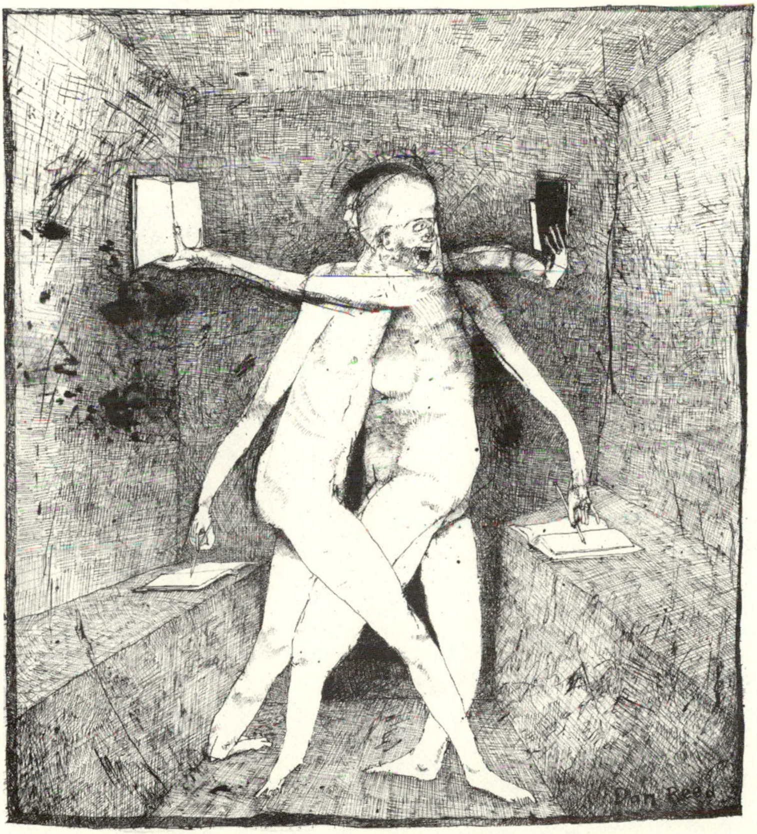

Princeton University Press · Princeton, New Jersey

Published by Princeton University Press,
41 William Street, Princeton, New Jersey 08540
In the United Kingdom:
Princeton University Press, Guildford, Surrey

This book has been composed in Linotron Galliard type

Clothbound editions of Princeton University Press books
are printed on acid-free paper, and binding materials are
chosen for strength and durability. Paperbacks, although satisfactory
for personal collections, are not usually suitable for library rebinding

Printed in the United States of America by Princeton University Press,
Princeton, New Jersey

Library of Congress Cataloging-in-Publication Data

Weinstein, Arnold.
The fiction of relationship / illustrations by Dan Reed.

p. cm.
Bibliography: p.
Includes index.
ISBN 0–691–06751–1

1. Fiction—History and criticism. 2. Interpersonal relations in
literature. 3. Self in literature. 4. Sex in literature.
I. Title.
PN3352.I56W45 1988
809.3′9355—dc19 88–5920
CIP

C O N T E N T S

PREFACE

All books are doubtless personal, and we now know that the distinctions between scientific and "private" writing are dubious at best, specious at worst. Language has its way with us, so that our most intimate, immediate disclosures fall into generic frames, while our most distanced, professional transactions are unwitting self-portraits. But a book on relationship is even more personal than most, and I am happy to situate this book, insofar as I can.

As someone who has spent his adult life teaching and writing on texts from different backgrounds, as a practicing comparatist, I have always been struck by the inherent scandal of *comparison*, of bringing disparate things together and assessing them. In no small way, this book constitutes a reflection on my career. Yet, that is the least of it. The central theme of this study is the linkage of people, the ways in which people live and die "connected," despite our notions of self or individual hegemony. Those linkages are at the fore of most of the books discussed here, and they essentially constitute the basic human patterns of life and culture: marriage, coupling, murder, manipulation, control, even war. We live in relation.

And what I know of this theme, as it informs the books I read and the way I combine them, comes from my relationships. We learn, as we go on living, to measure the extent of our involvement with others, the manifold ways in which one's life—both personal and professional—is really a composite form, reflecting countless influences and stimuli, ascribable ultimately to the culture(s) in which we live and the planet we inhabit. There is little doubt in my mind that this book and its author owe a debt of gratitude to Brown University, where I have been teaching since 1968; the freedom to experiment and the opportunity to teach according to one's heart as well as one's mind are privileges that I have come to take for granted, and I am happy to acknowledge them here. Let me also thank the Wesleyan Center for the Humanities, and Khachig Tölölyan in particular, for arranging, some years ago, for me to talk about the fiction of relationship; that was the start of my book. Albert Sonnenfeld and Mary

Ann Caws lent an early, encouraging ear to my pairing of Laclos and Burroughs, and that essay informs the "linking" spirit of my book. The "letter" of my book, certainly the "look" of my book, owes a very great deal to Dan Reed's remarkable drawings; his skill and his friendship are equally valuable to me.

Finally, even closer to home, there are people who have helped me to understand what relationship is, because their lives are bound up with mine, and I am pleased to acknowledge here the shaping influence of my family: my brother Philip, whose life is twinned with mine in more ways than one; my children, Catherine and Alexander, whose beauty and mystery have always moved me; and especially my wife, Ann, who knows what I do not know and whose life is interwoven with mine in ways beyond notation. To see the larger family is really what this study is about. Because the very writing of a book is a relentlessly private affair, because the profession comes so insidiously between our loved ones and us, I have wanted in this book to begin to even the score, to bring into some tandem the truths of my life and the texts that I read. I hope that those others whose lives I share will see themselves here.

On the more technical side, I would like to thank Ineke Van Dongen and Elke Freccia for their valuable assistance in preparing this manuscript for print. A word of thanks is also due to Robert Mueller for his help in proofreading and compiling the Index.

On a much less personal note, a word is in order concerning the use of foreign-language quotations in the body of this text. All material from French, German, Spanish, and Italian is given both in the original and in English. I have translated the French and German passages myself. I do not claim to be a Hispanist or an Italianist, and there I have relied on published translations for the English versions. Sophocles, Ibsen, and Strindberg have been cited from English translations, but there are occasional references to the Norwegian or Swedish in the notes. My reason for "thrusting" the foreign languages at my reader is simple: my book is about bringing disparate things together, and since the world is not "Englished," it seems worthwhile to make the different linguistic provenances of these materials *visible*, to allow my reader to see as much as possible that encounter of languages and cultures which comparative literature entails.

The Fiction of Relationship

INTRODUCTION

My title, *The Fiction of Relationship*, is something of a pun, and it is meant to express two fundamental notions: (1) the narrative literature of relationship, and (2) the view that relationship may be a fiction, something made rather than given, built out of belief, not fact. These two notions constitute both the ground and the horizon for the book that follows. Literature—essentially prose fiction, but also some dramatic texts—will be the material under study, but the larger thrust of my inquiry is about the mystery of relationship. To call my topic a mystery is to announce, straight out, that the ways in which the individual discovers and experiences linkage are anything but clear to most of us. To be coupled, to seek connection, to encounter kinship or even bondage, all are manifestations of relationship, and the range of issues embodied here is enormous: erotic, psychological, aesthetic, moral, even social and political.

This topic, so broad as to defy any single principles of inclusion or exclusion, has been strangely underutilized as a "rubric" or specific rationale for looking at literature and lining up texts, although writers and critics have forever been dealing with this issue. I want to acknowledge, at the outset, a general debt to Rougemont's pioneering study, *Love in the Western World*, and to indicate just how I part ways with him and with studies that have followed in his wake.[1] Rougemont is fundamentally concerned with the wellsprings of desire, and he makes a strong case for an entire occulted tradition of human connection that begins with the troubadours and continues into our day. My interests are less in the rationale of desire, or the secret reasons that draw people together, than in the bizarre spectacle of connection itself, the strange forms of linkage that are discernible in literature. Thus, René Girard's ground-breaking *Mensonge romantique et vérité romanesque* is working with issues very different from the ones I want to illuminate; Girard's theory of triangulated desire and his insistence on mediation at the heart of much narrative litera-

1. Denis de Rougemont, *Love in the Western World*, trans. Montgomery Belgion (New York: Pantheon, 1956).

ture have doubtless opened our eyes to the complex machinations at hand in Cervantes, Stendhal, Dostoevsky, and Proust, but he is largely unconcerned with the figural drama that engages me.[2] To put it simply, I am willing to trust my characters when they desire connection (whereas Girard wants to deconstruct the very notion of *le désir spontané*); my sights will be focused on the obstacles that prevent union, the transformations brought about by linkage, and all those couplings that are either unconsented or unsuspected. Another major study that must be mentioned is Tony Tanner's *Adultery in the Novel*; Tanner's book is appropriately subtitled *Contract and Transgression*, and it is a remarkable meditation on the psycho-social dynamics of adultery.[3] By dint of shrewd, often ingenious analyses of Rousseau, Goethe, and Flaubert, Tanner is able to sketch out a veritable dialectic between the play of desire and the weakening of those traditional codes that formerly governed the psychic, moral, and legal affairs of the bourgeoisie. "Pairing," in the sense that I want to examine it, as the connective career of the subject, does not interest Tanner, and whereas I am in his debt for "unpacking" some of the implications of adulterous desire, I do not feel that we are covering the same ground.

If there is a model I have emulated, it might be Leo Bersani's provocative essay on "coupling" in *Wuthering Heights* and *Les Chants de Maldoror*, which is found in his fine book, *A Future for Astyanax*; Bersani is drawn precisely to the spectacle of pairing, and his very rationale for juxtaposing Lautréamont's quasi-surrealistic procedures with those linking Catherine and Heathcliff is strategic in the same way I would like this book to be strategic: to oblige us to rethink the nature and limits of individuation, to rediscover the oddness and

2. René Girard, *Mensonge romantique et vérité romanesque* (Paris: Grasset, 1961). There is little doubt that Girard would consider my approach naive, especially insofar as it "trusts" the texts at hand to show us connections; as he points out, we are never willing to acknowledge the presence of the mediator: "Subjectivismes et objectivismes, romantismes et réalismes, individualismes et scientismes, idéalismes et positivismes s'opposent en apparence mais s'accordent secrètement pour dissimuler la présence du médiateur. Tous ces dogmes sont la traduction esthétique ou philosophique de visions du monde propres à la médiation interne. Ils relèvent tous, plus ou moins directement, de ce mensonge qu'est le désir spontané. Ils défendent tous une même illusion d'autonomie à laquelle l'homme moderne est passionément attaché" (p. 24).

3. Tony Tanner, *Adultery in the Novel: Contract and Transgression* (Baltimore: Johns Hopkins University Press, 1979).

scandal of coupling itself.[4] In this sense, adultery or even sexual congress are ultimately variations on a theme, and it is the theme that I wish to illuminate.

The search for linkage and pattern is as old as criticism itself, but what differentiates this study from others is its dual insistence that relationship is stranger than we realize and that there is common ground between the linking of people and the linking of texts. Like everyone who has ever written anything, I feel that these things need saying; given the centrality of my subject (relationship) in one's personal life, and given that I have spent many of my adult years linking texts, it follows that this is a personal study in more ways than one. The ensuing essays can be said to have common cause with Forster's brief, overworked dictum, "Only connect"; but whereas Forster exhorts us to connection, thereby implying that we are free to choose, I have come increasingly to the belief that we are connected in myriad ways beyond our immediate knowledge or control. Hence, my book deals with consented relations and also with those we did not know we were having. It will be seen that I go as far afield with this theme as I am able to, but I would like to feel that I am always tending to the central business at hand, shedding light on the fiction of relationship. And I can only hope that these pages demonstrate in variety, coloration, and extended argument just how central that impulse to connection is in human affairs and in the act of criticism.

To locate "relationship" at the heart of both literary criticism and human affairs is to acknowledge that the governing assumptions of this study are distinctly humanistic in nature. Literary texts will be analyzed, juxtaposed, combined, and recombined in the name of a belief that is embarrassingly simple: literature tells us how we live, puts on record and makes visible what we fail to hear or to see in our own lives. This belief will doubtless appear naive in today's critical culture, and there are many irrefutable reasons why literature should not be read as a guidebook to life. But all these reasons still seem "mind's reasons" to me, logically airtight but emotionally and experientially unsatisfying. The sustaining conviction of this book is that great literature performs a unique service for us, for it seems to have a scope and a depth to which we rarely attain in our own lives: its temporal sweep, its psychological probing, and its peculiar configurations expand, intensify, and challenge our sense of what life portends, and of the figure we ourselves are making.

4. Leo Bersani, *A Future for Astyanax* (Boston: Little, Brown, 1976).

We have heard a great deal in recent years about the deconstructionist claim that texts are far more open, unbounded, and indeterminate than traditional criticism has allowed. Redefining closed *works* as open *texts*, as porous and reflective of the binds and paradoxes that inform all culture, has led to a salutary reevaluation of literary statement. Arguably the most appealing feature of such criticism is its commitment to freedom, its principled suspicion of closure and unity. There is nothing deconstructionist in this book, as the reader has doubtless already surmised, but there is an equally radical commitment to a freer criticism, a coming to terms with art that opens it up rather than closes it down, a liberating rather than a legislating operation. What follows may seem "lawless" to some readers, especially those who insist on "legitimacy" as a basis for argument. I am not overly interested in defending or enshrining my practice, nor in laying down a new set of "comparatist" laws for valid interpretation. Such critical legalisms, it seems to me, have little to do with the appreciation and excitement of art, or with its wider reach and deeper pleasures, and they invariably centralize their own interpretive procedures, as if what most counted were the irrefutability of the critical method. We have, in my view, perhaps too much method and theory today, too much critical narcissism—although even to make this allegation is to be guilty of it—and this introduction is meant to be just that: a lead-in to the analyses that follow, not a critical manifesto.

The most obvious fictions that one would want to examine in a study of relationship would be novels of love and marriage, since much of their motive power derives from relationship (the desire for it, the results of it). It is equally the case, however, that narratives of human connection are imbued with a significant political dimension, in that high and low, powerful and disenfranchised find themselves linked in ways beyond their ken (one need merely think of Dickens here). Both sets of texts dwell insistently on the epistemological issues at hand, the process of coming to know how and why and if one is bound or free. One's sense of these matters (the sense of the protagonists and also the sense of the reader) depends, in large measure, on philosophical principles as much as on intellectual or moral acuity, or indeed empirical data. Such novels inevitably raise questions about the so-called sovereignty of the self, indeed about the very concept of an integral self that has its own contours and career. By focusing on "relationship," a view that must be pluralist even though it cannot be panoptic, we will get a special purchase on the crisis of individuation, and it will be seen that novels are peculiarly rich in lessons about hegemony and maneuvering room.

Another major issue that presses for consideration is the old bugbear, Time. There is doubtless an entire industry of critics who examine the issue of time in literature, particularly narrative literature, and such investigations often raise intriguing philosophical and metaphysical questions. My concern with time is much simpler: time is the medium of relationship, one of the basic units of measure for gauging human connectedness. Not only is relationship inherently a dynamic construct (as most of us learn over and over throughout our lives), but novels are especially geared to tell this kind of story (a story that invariably eludes our fragmentary grasp of things). Thus, in an unprogrammatic sort of way, this study aims at delivering a kind of anatomy of the novel form, or at least a sketch of its parameters and peculiar virtues. To analyze a broad spectrum of novels from the eighteenth century to the present in terms of how they depict relationship will ultimately tell us something intriguing about the development and resources of fiction, namely that narrative technique evolves in bizarre tandem with the relationship theme: epistolary fiction, point-of-view narrative, visceral realism, *style indirect libre*, encyclopaedic distancing, and Surrealist fantasy; all these modes of writing are also modes of seeing, and as such, they ineluctably disclose what can and what cannot go together, what alignments, allegiances, and traffic the protagonist is either able or unable to take in. But my study is not conceived as a compendium of narrative tactics, and it is meant still less to suggest the handbook or the taxonomy, since there is considerable fire and drama in my topic. Relationship has a centrality and an immediacy that few other themes can claim, and it is important to remember that it is not only an essential "subject" of literature, a given, but also very often it is the very "goal" of the text, a goal pursued by readers and protagonists alike. To learn who is connected, and how so, has given rise to (and fueled) plots from Sophocles to the present.

There will be much talk of freedom in this book, and also of field-pictures and composite forms. For the most part, these issues will be located in the texts themselves, where they belong, but it will be more than obvious that such concepts fully inform the strategy and writing of the criticism itself. Having written on seventeenth- and eighteenth-century fiction, and on the development of the modern novel from Dickens to the *nouveau roman*, I have tried, in my earlier books, to mesh historical thinking with comparatist strategies, aiming at a pan-European view of the novel tradition seen at its beginnings and in its modernist phase.[5] This book is rather different. It is a fully comparatist study in which I have tried to be true to the demands of my subject, and this has led me to lift books out of their cultural matrix, to accentuate commonality of theme or design in materials divided by language and history. But one can hardly "unlearn" history, and the novels at hand will be seen to carry a good bit of "luggage" with them, even if they are put into surprising company; yet it has seemed worthwhile to create my own critical scaffolding for the fiction of relationship, to do some linking and relating of my own, drawing (cavalierly, it may appear) on radically disparate materials to fashion an argument or continue a line of reasoning. The rationale for the groupings at hand is always spelled out, and I hope these arrangements of texts will not seem unprincipled or whimsically associative in character. Indeed, such practice should ultimately be seen as more faithful to history than first appears, since a number of the essays seek to make visible a development, a parabola, a waxing and waning of an idea or theme, that cannot be "captured" by our traditional categories. Hence, it is permissible (and, hopefully, fruitful) to move from Kafka to Melville and thence to Faulkner, from Defoe to Proust and Robbe-Grillet, from Laclos to Burroughs, because there are strange affiliations here, points on a compass that mark the lines of force I am seeking to chart.

If such a procedure constitutes a redefinition of comparative literature, so be it. In thinking and writing this book, I have been struck by the exciting congruence between my subject matter and the possible ways of illuminating it, for I have come to see criticism itself as a (disguised) version of the fiction of relationship. What is *comparison* if not linkage, juxtaposition, connection? To contrast or compare two things (books, ideas, people) is to devise a new conceptual shape; there is something heady and inebriating about that activity, and I suspect that it calls into play some fundamental intellectual energies. I have chosen to exercise that shaping freedom to the hilt in this book, partly because orthodox literary pairings would have dreadfully restricted my field of operation; more essentially, however, I wanted to test and display the issues at hand, to show that the comparison of books can mirror the way we move about reality, moving

5. Arnold Weinstein, *Vision and Response in Modern Fiction* (Ithaca: Cornell University Press, 1974) and *Fictions of the Self: 1550–1800* (Princeton: Princeton University Press, 1981).

from discrete fragments to connections and syntheses. The novelist, as James once said, is the man for whom nothing is lost, and he surely had in mind a man who made connections, who saw that fascinating bridges can be made (or imagined) between the seemingly disconnected stuff of experience. This is not to say that the "world" falls into place and behaves according to such ordering principles; on the contrary, connections are often most fascinating when they are most fictive, most imbued with a sense of their tentativeness. So it follows that the groupings of texts here are tentative, worth what they are worth, markings in a field that is limitless. Comparative criticism need not, in my judgment, be bound by documentable ties and bonds; on the contrary, it offers a rare opportunity for new constellations, for rethinking the canonical texts and stretching one's mind, for making new designs out of old fabric. It is not a question of iconoclasm for its own sake, so much as a fresh look, a willingness to abandon the established categories.[6] Relationship itself is a drawing out of the self, an extension of boundaries; I have tried to make that exploratory spirit central to this book, in every way that I responsibly could do so. Novels themselves, I am arguing, perform such functions for us: they illuminate the terrain we inhabit, and they make it seem a larger place than we had thought.

Such a procedure does not merely celebrate exploration for its own sake, although that is worth celebrating; but there is another reason as well for widening our sense of what fits together, and that has to do with the complacency of our existing categories and groupings. These structures serve all too often to deaden rather than to enliven the materials they frame, and it has seemed worthwhile to build new houses for the texts at hand, to imagine new fits, new relationships. Hence, the pairings of this study should surprise, should seem (at least on the face of it) outlandish or arbitrary, thereby forcing the reader to question what such materials might possibly have in common. To seek or discern commonality where one had not thought to locate it is not only the method but also the goal of this study, the outcome it would like to advance.

Routine, habit, and inertia operate everywhere, within texts and

6. The kind of "legislating" comparatist work I have in mind can be seen in Ulrich Weisstein's influential *Comparative Literature and Literary Theory* (Bloomington: Indiana University Press, 1973) or Robert J. Clements' *Comparative Literature as Academic Discipline* (New York: Modern Language Assocation of America, 1978).

within readers, narrowing the world into tidy, predictable categories, bathing the world in a soothing overlay of logic and propriety. All of the texts studied here have an explosive dimension, because they invariably wreck the protagonists' initial sense of how things fit, of where they themselves fit. There is the potential for great shock here, an awakening to a larger picture of causality and connection, a chastened sense that one is implicated where one thought oneself free. Consider, in this light, the following passage from Carlyle:

> One of Dr. Alison's Scotch facts struck us much. A poor Irish Widow, her husband having died in one of the Lanes of Edinburgh, went forth with her three children, bare of all resource, to solicit help from the Charitable Establishments of that City. At this Charitable Establishment and then at that she was refused; referred from one to the other, helped by none,—till she had exhausted them all; till her strength and heart failed her; she sank down in typhus fever, died, and infected her Lane with fever, so that 'seventeen other persons' died of fever there in consequence. The humane Physician asks thereupon, as with a heart too full for speaking, Would it not have been *economy* to help this poor Widow? She took typhus-fever, and killed seventeen of you!—Very curious. The forlorn Irish Widow applies to her fellow-creatures, as if saying, "Behold I am sinking, bare of help; ye must help me! I am your sister, bone of your bone; one God made us; ye must help me!" They answer, "No, impossible: thou art no sister of ours." But she proves her sisterhood; her typhus-fever kills *them*: they actually were her brothers, though denying it! Had man ever to go lower for a proof?[7]

The illumination that emerges from this passage stems from a drastic reconceiving of the world, a necessary restructuring of one's environment and the place one occupies in it. Relationship is a drawing out of the self, an incessant challenge to privatist enclosure. One is hard put to distinguish between the intellectual and the moral here, in that the self-made man, the independent individual, is as much an ethical as a philosophical or economic proposition. Typhus fever announces a reign of linkage that makes a mockery of individuation, just as the plague in Thebes and the rottenness in the state of Denmark betoken

7. Thomas Carlyle, "Typhus Fever in Edinburgh," quoted in the Norton edition of Dickens' *Bleak House*, eds. George Ford and Sylvère Monod (New York: Norton, 1977), p. 912.

a radically collectivist view of life. Carlyle is out to show just how confining, self-indulgent, and *wrong* the quotidian logic of the Edinburgh community is, that familiar logic of individual hegemony which says "this is me and that is you," not recognizing that the operative word of the phrase is "and." The broader family that Carlyle points to is emblematic of that larger constellation to be charted in these analyses. That charting process is one of opening up and moving out, of discerning kinship and connection in many arenas at once: between books that seemed to have nothing in common, between characters that seemed integral and free.

There can be no proper history for the fiction of relationship, and my chapters aim more for a local cogency than for some larger global design. I want, in these forays, to move horizontally, to indicate something of the richness and challenge that such a theme offers. My first chapter constitutes a kind of mini-history of the couple in fiction, ranging from the epoch-making *Manon Lescaut* and *Werther* on to modernist texts of Virginia Woolf and Boris Vian. In this essay, a number of concerns are played off against each other: the development of point-of-view narrative, the authority given to subjective desire, the huge areas of darkness and blindness that accompany such a narrational stance, the challenge of depicting reciprocity or mutuality through fictional means, the idealist tradition and the rise of the novel. In particular, this discussion lays out some of the generic constants of relationship fictions: the single perspective, the curve of time, the inner/outer dialectic, the challenge posed by the couple. From the outset, we see the peculiar role that the novel is called on to play: to record the hunger of the self for union, and at the same time to illuminate the spectacular subversion which is at work, since the greatest single impediment to mutuality is precisely the hungry self. As point-of-view narrative begins to develop, as the novelist discovers common cause with the yearnings and inside picture of the protagonist, the story of relationship becomes one of frustration, of crossed purposes, of incomprehension, of incompatibility. I move from the paradigmatic erotic quests of Prévost and Goethe to Flaubert's seminal "crossroads" text, *Madame Bovary*, and then on into the modernist, stereophonic renditions of the theme in Ford's *The Good Soldier*, with final stopping points at Woolf and Vian. Other candidates for this chapter are, of course, possible, and the reader might well consider the epistolary tradition in this light, or indeed an entire host of psychological novelists such as Austen (whose marriage scenarios depend precisely on overcoming the dynamic in question) or James (who invented the fullest arsenal of techniques to carry out his subjective mission) or, ultimately, Proust (who carries the idealist banner to its most ecstatic collison with the opacity of the other).

My second chapter focuses more on the unseen, and I call it "Memory and Multiplicity." In the modern world human relationships, especially those formalized, long-duration ones we call marriage, end up being notoriously precarious and mobile; the threat I am alluding to is not primarily that of incompatibility as such, but rather the pervasive and shaping role of time. The self changes over time, and this personal evolution makes of human relationship an almost impossible balancing act. This kaleidoscopic view of the self is not easy to render in fiction, but it is possible to compare a group of novelists—themselves widely separated in time and space—who are especially concerned with the multiplicity of the self, the many people that one is and was over a lifetime, and the ensuing, inevitable jolts that multiplicity poses for binding relationships. One might argue that the novel form itself emerges here as a privileged record or custodian of one's inner states, one's inner metamorphoses that are inevitably hidden to the outside world. In these texts the novel assumes as its mission the depiction of the inner life, and there is much old-fashioned drama in the fact that such an agenda is (thankfully? tragically?) invisible. But, then, what is the status of that which cannot be seen? Is the shape of one's life something one puts together with mirrors and glue, or is it the spiritual configuration that is truer than the banal data of one's so-called résumé (a disquieting term, if ever there was one)? Is literature crucial to the enterprise of making this shape known? By spreading our critical nets wide enough, by beginning with the "birth" of such fiction in Defoe, then examining its fullest apotheosis in Proust, and finally querying its odd reappearance as mirage and con game in Robbe-Grillet, we will be able to raise some central questions about the ultimate status (verbal and psychic) of this "inner realm."

My third chapter is devoted to a contrastive study of two extremist texts, Laclos' *Liaisons dangereuses* and Burroughs' *Naked Lunch.* It is here that those aforementioned principles of comparatism are given fullest play, since no sane person (that I know of) has seen fit to compare these two works. We must move beyond traditional categories and psychology in these works, if we are to understand their joint views of the self as object of desire and manipulation, as body-machine that can be programmed and controlled by the other. There is also an ethos of cruelty here, a radical form of scientism that presents the erotic plot (the control of another's body) in terms of a behavioralist experiment. This view of human connection, crude though it is, makes exploitation the single aim of relationship, and it contrasts sharply with the love-fictions studied up to now. Laclos and Burroughs have much to tell us about the dynamics of bonding, about the ferocity of human hunger and the kinds of exposure and violation that the relationship text courts. Finally, these texts image, on the one hand, the drama of the closed versus the open self, with the attendant notion of a hidden core of identity that must be protected, and on the other hand, the countless ways in which the self is opened, penetrated, invaded, taken over. Underneath the flowery eighteenth-century rhetoric of Laclos' seduction novel, one sees a rawer spectacle of sadistic control, and from here it is possible to move to Burroughs' junkie scene, where the self is everywhere invaded, raped, or pillaged, whether it be sexually, chemically, or ideologically. In *Naked Lunch* "relationship" is a euphemistic Old World concept for the "algebra of need" that underlies and underwrites the body's dealings with others; here, the elitist pairings that ordinarily frame the erotic career are dazzlingly exploded and democratized: connection and coupling are everywhere in this viral world, showing the self to be enmeshed in an endless morass of signs, chemicals, limbs, and impulses. Burroughs' book is dealt with roughly in the middle of this study, and it is intended to be an extreme promontory for the ventures at hand, a brutal, dreadfully egalitarian text that attacks the privileges of the aristocratic individual as sharply as the events of 1789 to which Laclos' novel pointed.

The perils of connection need not be as bestial as those imaged in Laclos and Burroughs, but they will always be dangerous, nonetheless. Whether it be physical or emotional, linkage can kill. My fourth chapter deals with a form of relationship that can be loosely termed "metamorphic." Here we will be examining texts that uncover unsuspected bonds between improbable, often radically disparate individuals, often "coupling" them in grisly ways. The discovery of this link, at its most extreme limit, is utterly traumatic because it entails no less than enactment, *becoming* the other. The traditional motif of the double, such as one sees it in Dostoevsky or Conrad, underlies these fictions, but the works to be analyzed here are more drastic in their insistence on kinship, their annihilation of the myth of integrity or independence or closed selfhood. Kafka's "In der Strafkolonie" will be viewed as an exemplary tale, as its initial emphasis on crime and punishment yields to its even darker truths of displacement and transformation: in the end, the officer *becomes* the prisoner, and that fundamental metamorphic act is mirrored in the other extremist texts, to be compared with Kafka's: Melville's "Benito Cereno" and selected Faulkner texts. All of these fictions are about fraternal relations of a spiritual order which are socially unavowable, and it will be seen that these composite materials deal essentially with power and vision, the refusal to regard the other as human; ultimately, each of them centralizes linkage and relationship as the primary political act of comprehension. In a more indirect fashion, this chapter seeks to illuminate one of the major, unacknowledged purposes of fiction, namely the "altering" and coercing of the reader through the agency of the text. Although this entire study is grounded on the notion that reader involvement and empathy are good for the soul, these novels give us pause, in their relentless exposure of the cost involved with "merging," with an empathetic connection between self and other. Kafka's Machine has to be a writing machine, because it is through language and narration that the writer wields his power, enters into the neural circuits and blood streams of his readers. Such an entry can be graced with value, as these stories tell us, if it remains virtual, "merely" imaginative and cerebral. But, where does "merely" stop? At what point does the imaginative experience of the other begin to erode our own lines of identity? Kafka, Melville, and Faulkner, different though they are, have been obsessively drawn to this issue, and the darkness of their texts, the ominous and stark lines of their plots, the disturbing connections they draw between the writer's essential project (to draw you in), and the tragedies they narrate (to be drawn in) shed a disconcerting light on the relational power of literature itself and the vampirish nature of writing.

If the fiction of relationship carries out its goal of challenging all views of individual hegemony, it is by no means clear whether one is to be grateful for the favor. What does the discovery of that larger picture bring in its wake? The fifth chapter of this study, "Heaven and Hell," seeks to chart two extremist positions—the angelic and the infernal—as modes of assessing the relational scheme. There can be little doubt that all the fictions studied here *enlarge* the picture we have of our most intimate circumstances, in that they shed light on linkages we did not know we had. The "heavenly" mode is fundamentally celebratory: it finds these expanded parameters to be a challenging new home for the self, and although the shrinkage in private authority is the inevitable price paid for such aggrandizement, it is a price worth paying, because the larger realm promises rare harmonies and beauties, transforms one's murky brief life into a luminous part of something longer and larger than individual experience. The work of Borges seems exemplary for this angelic enterprise, and his short stories provide perhaps the cleanest, most elegant tribute literature can offer to relationship as something noble and grand. But there is another way of looking at these matters, and the widening stage and more intense light of relationship may betoken a radical threat to the self, who discovers the extent of his or her connectedness. This reappraisal of one's position can be properly infernal, if the contacts with others become "turned on" and vitalized, resulting, ultimately, in a kind of energized labyrinth, a world with flowing power and charged circuits whose mission is to inform the self—through pain—of its "fit" with others.[8] The work of Strindberg will be counterpointed with that of Borges, as an instance of this infernal mode, and also as an extreme view of relationship as torture. The plays will be briefly investigated along these lines, but the Strindbergian *pièce de résistance* will be his compelling—and largely unknown—novel, *Inferno*, a very special account of encroachment and invasion.

These five chapters have, with varying emphases, been in the service of a widening vision, a larger kind of ecosystem that would better display the involvement, often the entrapment, of the self within frames and nets it had not suspected. The novel form has been credited with special powers of illumination, and it is fair to say that the basic movement of these texts is one of increasing revelation and exposure. Not much irony or attitudinal maneuvering room has been managed in these novels, and the final emerging paradigms of linkage would seem to have the austere propriety of fate itself. There is a peculiar, haunting power embedded in such a revelatory poetics, and this quasi-apocalyptic vein has been with us since the Greeks and Hebrews; what moral or philosophical prestige literature has enjoyed over the centuries is doubtless to be ascribed, at least in part, to such a "curtain-raising" posture, a mix of entertainment and edification by which the reader comes to understand the laws of his world. To learn

8. In defining the operation of the modernist text that gratifies its reader, Roland Barthes has sketched the dynamic between *écriture* and character: "le texte se fait, se travaille à travers un entrelais perpétuel; perdu dans ce tissu—cette texture—le sujet s'y défait, telle une araignée qui se dissoudrait elle-même dans les sécrétions constructives de sa toile" (*Le Plaisir du texte* [Paris: Seuil, 1973], p. 101). This writerly encroachment on the subject may give pleasure to the reader, but it may be experienced as pure undoing by the subject itself.

to see connection—at the heart of most of the fictions studied here, and emblematic of analytic criticism itself—would seem to be one of the oldest missions of art. And the *fact* of connection is hardly more important than the *discovery* of connection: Sophocles' *Oedipus the King* stands as the archetypal example of a text that foregrounds the revelatory process itself, the drama inherent in man's progressive discovery of linkage where he thought himself free. Sophocles' formula includes all the elements that are to become staple items in modern literature: the quest for identity, the hidden crime, the sleuthing posture, the critique of knowledge and control, the emergence of a field-picture, of a damning pattern at the expense of individual autonomy. The Sophoclean scenario reaches its heyday in the work of truth-seekers such as Dickens, Ibsen, and James, all three intrigued with the cover-ups imposed by polite society, all three aware of the increasingly heavy price paid for knowledge and exposure. Modes change, but Strethers' apprehension of the true relationship between Chad and Mme. de Vionnet is a direct descendant of Oedipus' shattering discovery of his own kinships. Likewise, when Ibsen's Gregers Werle insists on illuminating the true ties that underlie the Ekdal family situation, he is ethically in line with an entire truth-seeking tradition. There is a Western imperative to *see*, and its frequent corollary is that we then can see into the true nature of things, the true, hitherto hidden structure of things, the underpinnings of Reality itself. Relationship, in such a scheme, is no less than the nature or arrangement of knowledge, the pattern we seek; we scrutinize and quest, so that we may discern the disposition of things, the operative connections between them, between them and us.

And, yet, other responses are both possible and real. Although it is rare, art sometimes shows us a willed evasiveness, a principled refusal of revelation. Art's entire educational agenda is challenged in this kind of work, and usually the challenge comes in the name of other values, notably happiness or survival. Little is more instructive, in this regard, than the behavior of Leopold Bloom in *Ulysses*, who is the premier literary representative of sidestepping-in-order-to-live. Relationship looms large for Bloom, and it noises home truths he would like to keep at a distance: his wife and Boylan, his dead father and his dead son. Bloom is certainly not the first character in fiction to prefer ignorance to knowledge, but he has developed a systematic ducking technique that puts him in a class by himself. His antics are particularly noticeable, of course, because Joyce has placed him in a fiction that works largely like a minefield, tripping him up at every turn. A comparison with Homer indicates how far we have come: from the bound but seeing Odysseus at the mast to the artful dodging of Bloom.

Humane (or cowardly, as the case may be) reasons are not the only ones for evading or rejecting Revelation in literature. There is also a kind of modern writer who decides that it is far more interesting to *make* truths rather than simply *revealing* them. Such a writer has no interest in being a sage or a remove-the-veil philosopher, but prefers, instead, to reinvent the world out of whole cloth. In these precincts, the search for Relationship is turned quite on its head, since the writer is now free to flaunt his own form-making powers, to pair and couple and bond, as he wishes. This kind of art is resolutely formal, in that it insistently posits its own kinships and linkages, knowing them to be fictitious and metaphoric, knowing them to be man-made, devised rather than decreed. No longer revelatory of some a priori Law or Pattern, art becomes overtly generative, even capricious. Causality becomes a meaningless term in this scheme of things, as the authoring mind spawns its own histories and harmonies at will. In the most radical examples of such art, Robbe-Grillet's X can actually create "last year" in *Marienbad*, much the way Borges allows Kafka to create, "pastward," his precursors, or indeed takes the peculiar liberty of creating his own footnotes and the fateful-but-invented harmonies of his work. There is frequently a ludic dimension to this kind of literature, for it celebrates its own form-giving powers; one might choose to view such texts as entirely self-reflexive, a form of writerly navel-gazing, an exercise with little or no referential or explanatory claims.[9] Even Proust's Elstir seems to revel in his own aesthetic prowess, his capacity to recombine the elements that nature presents to him, whether it be people or landscapes. In Joyce, one encounters something akin to a morphological fantasia, resulting in arrangements that can give us Blephen and Stoom. The writerly freedoms expressed in this kind of work remind us that literature need never be the lackey to philosophy or even to "truth." Notions such as causality and discovery become quaintly obsolete in a literature that invents its laws and itself as it goes, and it would seem to follow that the search for relationship via literature would thereby go out of business.

9. Barthes has located the essence of "textual pleasure" in this spectacle of "liberated" writing: "Le plaisir du texte, c'est ça: la valeur passée au rang somptueux de signifiant" (*Le Plaisir*, p. 103).

Yet, it is precisely in such generative art that the *fiction* of relationship acquires its deepest resonance. To see connections being visibly "forged" by the writer, breezily tossed off at will, leads only initially to a label of "art for art's sake"; the more one ponders this kind of insolent formalism, the more referential it all begins to look. We are made to consider the possibility of a world without causality, a world with rhyme indeed but no reason. To be people for whom nothing is lost, we need to see that these figural works catch us in their mirrors, show us also to be the inhabitants of "design." Such literature—again, Borges comes to mind, and one might enlist Joyce or Nabokov as well—can also be intensely moving, as we realize just how easy it is for one person's design to be another's experience, perhaps another's death. Much of the *nouveau roman* can be seen in this perspective, as a kind of interplay between the proprieties of language and of self; perhaps the handsomest, most seductive embodiment of these principles is to be found in the work of Italo Calvino. Hence, a final chapter devoted to these changing modalities of connection and design will offer something of a more speculative nature to follow the urgencies and ultimacies delineated in the first five chapters.

The working distinction between relationships that are discovered and those that are made also applies, as has been suggested, to critical practice as well, especially for the comparative critic who is at something of a crossroads here. Traditional influence study traces "operative" connections between artists, and whether one moves into its more cubist form of *Rezeptionsästhetik* or the more speculative, Freudian work of Bloom and his followers, one is always seeking to gauge impact and causality. But, it hardly seems necessary to state, comparative criticism can also *make* connections, by means of parallels, analogies, contrasts, and juxtapositions that are openly given as fiction rather than history. What authorizes this study and this method is the belief that art has a certain timelessness, that we may learn more, learn to see more, by daring to take writing out of its immediate history and inscribing it into a freer context, ideally a context of other art. The comparatist is likely to have common cause with this spatial view, not because he rejects history but because he seeks the larger arena where the critical act becomes most intense and most rewarding precisely when it is free to propose its own form. "Form," like "relationship," is really of the essence here, "form" as something lived, something encompassing at once the play of the mind and the career of the subject. The discovery of form and the making of form, the discovery and the making of relationship, are among the most intense and rewarding human activities, and there is no reason why *criticism* should not be defined in these terms. Hopefully, the following essays will demonstrate both the value and the pleasures of such an approach.

CHAPTER ONE

The Fiction of Relationship

"The fiction of relationship" is, as may be suspected, a loaded term, a double entendre that signifies at once the narrative literature of relationship and also the notion that relationship itself may be a fiction. On the one hand, there is no doubt about it, we do have a body of literature that deals with the couple; at the same time, the most memorable of these texts are invariably problematic at the core, issuing from a conflicted attitude toward relationship itself: is it possible? Equally crucial: is it narratable? How can the theme of human connection be rendered in literary texts? More basically still, do novels have something to show us in this area that we are unequipped to see on our own, not so much because of the author's wisdom, but precisely because of the virtues of his medium, the peculiar aptness of fiction to shed light on the enterprise of coupling. This light is, at its most luminous, directed both within and without, illuminating the need for union but also rendering the composite form of the couple, the figure they make. Who can see as much in real experience? In looking at several paradigmatic and a few lesser known novels of relationship—notably two eighteenth-century texts, Prévost's *Manon Lescaut* and Goethe's *Werther*; Flaubert's *Madame Bovary*; and three twentieth-century fictions of marriage, Ford's *The Good Soldier*, Woolf's *To the Lighthouse*, and Boris Vian's *L'Ecume des jours*—I would like to sketch a kind of generic history of incompatibility. It is a rich incompatibility, located sometimes between lovers, other times between the couple and their world; and finally it is to be seen, fruitfully and provocatively, in the narrative apparatus itself, the field where the text lives, a field that is both charted and mined. To be sure, my deck is stacked, and it is also very small, but I would hope that the particular discussion will buttress a larger argument about relationship and the novel tradition as we know it.

A few clarifications are in order. First, one must distinguish relationship from the more violent phenomenon of passion. In his classic study on love in the Western world, Rougemont elaborately makes the case that passion is a derived form of mysticism, that it is death-oriented, that it neither knows nor wants gratification. Relationship would seem to be the other side of things, and I would want to argue that it is profoundly life-oriented, that it, like all living phenomena, encounters death, but as nemesis, not as secret ecstasy. Relationships exist in time, they are made of time, and the pathos of much literature devoted to them has to do with the effects of time: either the cessation of love or, more poignantly still, the cessation of life. Passion may easily be construed as an individual feeling, and here too we reach the crux of relationship: it is insistently mutual, connective. The word itself suggests linkage, and this goes far in explaining why lyric poetry is a fitting locus for passion, but fiction (and, indeed, drama) is the more natural literary home for relationship. The novel has the kind of reach that is needed if relationship is to be "caught" within the artist's net: it has the requisite temporal span for depicting the curve of lives intertwined; it also does justice to that gritty societal world which may make things hard for lovers; finally, it is peculiarly suited to handle those central issues of mutuality and reciprocity, perhaps even more suited than theater, because it can at once accommodate the subjective view and still render the alterity and density of the loved one. This last dialectic is the Ariadne's thread of the argument that is to follow, because it encompasses the central tension at hand: the play between individual vision/desire and the opaqueness of the other. The rise of the novel, usually accounted for along sociological lines, is inseparably linked to this dialectic: from the eighteenth century on, fiction begins to focus more and more intensely on the inside picture, giving birth to what becomes point-of-view narrative and expressing the nature of human feeling and subjectivity with unprecedented immediacy and importance. Yet, the novel form is inherently environmental (even when it seems in the service of a despotic single vision), and it ineluctably "situates" its own speaker, delivering a world that contains that speaker, always acknowledging a reality scheme beyond that of desire. And, as if this were not enough in terms of checks and balances, the novel form also teaches us that subjectivity and blindness go hand in hand, that the single vision is every bit as cyclopic as it is delicious. We know, of course, that writers such as Ford and James exploited this dialectic for all it was worth, but so too did the earlier novelists of relationship. How could they not?

The novel is, then, especially formed for giving us the many optics we need to understand relationship. What I have called variously dialectic, tension and play, the tandem of subjective appetite and epistemological uncertainty, has a distinctly formal, generic appeal to the novelist; his is the medium in which it can be truly played out. But, we can hardly fail to observe that this dialectic between desire and knowledge is part and parcel of the motive force of love itself. Not only could it be taken as a working definition of jealousy (the loved one as unknowable), but it seems to be at the very pulse of human affection: the desire for union, for the lover to be bonded to the loved one. And the obstacles which are so congenial to the novelist (blindness, distortion, etc.) are the very real obstacles that people who love face throughout their lives.

"Throughout their lives" brings us back to the notion of time, and it allows for a final clarification of terms, this one perhaps more editorial than the others. To maintain a relationship over time (formerly known as the concept of marriage) entails energies other than passion, and indeed poses problems that are unknown to passion. The energies in question have to do with fidelity, evolving feelings, and the like; the problems involved concern the peculiar assertiveness, the quasi-insolence of imposing a human form, of stopping the entropic work of time, of making something stick. Coming together is possible for anyone; staying together is a challenge to all parties involved (the principals, perhaps the gods), for it is an act of volition, the foisting of a human-made pattern onto the heterogeneous randomness of the species. Relationship is an assertion, a construct; using this language, we are not far, as is tolerably obvious, from the view of relationship as a work of art, as a fiction: created by two people, it has a shape and may confer a meaning to the flux and atomization of individual experience. All these natural enemies—entropy, time, flux, fragmentation, change, death—make relationship a precarious affair, one easy to experience but hard to *see*, about which the novel has something to teach us.

To teach us these things, the novels in question must be examined in ways that are at once formal and substantive. Individuation is given, and connection is desired. That operation may bear many names and come in many colorations and hues, ranging from friendship to familial love to sexual desire; whatever the affective label is, the project itself entails an opening, an extension of the individual. This special dynamic and the meanings invested in it are at the heart of my inquiry, and it will soon enough be clear that my key notions—relationship, self, other—must be understood as both formal and thematic. Sartre once observed, with regard to Faulkner, that every aesthetic implies a metaphysic; in like manner, I want to insist that the authorial choices made in these fictions—point-of-view narrative, first-person lyricism, *style indirect libre*, delayed disclosures, stream of consciousness, surreal environment, even word play—both form and inform the story of relationship. Each text that I study was felt, in its time, to have broken new ground, to have created new voices and new ways of seeing; each novel, likewise, seems to be imbued with an urgency, a desire at once to take the measure of the self and to wed it to another. There is ultimately a situational drama at work here: individuals yearn to be completed by something or someone outside their precincts; once the linkage is made, the inner dynamics of the couple and the outer dynamics of the environment must be contended with. With this perhaps overly formulaic and schematic definition in mind, one can begin to look at some of the novels themselves.

1

There is no real starting point for love literature, although the troubadour lyrics and courtly romances of the medieval period certainly go a long way toward establishing its prominence. As for narrative proper, however, with its possibilities of temporal span and multiple point of view, we may properly turn to the eighteenth century, and we can begin to witness the fiction of relationship. This Age of Sensibility, moreover, was witness to a new concert of voices and needs; its literature—especially in Europe—centralizes and comes close to legitimizing human qualities that had been largely regarded as aberrant or peripheral in the past: desire, yearning, the affective in all its guises. In 1731 the Abbé Prévost published a novel whose full title is *Histoire du Chevalier Des Grieux et de Manon Lescaut*, a distinctly and tragically connective title. Prévost's novel describes, from the perspective of the lover, a young man's desperate efforts to hold onto his mistress. The woman, Manon Lescaut, is seen almost exclusively through the eyes of Des Grieux, and she is, therefore, in all senses, an object: an object of his gaze, his appetite, and an object on the Parisian market whose favors men can buy. Manon is a courtesan, or, as Montesquieu disdainfully put it, *une catin*, a trollop. The novel depicts a rampantly hypocritical setting, a vicious world that mouths old values but is up to its neck in exchange and barter. Des Grieux commits the grievous sin of loving Manon, wanting to marry her; whereas his father is perfectly prepared to buy him women, he finds marriage with such a creature unthinkable. Hence, the young aristocrat is on his own, without funds, wanting only to live with Manon.

She, however, needs money, and the plot is little more than a series of *coups de théâtre*, where Des Grieux loses the money he has either stolen or conned his friend out of, and thereby loses Manon in the bargain, for whom a wealthy suitor is always within reach.

Prévost's book, although outfitted with a proper preface that points to some kind of moral lesson in Des Grieux's tempestuous career, is nonetheless a splendidly subversive story. The young man is, to be sure, tarnished, even to the extent of becoming a cheat and a murderer, but he alone celebrates the power and the value of feeling. The first-person narration weds us to Des Grieux, grants immediacy and lushness to his affective wants, and nothing in the book remotely measures up against his new code; against everyone, he proclaims the authority of love, the nobility of love. But, these tidings are not only unheeded, they are, like those spoken by other love disciples, regarded as dangerous. The book is fueled by the most elemental plot imaginable, a bare-bones paradigm of relationship itself: will they stay together? can he keep her? Being with Manon is the goal of his life, and all social values are discarded in the process. But this society does not want this relationship, and the conflict is relentless. The older institutions of home and church function flagrantly as symbolic prisons where Des Grieux is confined; beyond that, he and Manon are whisked off to literal prisons more than once. The regularity and insistency of this kind of societal intervention begins to look like some kind of higher decree, one perhaps more metaphysical than social, a ban on connection, a green light for dalliance but an absolute denial of permanent cohabiting.

When one looks a bit more closely, one sees that the injunction to separate the lovers is writ small as well as large, written into the flesh as well as enforced by agents of authority. The pleasure-loving Manon is drawn to Des Grieux for many reasons, but one of them is indisputably sexual; he coyly informs us that she has informed him the he is "le seul qui pût lui faire goûter parfaitement les douceurs de l'amour" (the only one who could make her perfectly savor the pleasures of love).[1] Here is, of course, the region where the young man will be struck down. Three times, Prévost treats us to a replay of a thinly veiled coitus interruptus scene, and at each juncture, the young man is hauled out of bed by armed policemen. He is deprived, first,

1. Abbé Prévost, *Manon Lescaut* (Paris: Garnier Frères, 1965), p. 61. Subsequent quotations will be taken from this edition and noted parenthetically in the body of the text.

of his knife; secondly, he speaks of a blade suspended over their heads; and last of all, he jumps for his sword, which is portentously caught up in his belt. Even Des Grieux can tally it up: "Un homme en chemise est sans résistance" (A man in a nightshirt is without resistance [152]). *Manon Lescaut* is a diabolically cogent novel, and its subtext is clearly one of emasculation and castration, the final forms of action that society can take against the couple. The book is shot through with resonant sexual images: Des Grieux has to give Manon his pants for one of the escapes; he runs through Paris with loaded and unloaded guns, this too in the service of his mistress; he is able to open her cell door only by means of a key that is "effroyablement grande" (102); the appropriate culminating image for this history of sexual menace occurs when the young man tries to use his sword to dig a hole to bury Manon, and he breaks it. Without saying anything openly, perhaps without even knowing what he is saying, Prévost is showing us something of the scandal of coupling, and he is brilliantly bringing the lesson home, to the genitals, making it abundantly clear that the sensual education experienced by the young aristocrat carries in its wake something close to a sexual dismantling.

But, social and even sexual threats are not the only ones. The society most critical in a fiction of relationship is that smaller society of two, that Other, the genuine New World that Des Grieux has discovered but cannot colonize. For most of the book, the most perplexing enemy of relationship would appear to be Manon herself. Each time there is a shortage of cash, off she goes. Yet, she insists, honestly it would seem, that she never stops loving him. Relationship, she says in a memorable passage, is a spiritual, not a physical affair, "la fidélité du cœur"; the connectedness that counts is less that of the body than of the heart. Des Grieux, love apostle though he is, cannot quite manage this sublimated doctrine, and consequently a great deal of the novel shows us the two lovers confused and hurt, each baffled by the principles of the other. It is important, I think, to grant each of these positions a measure of sincerity, and one might even go much further and sketch out an ideological binary system with Des Grieux at the aristocratic, idealist end, and Manon at the materialist end, with her famous quip, "crois-tu qu'on puisse être bien tendre lorsqu'on manque de pain" (do you think one can be really tender when one is short of food [69]). For our purposes, what counts is to grasp the optical system of the novel form, to see how Prévost has presented the blindness theme most perfectly by having the blind man speak. Des Grieux never even comes close to an understanding of his mistress or his culture, and one might add that he is more than a little slack in matters of self-honesty: after all, he is a cheat, a pander, and a murderer, but the reader has to *see* it, since the young man never falters in his impeccable self-esteem. It is well known that Auerbach could not stomach so much self-deception, but it would seem that he missed the fun, the special fun that novels offer. *Manon Lescaut* is stereophonic even though Manon hardly speaks; the reader cannot avoid contrasting Des Grieux's intensely rhetorical, inflated love language with the nuts-and-bolts pragmatism of Manon. The grand imperative of the book is that of union, sexual union, maintainable sexual union over time, outfitted of course with the requisite high-flown moral sentiments. This may not be everyone's notion of relationship, but it is for real, and it commands considerable authority and pathos in Prévost's hands. What is so fine about the novel is its uncanny strategy of separation, a strategy that finds all means good, ranging from the political to the sexual to the more banal one of incomprehension. We are witnessing the algebra of relationship, and we are seeing the remarkable resources afforded by the novel form.

At its close, the novel comes dazzlingly close to resolving its dilemmas. The couple is expulsed from France, and the reader senses that this is right, that relationship needs the New World if it is to flourish. Inwardly, the changes are even more momentous: Manon becomes disciplined and orderly; Prévost even uses the word "réglé" to describe the conduct of this once wanton woman. Along with this change of habits is a perceptual change of real magnitude: Manon learns to *see*, to see Des Grieux, to think in terms of "we" instead of "I." She it is who suggests that they run away from the corrupt New Orleans, a flight that will lead to her death. Prévost has unmistakably "altered" Manon in New Orleans, only one is tempted to view it much the way one "alters" dogs or cats. The two lovers finally experience unity, a true entente, but one must ask : why is it so unconvincing? why so brief? why so doomed? One possible answer might be that there is a narrative penalty to pay, that to put Manon and Des Grieux on the same wavelength is to destroy as well as to resolve his story. There is doubtless much edification in the mutuality and reciprocity that are achieved at the novel's close. But this breakthrough, this triumph of relationship is singularly undramatic, almost uninteresting, and it brings me to my final point on *Manon Lescaut*: we still read this book today because it grants such power and authority to the hunger and wants of its troubled protagonist. The novelty of this book is inseparable from the consciousness of Des Grieux; his needs rule everywhere, not merely over his conduct, but over the narrative choices made by the author. The high drama of the novel is the double one of separation and blindness, of intervention and longing; perhaps the greatness of the book, for I think it is a great book, lies in its symbolic wars, its dim recognition that mature love means a brooking of appetite and doubling of vision, whereas the novel of feeling, as we are now beginning to see, may be narcissist and cyclopic at the core.

2

Goethe's relationship-seeking hero, Werther, whose sorrows became famous throughout eighteenth-century Europe, appears to be even more of a narcissist, more neurotic and checked by inner stresses than Des Grieux. Many find Werther hard to take seriously today. Yet, Napoleon insisted on meeting Goethe in person, on the strength of this novel. And, for the contemporaries, it was strong medicine indeed, producing a Werther craze, including even some real suicides committed in blue frock coat and yellow vest. Critics, beginning with the older Goethe himself, have not been kind to Werther, and he has become, for many, synonymous with the diseases of romanticism: cult of feeling, fascination with death, passion-sickness, lack of restraint and reason, yearning for the infinite, social double-talk. One recalls Goethe's own famous *mot*: "das romantische ist das kranke" (the romantic is the sick). Yet, there is something undeniably grand about this book, a fabulous sense of human promise, of the self taking measure of Nature's grandeur and of its own inner space as well. Werther is a character filled with both wonder and humility as he confronts people and things. The magnificent natural descriptions in the book express the same reverence and hunger for the Godhead, the same desire for union and fulfillment that Werther will transfer to Lotte under the name of human love.

The novel charts a grim education, one that is appropriately natural and social: the young man is increasingly aware of the brute unfair power of Nature, its random force, *its* endless cycle of growth, destruction, and future growth; Werther's awed sense of the potential power and the inevitable transiency of human life accounts for his uncompromising affective demands, demands that are everywhere thwarted by the *kleinbürger* mentality that surrounds him. More than Des Grieux, Werther is richly depicted as a person who loves. The same can hardly be said for Des Grieux, who comes across, despite his disclaimers, as cold and conniving toward most of the people that come his way. The pages Goethe devotes to Werther's courtship of Lotte have cloyed a good bit over the years, but Werther's capacity for connection, his championing of connection, extends far beyond Lotte herself. Hence, we see Werther befriending and empathizing with people at every end of the social spectrum: peasants and aristocrats, murderers and madmen. The book opens with his haunting memory of a dying first love, and his fervor as love apostle is directly nourished by his awareness of human solitude and fragility, of the ultimate precariousness and helplessness of the individual. Werther might be taken, in some odd way, as a sentimentalized version of Fielding's Parson Adams, a man who wanders through the societal desert, ready to love those he meets, encountering corruption or callousness wherever he goes. Adams is, to be sure, a comic vehicle, and there is no hint of farce in Goethe; instead, Werther runs into the primness and off-putting decorum of well-behaved Enlightenment society. Here, the comparison might shift from Parson Adams to Rousseau, who also hurled himself against the conventions of decorous behavior in his effort to make contact. There are no real villains in Goethe's novel, none of the downright evil that Fielding and Rousseau depict, but there is a pervasive sense that Werther is a diseased phenomenon, a wild figure who presses too hard, who wants "in," who is either unwilling or unable to maintain his distance.

Although Goethe took a rather jaundiced view of his youthful surrogate later in life, there can be no doubt that the social world depicted in *Werther* is marked by signs of frigidity and indifference. Werther's cult of feeling is an embarrassment to these good burghers, but their own scheme is in trouble. The story is rife with failed inheritances, with ominous outbreaks of violence, with persistent hints that polite behavior cannot permanently repress people's more elemental needs. The world that Albert is sanely managing and Lotte benignly mothering is actually rotting away; once one leaves their idyllic setting, one encounters madmen who yearn for the asylum, servants whom desire has chafed into rape. Wherever Werther turns his gaze, he sees coldness and self-sufficiency, and he cannot bear it:

> Ich möchte mir oft die Brust zerreißen und das Gehirn einstoßen, daß man einander so wenig sein kann. Ach, die Liebe, Freude, Wärme und Wonne, die ich nicht hinzubringe, wird mir der andere nicht geben, und mit einem ganzen Herzen voll Seligkeit

> werde ich den andern nicht beglücken, der kalt und kraftlos vor mir steht.[2]
>
> [Often I would like to tear open my breast and bash in my skull, because we mean so little to one another. Alas, the love, joy, warmth and bliss that I do not contribute myself, no one else will give me, and even with a heart full of happiness, I cannot make someone happy who stands before me cold and inert.]

It is a splendid image of *opening* the self ("die Brust zerreißen und das Gehirn einstoßen"), and, as such, it is a graphic protest against the enclosed nature of the individual.[3] We will encounter this imagery again, in a dreadful, literal manner in both Kafka and Burroughs, but it is rigorously apposite in Goethe's tale, and it is annunciatory of the drastic, primitive energies that human desire brings into play. On the one hand, there is a voracious appetite to merge with the other, to transcend one's epidermal and conceptual confines; on the other hand, the charged being who seeks this fusion usually encounters a kind of creatural indifference, inertia, and complacency that is death itself. The difficulty of loving is seen to be almost muscular, an indigenous defect common to the species. Werther's own death by suicide *might* have been prevented, if anyone had cared quite enough to make a move; Goethe's depiction of Albert and Lotte and a friend having supper together as Werther is preparing his death is absolutely grisly in its language of indifference and impersonality, and it constitutes, in its choice of pronouns at the end, something close to a sentence of death:

> Der Tisch ward gedeckt, und eine gute Freundin, dir nur etwas zu fragen kam, gleich gehen wollte—und blieb, machte die Un-

2. Johann Wolfgang Goethe, *Die Leiden des jungen Werther*, in *Gedenkausgabe der Werke, Briefe und Gespräche* (Zurich: Artemis Verlag, 1953), IV, p. 466. Subsequent quotations will be taken from this edition and noted parenthetically in the body of the text.

3. Thomas Mann dealt, some fifty years ago, with this dimension of *Werther*, applying the notion of prison-house to every aspect of the protagonist's dilemma: "Das Leben, die Person, die Individualität ist ihm ein Kerker" ("Goethes *Werther*," in *Goethe im XX Jahrhundert: Spiegelungen und Deutungen*, ed. Hans Mayer [Hamburg: Christian Wegner Verlag, 1967], p. 14).

terhaltung bei Tische erträglich; man zwang sich, man redete, man erzählte, man vergaß sich. [506]

[The table was set, and a good friend, who simply came to ask a question, wanted to go right away—and stayed, made the dinner conversation bearable; they forced themselves, chatted, told stories, forgot themselves.]

Die Leiden des jungen Werther is a prototypical fiction of relationship because it is epoch-making in its expression of human hunger against the backdrop of creatural inertia and social distance. Whereas Prévost is arguably the first to tell the story of the couple in its full problematic, Goethe is equally prophetic in fashioning a language of longing and desire, in advocating empathy as a cardinal human virtue. Those who regard *Werther* as a portrait of neurosis (and they are legion) frequently point to the built-in narcissism of the first-person stance, and one can hardly deny that this novel exploits point-of-view perspective to the hilt. As we know, this strategy inevitably carries a large dose of blindness with it. But there is much more that might and must be said about first-person narrative, especially here. Goethe's protagonist encounters distance everywhere, and although he cannot literally make contact, he does effectively bridge the gap between himself and his fellows in a profound way: he "first-personalizes" his world.[4] He has reverence for the inner workings and inner mystery of those he encounters. His accounts of the farmhand, the madman, the servant girl are remarkable in their "projective" character. The first person is singularly equipped to give as well as to take, and true generosity or empathy comes about precisely when "I" becomes, or tries to become, the other. When Albert speaks cold reason to him

4. Werther's proclivity for "first-personalizing" his world was noted long ago by Wolfgang Kayser in his "Entstehung von Goethes *Werther*," *Deutsche Vierteljahrsschrift für Literaturwissenschaft und Geistesgeschichte* 19 (1941), pp. 430–51. Needless to say, the entire "anti-romantic" reading of the text zeroes in on this feature of Werther as a liability, a form of blindness and egocentrism. A more recent view of these matters is to be found in Anthony Thorlby's fine essay, "From What Did Goethe Save Himself in 'Werther'?" in *Versuche zu Goethe: Festschrift für Erich Heller*, eds. Volker Dürr and Géza v. Molnár (Heidelberg: Lothar Stiehm Verlag, 1976), pp. 150–66; Thorlby sees Goethe's novel as a classic formulation of the romantic dilemma of the mind cut off from its world and seeking fusion with it, opting ultimately for an aesthetic solution.

about the absurdity of suicide, Werther denies the very ground Albert is standing on by his claim that nobody can be assessed by dispassionate, so-called objective standards, that we can understand the other only by merging with him, imagining his reality: "Denn nur insofern als wir mitempfinden, haben wir die Ehre, von einer Sache zu reden" (Then only insofar as we empathize, are we entitled to speak of something [427]). There is a code here. It is a moral code, and its first commandment requires that distanced, cool judgment be replaced by personal sympathy. Third-person understanding is not understanding. *Mitempfinden*, "to feel with," is a well-nigh perfect verb for expressing the pathway to knowledge. This code is also a writerly code: empathy must precede language itself, thereby legitimizing our right to speak ("von einer Sache zu reden"); our authority for turning the world into language is predicated on our involvement with the world, our connection to it. Werther is true to these principles; his capacity for self-projection and the "interested" nature of his language betoken connection and openness at once, whereas the play-it-safe closure of Albert and his kind figures forth the same sterility and barrenness that are imaged in the failed inheritances.

One can, I think, go even further in assessing the nature of empathy in this text. Werther may not "possess" Lotte sexually, but he does indeed get through to her, and the penultimate sentence of the novel, "Man fürchtete für Lottens Leben" (One feared for Lotte's life), indicates that she has, as it were, "caught" him, the way one "catches" typhoid or diphtheria. Finally, we are led back to the language itself, and from the language to the suicides it caused. The style of the book, its extended syntax, the primacy it grants to the affective over the rational, these are the revolutionary features of Goethe's prose, and they establish a disturbing bridge between text and reader. Language is the final conduit of relationship, the seemingly innocuous connection between dead letters and living readers. Those readers who responded to the text with swooning, even with suicide, experienced the relationship that fiction can offer; like Lotte, they too "caught" Werther.[5] Goethe's prose is in the service of Werther's em-

5. Goethe himself tended, in his later years, to regard *Werther* as an explosive, indeed a "contaminating" text, and in 1824, almost fifty years after its publication, he said: "Ich habe es seit seinem Erscheinen nur einmal wieder gelesen und mich gehütet, es abermals zu tun. *Es sind lauter Brandraketen!* Es wird mir unheimlich dabei, und ich fürchte den pathologischen Zustand

pathetic vision, and with it a whole new concept of language begins to appear in literature: organic, immediate, suffused with the vibrancy of emotion. We cannot fail to see that the letter form is a privileged form of release in this novel: Werther's feelings pour out in his letters, because they have no other outlet, giving us an eery analog of the dammed waters that must overflow, that appear throughout Goethe's work, from *Tasso* to *Faust*.[6] That act of flooding is a frightening image of the self's desire to spread, to become one with the other, emotionally, sexually, cathartically, verbally. We are doubtless close to one of the wellsprings of all art, namely that it provides a mode of connection, of relationship if you will, that is either unavailable or unimaginable or unacceptable in "life." In studying Goethe's novel, we begin to perceive the affective and neural crisscrossings, transactions, and trade-off's that fuel artistic expression: the impetus to relationship is all-powerful, situated not only between the lovers of the text but also in the crucial interstices between text and reader. One need not be Dr. Freud or Sherlock Holmes to suspect that these alternative strategies of contact and connection originate from a single energy source, thereby hinting to us that frustration and failure within the text are strangely redeemed by the text's dynamic with its readers. What is certain is that the inside picture, that special point of view that is to mark so much of the novel's history, may possess a wierd posthumous life of its own, recouping in its readership what it loses at home.

Let us recapitulate. In their time, *Manon Lescaut* and *Die Leiden des jungen Werther* were read and experienced as paradigmatic love stories, and indeed they are still read that way. Yet, each is rife with all those incompatibilities mentioned at the outset: *malentendu* or mis-

---

wieder durchzuempfinden, aus dem es hervorging" (quoted by Mann, "Goethes *Werther*," p. 17).

6. Thorlby, like many other critics, seizes on the passage where Lotte tells Werther that he loves her *because* she is betrothed to another and unavailable, and he goes on to argue, with considerable persuasiveness, that Werther's entire project is one of *aesthetic passion*, in which sexual union with Lotte herself is of little account, for the larger gambit is a kind of impossible fusion or fulfillment achievable, if at all, through language or art. This view successfully accounts for the displacements at the heart of the text, but it misses out on some of the urgency of the matter, the crucial issue of *release* (imaged in opening the veins of horses etc.) that has been designated as a possible outcome of art ever since Aristotle spoke of catharsis.

alliance between lovers, societal obstacles, barriers of perception. Each book is powerfully subjective in tone and technique; each expresses the dual wants of the self and the desire for union. One grants connection within the story, and the other images it largely through yearning and even through writing. Each recognizes, via its larger composite form, the possible narcissism of the self-flaunting lover. Each closes with the death of one partner. In sum, these are the salient features of the genre, and we will see them reappear, albeit clothed in new ways and handled with greater sophistication, in the nineteenth- and twentieth-century fictions to which we shall turn. Many of our initial questions, however, remain open: can mutuality be narrated? can the self reach knowledge of the other? can the self even perceive the fuller contours of the figure that it is making? Whatever the answers may be, the formula for successful love-fiction seems to be established: love is best conveyed by expressing the subjectivity, the desire of the would-be lover, whereas relationship seems to be not only beyond the reach of the characters, but beyond the precincts and modus operandi of the text.

3

Even the most impressionistic history of the novel of relationship is obliged to account for *Madame Bovary*, hazardous though it may be, in a few pages, to say anything worthwhile concerning a text that has been at the center of critical debate for more than a century now. Flaubert's book is an unavoidable *point de repère*, and it is particularly intriguing as a restatement of the eighteenth-century romance looking toward the modernist experimental fiction. The ostensible subject of the book is the frustrated romantic yearnings of Emma Bovary; like every Flaubert character, she desires the absolute, is splendidly equipped with longing and hunger, with dreams that are tacky and improbable, and the book's fable consists in her coming to terms, or not coming to terms, with the implacable mediocrity of French provincial life in general and Charles Bovary in particular. Now Flaubert, it would appear, had trouble sticking to his subject, so much did he loathe its dreariness and vulgarity; his real prey, as critics like Genette and Bersani have suggested, may have been the performance of his own style and language, the creation of a verbal artifact that contained his characters but had little allegiance to them.[7]

One can easily discern in this disposition an aesthetic imperative that celebrates authorial power at the expense of the author's creatures; we find an exact analog of this power scheme in Flaubert's famous pronouncement likening the artist to God: "L'artiste doit être dans son œuvre comme Dieu dans la Création, invisible et tout-puissant, qu'on le sente partout, mais qu'on ne le voie pas" (The artist must be in his work like God in the Creation, invisible and all-powerful, everywhere sensed, but nowhere seen). As we know, Joyce did a significant variation on this in the *Portrait of the Artist* when Stephen proclaims: "The artist, like the God of creation, remains within or behind or beyond or above his handiwork, invisible, refined out of existence, indifferent, paring his fingernails." It is very tempting to emphasize the Joycean turn of the screw, the suspicious variety of postures invoked (within or behind or beyond or above), the crucial shift from Flaubert's impersonality to Joyce's indifference (paring his fingernails), leading to the final verdict that Flaubert is being oracular while Joyce is winking at us the whole time.[8] Yet, there can be little doubt that Flaubert is among the first to exercise the kind of authorial maneuvering room that Joyce was to immortalize, and one finds in *Madame Bovary* a spectrum of narrational gambits that makes *Portrait* look monochromatic (*Ulysses* is another matter). Flaubert seems to be all over the map, both inside and outside, laughing, yawning, and weeping. Bersani tells us that Flaubert's characters are ideally suitable for a suspension of our interest in them, and Genette has catalogued the "silences of Flaubert," those moments of verbal take-over, where plot and characters fade into the background as the descriptions become autonomous and liberated from the tedious business of telling a story.

Flaubert's attitude toward his materials constitutes, as is well known, one of the thresholds of modern literature, analogous to Mallarmé's "liberation" of the word in poetry, but less attention has been focused on the power dialectic that he inaugurates. We saw, in

7. Gérard Genette, "Silences de Flaubert," in *Figures* (Paris: Seuil, 1966) and Leo Bersani's chapter on Flaubert in *Balzac to Beckett: Center and Circumference in French Fiction* (New York: Oxford University Press, 1970).

8. I am indebted to my brother Philip for initially drawing my attention to the differences expressed in these two similar manifestoes.

Goethe's *Werther*, that the verbal performance of the work enables triumphs that are denied in the plot; with Flaubert, we can begin to take full measure of just how far such transactions can go. There is something absolutely punitive in *Madame Bovary* (to which the author's famous phrase, "Madame Bovary, c'est moi," gives a twist but hardly a lie), and we see this dimension of the novel most sharply in such scenes as the famous *comices agricoles* episode, where Flaubert systematically "cuts" and "splices" the love discourse served up to Emma by Rodolphe in and out of the fatigued political clichés of the government speaker and the weights and measures of oxen and manure. The artist may be invisible in his person, but he is all the more potent in his doings, placing his pathetic heroine in countless squeezes, undercutting and mocking her by the very architecture of his work.

This kind of authorial bullying stems obviously from Flaubert's temperament, but its roots would appear to go deeper still, especially since it resurfaces in so much twentieth-century fiction. In fact, one would not be going far afield by stating categorically that the experimental novel systematically manipulates its characters, that it demonstrably supplants their authority with *its* verbal prowess. One thinks of the works of Joyce, Borges, and Robbe-Grillet as examples of textual worlds that operate much like minefields for the characters who have to negotiate them: Borges' people encounter dislocations of time and space, find themselves to be fodder for some larger unfurling; Joyce's Bloom is subjected, especially in chapters such as "Circe," "Cyclops," and "Ithaca," to an entire arsenal of tricks and devices, ranging from talking soap to arithmetic whimsy ("reduce Bloom by cross multiplication of reverses of fortune . . ."). And much, very much of these pyrotechnics is outright victimization; in Robbe-Grillet we witness the most extensive, most refined version of such exploitation, since his characters turn into photographs or figure eights at will (at the author's will), while the roads they travel and the goals they seek change shape and form with the regularity and ease of a kaleidoscope. Yet, even the most sadistic of these texts has a disturbing kind of referential power, as if it were saying, The world you live in is exactly the kind of prison you see in this text, and your maneuvering room in that world is precisely as limited and despotically controlled as it is in this text. Hence, the concentration-camp text suggests, somewhere, a concentration-camp world, and the most vicious narrative exploitation might be explained (away?) as an exposé of the various prison-houses where people live: verbal, political, biological, etc.

Such manipulation *might* be accounted for in such terms; after all, Robbe-Grillet once grounded his work on the observation that our contemporary culture is "celle du numéro matricule." There would seem, however, to be something disingenuous in such rationales, if for no other reason than the obvious exhilaration evidenced in the text, the manifest vigor and joy of the verbal high jinks themselves, the undeniable reek and flavor of assertion that emerges from the fictions of Joyce, Borges, and Robbe-Grillet. Perhaps they are showing us that verbal power is the last remaining power, that the artist is still in control of his own universe, and that he has the giddy privilege of making the laws and then making the people, and then bandying about the people in subservience to the laws. Is this not what it means when one proclaims, "L'artiste doit être dans son œuvre comme Dieu dans la Création, invisible et tout-puissant, qu'on le sente partout, mais qu'on ne le voie pas"?

But the victimization that is so brilliantly conceived and implemented in *Madame Bovary* does not seem entirely referrable to Flaubert's modernist narrational gambit, and if we look back to the models offered by Prévost and Goethe, we may be able to see the power dynamic in *Bovary* in yet another way, this time as a generic feature of the relationship text. The real target of the novel, the true victim of the text's unremitting narrative stratagems, seems to be human desire itself. The first-person yearnings of Prévost and Goethe have been dreadfully framed and tested by Flaubert; *Madame Bovary* is the grand arena where the one-eyed lyricism of desire is stereophonically put to death. When Emma begs for money from Binet, Flaubert positions himself at a neighboring window, not for reasons of *pudeur*, but to flex his narrative muscles, to show how much maneuvering room *he* has, in contrast to the *huis clos* she is in. Strangely enough, Emma gains in pathos what she loses in authority, a pathos we will meet again in Vian's *L'Ecume des jours*, where the narrational ante has been upped even further. The novel of relationship teaches its readers to expect such comeuppance, and the genre as a whole tends to work parasitically with the theme of desire, to fasten onto the affective and the lyrical while reserving in store the never-failing punishment for such effusion, the inevitable reality-lesson that exposes desire as a cheat. What is there in desire that cannot be abided? Keats once wrote that a street fight is deplorable but that the energies in it are fine. Emma and Frédéric and Félicité all yearn, but they do so "degradedly": they hunger variously for the sensual delights of the Orient, the religious bliss of the Christ-child-in-a-manger, the advertised ecstasies of romances and chivalric tales. The Keats question remains: must revery itself be diseased just because its "scenarios" are tarnished?

Perhaps it is. Emma dreams of emotional and sexual splendor, and her entire life is nothing but a search for "true relationship." The fusion that Des Grieux presumably experienced and Werther vainly sought reappears in Flaubert as problematic at the core, punishable as well as unattainable. The self in Flaubert's books, the famous realist novels and *Saint Antoine* as well, is prodigiously available, bent on projection, open for fusion. But that act of merging is sensed to be lethal, something that would *undo* the self that yearns for it. Again and again in Flaubert's work, as Jean-Pierre Richard has shown, we see the imagery and the thematics of dissolution, swooning, coming apart.[9] Orgasm betokens such loss of control, loss of contours; so too does seizure, notably the mysterious seizure experienced by Flaubert at a critical moment in his life, the event that some think launched him into writing as a form of religion. Very much like Rousseau, who was also disastrously "available" and volatile, who also turned his art into a kind of control that he lacked in life, so too does Flaubert pit the steely form of language and technique against the enemy within: the inflammable senses, the yearning soul, that fluid self that wants out. The desire for fusion is matched by a corresponding terror of fusion, and this helps to account for the blend of lyricism and contempt that marks the love scenes in *Madame Bovary* and *L'Education sentimentale*. One of the richest, most ingenious analyses of Flaubert along these lines is the magisterial essay on *Bovary* in Tony Tanner's *Adultery in the Novel*; Tanner gives us the full spectacle of Flaubert's verbal pyrotechnics, and he is especially good at showing the erasure of "difference," the ways in which the words "run together," call to one another by means of puns, anagrams, and "associative series."[10]

9. Jean-Pierre Richard, "La Création de la forme chez Flaubert," in *Littérature et sensation* (Paris: Seuil, 1954).

10. Although Tanner networks Flaubert into frequencies including Freud, Saussure, Lacan, and other moderns, he does not assess the writerly enterprise as inherently punitive or terroristic. Yet, his view of Emma being "liquefied" and "morselized" by the text would seem to announce a scriptural cannibalism of unusual proportions, and it seems appropriate to underscore the exploitative dimension of this kind of writing, an exploitation that will

What ultimately emerges from Tanner's reading is a writerly version of adultery, adultery defined as improper fusions (see his remarks on "fondre," "fonder," and "confondre"), as a monstrous scriptural bonding that signals the breaking of all "proper" contracts, ties, and relationships.

The easiest authorial way to punish desire is, of course, to satisfy it. What we have, in *Madame Bovary*, is a poignant drama of human longing worked over by technique, for technique is the author's distancing device for exposing the gulf between dream and reality. Flaubert takes the step Goethe refrained from, and he grants mates to his longing heroine. He dramatizes the life of the couple, converts passion into the temporal mode of relationship, and thereby proffers the ultimate realist lesson: actuality undoes desire. Once again the novel form proves its mettle, for its temporal span obliges Emma, whose desire was to be married at midnight in a torch-lit ceremony, to experience what time does to couples. Flaubert's relentless use of the imperfect captures with awful precision the unglamorous intimacy of life together, the prosaic, routinized dimension of marriage. Auerbach's brilliant analysis of Emma watching Charles eat is well known, and it beautifully illuminates the peculiar economy of Flaubertian prose, its capacity to render the prisonlike existence of an entire life in the depiction of a single scene.[11] But there is also an intolerable "closeness" in much of the description of this novel; here is a particularly merciless description of Charles:

> Il prenait, avec l'âge, des allures épaisses; il coupait, au dessert, le bouchon des bouteilles vides; il se passait, après manger, la langue sur les dents; il faisait, en avalant sa soupe, un gloussement à chaque gorgée, et, comme il commençait d'engraissir, ses yeux, déjà petits, semblaient remonter vers les tempes par la bouffissure de ses pommettes.[12]

> [As he aged, his features thickened; during dessert, he would cut up the cork of the empty bottle; after eating, he would roll his

---

be most fully actualized in Joyce's *Ulysses* half a century later. Flaubert is the gateway to modernism in more ways than one.

11. Erich Auerbach, *Mimesis: The Representation of Reality in Western Literature* (New York: Doubleday, 1957), pp. 426–29.

12. Gustave Flaubert, *Madame Bovary* (Paris: Garnier Flammarion, 1966), p. 95.

> tongue over his teeth; when swallowing his soup, he would make a gurgling noise with each spoonful, and, as he was beginning to put on weight, his eyes, already small, seemed pushed up to his temples by his puffed-out cheeks.]

One is hard put to distinguish between Flaubert and Emma here; the deadly imperfect verbs are his, but the ruthless precision, the anatomical knowledge of one's partner over time, these clearly reflect the vision of Emma. Flaubert's imperfects show us the very imperfections of relationship, and we understand why the novel is the ideal genre to depict failed marriages, to display the damage of time, the surfeit and disgust, the *écœurement* that can be felt only by people who live together. Charles is, of course, a poor candidate for passion in the first place; but the more glamorous types, Rodolphe and Léon, fare no better: for Emma, relationship would be sustained poetry, sustained peak moments, but what we see, instead, is the relentless movement from cheap lyrical beginnings to boredom and repetition. Relationship for Emma should be gloriously algebraic, passion times time; but time is a negative, a corrosive factor here, one that dissolves the initial equation into the peculiar flavor of waste and decay which constitutes the residue of all Flaubertian texts.

4

As we know, at the very close of *Madame Bovary*, after Emma is dead, Charles discovers the true nature of his wife's past nervous condition, and he more or less dies from it. To phrase it that way is to emphasize another dimension of the fiction of relationship, i.e., the blindness, the congenital blindness each of us has concerning the lives of others; to phrase it that way is also to introduce Ford's *The Good Soldier*, Ford's strange, dazzlingly modernist inversion of Flaubert's novel, the story told by the husband this time.

The blindness at the heart of *Manon Lescaut*, the enforced solipsism that binds Werther, the corrosive effect of time on relationship in *Madame Bovary*, all these features appear in Ford's book, but they are so heightened, exaggerated, caricatured and, above all, narrativized that the result is a kind of *grand guignol*, an epistemological funhouse, the subjective fiction of relationship *par excellence*. Ford is drawing on a very old tradition of love triangles and cuckolded husbands, but the twists that he gives to this tradition make his book look downright spectacular. After all, even a writer like Austen relies heavily on misunderstood motives and repressed information; she also gets considerable mileage out of the very conventions that govern her polite society, the conventions that allow a poem in *Emma* to be credibly misread because it is entirely ambivalent in its references, or indeed the restraints of well-behaved people who never ask each other something straight out, who are masters at whispers and smiles in crowded small rooms. The Frank Churchill–Jane Fairfax secret liaison is the kind of thing Ford inherited, and one could say that Austen works the notion of blindness about as finely as it can be done. The obvious follow-up to Austen, along these lines, is James, who constructs an entire *ars poetica* out of these issues, tapping the "center of consciousness" as a veritable lodestone for getting stories told with the right blend of light and darkness. Indeed, some of the later James, such as *The Sacred Fount*, resembles the Ford scenario very closely, especially along the lines of surface conventions whose deeper meanings are so buried that the effort to perceive them blends imperceptibly into the act of creating them out of whole cloth. Who is doing what to whom, vulgar though it is as a formula, is the endless subject of speculation, sleuthing, and inventing throughout the Jamesian corpus. But James was altogether too fastidious to come up with the kind of circuslike fiction we encounter in *The Good Soldier*; Ford brings to these epistemological dilemmas a sense of the garish, the grotesque, and the theatrical that James could probably never have stomached. Moreover, the uncertainty that fuels the work of Austen and James seems largely of a procedural nature, whereas Ford is depicting a world where no vision of order is quite imaginable, offering us, in its place, what has been called "an irresolvable pluralism of truths, in a world that remains essentially dark."[13]

The story, we know, is essentially that of Dowell, Ford's Prufrock-like narrator, and his efforts to understand the complex web of deceit and betrayal in which he has unwittingly participated for the past ten years. There is a good deal to unravel: the gross and grotesque infidelities of his wife, Florence, with whom he has an unconsummated marriage because of her so-called bad heart; the more profound and significant deceptions of Edward and Leonora; the tragicomic story of Nancy Rutherford, who ends up going mad. All is permissible in

13. Samuel Hynes, "The Epistemology of *The Good Soldier*," in *Ford Madox Ford: Modern Judgements*, ed. Richard Cassell (London: Macmillan, 1972), p. 102.

Ford's narrative, and he sovereignly mixes levels of discourse and chronology to bring his rabbits out of the hat with brio and dispatch. Much has been written about the irony of the book as well as its comic use of point-of-view narrative turned against the speaker himself.[14] But irony may simply be too short-winded a mode to take us through this text. Ford's novel has the remarkable economy of the nineteenth-century well-made play; its materials are few, but the connections forged, assumed, denied, and concealed between them are disturbingly many. Ford has tapped the structural and the sociomoral power of relationship itself, the human need for stable, enduring, unitary bonds versus the shocking variety of our actual liaisons, our multiple identities, the irreconcilable roles we play out. Ford's discovery is not that we are emotional chameleons, not even that our connections with others are both licit and illicit, thereby wrecking all conventional codes; Dickens and Balzac had already dramatized that story of connectedness. Ford's genius is to flaunt the process of discovery itself, to open his material endlessly, to turn upside down what seemed secure, to show ultimately that nothing is innocent in human intercourse. Hence, his world is drenched with coherence, with linkage, with characters who should be separate but who nonetheless merge. The code he breaks is not merely the Edwardian one; it is an older one whose transgressions have fascinated literature ever since Sophocles framed them in his Oedipal fable. Multiplicity is, in itself, untenable, and Ford bursts through the staid precincts of his narrator's mind by depicting a world that is emotionally energized to the point of scandal, a set of characters who are cancerously active and enmeshed with one another, a kind of musical chairs—or minuet as he calls it—that is forever forming new configurations. There is something exponential about *The Good Soldier*, for it charts and chronicles permutations that must destroy any fixed view of human

14. Almost all modern criticism of Ford's novel has had to contend with Mark Schorer's extremely influential "Interpretation" accompanying the Vintage edition of *The Good Soldier* in 1957, and still reprinted in that edition. Schorer's rather hostile view toward Dowell, and his assessment of the book as comic irony which targets its own speaker, have been challenged by a host of more sympathetic readers, starting with the work of John Meixner and Samuel Hynes and still represented in the very fine study by Ann Snitow, *Ford Madox Ford and the Voice of Uncertainty* (Baton Rouge: Louisiana State University, 1984). Snitow mediates very effectively between these two views, showing how the fusion of irony and sympathy is the hallmark of Ford's art and vision.

affairs. The beauty of the novel resides in the comedy and pathos that attend such mobility. Comic, indeed, is the obliteration of brittle, cardboard conventions, such as those which Dowell has esteemed and thought operative in the world of his fellows; but the view of relationship as plague, as contagion, as epistemological horror, carries considerable pathos as well.

Ford's initial title, "The Saddest Story," most aptly fits our topic; *The Good Soldier* is about manifold efforts to shield, to protect the heart, to take convention for reality itself. Dowell, in order to protect his presumably fragile wife, is obliged to exercise a certain amount of censorship: "For twelve years I had to watch every word that any person uttered in any conversation and I had to head it off what the English call 'things'—off love, poverty, crime, religion, and the rest of it."[15] On the face of it, this is a somewhat large number of issues to avoid, and in the course of the book these "things" will come to be more substantial, more imperious than the ghostly narrator himself. The irony of Ford's book changes to a deeper hue, a hue so deep that one is hard put to term it irony at all, as the fuller stories of Edward, Leonora, and Nancy rise to the surface. We begin to measure—not in the relentless manner of Flaubert, but via delayed disclosures—the connection between relationship and time, as we realize that the privileged arena for love, poverty, crime, religion, and the rest of it is precisely marriage, especially a bad marriage. At a dinner party or during a brief tryst, these sordid details can probably be screened out; during a life together, they not only filter through, but they demonstrate that they are the bedrock of reality, the very environment in which self has been formed, the actual constituents of personality and principle. The comedy of errors yields to a darker view of causes, of incompatibility and availability, of people doing what they did because they could do nothing else, being who they were. Edward's feudal view of his role in the community, his sentimental communal values, Leonora's Catholic sense of authority and individualism, her financial tightfistedness, Nancy's battered childhood, these features of the past have made these characters what they are; this is their flesh.[16]

15. Ford Madox Ford, *The Good Soldier* (New York: Vintage Books, 1951), p. 16. Subsequent quotations will be taken from this edition and noted parenthetically in the body of the text.

16. In defining the novel as "the interaction of Convention and Passion," Samuel Hynes has gone on to relate Passion to a larger story of suffering that

Dowell, the American without passion or past, has been unable to pierce the surface, but the larger picture he draws for us and himself during the book goes beyond the epistemological striptease many see in the novel: it is an eloquent indictment of specious surfaces, a grim picture of human relationships over time, a philosophy of human event that is causative rather than absurd, an aesthetic of delayed revelations and flashbacks that functions—much like Faulkner's—to implement and deepen the garish hues of the initial trauma.[17] Ford's book closes on a tone of fatigue and nihilism, the fatigue of a mind that has been stretched far beyond its customary borders, the nihilism of a spirit that has recognized how much luggage people carry with them, how powerless the individual is to shape or counter the potent, only apparently invisible forces of one's past, and how nothing can remain hidden as time actualizes one's repertory and effects its special composite of personal destinies. In Ford's text, ultimately, the *drama* of perception—played out for the reader with such dash and brio—becomes the *novel* of relationship, that complex weave of individuals inextricably linked in their lonely lives. *The Good Soldier* stands as the *ne plus ultra* of subjective fictions plotted by relationship. Whereas Flaubert brings actualization and entropy to the earlier romance scheme, Ford expands and explodes the whole consort, positing connection everywhere, making knowledge of such connection his form as well as his theme, culminating in a vision of disorder that borders on the apocalyptic.

---

goes well beyond sexual desire ("Epistemology," 103–104). Ann Snitow has acutely remarked that the increasingly emblematic nature of the story, the gradual transformation of profane characters into Passion Players ruled by divine judgment indicates something of Ford's dilemma in keeping the right balance between sympathy and irony (*Ford Madox Ford*, p. 185).

17. Snitow has remarked on Ford's admiration for writers who could manage closure, especially prose writers such as Maupassant, who could deal out final(izing) sentences with a poise that he, Ford, could only envy. Snitow feels that Ford's deepest truths are those of ambiguity and uncertainty, and that he is, consequently, weakening his novel by moving beyond the ironic into the sentimental or melancholic at the close (*Ford Madox Ford*, pp. 184–90). But I think Snitow remains closer to Schorer than she herself realizes, and this leads her to assess the book's final movement in terms of "taking sides" or abandoning "uncertainty," whereas it can also be seen as Ford's special way of "unpacking" his garish materials, showing just how much resonance and plenitude they have in a fiction that broods endlessly over them.

5

How does one move out of Ford's labyrinth of misconceptions? Can the novel embody the subjective need for relationship and yet move beyond narcissism and solipsism? Can point-of-view narrative be made compatible with mutuality? A final consideration of two twentieth-century texts will not so much close this argument as open it, suggesting that the tandem of fiction and relationship is still free to move down roads hitherto untaken.

Virginia Woolf's *To the Lighthouse* is arguably the most perfect and beautiful marriage-text in the English language; it succeeds in mediating all the diverse strands of my argument: man and woman, relationship over time, subjectivity and reciprocity, life and art. Mrs. Ramsay is the high priestess of relationship, and she is prepared to exercise that function in the most mundane circumstances: isolated selves around a table must be brought together:

> Nothing seemed to have merged. They all sat separate. And the whole of the effort of merging and flowing and creating rested on her. Again she felt, as a fact without hostility, the sterility of men, for if she did not do it nobody would do it, and so, giving herself the little shake that one gives a watch that has stopped, the old familiar pulse began beating, as the watch begins ticking—one, two, three, one, two, three.[18]

There is something fine at work in this passage, a readiness to grasp social life at its most basic level, something almost as elemental as a blood transfusion; and on this humble stage the simple figures come, the pulse and the watch, the signs of human life and the time bomb of the human body. "Marry, marry" are the words with which Lily Briscoe fixes Mrs. Ramsay's image in her mind, and no character has ever done more credit to the institution: her understanding of and devotion to her husband is conveyed with great delicacy and great richness by Woolf, and that is no mean feat, given the frequently caricatural and absurdist depiction of Mr. Ramsay. When he ponders, with trembling seriousness, whether he will ever adventure beyond Q, he seems as solid a candidate for ridicule as Charles Bovary ever was. No touch is perhaps more perfect than Woolf's handling of

18. Virginia Woolf, *To the Lighthouse* (New York: Harcourt, Brace & Co., 1927), p. 126. Subsequent quotations will be taken from this edition and noted parenthetically in the body of the text.

the walk they take together; Mr. Ramsay remains obsessed with his "stock" in the intellectual community because he is what he is, but that does not prevent him from trying to commune with his wife; she is looking at flowers, and therefore he will too, albeit in his own way:

> He did not look at the flowers, which his wife was considering, but at a spot about a foot or so above them. There was no harm in him [Charles Tansley], he added, and was just about to say that anyhow he was the only young man in England who admired his—when he choked it back. He would not bother her again about his books. These flowers seemed creditable, Mr. Ramsay said, lowering his gaze and noticing something red, something brown. [102]

Unspectacular perhaps, nonetheless this little notation of creditable flowers renders point-of-view narrative in an exquisite fashion, but the whole passage is bathed in generosity and sympathy, depicting the mundane but nonetheless epic journey required to move from one person to another. The colors of the flowers reappear in that reddish-brown stocking Mrs. Ramsay is constantly knitting, and they become almost emblematic for an entente beyond language, for what will also be called "the thing that endures." At the close of the first section of the novel, he is watching her knitting, telling her she will not finish the stocking tonight, much the way he opens the novel by telling James that it will not be fine tomorrow, that there will be no expedition. Words separate Mr. and Mrs. Ramsay, but they are united beyond the words:

> Then, knowing that he was watching her, instead of saying anything she turned, holding her stocking, and looked at him. And as she looked at him she began to smile, for though she had not said a word, he knew, of course he knew, that she loved him. He could not deny it. And smiling she looked out of the window and said (thinking to herself, Nothing on earth can equal this happiness)—
>
> "Yes, you were right. It's going to be wet tomorrow. You won't be able to go." And she looked at him smiling. For she had triumphed again.
>
> She had not said it: yet he knew. [185–86]

There is doubtless a certain cunning in this passage, and it is possible to see Mrs. Ramsay as a manipulative, shrewd wife; but the overriding sentiment that emerges is one of mutuality and consent, the pleasure that comes from pleasing, the pleasure that comes from a shared bond, a shared base against which local disturbances are as nothing, at worst a minor irritant, at best a stimulus for better things.

In Mrs. Ramsay, Woolf has created one of the richest characters in literature, and for once, all those properties of fiction which have militated against relationship—inner versus outer, self versus other—are brought together in a rare kind of harmony. Mrs. Ramsay's devotion to others is seamlessly wedded to a well-nigh infinite inner expansion as well; her life perfectly balances relationship and self, and it does so in the limpid, almost monosyllablic language of children and of poetry:

> No, she thought, putting together some of the pictures he had cut out—a refrigerator, a mowing machine, a gentleman in evening dress—children never forget. For this reason, it was so important what one said, and what one did, and it was a relief when they went to bed. For now she need not think about anybody. She could be herself, by herself. And that was what now she often felt the need of—to think; well, not even to think. To be silent; to be alone. All the being and the doing, expansive, glittering, vocal, evaporated; and one shrunk, with a sense of solemnity, to being oneself, a wedge-shaped core of darkness, something invisible to others . . . and this self having shed its attachments was free for the strangest adventures. When life sank down for a moment, the range of experience seemed limitless . . . our apparitions, the things you know us by, are simply childish. Beneath it is all dark, it is all spreading, it is unfathomably deep. [95–96]

This passage—usually quoted only in its famous final phase, but most fully reflective of the Woolfian synthesis when the children and the refrigerator and the mowing machine assume their rightful places as well—moves effortlessly beyond binarisms and incompatibilities and polarities, all those conflictual arrangements at the heart of the work we have examined up to now, and it shows us the wonderful connection between love for others and self-exploration.[19] The maturity of

19. That "wedge-shaped core of darkness" has been interpreted in many

Woolf's work lies in its capacity for assent, its firm sense that generosity is always of a piece, that "inner" and "outer" are not opposed, but rather twin routes, allied realms into which the self moves jointly. The descent into reverie, into the unconscious, is always wedded to the daytime agenda, to the no-less-important needs and precious lives of others. Woolf's narrative finds voices for all this.

For many readers, however, the regnant relationship in the novel is not that between the Ramsays, but between Mrs. Ramsay and Lily Briscoe. By imaging herself in the novel as Lily, Woolf has beautifully fused the filial and the artistic themes, and as a result, Lily poses the questions that are central to this entire study. What, Lily wonders, is the ultimate price of relationship; i.e., what does one pay, in order to have it, and what is its true value, when one has it? Is the human bonding that Mrs. Ramsay epitomizes not futile, even a trifle ridiculous, given the lackluster quality of her materials? Art, it would seem, at least for Lily, promises more than marriage, provides a better arena for fulfillment and enactment, has stronger chances for survival. Lily's views, like those of Mrs. Ramsay, are a matter of temperament as much as of philosophy, and it is a tribute to Woolf's own artistic reach that she is able to embody these two modes of being with such integrity, so much so that each appears more than a little quaint in the eyes of the other.

Life has taught Lily that relationships do not hold up. Whereas Flaubert was concerned to depict the death of romance and the boredom of connection in terms of entropy and *grisaille*, Woolf probes the effects of time on marriage in a far more impassioned manner. Consider, for example, the Rayleys, whom Lily considers when she is measuring Mrs. Ramsay's marriage doctrine and finding it quite defective. After all, the Rayley's marriage "had turned out rather badly"; "things had worked loose after the first year," Woolf writes, and her discreet metaphor calls to mind both the stocking that was being knitted and the shawl that is under siege in the "Time Passes" chapter. The Rayleys did not work out, and Lily feels that time has

---

ways, and James Naremore has built an entire reading of Woolf in terms of a "world without a self," a form of subjectivity that is strangely impersonal, frequently in collusion with death and extinction (*The World without a Self* [New Haven: Yale University Press, 1973]). Naremore's contention that Woolf offers us a "sense of multipersonal subjectivity" (p. 122) is carefully borne out by his close readings, but I feel that he understates the peculiar generosity and fusions that are at the moral heart of *To the Lighthouse*.

proven Mrs. Ramsay wrong, that "this mania of hers for marriage" bordered on the absurd. As she then thinks of her own tranquil arrangements with William Bankes, Woolf introduces the following:

> (Suddenly, as suddenly as a star slides in the sky, a reddish light seemed to burn in her mind, covering Paul Rayley, issuing from him. It rose like a fire sent up in token of some celebration by savages on a distant beach. She heard the roar and the crackle. The whole sea for miles around ran red and gold. Some winey smell mixed with it and intoxicated her, for she felt again her own headlong desire to throw herself off the cliff and be drowned looking for a pearl brooch on a beach. And the roar and the crackle repelled her with fear and disgust, as if while she saw its splendour and power she saw too how it fed on the treasure of the house, greedily, disgustingly, and she loathed it. But for a sight, for a glory it surpassed everything in her experience, and burnt year after year like a signal fire on a desert island at the edge of the sea, and one had only to say "in love" and instantly, as happened now, up rose Paul's fire again. And it sank and she said to herself, laughing, "The Rayleys"; how Paul went to coffee-houses and played chess.)
>
> She had only escaped by the skin of her teeth though, she thought. [261–62]

The novel's many pagan elements are visibly on display here, and their purpose is to image passion, passion that strangely remains intact long after its celebrants have separated. Somewhat like Ford's minuet that danced itself forever, affections have an eternal life; only the humans, the "occupants" of the affections, wax and wane, love and stop, stop and remember. Note that the pallid word "memory" is unused by Woolf; instead, the scene magically and despotically reappears, in all its fervor and raw force. The Rayleys' former passion explodes into Lily's mind, much the way a flaming meteor might reenter the earth's atmosphere, causing those who see it to ask where it could have been for all this time. There is a mystery here, a riddle: does love stop? can people somehow still be together even though life pulls them apart?

Who can forget when first reading, on page 194 of a 310-page book, enclosed in brackets, almost as an afterthought, the following words: "[Mr. Ramsay, stumbling along a passage one dark morning, stretched his arms out, but Mrs. Ramsay having died rather suddenly the night before, the arms, though stretched out, remained empty.]"

One is stunned by the brutality of these lines, the sheer disproportion between Mrs. Ramsay's beauty and the great force of death that took her. In this brief middle section of the novel, other Ramsays too, the children Andrew and Prue, will die, in brackets as well, as the war goes on and anarchy reigns.[20] Once again we encounter the condition and test of relationship: time itself. Here is also the absurd contingency of all human constructs. Woolf's book tests whether relationship can survive time as well as subjectivity.

Death separates definitively. Ten years later, at the same summer house, Lily experiences Mrs. Ramsay's intolerable absence:[21]

> To want and not to have, sent all up her body a hardness, a hollowness, a strain. And then to want and not to have—to want and want—how that wrung the heart, and wrung it again and again! [266]

Time does not merely alter and destroy us individually, although that is already a great deal to contend with; its most heinous power lies in its assault on those we love, its capricious dismantling of the human family.

We return to the impasse: individuation is given, and connection is desired. Death radicalizes the issue, flaunts our islanded condition, but are we not equally stymied, equally locked out, even in life? Ten years earlier, with her head on the living Mrs. Ramsay's knee, Lily wrestled with the same enigma:

> Sitting on the floor with her arms around Mrs. Ramsay's knees, close as she could get, smiling to think that Mrs. Ramsay would

20. Those brackets have always seemed merciless to me, but Maria Dibattista sees them as graphic forms of human assertion, "the victory of the narrator in rescuing humanly decisive events from the vast stretches of indifferent time that surround them" ("*To the Lighthouse*: Virginia Woolf's Winter's Tale," in *Virginia Woolf: Revaluation and Continuity*, ed. Ralph Freedman [Berkeley: University of California Press, 1980], p. 180).

21. One of the most intriguing and thoughtful accounts of Lily Briscoe's "extreme" reaction to the loss of Mrs. Ramsay can be found in Mark Spilka's "On Lily Briscoe's Borrowed Grief: A Psycho-Literary Speculation," *Criticism* 21 (Winter 1979). Spilka reads sensitively and provocatively between the lines, and his biographical explanation, although too "extra-textual" for my taste, goes a long way toward grounding Lily's crucial responses in the third section of the novel. Oddly enough, Spilka's view of *Trauerarbeit* is very close, indeed, to the Freudian "dream work" that Dibattista sees as the burden of the novel.

> never know the reason of that pressure, she imagined how in the chambers of the mind and heart of the woman who was, physically, touching her, were stood, like the treasures in the tombs of kings, tablets bearing sacred inscriptions, which if one could spell them out, would teach one everything, but they would never be offered openly, never made public. What art was there, known to love or cunning, by which one pressed through into those secret chambers? What device for becoming, like waters poured into one jar, inextricably the same, one with the object one adored? Could the body achieve, or the mind, subtly mingling in the intricate passages of the brain? or the heart? Could loving, as people called it, make her and Mrs. Ramsay one? for it was not knowledge but unity that she desired, not inscriptions on tablets, nothing that could be written in any language known to men, but intimacy itself, which is knowledge, she had thought, leaning her head on Mrs. Ramsay's knee. [78–79]

There can hardly be a passage in all of literature that more perfectly expresses the mystery of relationship: its appeal, the insurmountable barriers (both physical and mental), the very confines of the soul that wants fusion. This passage begins and ends in the soft darkness of Lily's head resting on Mrs. Ramsay's knee, and it strives to state the ineffable by means of images: waters poured into one jar, mingling in intricate passages. The most arresting image is doubtless the sacred inscriptions with their initial conception of merging with the other as a *reading* of the other, but this view of "knowledge" yields to something beyond "any language known to men," pointing toward a state on which language can have no purchase. Some feminists might want to italicize "men" in that passage, with its possible suggestion of a different language known to "women," but the issue is perhaps not gender-specific at all. Woolf seems to intuit that language is only a threshold for what is ultimately desired. Perhaps that final union, like the orgasmic flooding of pleasure induced in Mrs. Ramsay by the lighthouse beam, would dissolve the self permanently into nothing, and must forever remain—certainly for the novelist, perhaps even for the individual—on the far side of things.

And yet, connection is achieved. The final chapter of *To the Lighthouse* makes good on all its postponed or doomed expeditions. The lighthouse is reached, and with it we may say that the knitting is completed, the web woven. Mr. Ramsay and James and Cam *live* their connection with the dead Mrs. Ramsay, live it through their act of solidarity. And Lily, who entered that house ten years later and saw that it was a "house of unrelated passions," makes her trip through art. "Tunneling her way into her picture, into the past," Lily fuses the processes of memory and creation, each a form of retrieval, of restoring what time removes. Woolf emphasizes this fusion between the aesthetic and the experiential; Lily's materials are not so much her colors and lines as they are her past, her life: "She was not inventing; she was only trying to smooth out something she had been given years ago folded up; something she had seen" (295). The extraordinary domestic metaphor of life as something folded up that the artist unfolds and makes visible is a humble image of resurrection.

One cannot stop death, but the severed ties can be refused, indeed re-fused into something again living and whole. It is a question of vision. Just as "nothing was simply one thing" (277), so too can Lily look out at the sea and grasp its terrible harmony, its human pattern:[22]

> She seemed to be standing up to the lips in some substance, to move and float and sink in it, yes, for these waters were unfathomably deep. Into them had spilled so many lives. The Ramsays'; the children's; and all sorts of waifs and strays of things besides. A washerwoman with her basket; a cook, a red-hot poke; the purples and grey-greens of flowers; some common feeling held the whole. [286]

Feeling unites the discrete parts into a tapestry that time cannot take apart. But feeling itself is evanescent, so art alone fixes it forever. One's art, like the knitted stocking and the shawl on the hook, must hold:

> Beautiful and bright it should be on the surface, feathery and evanescent, one colour melting into another like the colours on a butterfly's wing; but beneath the fabric must be clamped together with bolts of iron. It was to be a thing you could not dislodge with a team of horses. [255]

22. Dibattista makes some suggestive parallels to Freudian dream interpretation here, especially the crucial characteristic that dreams have of representing opposites as the same thing ("Winter's Tale," p. 186). It seems essential to appreciate not only the "therapeutic" dimension of such "doubleness," but to grasp the aesthetic principles as well; Woolf is looking for "the thing that endures," and a multivalent language endows its referent(s) with a very special life of their own.

"We perished, each alone" is the message of the sea and the air, as well as the litany of Mr. Ramsay. But the book brings them back to life, just as memory resurrects the absent and the dead. As the darkness comes, early in the book, and Mrs. Ramsay is reading a bedtime story to James, in that room with the mocking pig skull, thinking of Andrew perhaps falling off a cliff, totally enmeshed with loved ones, Woolf writes the following:

> But she did not let her voice change in the least as she finished the story, and added, shutting the book, and speaking the last words as if she had made them up herself, looking into James' eyes: "and there they are living still at this very time." [94]

Fairy tale? Art and human memory. Here is the life-giving power of the self. Through memory and art, the dead may continue to live, and our relationship with them enjoys or suffers thereby a strange half-life of its own. The subjective barriers to reciprocity—so highlighted in most of the fiction of relationship—have become the life line of connection, the spiritual continuation that goes on when the pulse has stopped and the clock no longer ticks.

6

To follow the discussion of Woolf's *To the Lighthouse* with Boris Vian's *L'Ecume des jours* is to append a bizarre *postscriptum* to the idealist argument that has come full circle. In Woolf, the inside world is beautifully wedded to the external scene, and we see that the virtues of relationship that we have been seeking—reciprocity, mutuality, generosity, permanence—are indeed compatible with narrative literature. Nonetheless, Vian's strange novel is worth including, because it sharply challenges the entire idealist tradition that has been sketched, those fertile emotive and narrative connections between subjectivity and relationship, that final transcendence offered by the mind. In *L'Ecume des jours*, that venerable pair—subjectivity and narrative—become unstuck, breathtakingly unstuck, as narrative control becomes empowered and energized in a surreal manner, while subjectivity disappears altogether. The Flaubertian scorn for Emma and the Ford manipulation of Dowell are spectacularly brought to completion in Vian's fantasy text, where the wants of the couple are glaringly incommensurate with the writerly and phenomenal world in which they have been placed. Whereas point of view still constitutes the authority of Woolf's book, it is radically eclipsed in *L'Ecume des jours*; but, proving that peculiar law of fiction that we have seen before, the story of the couple is all the more poignant, all the more compelling, even though it has lost its voice. Vian's book concludes my argument, in that it announces the death of a number of staple items: personal perspective, fixed world, a fair chance. Here, we see a frightening picture of some future, perhaps indeed the present, but shorn of its routinized façade and endlessly threatening. We can measure here, as never before, just how precious and precarious relationship is.

The first thing one has to note about *L'Ecume des jours* is the status that language enjoys within it. Words are marvelously potent here: metaphors are literalized, clichés are "activated," a ticket that is punched is blinded, a prescription that is, as the French say, "executed," is in fact guillotined. On some level, there can be no doubt that such a world represents every writer's dream, the dream of a magic language that would be immediate and energized, rather than figurative and mediated. Yet, this sorcerer's-apprentice realm is more than a tribute to language; it is also a remarkable medium through which Vian can display the violence and monstrosity of our everyday lives. The door that is slammed slams back, the tie that refuses to stay knotted has to be gunned down; the resistant sausages will not cook. At the skating rink, people are mutilated in swarms and then cavalierly dumped into large holes; the welfare literature displays butchers strangling children; at work, people are chained to machines, and they are routinely decimated, sectioned into pieces. There is clearly something demonic about this book, as if Vian discovered the murderous velocity of the planet's pull, the abrasive power of the wind, the ungiving hardness of the earth, the cosmic indifference that bathes human life. The doctor rightly thinks of his universe as shark-infested, of himself as the "malheureux naufragé dont les monstres voraces guettent la somnolence pour retourner le fragile esquif" (the unfortunate shipwrecked person threatened by voracious monsters who wait for him to fall asleep so they can capsize his fragile boat).[23] One reads this novel anthropologically, trying to decode the strange operational laws of this society: eels come out of faucets, windows

23. Boris Vian, *L'Ecume des jours* (Paris: 10/18, 1963), p. 92. Subsequent quotations will be taken from this edition and noted parenthetically in the body of the text.

that are broken grow back, leather is still alive. This is our world, if you will, but exponentially vitalized, its mechanical and industrial gadgets possessed of a life of their own, its natural and botanical features turned free and hostile.

At the beginning, this violent world is manageable: the very first scene shows us the protagonist ordering his blackhead to retreat back underneath the skin, out of sight; the gadgets serve the people, culminating in culinary and aesthetic delights. But all goes awry. Colin wants to fall in love. He yearns for nothing other than relationship, but in its simplest, most amoeba-like terms. Nonetheless, this is to be his transgression. Vian himself said that life is divided into two phases:

> celle où l'on s'habille soigneusement, et alors la vie consiste à s'habiller presque tout le temps, c'est avant qu'on soit marié, et on guette, le samedi soir, la venue du bouton qu'on aura sur le nez le dimanche, et ensuite on est plus tranquille, c'est-à-dire qu'on commence à avoir des malheurs parce qu'on a cessé de ne penser qu'à soi. [184]

> [the phase when one dresses with care, and life consists then of dressing up almost all the time, that's before one is married, and one is on the lookout, Saturday night, for the pimple one will have on the nose on Sunday, and afterward one is more relaxed, that is, one begins to have troubles because one no longer thinks only about oneself.]

The egoist alone is safe. Linkage is the danger. Vian treats us to linkage of the most basic, undiscriminating kind. Colin wants connection, and virtually any girl will do. In fact, the young men and young women of this novel are more or less interchangeable. More to the point, they have no psychology, no inner life or thoughts to speak of. We are at the antipodes of the subjective tradition, yet Vian is going to show us that relationship has a peculiar poignancy all its own, a pathos that is, as it were, structural, rather than dependent on the merits or souls of the individuals in question. To be joined to another alters the organism, changes (indeed, becomes) one's fate, and constitutes value. The courtship between Colin and Chloé is imaged in terms that are at once infantile and moving:

Le banc paraissait un peu humide et vert foncé. Malgré tout, cette allée n'était pas très fréquentée et ils n'étaient pas mal.

—Vous n'avez pas froid? demanda Colin.

—Non, avec ce nuage, dit Chloé. Mais . . . je veux bien me rapprocher tout de même.

—Oh! . . . dit Colin et il rougit.

Ça lui fit une drôle de sensation. Il mit son bras autour de la taille de Chloé. Sa toque était inclinée de l'autre côté et il avait, tout près des lèvres, un flot de cheveux lustrés.

—J'aime être avec vous, dit-il.

Chloé ne dit rien. Elle respira un peu plus vite et se rapprocha insensiblement.

Colin lui parlait presque à l'oreille.

—Vous ne vous ennuyez pas? demanda-t-il.

Elle fit non de la tête, et Colin put se rapprocher encore à la faveur du mouvement.

—Je . . . dit-il tout contre son oreille, et, à ce moment, comme par erreur, elle tourna la tête et Colin lui embrassait les lèvres. Ça ne dura pas très longtemps; mais, la fois d'après, c'était beaucoup mieux. Alors, il fourra sa figure dans les cheveux de Chloé, et ils restèrent là, sans rien dire. [43]

[The bench seemed a little humid and dark green. Nonetheless, this pathway had few people and they were okay.

"Aren't you cold?" asked Colin.

"No, with this cloud," said Chloé, "but . . . I would still like to get closer."

That gave him a funny feeling. He put his arm around Chloé's waist. Her hat was turned to one side, so he had, near his lips, a rush of shiny hair.

"I like being with you," he said.

Chloé said nothing. She breathed a little faster and moved slightly closer.

Colin was practically speaking in her ear.

"Are you having a good time?" he asked.

She nodded her head, and Colin was able to move still closer.

"I . . . ," he said, against her ear, and just then, as if by accident, she turned her head, and Colin kissed her lips. It didn't last long, but the next time it was much better. Then he buried his head in Chloé's hair, and they remained there, saying nothing.]

There is a certain coyness in these lines, but it is the coyness of children, the coyness of animals snuggling together for warmth and pleasure. Language is almost to no avail here, but the two bodies know precisely what they are seeking (the verb "rapprocher" is used three times), and any means of achieving touch is good. Something of the splendor and excitement of physical closeness is rendered here, the shimmering hair, the quickness of breathing, the inexorable rush of the senses seen close up, seen almost microscopically as one face takes in and merges with the other. This exquisite evocation of human tenderness and fragility will be systematically played in reverse by the novel's close as we see Alise's hair on fire and the tortured lungs of Chloé who can no longer breathe; but, for the present, Vian gives us the freshness and beauty of youth and desire. "J'aime être avec vous" is the elemental pulse of relationship, and the closing image of the boy's face buried in the girl's hair, utterly silent, tells us something about the mystery and appeal of oneness. This fragile human tenderness, the beginnings of intimacy, the touching of bodies, the tiny shelter of love is placed by Vian in the no-holds-barred, utterly demiurgic world that has already been described. In so doing, he exposes the vulnerability that is the condition of relationship, a vulnerability intolerably magnified by the surreal setting in which the lovers are put.

Perhaps the best way to describe this surreal setting is to say that people wear out, whereas things get stronger. "S'user" is a grisly verb, but it effectively characterizes what happens to humans in Vian's story. Not only does human flesh sicken and die, but everything connected with humans seems condemned: Nicolas ages, merely because of his connection with Colin and Chloé; the apartment systematically shrinks into one dimension as the death saga is played out; light is withdrawn from their world. Vian achieves striking effects by juxtaposing the people and the things: when Chloé coughs, it is "comme une étoffe de soie qui se déchire" (like the ripping of silk cloth [71]); on the same page, a window is broken but we then read, "Le carreau cassé commençait à repousser" (the broken pane began to grow again). This tenacious power and endurance of things is not only counterpointed by human fragility, but is heinously inscribed within the human realm, sabotaging human values at every turn. The window grows back, the leather is alive, the sausage is unkillable; the animal and the vegetable and the mechanical cohabit, and they do so *inside*. Chloé, ill, takes strange medicine, and Vian gives us a close-up of the new pharmaceutical mode:

Il y avait, sur des tables, une multitude de machines à faire les pilules et certaines fonctionnaient, bien qu'au ralenti.

Les pilules, sortant d'une tubulure de verre bleu, étaient recueillies dans des mains de cire qui les mettaient en cornets de papier plissé.

Colin se leva pour regarder de plus près la machine la plus proche et souleva le carter rouillé qui la protégeait. A l'intérieur, un animal composite, mi-chair, mi-métal, s'épuisait à avaler la matière de base et à l'expulser sous la forme de boulettes régulières.

—Vien voir, Chick, dit Colin.

—Quoi? demande Chick.

—C'est très curieux! . . . dit Colin.

Chick regarda. La bête avait une mâchoire allongée qui se déplaçait par rapides mouvements latéraux. Sous une peau transparente, on distinguait des côtes tubulaires d'acier mince et un conduit digestif qui s'agitait paresseusement.

—C'est un lapin modifié, dit Chick.

—Tu crois?

—Ça se fait couramment, dit Chick. On conserve la fonction qu'on veut. Là, il a gardé les mouvements du tube digestif, sans la partie chimique de la digestion. C'est bien plus simple que de faire des pilules avec un pisteur normal.

—Qu'est-ce que ça mange? demanda Colin.

—Des carottes chromées, dit Chick. [95–96]

[There were, on the table, a number of pill-making machines, and some were in operation, although at a slowed pace.

The pills came out of a tube of blue glass and were received by wax hands that put them into pleated paper cones.

Colin stood up to look more carefully at the closest machine and he lifted up the rusted gear-case that protected it. Inside was a composite animal, half flesh, half metal, laboring to ingest the raw materials and then to expel them in the form of even little pills.

"Come look, Chick," said Colin.

"What?" asked Chick.

"That's interesting," said Colin.

Chick looked. The animal had an elongated jawbone that moved in a rapid lateral fashion. Underneath its transparent skin

> could be seen tubular ribs of thin steel and a digestive tract that was in idle motion.
>
> "It's a modified rabbit," said Chick.
>
> "You think so?"
>
> "There are lots of them," said Chick. "You retain the function you want. This one has kept the dynamics of the digestive tract, but without the chemical process of digestion. It is certainly simpler than making pills with a normal pill gun."
>
> "What does it eat?" asked Colin.
>
> "Chrome carrots," said Chick.]

The "lapin modifié" testifies to an amalgamated world that relegates any purist notion of humanism to the past. Things are mixed here, and people are a hodgepodge of heterogeneous systems, each having its own dynamic, none necessarily subservient to human will. At first glance, Vian's arrangement seems wildly improbable, but the more one understands the systemic nature of the human body, or the electric circuitry of the neural and cardiac systems, or the vagaries of genetic engineering, or the encroachment of the chemical-laden atmosphere into our lungs and lives, the more "at home" Vian seems, the more of a realist he becomes.

The setting of *L'Ecume des jours* refuses to remain a setting; it reveals itself as the very medium of life, and the barbaric energies and aggressions that can be seen at skating rinks, factories, and laboratories are also to be found within the human body. But, they cannot always be kept within. Vian's characters have no "inner life" only in the psychological sense of the term; biologically, however, they have a teeming, cancerous inner life. The book starts with a blackhead that wants out, and although Colin is able to chase it back, we see the onset of a war that cannot be won; that erupting blackhead is monstrously re-imaged in the environs of the doctor's office, and Vian treats us to a full landscape of internal matter, things that either grow within the body or are stuffed in there to plug it up:

> Sous les barreaux, coulait de l'alcool mélangé d'éther qui charriait des tampons de coton souillé d'humeurs et de sanies, de sang quelquefois. De longs filaments de sang à demi coagulé teignaient çà et là le flux volatil et des lambeaux de chair, à demi décomposée, passaient lentement, tournant sur eux-mêmes, comme des icebergs trop fondus. On ne sentait rien que l'odeur de l'éther. Des bandes de gaze et des pansements descendaient

> aussi le courant, déroulant leurs anneaux endormis. Au droit de chaque maison, un tube de descente se déversait dans le canal et l'on pouvait déterminer la spécialisation du médecin en observant, quelques instants, l'orifice de ces tubes. Un œil roula sur lui-même, les regarda quelques instants, et disparut sous une large nappe de coton rougeâtre et molle comme une méduse malsaine. [103–104]
>
> [Underneath the bars there was a flow of alcohol mixed with ether, and floating in it were cotton pads stained with discharge and menstrual flow, sometimes with blood. Long filaments of half-coagulated blood mixed here and there with the volatile flux, and scraps of decomposing flesh eddied slowly by, turning in circles, like melting icebergs. There was a smell of nothing but ether. Pieces of gauze and bandages also came down the current, uncoiling their lazy circles. At the right of each house a tubelike gutter emptied into the canal, and one could make out the specialty of the doctor by looking, for a few seconds, at the opening of these tubes. An eye turned about itself, looked at them a few moments, and disappeared under a layer of soft, reddish cotton, like a sickly medusa.]

This charming, leisurely evocation is in the grand line of such texts as Baudelaire's "La Charogne," although Vian is significantly unable to manage the nineteenth-century poet's "carpe diem" response to the fate of flesh. Whereas Baudelaire merely puts his rotting carcass on his lovers' agenda, Vian reinvents the very world we live in, inverting the traditional inner/outer scheme and thereby putting the miasmic, viscous material flux up front, visible to all, inescapable. He has "liberated" the inner world of organs and discharges and tumors, spilled it out into the landscape, turned it into the landscape.[24] And, indeed, is it not that? In life, we cannot *see* the cancer that is growing within, the mucus that coats our passages, the massing obstruction in our veins, the aneurysm that is about to come; it is doubtless a

24. Michel Rybalka has very appropriately referred to Roland Barthes' desire for a new kind of science fiction as a way of describing Vian's exploratory program: "Ce que j'aimerais [Barthes], c'est une science-fiction qui ne porterait pas . . . sur des inventions d'ordre technique, physiologique ou biologique même, mais plutôt sur des imaginations d'ordre affectif: un fantasme-fiction, un amour-fiction, si j'ose dire" ("*L'Ecume des jours*: Amour-fiction," in *Boris Vian: Colloque de Cérisy 1* [Paris: 10/18, 1977], p. 213).

blindness to be thankful for. However, that eye which turns about itself, takes *us* in, makes us the spectators of our own innards. *L'Ecume des jours* gives this organic realm its due, puts it center-stage. Seeing this so close up, one realizes that, at the slightest provocation or loss of balance, these "natural" forces will turn against you, wipe you out.

Marriage is such a provocation. Chloé falls ill on her honeymoon, and the medicine she takes, which makes her feel "comme si deux bêtes se battaient dans [sa] poitrine" (as if two animals were fighting in her chest [100]), is devised to kill the lily that is growing in her chest.[25] The lily is growing and must not be allowed to flower; for this, she must be surrounded by other flowers and abstain from drinking. The lily does flower, after reaching a size of one meter; it is removed, but later Chloé has one in her other lung, and this one will kill her. Colin, who was rich and vain at the beginning—remember the blackhead—is now poor and desperate, for he needs money to keep Chloé alive as long as possible. Jobs are hard to find; here is one that he lands:

> —Voilà, dit l'homme. Entrez, je vais vous expliquer le travail.
>
> Colin entra. La pièce était petite, carrée. Les murs et le sol étaient de verre. Sur le sol, reposait un gros massif de terre en forme de cercueil, mais très épais, un mètre au moins. Une lourde couverture de laine était roulée à côté par terre. Aucun meuble. Une petite niche, pratiquée dans le mur renfermait un coffret de fer bleu. L'homme alla vers le coffret et l'ouvrit. Il en retira douze objets brillants et cylindriques avec un trou au milieu, miniscule.
>
> —La terre est stérile, vous savec ce que c'est, dit l'homme, il faut des matières de premier choix pour la défense du pays. Mais, pour que des canons de fusil poussent régulièrement, et sans distorsion, on a constaté, depuis longtemps qu'il faut de la chaleur humaine. Pour toutes les armes, c'est vrai, d'ailleurs.
>
> —Oui, dit Colin.

25. This lily has been the object of considerable critical scrutiny, and Alain Costes has seen fit to call it even a fetus: "Si en effet la toux survient immédiatement après le mariage, c'est qu'elle est sans doute liée intimement à la vie sexuelle du couple. Encore faudra-t-il rendre compte de la voracité de ce fœtus-nénuphar qui doit dévorer sa mère pour naître dans le marécage des derniers chapitres" (*Colloque de Cérisy* I, p. 119).

> —Vous pratiquez douze petits trous dans la terre, dit l'homme, répartis au milieu du cœur et du foie, et vous vous étendez sur la terre après vous être déshabillé. Vous vous recouvrez avec l'étoffe de laine stérile qui est là, et vous vous arrangez pour dégager une chaleur parfaitement régulière. [142–43]
>
> ["Here we are," said the man. "Come in, I'm going to explain the job to you."
>
> Colin went in. The room was little and square-shaped. The walls and the floor were made of glass. On the floor there was a big mound of earth in the shape of a casket, but very thick, at least a meter. A heavy wool cover was rolled next to it on the ground. No furniture. A little slot in the wall contained a blue steel box. The man went to the box and opened it. He took out twelve shiny, cylindrical objects with a tiny hole in the middle.
>
> "The earth is sterile, you know what that means," the man said."We need first-class raw materials for our national defense. But the only way to make the gun barrels grow evenly, without irregularities, is, as we learned a long time ago, to supply human heat. This is true for all weapons, you know."
>
> "Yes," said Colin.
>
> "You make twelve small holes in the earth," said the man, "corresponding to your heart and liver, and you lie down on the ground after taking your clothes off. You cover yourself up with this sterilized wool blanket, and you proceed to transmit a perfectly even heat."]

This hallucinatory sequence allows us, I think, to measure the abyss between tired cliché and visionary literature, for Vian is giving us, decades before it became current, a rigorously exact version of the slogan Make Love, Not War, but expressed as pure image, uncontaminated by moralizing or labeling. Yet, Vian's admixture of sex and guns announces the death of relationship. The mechanical world not only enslaves, but it requires human seed. It is a small step from this scene to a retrospective reading of the novel, whereby Colin's seed is equally mis- or dis-placed, leading, at least figuratively, to the creation of a lily in Chloé's chest rather than a child in her womb. There is a frightening meditation here about human impulse and energy, the deadly outcomes produced by sexual desire. Lilies in chests and steel flowers on rifles (for that is all that Colin can produce) are dreadful images of creativity gone amuck, turned against the creature, feasting on it. One can see the extraordinary logic of Vian's conception; he has found images for our poor words: cancer, alienation, dehumanization. The entire novel is an explosion of light, a literal re-forming of our deadened world of abstractions. We have doubtless *known* the things he says: that the pills we take alter our chemistry and assert their molecular will within us, that we are bound to the powerful machines we build, that we do routine violence to the natural world, that our best energies and sap of life are channeled technically away, that organic monsters breed within our bodies and grow us into death, that the bond between people is, as Faulkner would say, a bond floated by the gods, that they may take away, not because we stop loving, but because we stop living. These tidings are not ultimately new, but it is still not certain that we have ever seen it in literature rendered with such keenness.

With this in mind, we can return to the plight of the couple. My point is elementary: the fiction of relationship need not wallow in subjectivity or chart the inner vision of loving characters; Vian's novel insistently foregrounds the setting, adopts a perspective that is not only external but virtually extraterrestrial. Joyce's reworking of the Flaubert dictum on authorial maneuvering room—within or behind or beyond or above—announces, to be sure, a kind of rhetorical Magna Charta of modern fiction, with all the rights being in the hands of the writers. Seen from our angle, however, it is worth adding that such situational freedom adds great poignancy to the story of the couple, illuminating, as it does, their precious stasis by its sovereign mobility. Nothing could more powerfully underscore the fragility of relationship than the energized, utterly free world into which Vian has inserted it.[26] None of the consolations of the other novels will do here; neither language nor memory offers a reprieve. The connectedness of the heart is torture when the loved body is annihilated. Vian seems to be saying, with a rare narrative eloquence, that our bodies are our first and our last frontier. Devoid of personality, barely differentiated from one another, wanting only to continue living, Vian's characters are horrendously exposed. But their ultimate

26. Marguerite Nicod-Saraiva has argued that the fantasy and linguistic reflexivity of Vian's novel are meant to palliate, to "couper court" on the tragic issues at hand: "Mis en présence d'une peinture intolérable de la condition de l'homme, le lecteur est entraîné dans une bataille endiablée pour fuir cette vision" (*Colloque de Cérisy 1*, p. 148). Obviously, my view is that the tragic is heightened and enhanced by Vian's strategy.

vulnerability comes through relationship: Colin's miseries followed his marriage; his union with Chloé is unlike every other union I have mentioned: it brings forth neither the lyricism of Des Grieux nor the worship of Werther, neither the boredom of Emma nor the paranoia of Dowell; not even the selflessness and inward turn of Woolf. The marriage of Colin and Chloé, their relationship, seems to be a metaphysical scandal in their strange world, a vain and punishable act of human assertion, an act of hubris equivalent to answering the riddle of the sphinx. Their being together offends, and they will be struck down by the entire surreal arsenal at Vian's disposal. But only one of them is struck: the book's pathos hinges entirely on the fact that *he* suffers *her* death. Here is the reciprocity of relationship, here is "Mitempfinden" with a vengeance.[27]

Relationship, then, to begin summing up, is a physical as well as a mental construct. Not so much clocks as bodies record the passing of time. While we live, we float on the surface, the froth of days, "l'écume des jours," but Vian, like Woolf and all the writers I have dealt with, knows that "we perish, each alone." Two subjects cannot be one, but two bodies can, at least momentarily, unite. Little is more "touching" in *L'Ecume des jours* than the moment when Chloé asks Colin to love her diseased and dying body:

> —Tiens-moi, Colin. Je vais tomber!
> —C'est le lit qui t'a fatiguée . . . dit Colin.
> —Non, dit Chloé. C'est les pilules de ton vieux marchand.
> Elle essaya de se tenir debout toute seule et chancela. Colin la rattrapa et elle l'entraina dans sa chute sur le lit.
> —Je suis bien comme ça, dit Chloé. Reste contre moi. Cela fait si longtemps que nous n'avons pas couché ensemble!
> —Il ne faut pas, dit Colin.
> —Si, il faut. Embrasse-moi. Je suis ta femme, oui ou non?
> —Oui, dit Colin, mais tu ne vas pas bien.

27. Alain Costes has made an intriguing argument for ambiguity and conflict at the instinctual level in *L'Ecume des jours*; hence, he feels that Colin hates as well as loves Chloé, and that Vian is out to show that he must "destroy" her by his "love": "A l'image d'une fleur carnivore dont l'évocation nous fige entre beauté et horreur, *L'Ecume des jours* entrecroise constamment les affects les plus contradictoires, les plus fondamentaux aussi. Piégé entre rire et sanglot, bonheur et désespoir, le lecteur retrouve en lui, en toute méconnaissance, les échos d'émois primitifs qui lui parlent d'un temps où amour et haine filaient le même cocon" (*Colloque de Cérisy I*, p. 177).

—C'est pas ma faute, dit Chloé et sa bouche frémit un peu, comme si elle allait pleurer.

Colin se pencha vers elle et l'embrassa très doucement, comme il eût embrassé une fleur.

—Encore, dit Chloé. Et pas seulement ma figure . . . Tu ne m'aimes plus alors? Tu ne veux plus de femme?

Il la serra plus fort dans ses bras. Elle était tiède et odorante. Un flacon de parfum, sortant d'une boite capitonnée de blanc.

—Oui, dit Chloé en s'étirant . . . encore . . . [101–102]

["Hold me, Colin, I'm going to fall!"

"It's the bed that exhausted you," said Colin.

"No," said Chloé, "it's your old peddler's pills."

She tried to stand up on her own and wavered. Colin grabbed her, and she pulled him down with her on the bed.

"I'm fine just like that," said Chloé. "Stay with me. It's been such a long time since we've slept together."

"We shouldn't," said Colin.

"Yes, we should. Kiss me. I'm your woman, yes or no?"

"Yes," said Colin, "but you're not well."

"That's not my fault," said Chloé, and her mouth trembled a little, as if she were going to cry.

Colin leaned toward her and kissed her very tenderly, as he would have kissed a flower.

"More," said Chloé. "And not only my face . . . Don't you still love me? Are you tired of your woman?"

He held her more closely in his arms. She was warm and fragrant. A bottle of perfume, coming from a white padded box.

"Yes," said Chloé, stretching out, "More . . ."]

The body is the doomed *terra firma* of relationship; language itself stops here, as discourse is completed by intercourse. So too, Boris Vian completes as well as challenges the idealist tradition that culminates in Woolf. *To the Lighthouse* and *L'Ecume des jours* present the life-and-death stories of the mind and the body; they show us, as fictions, that relationship is not a fiction.

CHAPTER TWO

Memory and Multiplicity

It is hard to imagine the fiction of relationship without referring repeatedly to the "inner life." Every text studied in this book has a complex (or, at least, problematic) view of that perhaps mythic realm. We have seen that the inner life carries an essential, inherent blindness with it as the price of its authenticity: to feel and know what is inside amounts to not being there outside. We have seen in Boris Vian's work, and we will encounter in subsequent chapters, a view of the inner life that is devastatingly literal, a matter of organs and blood and cells and humors. For most of us, however, as readers of literature, the inner life signifies the psychic activity within that consort (or construct) that we call a self. This psychic activity is distinguished by consciousness, and one of its chief pursuits is to comment on and interpret the events that befall the body it inhabits. At the center of this essay is the peculiar shaping and caretaking role assumed by consciousness, the work it performs as guarantor and retainer, the labor of identity. In this light, consciousness may be said to maintain our form, recall what is over, await what may come, imagine what might be or have been, always referring these psychic "events" to a proprietary center (or, indeed, circumference) of self. Such ventures would seem to constitute self; they compose its estate. Names used for denoting this realm range from self to identity to spirit to soul.

It can hardly surprise us that writing in general, and literature in particular, have frequently had common cause with the activity of charting, inventorying, expressing, and sharing this inner realm. The novel, especially, has often been devoted to recording the adventures of consciousness, to pruning the indiscriminate facts and stimuli of life into some kind of composite figure. That process of pruning and shaping, of positing a kind of glue or continuum between the discrete events and episodes of experience, is a fascinating activity, all the more fascinating when the writer experiences it as problematic, as openly fictive. The study that follows seeks to identify three special moments in the novel's evolution vis-à-vis the charting of the inner life: notably, its rudimentary beginning (Defoe), its teeming plenitude (Proust), its strange demise (Robbe-Grillet).

What, it may be asked, does relationship have to do with these matters? The answer is: it complicates, enriches, and ultimately adds pathos and urgency to the processes of self-portraiture. Relationship is not only the contextual ground on which the subject exists, but, often enough, the very fabric of which the self is made. Short of being a hermit, few people take stock of their inner life in isolation, *in vacuo*. One is always, willy-nilly, taking joint measures, both of oneself and of others. These two spectacles may look very different, since we are endlessly present at the former and sporadically peering at the latter. Even the thickest among us hears his or her inner tune, whereas even the finest may be inventing the other's tale. And, of course, one's own life must dwarf that of the other, in all ways: size, complexity, significance. Yet, however kaleidoscopic one's inner life is, however multiple and discontinuous one may seem to oneself, from the "inside," the very fixity of the body (an apparent fixity, to be sure) can make us appear monolithic to others, can make them seem "unitary" to us. This is, of course, largely a question of vision: we see our own pluralism; as for that of others, we are obliged to guess, to sort it out, because we are radically in the dark here, on the outside looking in.

This business of looking "in," taking stock of one's own states and trying to assess those of others, is the stuff of fiction. Composed both of tally sheets and guesswork, this odd stock-taking is a key activity, constitutive of all identities, our own and our estimate of others' as well. On the face of it, couched in such analytical language, these matters may seem highly abstruse, the sort of thing one ponders once a month, in one's study, as material for a sermon or an essay. But little is more immediate, continuous, vital, and unnerving than this tandem of light and dark, this mix of personal inventory and assessment of others. Both ventures are navigational, a measuring of the weather within and without. The novelists in question—Defoe, Proust, and Robbe-Grillet—provide three different ways of taking these "markings"; seen together, they make up a map.

1

Everyone knows Mark Schorer's famous assessment of *Moll Flanders*: "It is the morality of measurement, and without in the least intending it, *Moll Flanders* is our classic revelation of the mercantile mind: the morality of measurement, which Defoe has completely neglected to measure."[1] Defoe's novel, Schorer persuasively argues, is committed to measuring and counting, and it follows that what cannot be counted or measured is not caught within its nets. Damask, plate, lace, shillings, and guineas can be counted; so too can husbands, especially insofar as they represent damask, plate, lace, shillings, and guineas. These items loom large in Defoe's repertory, so large that many readers have felt that they—the things—constitute the sole authority in Defoe's scheme, and that all talk of spirit, soul, values, and the like is twaddle, not measurable and not serious. It is not so much a question of the "inner" life going out of business, but rather a kind of ongoing algebra whereby everything is transformed into the measurable, whereby the intangible and the immaterial are persistently reified if they are to command any credence. Dorothy Van Ghent's well known critique of the novel toils in much the same vineyard, and she is especially good at indicating just what Moll does and does not attend to; thus, low-key passages in Defoe become high-key passages for Van Ghent, such as the following:

> It concerns the Story in hand very little to enter into the farther particulars of the Family, or of myself, for the five Years that I liv'd with this Husband; only to observe that I had two Children by him, and that at the end of five Year he Died: He had been really a very good Husband to me, and we liv'd very agreeably together. But as he had not receiv'd much from them, and had in the little time he liv'd acquir'd no great Matters, so my Circumstances were not great, nor was I much mended by the Match; Indeed I had preserv'd the elder Brother's Bonds to me, to pay me 500 *l.* which he offer'd me for my Consent to Marry his Brother; and this, with what I had saved of the Money he formerly gave me, and about as much more by my Husband, left me a Widow with about 1200 *l.* in my Pocket.
>
> My two Children were indeed taken happily off of my Hands by my Husband's Father and Mother, and that by the way was all they got by Mrs. Betty.[2]

1. Mark Schorer, "Technique as Discovery," in *Forms of Modern Fiction*, ed. William Van O'Connor (Bloomington: Indiana University Press, 1959), p. 12.

2. Daniel Defoe, *Moll Flanders*, ed. Edward Kelly (New York: Norton, 1973), pp. 46–47. Subsequent quotations will be taken from this edition and noted parenthetically in the body of the text.

Commenting on this passage, Van Ghent says:

> What five years of her young womanhood, marriage, domesticity, and motherhood mean to Moll are certain finances, certain bonds amounting to so much, a certain quantity of cash in her pocket. . . . The statement informs us, with powerful obliquity, that the way to be happy through children is to have them taken off one's hands; it informs us also that children may be useful in settling family debts. With the greatest placidity and aplomb on Moll's part, the children are neatly converted into a shrewd price by which she gets out of a bad bargain with clean skirts. Schematically, what has been happening here is the conversion of all subjective, emotional, and moral experience—implicit in the fact of Moll's five years of marriage and motherhood—into pocket and bank money, into the materially measurable.[3]

Schorer and Van Ghent are not wrong about *Moll Flanders*, and it is one of the most "externalized" novels that exists. Intangibles are made tangible, and what counts is what is happening NOW, not the five years past or the five years to come. The passing of time would seem to count for little in Defoe's scheme, although he is remarkably aware of what time does to people. The changes that count are the material ones (Moll is either enriched or impoverished by each new episode), and ultimately Moll herself is included in this strange countdown. Nothing is more revelatory in this regard than the long title of the novel:

> The Fortunes and Misfortunes of the Famous Moll Flanders, etc. Who was Born in Newgate, and during a Life of continu'd Variety for threescore Years, besides her Childhood, was Twelve Year a *Whore*, five times a *Wife* (whereof once to her own Brother) Twelve Year a *Thief*, eight year a Transported *Felon* in *Virginia*, at last grew *Rich*, liv'd *Honest*, and died a *Penitent*.

Even granting the particulars of an eighteenth-century journalistic plain style, one is struck by the numbers here, the tally sheet that serves as a portrait of Moll. One is also struck, perhaps more after finishing the novel than when one initially opens it, by the categorical imperatives that seem to dominate here. Almost two hundred years later, Proust was to speak of the barricaded parts of one's experience

3. Dorothy Van Ghent, *The English Novel: Form and Function* (New York: Harper & Row, 1953), p. 53.

as *vases clos*, but Defoe's title page is staggering in its list of discrete, sealed-off particulars, of all-powerful codes between which little commerce is imaginable: Whore-Wife, Thief-Honest, Felon-Penitent. Names and labels have a forbidding autonomy, and they create, at certain charged moments, a peculiar form of melodrama; for example, after countless chaste nights in bed naked together, Moll finally "indulges" in sex with her married friend, and she puts it in the following way: "Thus the Government of our Virtue was broken, and I exchang'd the Place of Friend for that unmusical harsh-sounding Title of WHORE" (92). Although such heavy machinery does not seem designed for gradations or subtle effects, it does render the bald contours of Defoe's psycho-moral landscape. In this realm, things predominate, and when it comes to tagging Moll's behavior with an ethical label, the job is carried out with the straightforwardness of allegory.

What one misses, of course, are the possible connections between these terms, the human drama of negotiating such an itinerary. Instead, *Moll Flanders* is larded with non sequiturs, with dangling episodes and husbands, with abandoned children and altered stations. Whereas Fielding will sovereignly orchestrate his disguised men and women into a round of musical beds, Defoe opts for the comedy of disunion:

> And as we kept always together, so we grew very intimate, yet he never knew that I was not a Man; nay, tho' I several times went home with him to his Lodgings, according as our business directed, and four or five times lay with him all Night; But our Design lay another way, and it was absolutely necessary to me to conceal my Sex from him, as appear'd afterwards. [168]

In such a novel it is fitting that Moll and her friend lay naked in bed together many nights, unjoined, just as she lay "separately" four or five times with her accomplice in the passage just quoted. One of the nicest images of gratuitous separation is to be seen when Moll tracks her sick friend to his house in Bloomsbury, "whither he had, a little before he fell Sick, remov'd his whole Family; and that his Wife and Wife's Mother were in the same House, tho' the Wife was not suffered to know that she was in the same House as her Husband" (95). Each of these episodes reveals the isolated, disconnected nature of Defoe's people; even in a setting of sexual or familial mesh, they are strikingly alone, always widowed or orphaned in some sense.

Connectives lack in this world. Children are among the most tangible connectives, as are mates, but Moll's experience here is what it is elsewhere: numerical and nominative rather than substantive and binding. She goes through many men, but do we remember them? As for her children, there is the Van Ghent criticism, but perhaps we get a still sharper sense of her perspective in the elaborate preparations made for lying-in. Having a child paves the way for a comparative data-based analysis of midwifing possibilities, replete with three full bills of fare furnished by Mother Midnite, running from the most modest *prix fixe* to the much grander *repas gastronomique*. This is indeed the "conversion of all subjective, emotional and moral experience . . . into the materially measurable," and it testifies to the kinds of things Defoe's grid can take in. Children and husbands become as dimensionless and reified as the china and plate and cloth that are so desirable. Whatever spiritual or moral or emotional or temporal "outreach" these items might have is removed from the equation, seems beyond imagining. They have no meaning other than their presence. *Moll Flanders* is an ongoing tribute to the *presence* of things, as opposed to their transcendence or their history. We can see it happening. The child-to-be-born becomes a lying-in synopsis. The husband who is not there is replaced by the next available suitor. The family fleeing the fire with its precious heirlooms falls perfectly and ineluctably into Moll's hands, for in her hands those time- and emotion-drenched items will become just so many pounds of sterling or cloth. Can it be surprising that children will also be traded and stolen in such a text, that Mother Midnite "had been sued by a certain Gentleman who had had his Daughter stolen from him, and who it seems she had helped to convey away" (154). All of life becomes negotiable goods in this kind of scheme, and Defoe's rendition of the material life has a kind of innocence and vigor and animal health that we rarely encounter in fiction.

Defoe is patently vulnerable to the "morals" charge, as it has been articulated by Schorer, Van Ghent, and many others. For those who uphold, in Barthes' condescending term, "la civilisation de l'âme," Defoe is something of a monstrosity, offering us either nothing or else such huge but empty monolithic constructs as Wife versus Whore and the like. But, an argument can also be made that his way of presenting things has a rare kind of honesty—both moral and conceptual—that one would do well to examine. As far back as 1957, Ian Watt re-evaluated Defoe's famous egotism, and he saw in the author's "concentration on isolated individuals" a peculiarly modern view of life, a view so modern that he suggested, with considerable eloquence, that Defoe's time may now be coming:

> . . . it is certain that, at the end of the long tradition of the European novel, and of the society whose individualism, leisure and unexampled security allowed it to make personal relations the major theme of its literature, Defoe is a welcome and portentous figure. Welcome because he seems long ago to have called the great bluff of the novel—its suggestion that personal relations really are the be-all and end-all of life; portentous because he, and only he, among the great writers of the past, has presented the struggle for survival in the bleak perspectives which recent history has brought back to a commanding position on the human stage.[4]

In contrast to the high-sounding moral niceties of the "great tradition," Defoe was seen to have the virtue of describing the human animal as a self-enclosed creature, bent on living, focusing on the here-and-now, negotiating—usually with relish—the innumerable bargains and deals that life offers to the living.

If Watt's view has a certain unsweetened, tonic taste of truth to it, the other defense of Defoe is a theoretical one, and may be linked with the name of Robbe-Grillet. Now, Robbe-Grillet never wrote about Defoe (and may never have read him), but in his sauciest early essays—roughly contemporaneous with Watt's *Rise of the Novel*—he brilliantly called into question the never-never world of content and interiority that literature customarily serves up. In Robbe-Grillet's phenomenology, man is a thing among things, and the task of art is to make us rediscover our unprivileged place in the world. That world was to be delivered verbally by means of a meticulous "objectal" style that relentlessly stuck to surfaces. That Robbe-Grillet's own work does not behave as it should is less central to our purposes than the vantage point his prescriptive theory offers on *Moll Flanders*. The French *nouveau romancier* was also, to re-use Watt's language, calling the bluff of the European novel, not so much in terms of its traffic with relationship as with meaning itself, the underlying, never-visible, yet exclusively prized "essence" of things. Robbe-Grillet, like Defoe, entrusts his narrative to surfaces and to things, and he too is suspicious of that spirit realm that can never be seen, touched, or

4. Ian Watt, *The Rise of the Novel* (Berkeley: University of California Press, 1957), pp. 133–34.

smelled. To be sure, the eighteenth-century English writer does not indulge in geometry or the kind of figural landscapes dear to the French modernist; but the Frenchman does indeed provide a strange underpinning to Defoe, a philosophy of surfaces that is marvelously adumbrated in the materialist fiction of Defoe.

The case should be acquiring some contours by now. Defoe's presumable morality of measurement may be more than ethical abdication; it can also be seen as a special form of innocence, a refusal to truck with the so-called inner world and a brash certainty that the individual is on his own, for better or for worse. The pragmatic and the here-and-now seem to rule, and the novel's unswerving focus on the visible seems purchased at the cost of any real interest in the realms of spirit or the past. This argument is susceptible, as we have seen, to praise as well as criticism, and no reading of Defoe can afford to ignore these constitutive features of his art. But, what is fascinating, and much less examined, is the way Defoe manages to *work* this construct of his, the way in which Moll Flanders—unidimensional and object-oriented though she is—stumbles onto and reveres all those items presumably beyond her reach: spirit, past, connection. The atomized, surface world of the present—so evidently the abiding authority in Defoe's scheme—becomes, at special moments, luminous and echoing. To understand and to measure that aura and that echo are the burden of the following analysis.

Consider, for example, the following rumination, which occurs precisely after Moll's crass calculation regarding the foisting of her children onto her in-laws:

> I confess I was not suitably affected with the loss of my Husband; nor indeed can I say that I ever Lov'd him as I ought to have done, or as was proportionable to the good Usage I had from him, for he was a tender, kind, good humour'd Man as any Woman could desire; but his Brother being so always in my sight, *at least*, while we were in the Country, was a continual Snare to me; and I never was in Bed with my Husband, but I wish'd my Self in the Arms of his Brother; and tho' his Brother never offer'd me the least Kindness that way, after our Marriage, but carried it just as a Brother ought to do; yet, it was impossible for me to do so to him; In short, I committed Adultery and Incest with him every day in my Desires, which without Doubt, was as effectually Criminal in the Nature of the Guilt, as if I had actually done it. [47]

This splendid passage flaunts the authority of the unseen and the past. The husband in bed is ghosted and cuckolded by the ever-present, yet absent older brother; the present things are inhabited by past spirits. Desire re-scripts the world, and the conjugal sex is transformed—at least, psychically—into adultery and incest. Nothing is what it appears; the past lives, and the yearned-for competes with the actual. The virtual rivals with the recorded, and the here-and-now is a spectral enactment of the was-or-will-be. Such a scene is a textbook case of libidinal displacement, and it operates a kind of cubist explosion on the static surface world.

Doubtless the most celebrated triumph of desire over things occurs in the remarkable parting scene between Moll and her Lancashire husband, Jemy. The reader who is accustomed to Moll's strategical gambits encounters the emotional violence of this episode with surprise. Logic and self-interest dictate that the two deceivers will part, once they have nothing left to gain, but logic is to no avail as Moll suffers Jemy's absence: "I eat but little, and after Dinner I fell into a violent Fit of crying, every now and then, calling him by his Name, which was *James. O Jemy!* said I, *come back, come back*, I'll give you all I have; I'll beg, I'll starve with you"(120). If time was overcome by Moll's desire for the older brother, space will be transcended here, as Moll's call for connection carries twelve miles, reaches Jemy and brings him back. Why the magic? Surely, Defoe would not break his empirical code if he were not at pains to show that strong feeling has a shaping power, a dimensionality all its own. The beauty of *Moll Flanders* lies in its moments of magic and transcendence that are wholly inscribed within the phenomenal world even as they suffuse it with spirit. To borrow, prematurely, from Proust, it is as if Defoe were writing a kind of palimpsest wherein the surface script is periodically shot through with the luminosity of an older language.

The unseen does exist in *Moll Flanders*, and it enjoys a crucial dialectical relationship with the visible. Nowhere does this dialectic count more than in Moll's fabulous successes in disguise and impersonation. Much has been written about the relative authenticity or inauthenticity of Moll, as she plies her trade as thief and con woman, but this whole line of thinking hinges on Moll's *doubleness*, her strategic appearance (beggar woman, rich dowager, woman of property, man) and her "true" self (thief), which is invisible.[5] Let us state the

5. Most Defoe critics have addressed this issue of Moll's doubleness, and it has received all manner of interpretation, ranging from casuistry to "indif-

obvious: the people whom Moll gulls do not perceive this doubleness. We, who watch her, know better. Or do we? Can Moll tell us what she is? Does she even know what she is? Do her performances indicate "truths" beyond her ken? Will it really suffice to label her "thief" (or, indeed, Whore or Felon or Penitent or the like)? Let us recall Robbe-Grillet and refocus on what we actually see: a woman intricately embroiled with others. To deceive others, you have to be *with* them; is it possible that being *with* them counts as much as deceiving them? What is the reader to make of Moll speaking to the child in the park, helping the family flee the burning house, planning her future with the banker or letting herself be wooed by Jemy? All of these episodes could be said to constitute a *ballet* of relationship, a peculiar *pas de deux* in which the gestural alone counts for the partner whereas the verbal (the private, hidden truth) alone counts for the reader. Are these gestures inauthentic? Whatever they might *mean*, they *show* the loner linked, entangled with others, at times feverishly social and familial. One initially interprets such a discrepancy between motive and performance as one of the ironic trumps of art, its capacity to cut through appearances and reveal what is hidden to the eye. Initially. But, soon enough either/or yields to both/and, and one interprets these masquerade scenes doubly, in two crucial senses, as both concealing and enabling. The gestures and performances of *Moll Flanders* come to be, as is doubtless true of our own gestures and performances, modes of enactment, ways of being ourselves, a kind of speech for which words will not and cannot do. The moment we see this, we realize that Defoe's novel is wonderfully ambivalent, shot through with a language of plot and image that is raucously at odds with its overt verbal and moral homilies. The verbal will take us only so far in this novel.[6] We never do truly know *why* Moll does what she

---

ferent monitoring." In arguing for the patterning in Defoe's work, David Blewett has perceptively pointed out that "truth" is too restricted a grid for the character which Defoe has created, and that we often encounter a vocabulary of equivocation that will accommodate Defoe's vision: "There is one truth that operates in the conscience or at moments of self-accusation, but there is another 'truth' that exists only in the world of appearance and deception" (*Defoe's Art of Fiction* [Toronto: University of Toronto Press, 1979], p. 89). Blewett does not assess this manipulation of appearances in the light of what the novel form is able to display, nor does he discern in it the humanist, caretaking ethos that I am at pains to elaborate.

6. Martin Price has, better than anyone, made the argument that Defoe's celebration of "energies" seems to have an ethos of its own (*To the Palace of*

does, although we soon enough see that it is not for the money. Sooner or later, one is obliged to recognize that Moll revels in disguise because it suits her, because it completes her. She is not hiding behind her masks; she is her masks.

There is something of a visual extravaganza here. We *see* the playing out of a repertory. Wife-whore-thief-dowager-man, each avatar is actualized before our eyes, and dissolved shortly afterward. Each picture, each coming together of man and woman, thief and victim, achieves its focus, its contact, its pathos only insofar as the past roles, the hidden motives remain unseen. Her public must think each instance enduring, each part the whole. For others, Moll is exclusively the present performance, the visible moment. There is something enormous in Defoe's project here, for he is tackling the elemental theatrics and duplicity of all social life. The laws of visibility coerce, but only so long as someone is looking; yet, how unguarded, unwatched, scandously free most lives are, most of the time. Who does not cheat? Moll is the consummate chameleon, metamorphosing at will, reveling in multiplicity, sagely aware that no one ever knows the difference, that no one is keeping score. There is a real scandal in Moll's behavior, because it seems offensive and intolerable that a character could be so varied and innocent at the same time, could refuse to assimilate experience, refuse to remember, refuse to *interpret*. Instead, Moll is insistently multiple, doing her numbers, blatantly surface, cheerfully discontinuous. Such behavior would seem to constitute a fundamental human crime (such as that which Schorer and Van Ghent accuse her), but, as we have said, the unseen is not absent from the scene. Moll understands to perfection the laws of visibility, the authority of appearances. She knows the extraordinary freedom of performance that presents her exclusively in the here-and-now, and leaves everything else in the dark. Defoe is encountering here nothing less than the sovereign and tragic freedom of life itself: what we think, what we have been, can never show; the surface and the moment alone can be seen. Sovereign, because the avenues for

---

Wisdom: Studies in Order and Energy from Dryden to Blake [New York: Doubleday, 1964]). "Energy" might be a better road into the dynamics of the novel than "irony" has proved to be; Laura Curtis, in *The Elusive Daniel Defoe* (London: Vision Press, 1984), has tried to find a way out of the "debate" between the "controlled" reading of Novak and the "unintentional irony" reading of Watt by developing an intriguing view of *Moll Flanders* as a "hoax" narrative, one that never does reveal its "bottom line" (unlike irony, which depends on critical readjustment).

self-creation and deceit are virtually endless; tragic because we are doomed to opacity. As performer and woman-on-the-make, Moll exploits such duplicity; as moral consciousness, however, Moll measures it.

One attends to something very nigh to the birth of the novel, as Moll, skilled at all manner of weights and measures, at last inventories what Montaigne called *l'arrière boutique*, the private chamber of time, thought, and consciousness, whose records are kept in the dark. But they can be kept. At signal moments in the novel, the door to this chamber opens:

> Then it occur'd to me what an abominable Creature am I! and how is this innocent Gentleman going to be abus'd by me! How little does he think, that having Divorc'd a Whore, he is throwing himself into the Arms of another! that he is going to Marry one that has lain with two Brothers, and has had three Children by her own Brother, one that was born in *Newgate*, whose Mother was a Whore, and is now a transported Thief; one that has lain with thirteen Men, and has had a Child since he saw me! poor Gentleman! *said I*, What is he going to do? After this reproaching myself was over, it followed thus: Well, if I must be his Wife, if it please God to give me Grace, I'll be a true Wife to him, and love him suitably to the strange Excess of his Passion for me; I will make him Amends, if possible, by what he shall see, for the Cheats and Abuses I put upon him, which he does not see. [142]

Although this extended curriculum vitae unmistakably parallels the title page, there is quite a difference between us seeing it and Moll reflecting on it. With little fanfare and characteristic plain-speaking, Moll moves from breast-beating to calm assessment, but no matter how calmly she goes about it, Moll is making the rather awesome discovery that one's self is strangely constant although one's experiences never stop, and this discovery is followed by a moral resolve to establish some kind of harmony or equilibrium between the visible present and the invisible past. In owning her episodes, Moll is proprietary in the finest sense: her purchase on experience, for once, is temporal rather than spatial, collectivist rather than privatist. She has always wonderfully understood that the present performance is alone visible, visible to the spectator; she now realizes, with considerable acuity, that *all* performances are visible, visible to the performer.

Defoe has all along tapped the high drama of perception that renders our thoughts and our past invisible to others, and his heroine's professional artistry consists in exploiting this discrepancy. By making Moll now take her own measure, he reminds us that the wildest external disguises pale before the unseen transformations that time deals out to all living creatures. We change, but who knows? The body alters so slowly, shows so little; the mental life is, for the outsider, so muted and muffled; the past does not show. Moll Flanders would seem to be the last character in fiction to appreciate this inner realm, these private alterations, but nonetheless, there she is, charting the great divide between one's sensed-and-lived variety and one's visible sameness. The navel-gazing protagonists of modern fiction could hardly command the same respect, for they routinely truck with such alterations; for Moll, it is something new. In pledging to "make him Amends, if possible, by what he shall see, for the Cheats and Abuses . . . which he does not see," Moll announces a code of human responsibility and posits the hegemony of self. The self contains and assesses its episodes, past as well as present, mental as well as gestural. Defoe has created in Moll Flanders something rich and capacious.

And one must look for that self sometimes in strange places. Moll rarely achieves the level of lucidity and self-knowledge mirrored in the passage just discussed, and for the most part, her self-reflexiveness is minimal. But Defoe has several languages at his disposal, and they all speak Moll. At each crisis, for example, Moll experiences acute visceral distress, ranging from nausea to revulsion to sickness to fits of crying. These are all elemental expressions of character. At other junctures, Defoe displaces Moll's emotional or spiritual activity onto the scene itself, and we must learn to see it there. Consider, in this regard, the amazing sequence that recounts Moll's first theft; i.e., her entry into a new life. We may recall that she has been wasting away for two years, "as if it were only bleeding to Death," and in this state of distraction she passes "a little Bundle wrapt in a white Cloth"; something very deep within Moll emerges here, as she steals the bundle, succumbing to the Evil One, whose appeal is like "a Voice spoken to me over my shoulder." Up to now, the language is conventional enough, but Moll then enters a veritable labyrinth of Defoe's making:

> It is impossible to express the Horror of my Soul all the while I did it: when I went away I had no Heart to run, or scarce to mend my pace; I cross'd the Street indeed, and went down the first turning I came to, and I think it was a Street that went thro'

> into *Fenchurch-street*, from thence I cross'd and turn'd thro' so many ways and turnings that I could never tell which way it was, nor where I went, for I felt not the Ground, I stept on, and the farther I was out of Danger, the faster I went, till tyr'd and out of Breath, I was forc'd to sit down on a little Bench at a Door, and then I began to recover, and found I was got into *Thames-street* near *Billingsgate*. I rested me a little and went on, my Blood was all in a Fire, my Heart beat as if I was in a sudden Fright: In short, I was under such a Surprize that I still knew not whither I was going, or what to do. [150]

The self is being "unpacked" in this passage, and the mazelike setting where Moll loses herself corresponds to the new space she is now to enter, an uncharted new terrain for self-enactment via mask and theft. We witness on these pages the murky gestation of a self, and it does not surprise us that Moll is in a trancelike state: "I knew not what to do, it was all Fear without, and Dark within," and "I . . . wandered about I knew not whither, and in search of I knew not what" (151). There will not be much psychologizing in Defoe's novel, but he does indeed chart the path from Wife to Whore, from Felon to Penitent. But that path is not, as we might anticipate, a simple linear path; instead, it is more like a spiral, a series of unfurlings and unpackings, beckoning already to that famous "forking path" which Borges was to use as a figure for the strange instancing of the self over time. "In the work of Ts'ui Pên, all possible outcomes occur," Borges writes; "each one is the point of departure for other forkings. Sometimes, the paths of this labyrinth converge: for example, you arrive at this house, but in one of the possible pasts you are my enemy, in another, my friend."[7] Whereas Borges set out willfully and ingeniously to explode the barriers of time and space, Defoe seems to have stumbled onto his discovery of freedom and volume, as if one lurched, in spurts and off balance, into new realms where one's future is waiting.

At climactic moments, Moll's self so completely exits from its here-and-now precincts that it "abrupts" onto the eternal. Grave illness can provoke such a change of venue, and Moll's Bath lover has ample occasion to change his vision: "It is true that Sick Beds are the times when such Correspondences as this are look'd on with different Countenance, and seen with other Eyes than we saw them with, or

7. Jorge Luis Borges, "The Garden of Forking Paths," in *Labyrinths: Selected Stories and Other Writings*, eds. Donald Yates and James Irby (New York: New Directions, 1964), p. 26.

than they appear'd with before: My Lover had been at the Gates of Death, and at the very brink of Eternity" (97). There are portals and thresholds in *Moll Flanders*, and it is rigorously appropriate that Moll widens her own optic at Newgate; her shocked awareness of a new scheme of things is consistently rendered by Defoe in terms of perspective itself:

> I now began to look back upon my past Life with abhorrence, and having a kind of view into the other Side of time, the things of Life, as I believe they do with every Body at such a time, began to look with a different Aspect, and quite another Shape, than they did before. [225]

We are dealing with more than a moral transformation here.[8] Moll has run headlong into a world where nothing is simply itself, now; instead, all things are inscribed in time and spirit. The old language, which was quite adequate for counting silver and coveting cloth, will no longer suffice:

> I am not capable of reading Lectures of Instruction to any Body, but I relate this in the very manner in which things then appear'd to me, as made on my Soul at that time; indeed those Impressions are not to be explain'd by Words, or if they are, I am not Mistress of Words enough to express them; It must the Work of every sober Reader to make just Reflections on them, as their own Circumstances may direct; and without Question, this is what every one at sometime or other may feel something of; I mean a clearer Sight into things to come, than they had here, and a dark view of their own Concern in them. [225]

This great passage has a starkness and power that have been completely "earned" by Defoe's plain style. The vision is now so broad and deep that it not only encompasses the artist's medium, but even reaches out to the reader, hinting that the words on the page are, if

8. David Blewett offers some arresting remarks about the way in which Moll changes shape in Newgate, notably how she, like the action of water in caves which "petrifies" and "turns into stone," also "degenerated into Stone." Blewett effectively compares this figure with the transformative activity that has marked her career, and he interprets this final stage as an end to her career (*Defoe's Art of Fiction*, pp. 91–92). My own view of transformation is a bit different from Blewett's, and I obviously feel that there are moments of epiphany and illumination in the novel that ultimately operate a metamorphosis on the phenomenal world.

truly seen, counters to a much larger realm. The widening of perspective can go no further than this: all the readers to come will take their place in Moll's forking path, see how her story is theirs, how nothing is simple or single or over. Such passages are a far cry from the three menus for lying-in, but they punctuate Defoe's materialist fiction with hints of larger things. These epiphanies are jolting, even searing; one is penetrated by them, somewhat as Moll herself experiences the very feel of her soul once it has been pierced by the minister: "This honest friendly way of treating me unlock'd all the Sluices of my Passions: He broke into my very Soul by it; and I unravell'd all the Wickedness of my Life to him: In a word, I gave him an Abridgement of this whole History" (226). Soul is unseen, hidden, beneath the play of appearances, of difficult and arduous access, needing to be "unlocked" if it is to be touched or engaged. Soul is tantamount to history, to narrative; it is the self over time.

In Defoe, the soul does not have an easy time of it, since the phenomenal world appears to be so authoritative. But moments of vision and transcendence do come. Somewhat akin to "the Men of whom *Solomon* says, *they go like an ox to the Slaughter, till a Dart strikes them through their Liver*" (176), so too is Moll struck by the piercing awareness of Eternity. These moments do not last. Moll goes on to America with her Lancashire husband, and she moves right into the American Dream, busy once again counting, weighing, and measuring. Yet, as we have had ample opportunity to see, even this heroine of presence has occasion to ponder the figure of her life. Moll's modest, rudimentary *prise de conscience* heralds the centrality of character in fiction, even as it intimates, in somewhat less obvious tones, that all identities require caretaking, are constructs, that the most homogeneous lives may be, at bottom, picaresque. Defoe, comfortable with surfaces and episodes, seems to enter upon the threshold of self virtually by accident. He adumbrates its integrative charge, its mission of linkage, but he evinces little anguish in the matter. If, in addition to surviving, one can also be coherent, so much the better.

For later writers, "survival" becomes strangely obsolete, inoperative as a pressure or stress for character. But, the figure of the life, the identity that is revealed or forged, takes on increasingly central authority in Western narrative. Pip, Rastignac, the Emma's of Austen and Flaubert, Julien Sorel, Raskolnikov, Conrad's Jim, all are seeking the figure in their own carpet, all are placed in fictions that probe into the mesh between external event and inner motive. Toward the end of the nineteenth century, this schema is more and more in trouble:

Dostoevsky's Underground Man is a psychic chameleon, a man without character; Flaubert's Frédéric Moreau experiences something akin to leakage as he measures the incompatibility between himself and the events of life; Conrad's Jim and Nostromo and Razumov encounter downright fissure between their inner and outer lives. That central proprietary drama—taking measure of one's life over time and gauging the contours of a self—finds a privileged home in the novel, even when events crush the self, even when the self goes out of business or shuts out the world. The transactions themselves are equally imperious, whether the resulting tally is in the red or the black, for the novel form has proved itself indispensable for the bookkeeping that characterizes the career of consciousness in the world. But, as all commentators have agreed, the novel goes "in," and this inward turn is doubtless prophetic; whereas Conrad and Dostoevsky chart a crisis, a kind of collision course between consciousness and event, what happens when the inner self swallows the world whole, when the activities of the self usurp the entire stage, making the present scene a tiny part of its immense panoramic purview of time and space?

2

Proust is indisputably the Rome to which these roads lead. In his great novel, external event—the abiding authority in Defoe—almost disappears, whereas motive is everything.[9] Yet, Proust, more than any writer before or since, knew that motive is not visible, that the figure of our life exists for us alone. Hence, his work is peculiarly apposite to Defoe's: much like Moll and her repertory, his characters are also disguised and episodic. Whereas Moll confusedly grasps that there must be linkage between her present and past, Marcel devotes his life and art to pondering and establishing these linkages: his truest *recherche* is for the shape of his life, initially and vainly sought in the trajectory of his social and sexual career, ultimately found in the web of his consciousness and art. The vista that Defoe's novel just points to has been opened wide, has become limitless, in Proust.

9. For a suggestive interpretation of the Proustian "inward turn," one should consult Richard Terdiman's *The Dialectics of Isolation: Self and Society in the French Novel from the Realists to Proust* (New Haven: Yale University Press, 1976).

Moll Flanders starts as an orphan, and that is the fact of her life; Proust's Marcel lives his sorry life as one haunted by an almost Edenic, prenatal form of bonding and union, a dream of pure transparency where the loved one is fused with oneself, connected soul to soul, free at last of alterity and opacity. The most perfect instance of such seamless union (for it is not merely a fantasy) occurs when the grandmother embraces the frightened, precarious child at Balbec; it is a moment of pure nurturance and connection:

> . . . et mes pensées se prolongeaient en elle sans subir de déviation parce qu'elles passaient de mon esprit dans le sien sans changer de milieu, de personne. Et—comme quelqu'un qui veut nouer sa cravate devant une glace sans comprendre que le bout qu'il voit n'est pas placé par rapport à lui du côté où il dirige sa main, ou comme un chien qui poursuit à terre l'ombre dansante d'un insecte—trompé par l'apparence du corps comme on l'est dans ce monde où nous ne percevons pas directement les âmes, je me jetai dans les bras de ma grand'mère et je suspendis mes lèvres à sa figure comme si j'accédais ainsi à ce coeur immense qu'elle m'ouvrait. Quand j'avais ainsi ma bouche collée à ses joues, à son front, j'y puisais quelque chose de si bienfaisant, de si nourricier, que je gardais l'immobilité, le sérieux, la tranquille avidité d'un enfant qui tète.[10]

> [. . . and my thoughts extended into her without deflection because they passed from my mind into hers without any change of place or person. And—like someone who wants to tie his tie in front of a mirror but doesn't understand that the end which he sees reflected is not on the side to which he raises his hand, or like a dog who chases along the ground the dancing shadow of an insect—deceived by the appearance of the body, as one is in this world where we do not directly perceive souls, I threw myself into the arms of my grandmother, and I pressed my lips to her face, as if I were thus gaining access to that immense heart she opened to me. When I had my mouth glued to her cheeks, to her forehead, in this way, I derived something so beneficial,

10. Marcel Proust, *A la Recherche du temps perdu* (Paris: Edition de la Pléiade, 1963), I, p. 668. Subsequent quotations will be taken from this edition and noted parenthetically in the body of the text.

so nurturing, that I remained as motionless, as solemn, as calmly gluttonous as a suckling child.]

Calling to mind Plato's famous cave allegory of blind men grasping shadows, Proust's figures of the man knotting his tie and the dog chasing the insect's shadow announce at once the world of human error and also the miraculous transcendence that is at hand here; moving from philosophy to fiction, from thought to action, from perception to behavior, the child embraces and becomes one with the grandmother, goes right through the envelope of flesh and bones into the nourishing heart of the loved one. Such triumphs of contact and fusion are rare, since, for the most part, the phenomenal world is neither penetrable nor decipherable by spirit. But the mother and the grandmother are sublime exceptions, for only there does the narcissist dream of the loved one as self-extension seem achievable. The second body magically completes the first one here, and the imagery of the suckling infant calls to mind a state prior to the sundering and weaning of individuation itself.[11] Every bit as miraculous and arresting as the embrace itself is the communication code established by Marcel and his grandmother at Balbec; for once, a language is devised that is immediate and at one with its referent, a univalent language that consists of tapping on the wall that divides the two rooms. There is something almost mythological in this beautiful sequence, a Proustian inversion of the Tower of Babel story, where we see the fashioning of a transparent language that connects rather than divides, a membrane between lovers that unites rather than separates. As we know, this perfect intercourse is short-lived; soon enough, the boy "toughens" and moves out into the world of Albertine and her friends, more or less abandoning the grandmother, misreading the signs of her illness (which we learn only much later in the novel).

Union through body or world is, for the most part, not to be had; that is what Marcel's experience teaches. One thinks of the delicious meeting between Albertine and Marcel where she "offers" herself to him, but it turns out to be an offer that he seems to be unequipped to accept; none of his organs is suited for the type of possession he

11. In his treatment of desire in the *Recherche*, J.-Francis Reille has not hesitated to label the grandmother herself as a neurotic, and to see in this passage evidence of the infantile need of nourishment and "idolatry" that characterizes Marcel's relationships (*Proust: Le Temps du désir* [Paris: Editeurs Français Réunis, 1979], p. 172).

has in mind, and instead he more or less crashes into her docile body, quarantined to her surface and powerless to go "inside."[12] Not only is Marcel doomed to the periphery, but he also discovers that there are more Albertines than he had reckoned with: ". . . dans ce court trajet de mes lèvres vers sa joue, c'est dix Albertines que je vis; cette seule jeune fille étant comme une déesse à plusieurs têtes, celle que j'avais vue en dernier, si je tentais de m'approcher d'elle, faisait place à une autre" (in the short journey of my lips to her cheek, there were ten Albertines that I saw; this single young girl being like a goddess with several heads, so that the one I had just seen, if I tried to get closer, yielded to still another [*Recherche*, II, 365]). Proustian characters are spawning and spilling all the time, possessed of avatars and secret lives, posing an epistemological riddle to the person who would know or "fix" them. Defoe is already aware that most lives will not bear much looking into, because most people's pasts are checkered, and therefore strenuous efforts are made to squelch those data in order to arrive at a "character"; in Proust, only the folks in Combray believe in such fixities as character, and we are told, soon enough, that Swann only *appears* to be a bourgeois progeny of bankers and barristers, that Charlus is not quite the gallant figure heralded by Saint-Loup, that Vinteuil may be more than the trifling country composer he seems.

This multiplicity is everywhere in Proust's world, like a cancer that has spread to every realm of activity. The perfect fit between sign and meaning that is enacted through the wall-tapping at Balbec is nowhere to be found in most of the exchanges the novel depicts. Some of Proust's finest satire emerges through his play with defective or abused sign systems, ranging from Mme. Verdurin's famous laughter to the complex verbal jousting between Faffenheim and Norpois

12. The Proustian handling of sexual love has been discussed by countless critics, but the most vehement and vituperative indictment of Marcel's arrangements with Albertine is to be found in J. Theodore Johnson, Jr.'s "Against 'Saint' Proust," in *The Art of the Proustian Novel Reconsidered*, ed. Lawrence D. Joiner (Medford, Mass., 1980). Johnson's lengthy essay is doubtless the most sacrilegious piece of Proustian scholarship in the past several decades, but even when it is most militantly biased in its critique of Proustian foibles, it is nonetheless a refreshing and eye-opening reading. Johnson does not tackle the passage I deal with, but reserves his wrath, instead, for the famous sequence where Marcel "embarks" on the sleep of Albertine (pp. 119–21).

concerning their respective social ambitions.[13] The mechanics of sleuthing and decoding are funny when it is a question of Bloch trying to make sense of Mme. de Villeparisis' odd torpor or Legrandin's declaration of love out of the pupil of his eye, but one laughs rather less when the setting becomes affective and urgent, as when Swann interrogates Odette or Marcel grills Albertine; in these latter instances, the loved one's double-talk and multiplicity cause great pain, and we begin to realize that certain kinds of spectacles—the duplicities and metamorphoses of others—are congenial to art but devastating in life. Proust frequently takes the high road in depicting this strange mobility—we see clearly enough, for instance, what Elstir is doing when he inverts land and sea motifs in his paintings—but he can also be delightfully arch in the way he sneaks much of this material in. Consider, for example, the following scene in "Combray" where the curé is explaining to Eulalie and Tante Léonie the hidden treasures of the stained-glass windows:

> . . . dans le coin du vitrail, vous n'avez jamais remarqué une dame en robe jaune? Hé bien! c'est saint Hilaire qu'on appelle aussi, vous le savez, dans certaines provinces, saint Illiers, saint Hélier, et même, dans le Jura, saint Ylie. Ces diverses corruptions de *sanctus Hilarius* ne sont pas du reste les plus curieuses de celles qui se sont produites dans les noms des bienheureux. Ainsi votre patronne, ma bonne Eulalie, *sancta Eulalia*, savez-vous ce qu'elle est devenue en Bourgogne? Saint Eloi tout simplement: elle est devenue un saint. Voyez-vous, Eulalie, qu'après votre mort on fasse de vous un homme? [*Recherche*, I, 105]

> [. . . in the corner of the stained-glass window, you've never noticed a lady in a yellow dress? Well then, that's Saint Hilaire, who, as you know, is called in certain provinces Saint Illiers, Saint Hélier, and even, in the Jura, Saint Ylie. Moreover, these various corruptions of *sanctus Hilarius* are not even the strangest among those that have taken place within the names of the blessed. Hence, your patron saint, my dear Eulalie, *sancta Eulalia*, do you know what she has become in Burgundy? Saint Eloi quite simply: she has become a male saint. Do you think, Eulalie, that they will make a man of you after your death?]

13. The classic study for this issue is Gilles Deleuze's *Proust et les signes* (Paris: P.U.F., 1970).

A great deal is on show here, even if it is beyond the ken of Eulalie and Tante Léonie. Proust is enamored of etymology, because it flaunts the historical mobility of language, the astounding metamorphoses undergone by names over time; and the reader who finds the lectures of the curé and Brichot tedious is missing some of the Proustian fun. The "corruptions" noted in this passage are fun, they are even "hilarious," although the curé is not laughing. He is, after all, using good linear logic when he slyly suggests that the woman will become a man, after death, in Burgundy, through etymological fiat. But, the novel undercuts the curé, because one need not die or go to Burgundy to change sex, and it can be done in the flesh as well as in the word. It will be one of the chief pastimes of the novel.

Sex change never quite leaves the province of disguise in *Moll Flanders*; in Proust we are dealing with morphology, not masquerade. Hence, Elstir's portrait of the young Odette, Miss Sacripant, focuses primarily on the ambivalence principle, less interested in any moral implications than in the aesthetic richness she can (be made to) display: "Le long des lignes du visage, le sexe avait l'air d'être sur le point d'avouer qu'il était celui d'une fille un peu garçonnière, s'évanouissait, et plus loin se retrouvait, suggérant plutôt l'idée d'un jeune efféminé vicieux et songeur, puis fuyait encore, restait insaisissable" (Along the lines of the face, the sex seemed to be at the point of confessing that it belonged to a somewhat boyish girl, but then it disappeared, and then elsewhere could be seen again, suggesting rather the idea of an effeminate, corrupt and pensive young man, but then it fled again, and remained ungraspable [*Recherche*, I, 849]). Just as the etymologist views "proper" names of people and places as a "cover" behind which he perceives the full play of history and language, so too the reader of Proust must regard the sexual identity of all characters as temporary, as simplistic counters for an erotic life that is bewilderingly complex and multiple. "Masculine" and "feminine" lose whatever unitary meaning they may have had, as Proust transforms them into a dizzying array of admixtures and distillations. And the whole consort moves, rendering it impossible to pin down any of these chameleons in their sexual habitat. Fluidity is the hallmark of such behavior, and that is what Elstir has brought off in his portrait of Odette: the identity refuses to give itself, and, somewhat like a striptease, it hints and exhibits but also dodges and evades, suggesting through its very elusiveness (être sur le point d'avouer, s'évanouissait, se retrouvait, fuyait encore, restait insaisissable) the anguished pursuit of the lover who seeks to know.

The multiplicity and mystery of character in Proust is well known; like Defoe before him, however, Proust retains an ambivalent attitude toward the chameleon self. Both authors know that consistency and integrity are morally indispensable: in Defoe, one's "reputation" depends on having followed a straight path, and the Proustian lover experiences pure anguish when he encounters duplicity. Nonetheless, Defoe is irresistibly drawn to types such as Moll and Jemy, and the Elstir passage indicates the kind of fascination, indeed the kind of freedom, that is enjoyed by the multiple self. But, where Defoe images Moll's repertory through disguise and event, Proust works "vertically," dismissing the here-and-now as *trompe-l'œil*, bent on reconnoitering the real quarry: the unseen enigma behind the envelope. Hence, Marcel can hold Albertine, can possess what is tangible about her, but her mysterious, unplumbable fullness escapes, haunts and dwarfs him:

> Par instants, dans les yeux d'Albertine, dans la brusque inflammation de son teint, je sentais comme un éclair de chaleur passer furtivement dans des régions plus inaccessibles pour moi que le ciel, et où évoluaient des souvenirs, à moi inconnus, d'Albertine. Alors sous ce visage rosissant je sentais se réserver comme un gouffre l'inexhaustible espace des soirs où je n'avais pas connu Albertine. Je pouvais bien prendre Albertine sur mes genoux, tenir sa tête dans mes mains, je pouvais la caresser, passer longuement mes mains sur elle, mais, comme si j'eusse manié une pierre qui enferme la salure des océans immémoriaux ou le rayon d'une étoile, je sentais que je touchais seulement l'enveloppe close d'un être qui par l'intérieur accédait à l'infini. [*Recherche*, III, 386]

> [At certain moments, in Albertine's eyes, in the sudden inflammation of her skin, I felt something like a ripple of heat pass furtively into regions more inaccessible to me than the heavens, regions where Albertine's memories, unknown to me, lived and moved. Then, beneath that blushing face, I felt the opening, as of an abyss, of the limitless space of the evenings when I had not known Albertine. I could easily take Albertine on my knees, hold her head in my hands, I could caress her, run my hands slowly over her, but, just as if I had been handling a stone that encloses the salt of immemorial oceans or the light of a star, I

> felt I was touching merely the closed envelope of a being who extended inwardly to infinity.]

Proust, like Defoe, has stumbled onto the infinite, but he locates it unmistakably inside the Other, rather than being an illumination of the scene. The eternal has for Defoe a spiritual significance, for it situates the Things in their larger frame. The infinite strikes terror in Proust, because it is an epistemological scandal, because it defies the questing lover who wants to inventory his goods; as defying riddle, it triggers the very fiction-making process that undergirds the twin operations of narrative and jealousy. It is perhaps instructive to consider Pascal's famous dictum regarding the intrusive place occupied by infinity in the modern consciousness: "le silence éternel des espaces infinis m'effraie" (the eternal silence of infinite space frightens me). Pascal strikes the modernist note (this, in mid seventeenth century) in expressing his fear of the immeasurable, his terror in the face of the unchartable, but Proust prophetically inverts Pascal's paradigm by claiming that human relations are now the proper sphere for the kind of metaphysical awe and magnitude formerly reserved for the cosmos. Pascal looked, with anguish, at the infinite sky; Marcel holds, with anguish, the girl who reaches inwardly to infinity. The realm of the interpersonal has literally become the New World whose boundaries must, but cannot, be charted.

A la Recherche du temps perdu hovers not infrequently on the edge of madness, and it is sometimes quite unperceived by the narrative voice. Marcel himself withdraws to a sanatorium for a period of years, but we are able to witness, at more than one juncture and up front in the text, the cracking of this mind as it wrestles with the infinite, does battle with dragons of its own devising. The jealous Swann and the jealous Marcel are among the most inventive and beleaguered characters in fiction, as they go about imagining countless masochist scenarios out of the very freedom offered them by their loved one's mystery. One can see, in the following evocation of jealousy, the manic creative process itself, the spewing forth of metaphors and the relentless tracking that goes nowhere, that feeds on itself and dissolves all prior boundaries between inner and outer, fantasy and fact:

> . . . toujours rétrospective, elle [la jalousie] est comme un historien qui aurait à faire une histoire pour laquelle il n'est aucun document; toujours en retard, elle se précipite comme un tau-

reau furieux là où ne se trouve pas l'être fier et brillant qui l'irrite de ses piqûres et dont la foule cruelle admire la magnificence et la ruse. La jalousie se débat dans le vide, incertaine comme nous le sommes dans ces rêves où nous souffrons de ne pas trouver dans sa maison vide une personne que nous avons bien connue dans la vie mais qui peut-être en est ici une autre et a seulement emprunté les traits d'un autre personnage, incertaine comme nous le sommes plus encore après le réveil quand nous cherchons à identifier tel ou tel détail de notre rêve. Quel air avait notre amie en nous disant cela? N'avait-elle pas l'air heureux, ne sifflait-elle même pas, ce qu'elle ne fait que quand elle a quelque pensée amoureuse et que notre présence l'importune et l'irrite? Ne nous a-t-elle pas dit une chose qui se trouve en contradiction avec ce qu'elle nous affirme maintenant, qu'elle connaît ou ne connaît pas telle personne? Nous ne le savons pas, nous ne le saurons jamais; nous nous acharnons à chercher les débris inconsistants d'un rêve, et pendant ce temps notre vie avec notre maîtresse continue, notre vie distraite devant ce que nous ignorons être important pour nous, attentive à ce qui ne l'est peut-être pas, encauchemardée par des êtres qui sont sans rapports réels avec nous, pleine d'oublis, de lacunes, d'anxiétés vaines, notre vie pareille à un songe. [*Recherche*, III, 147]

[. . . always retrospective, it (jealousy) is like a historian who would have to compose a history for which there are no documents; always too late, it rushes forth like an enraged bull, to the spot where can no longer be found the proud and dazzling creature who torments it with his thrusts, whose magnificence and cunning are admired by the crowd. Jealousy thrashes about in a void, uncertain just as we are in those dreams where we are pained at not finding in his empty house someone whom we have known well in life but who may be someone else here and has merely borrowed the features of another, uncertain as we are, especially, upon waking up and seeking to identify this or that detail of our dream. What was our friend's expression when she told us that? Didn't she seem happy, wasn't she even whistling, something she does only when she is thinking about love-making, and when our presence disturbs and irks her? Didn't she tell us something that is contradicted by what she is saying now, about knowing or not knowing a certain person? We don't know; we'll never know; we persist in chasing the unsubstantial

> fragments of a dream, and during the whole time our life with our mistress goes on, our life which passes by what may be of real importance, which is attentive to what may have no significance, which is haunted by creatures who have no real relation to us, which is full of lapses of memory, gaps, futile anxieties, our life which is like a dream.]

Every conceivable variety of maddened and futile quest seems registered here: the historian who must compose his narrative but has no data; the bull who seeks his matador-torturer to no avail; finally, and most fatefully, the interpreter of dreams whose materials are endlessly fluid and interchangeable, for whom people and things glide into each other, wear masks, taunt us with their inaccessbility. The project of "fixing" the other's life is daunting indeed, since all the signs are ambiguous, all the languages foreign languages. Given this kind of ontological morass, it is hardly surprising that the Proustian lover resorts to abduction, knowing that even if the "core" of the mistress is infinitely free, at least the shell is in secure hands. The novel does not appear to consider it in the least odd that one might go to such measures, and the reader of *La Prisonnière* encounters a world where most normative codes have disappeared.

But, if you close the door on morality, it comes in through the window. To be sure, the scene and its people are kaleidoscopic, on the one hand, and the urgency of "knowing" is so imperious, on the other hand, that no traditional ethos could possibly rule here. But, Proust is, at some level, no less severe than Kafka, and his characters' "crimes" do, in fact, bring their own punishment, in predictable narrative ways and also in less predictable stylistic events. Mlle. Vinteuil and friend do penance for making a hell of the old composer's final years and desecrating his memory, for it is they who will devote their lives to publishing his posthumous work. Moreover, immediately after the melodramatic and voyeuristic discovery of their lesbian activities, the book itself launches into an impassioned, multilayered discussion of sadism, seeking, desperately it would seem, to bathe the intolerable sexual act in a rich philosophical ambiance; much later in the novel, this key scene will come back to haunt Marcel, to empty out, in delayed fashion, its still potent venom. In similar manner, the much-heralded exposé of the homosexual ethos, as it finally appears in the first part of *Sodome et Gomorrhe*, is accompanied by a strange verbal urgency, a heated-up prose that breathlessly and brilliantly paints its epic picture of inverts, in long, torturous sentences, larded with metaphysical overtones, as if syntactical and intellectual weightiness might atone for the transgressions at hand. There is a kind of umbilical cord, in Proust's novel, that binds narrative event to philosophical reflection, and it is the connection itself that is most shocking, because the language and assumptions of philosophy must appear to be disinterested and free; yet, in the *Recherche*, the tallying that consciousness provides as a follow-up or assessment to event is profoundly implicated, sucked into the dramas it pretends to judge at a distance. There is a pathology of narrative here, a loss of innocence that extends to the very principles of the work, so that everything is contaminated, even the most innocuous truisms and reflections.

At some point, one is forced to see the profoundly punitive dimension of the *Recherche*. In the last volume, the narrator will state, straight out, that analysis is lethal, that the writer kills the creatures of his fiction, that he himself has destroyed those he loved, destroyed them through writing. Each death within the fiction can be seen as a murder, each living character as a condemned character. Of course, the whole enterprise can ultimately be viewed as penance, just as Vinteuil's daughter and friend do penance, and perhaps, in some far-off realm, such penance will suffice. But, within the fiction itself, there is no reprieve, no way at all to get off the hook. At the core of it, we are dealing with a psychology of relentless torture. Love is merely the threshold of anxiety at best, and misery at worst. Swann remembers his sexual intimacy with Odette, and each pleasure, each caress, comes back to haunt him, to provide the very script of betrayal.

Marcel's love for Albertine epitomizes this kind of psychic entrapment. The protagonist imprisons Albertine, for all the reasons we have noted: to hold the other, to lock her in, to prevent her evolution, in a desperate bid for fixity. But it becomes manifestly clear that Albertine resides *inside* Marcel's lodging in more ways than one: true enough, he has no access to her inner life, but she, on the other hand, invades him, lives, lives "freely" inside him. Love itself is imaged, with a kind of surgical realism, as an act of *internement*, a displacement of the loved one from "outer" to "inner." At crucial moments in the latter volumes, usually triggered by unbearable revelations concerning Albertine's sexual licence, the young woman comes to be experienced as pure pain, inner presence. Contrary, he says, to photographic realism, which would have pictured Albertine at some measurable space from him ready to descend from the train, the new psychic truth was quite different in its disposition of objects. Within his very body, yet horrendously mobile at the same time, Albertine is the very picture of love as disease, a poison, a "foreign body" inside one's own, and monstrously potent in its capacity to inflict pain, for in these corporeal precincts, an altered glance, a blink of an eye, a trace of a smile acquire a well-nigh lethal power. The earlier dilemma of holding the loved body and suffering its infinite inward extension has now become, if possible, still more painful: that body is now displaced, inside oneself, yet still free to do endless harm. Marcel finally *possesses* his mistress, in the worst kind of way, as we measure the strange emotional boomerang that Proust has dealt out to his protagonist. Inside Marcel, finally, Albertine dies, but much later than the girl herself dies, for the internalized, "bacterial" Albertine is not bound by the same laws as the flesh-and-blood one; her life is like that of a poisoned rat under the floorboards, and the stench of her long passing permeates all of *Albertine disparue*.

"Inside" is the final reality-terrain in Proust. Albertine lives there, and that is where she must die if Marcel is to be free of her. One can say that the grandmother finally dies there as well, in that the beautiful sequence of "les intermittences du cœur" bestows on the grandmother the dignity of death and farewell that she is brutally denied in her "actual" death a year earlier. Knowledge itself comes to be defined as the residue of experience, the often poisonous materials that we have ingested in our lives and dealings with others, and Proust goes on to state that any other kind of claim to truth is spurious, that we can only *know* what is inside us, what life has deposited in us, written on and in us. But this act of knowing would seem to resist us at every turn, resist our language, defy our will, lie beyond our ken. Thus, Marcel sets out to inventory his domains and to possess the one thing possessable: the figure of his life.[14] In this scheme of things, the grand villain is *oubli*, which is the great erosive fact of life, the progressive dismantling of one's only estate. *Oubli* is variously conceived in the *Recherche*: occasionally almost surgical in its removal of experience, usually it is incremental and organic, substituting new tissue for old, new selves for old ones. We pay the price of this operation (which we call living) in terms of a perpetual am-

14. I am indebted to the work of Leo Bersani on Proust, as regards this issue of self-knowledge; see *Marcel Proust: The Fictions of Life and of Art* (New York: Oxford University Press, 1965) and *Balzac to Beckett: Center and Circumference in French Fiction* (New York: Oxford University Press, 1970), pp. 192–240.

nesia, a radical discontinuity. Proust's project is repossession. It is arguable that nothing more heroic has ever been attempted in literature than this Promethean effort to retrieve, to resurrect, and to do so as imperialist rather than antiquary. Proust's book will record—and, if necessary, create—the inner script of a life in time, that very vista whose threshold Moll Flanders begins to approach. Proust's detractors deplore the subjectivism and the alleged self-indulgence of such a venture, but all too often Marcel is envisaged as an idle narcissist. On the contrary, this novel is epic in its territorial charge, and it sets out to discover and colonize a New World every bit as much as the Renaissance explorers did. It is simply that Proust has turned things inside out. In us, rather than beyond us, is the world; our comings and goings, our bonds and our sunderings, our density and duration, are recorded in us. Nothing need die, because this lifelong performance can be activated and replayed at any moment, illuminating and even electrifying our present. After Albertine's death, Marcel discovers how banal and how sublime it all is, how nothing can ever be innocuous for the associative mind, how resonant and bristling his life still is, how nothing is ever over:

> En effet, en nous, de chaque idée, comme d'un carrefour dans une forêt, partent tant de routes différentes, qu'au moment où je m'y attendais le moins je me trouvais devant un nouveau souvenir. Le titre de la mélodie de Fauré, *le Secret*, m'avait mené au *Secret du Roi* du duc de Broglie, le nom de Broglie à celui de Chaumont. Ou bien le mot de Vendredi Saint m'avait fait penser au Golgotha, à l'étymologie de ce mot qui, lui, parait l'équivalent de *Calvus mons*, Chaumont. Mais par quelque chemin que je fusse arrivé à Chaumont, à ce moment je fus frappé d'un choc si cruel que dès lors je pensais bien plus à me garer contre la douleur qu'à lui demander des souvenirs. Quelques instants après le choc, l'intelligence qui, comme le bruit du tonnerre, ne voyage pas aussi vite, m'en apportait la raison. Chaumont m'avait fait penser aux Buttes-Chaumont, où Mme. Bontemps m'avait dit qu'Andrée allait souvent avec Albertine, tandis qu'Albertine m'avait dit n'avoir jamais vu les Buttes-Chaumont. A partir d'un certain âge nos souvenirs sont tellement entrecroisés les uns sur les autres que la chose à laquelle on pense, le livre qu'on lit n'a presque plus d'importance. On a mis de soi-même partout, tout est fécond, tout est dangereux, et on peut

> faire d'aussi précieuses découvertes que dans les *Pensées* de Pascal dans une réclame de savon. [*Recherche*, III, 543]
>
> [In fact, within us, from each of our ideas, just as from a crossroads in a forest, so many paths branch out in different directions, that at the moment when I least expected it I found myself confronted by a new memory. The title of Fauré's melody, *The Secret*, had led me to *The King's Secret* of the Duke of Broglie, the name Broglie to that of Chaumont. Or else the words "Good Friday" had made me think of Golgotha, Golgotha whose etymology appears to be the equivalent of *Calvus mons*, Chaumont. But, whatever the path that took me to Chaumont, at that moment I was struck by a blow so cruel that from then on I sought more to ward off the pain than to seek out memories. A few moments after the blow, my intelligence, which, like the noise of thunder, doesn't travel quite so fast, brought me the explanation. Chaumont had made me think of Buttes-Chaumont where Mme. Bontemps had told me that Andrée often went with Albertine, whereas Albertine had told me she'd never been to Buttes-Chaumont. At a certain point in life our memories are so intertwined with one another that the specific thing one is thinking of, the book one is reading, is of practically no importance. We have put something of ourselves everywhere, everything is fecund, everything is dangerous, and one can make discoveries that are every bit as precious as in the *Pensées* of Pascal, in an advertisement for soap.]

In this passage we see with utmost clarity that inner cosmos which the artist can reveal. Our neural circuitry appears to remember what we have forgotten, and it networks the external scene into its own wondrous arrangement, "using" the Things and Names only as supports for private investments and associations, then communicating the pattern to us through pain (or, as the case may be, joy). External categories and cultural hierarchies mean nothing here, for Pascal and the soap advertisement are equivalent receptacles or mirrors for the itinerant self that has been collecting and disseminating all its life. In Marcel's case, it is all there: the etymology, the multiple sexuality, the lie, the past. This is a world drenched with cogency and bursting with volume, in which the humblest details can resonate. Everything is related to us—"on a mis de soi-même partout"—everything is fecund; every teacup contains, if we know how to look and listen, Combray.

Marcel's life is shown to be a veritable minefield. Not unlike Joyce's Bloom, he too runs into himself constantly, finding the longest way around to be the shortest way home, recognizing and fulfilling his indigenous pattern at all times, doomed to coherence. But it is all private, hidden: the sequence *Calvus mons* – Chaumont – Buttes-Chaumont does not mean for Brichot what it means for Marcel. Each person's *carrefour* is unique, and our peculiar universe of associations and contexts, the odd narrative of our life that any event at any time can flash upon our mental and neural screen, this constellation is the least public thing on earth. The artist can make it public, however, and Proust depicts this revelation as no less than the sighting of a new continent. Hence, Vinteuil delivers his homeland in his great septuor, a homeland that he can visit and know and reveal only through his art.

> [Cette patrie perdue, les musiciens ne se la rappellent pas, mais chacun d'eux reste toujours inconsciemment accordé en un certain unisson avec elle; il délire de joie quand il chante selon sa patrie, la trahit parfois par amour de la gloire, mais alors en chantant la gloire il la fuit, et ce n'est qu'en la dédaignant qu'il la trouve, quand il entonne ce chant singulier dont la monotonie—car quel que soit le sujet qu'il traite, il reste identique à soi-même—prouve chez le musicien la fixité des éléments composants de son âme. Mais alors, n'est-ce pas que ces éléments, tout ce résidu réel que nous sommes obligés de garder pour nous-mêmes, que la causerie ne peut transmettre même de l'ami à l'ami, du maître à la maîtresse, cet ineffable qui différencie qualitativement ce que chacun a senti et qu'il est obligé de laisser au seuil des phrases où il ne peut communiquer avec autrui qu'en se limitant à des points extérieurs communs à tous et sans intérêt, l'art, l'art d'un Vinteuil comme celui d'un Elstir, le fait apparaître, extériorisant dans les couleurs du spectre la composition intime de ces mondes que nous appelons les individus, et que sans l'art nous ne connaîtrions jamais. [*Recherche*, III, 257–58]

> [This lost homeland, the composers cannot actually remember it, but each one of them remains always unconsciously attuned to it; he is delirious with joy when he sings in harmony with his

> homeland; he may betray it sometimes by pursuit of glory, for he turns his back on it when seeking fame, and it is only when he scorns fame that he finds it, when he breaks out into that distinctive song whose sameness—for, whatever its subject it remains true to itself—proves the permanence of the elements that constitute his soul. But in that case, is it not true that those elements, all this residue of reality that we are obliged to keep to ourselves, which talk cannot transmit, even from friend to friend, master to disciple, lover to mistress, that ineffable something which differentiates qualitatively what each person has felt and what he is obliged to leave behind at the threshold of phrases where he can communicate with others only by limiting himself to external points common to all and without interest, this can be made visible by art, the art of a Vinteuil or that of an Elstir, exteriorizing in the colors of the spectrum the intimate composition of those worlds that we call individuals, and that we could never know, without art.]

It is not hard to understand Proust's polemic against photographic realism, or even against the cinema itself, arguing that they can lead only to the shabbiest, poorest art, since the Things in themselves—that objectal world so central to Defoe and, as we shall see, to Robbe-Grillet—are of virtually no significance. What counts is the odd mesh into which we put them, the mental set that links a particular moment or a special face with a cold wind or a diphthong or the smell of hot chocolate. This inner constellation is, by necessity, orderly, for it is the record we cannot avoid establishing of our passing through, and it recoups *our* world, preserves, like wax, almost like flypaper, the strange, unique impressions made on and in us by experience. It might easily be thought that the Proustian venture has a museumlike aspect, culminating in a showcase display of all one's avatars and episodes, more than a little ghoulish in its mania for digging up and preserving. This "Madame Tussaud" reading is possible, but it seems seriously flawed, because it misses precisely the things that count: the magic connections between isolated moments, the remarkable power that is brought to the fore, a kind of "boosting" power that lifts the here-and-now organism into its true spatio-temporal homeland. Discovering one's fullness over time, one's odd tapestry of linkage and connection, one's indigenous song, is akin to ecstasy, for, like ecstasy, it moves the self out of its envelope. Recovering this "set" can thus be likened to nuclear fission, to an unprecedented release of energies that now course through the body, the result of a neural implosion of extraordinary intensity. In such moments, the self is not only re-experiencing its past career(s); more crucially, it is at long last assimilating its fuller form, taking into itself, consciously and deliciously, its essential multiplicity.

One of the more obvious and salient features of this inner composite is that it cavalierly dispenses with time and space, charting alignments and coalitions of a new type. Approximating, in computerlike fashion, the circuits and traces of the human brain, this new constellation records and thereby resurrects what we had thought dead. Memory, as it is ordinarily conceived, is too narrow, too directional a term to apply to this retrieval. Of primordial significance to Proust is the enrichment process itself, a visceral, well-nigh sexual experience of creation, constituting the self's *real* estate, that authentic inheritance of what was ours which comes, miraculously, to us rather than to our survivors, indeed, comes to us as our own survivors. It is here that the erosion, discontinuity, and hiatuses of habituated, anesthetized lives can be overcome. The gambit is remarkable: through consciousness and through writing, those *moi successifs* can be not only recorded, but even connected. The most luminous instance of this internal salvaging occurs in *Albertine disparue*, in a passage where that so-called simple notion—forgetting—is at last imaged as the life-and-death affair that Proust takes it to be:

> [L'être nouveau qui supporterait aisément de vivre sans Albertine avait fait son apparition en moi, puisque j'avais pu parler d'elle chez Mme. de Guermantes en paroles affligées, sans souffrance profonde . . . Or il m'apportait au contraire avec l'oubli une suppression presque complète de la souffrance, une possibilité de bien-être, cet etre si redouté, si bienfaisant et qui n'était qu'un de ces moi de rechange que la destinée tient en réserve pour nous et que, sans plus écouter nos prières qu'un médecin clairvoyant et d'autant plus autoritaire, elle substitue malgré nous, par une intervention opportune, au moi vraiment trop blessé. . . . mais nous n'y prenons garde que si l'ancien contenait une grande douleur, un corps étranger et blessant, que nous nous étonnons de ne plus retrouver, dans notre émerveillement d'être devenu un autre, un autre pour qui la souffrance de son prédecesseur n'est plus que la souffrance d'autrui, celle dont on peut parler avec apitoiement parce qu'on ne la ressent pas . . . Sans doute, ce moi gardait encore contact avec l'ancien, comme un ami, in-

différent à un deuil, en parle pourtant aux présents avec la tristesse convenable, et retourne de temps en temps dans la chambre où le veuf qui l'a chargé de recevoir pour lui continue à faire entendre des sanglots. J'en poussais encore quand je redevenais pour un moment l'ancien ami d'Albertine. Mais c'est dans un personnage nouveau que je tendais à passer tout entier. Ce n'est pas parce que les autres sont morts que notre affection pour eux s'affaiblit, c'est parce que nous mourons nous-mêmes. Albertine n'avait rien à reprocher à son ami. Celui qui en usurpait le nom n'était que l'héritier. On ne peut être fidèle qu'à ce qu'on a connu. Mon moi nouveau, tandis qu'il grandissait à l'ombre de l'ancien, l'avait souvent entendu parler d'Albertine; à travers lui, à travers les récits qu'il en recueillait, il croyait la connaître, elle lui était sympathique, il l'aimait; mais ce n'était qu'un amour de seconde main. [*Recherche*, III, 595–96]

[The new creature who could easily bear to live without Albertine had made his appearance in me, since I had been able to speak about her to Mme. de Guermantes in words of grief, but without real suffering . . . On the contrary, he brought to me, this new creature, along with oblivion an almost total suppression of pain, a possibility of happiness, this creature so fearsome, so soothing, who was none other than one of those spare selves that fate holds in reserve for us, whom fate sends in against our wishes, like the lucid and altogether authoritarian doctor who does not heed our requests, as a replacement, at the opportune moment, for the self who has been truly too injured. . . . we are aware of it only if the former self suffered great pain—a wound, a foreign body—which we are astonished to find no longer there, in our amazement at having become someone different, someone for whom the suffering of his predecessor has become the suffering of another, a pain one may describe with commiseration because one does not feel it . . . Of course, this self remained in touch with the former self, just as a friend, unmoved by bereavement, can nonetheless discuss it in the proper tone of sorrow to the persons present, and can go from time to time back to the room where the widower who has asked him to receive the company for him can still be heard weeping. I too still wept when I became again, momentarily, the former friend of Albertine. But it was into a new personality that I was in the process of changing. It is not because others are dead that our

> feeling for them weakens, it is because we ourselves die. Albertine had no reason to reproach her friend. He who had usurped the name was actually only the inheritor. One can be faithful only to what one remembers, and one remembers only what one has known. My new self, in growing up in the shadow of the former self, had often heard him speak of Albertine; through him, through the stories he recalled, he thought he knew her, he found her appealing, he loved her; but it was only a secondhand love.]

It would, I think, be no exaggeration to say that a full study of Proust could be devoted to this passage alone, so telling are its metaphors, its philosophy of life and death, its contrast of inner and outer realms. If we contrast this passage with Defoe's title page, we are in a position to measure the territory that each author has chosen to explore. Moll's repertory is wildly picaresque: wife, whore, felon, and penitent rupture any stable view of self; and yet, Defoe's triumph is to demonstrate that seventy years of living can indeed produce such variety, and that one's fellows are wonderfully blind to one's checkered past. Moll alone sees the final tally, and her narrative itself—most especially the confession at Newgate—is her way of putting the parts together. In Proust, however, that act of linkage is quite different. Against the crude contours of wife, whore, felon, and penitent, Proust is at pains to articulate a far more nuanced evolution of character and inner career, a parade of selves that disclose the unshared, unwitnessed psychodramas and crises of the passional life. Here is the ultimate Proustian inversion: on the surface, we remain unitary, but inwardly we are metamorphosed into a host of teeming figures, each with its peculiar destiny and coloration. There is something at once gargantuan and outlandish in this maniacally close-grained view of the shifting, evolving emotions. This is quite literally a life-and-death story, a zoomlike close-up of the affections in their natural habitat, but trumped up elegant and given domestic form, thanks to the friend-widower metaphorical scenario. Like an EEG, the Proustian machine renders the pulsations of the brain and heart, the alarming spikes and sharp loops registered by lifting an eyebrow or belching, measures their brief but poignant trajectory, renders them startlingly visible to the reader's eye. Would we know them otherwise? This closet-drama has all the specificity of Defoe's plate and damask, but it is entirely virtual, "the stuff dreams are made of." In this new scheme, one is pure change, pure process, and this incessant, cellular activity is a relentless agent of fragmentation and hiatus. But, if life is entropic, art is assimilative. And it is here that the Proustian generosity (a virtue rarely granted to him) shows. Only the inner conscience knows that the *paroles affligées*, spoken to Mme. de Guermantes concerning the death of Albertine, were hollow words, *sans souffrance profonde*. Only a writer for whom the self is endlessly dying and birthing could coin the brilliant phrase, the *moi de rechange*, the spare self that, much like the spare tire, will be enlisted to keep us going, in moments of emergency.

This view of the person as an unending series of deaths and metamorphoses emerges naturally enough from Proust's vertical fix on life. Sameness and continuity are fictions, the lazy lies of the habituated surface-dwellers who never take the trouble to look "in," to measure their alterations and acknowledge their dead. Fidelity is laudable, and Proust supports it, but one can be faithful only if one lives; the person who no longer loves is no longer the person who loved, is indeed the successor of that person, the radically different successor who follows a dead man. This view of the self is so prodigiously mobile, so atomistic and discontinuous, that any discussion of permanent bonds, of enduring love, would seem to be hopelessly naive. To love another presupposes a minimum fixity of selves that seems denied from the outset. It would therefore be easy enough to assume that the outside world is lost for good, traded against the inner repertory. After all, could you expect someone autistic to deliver a speech, or a person with palsy to run the marathon, or a person who could see only his own bloodstream to paint a picture of the city?

But look once more at the metaphors. The spectacle of forgetting is imaged entirely in societal terms.[15] The lucid and authoritarian doctor, the friend who receives guests at the wake while the bereaved widower mourns, the younger sympathetic listener who tries to love what he has heard: the whole social paraphernalia of the *Recherche* seems present and accounted for, albeit in internalized form. Yet, and this cannot fail to surprise us, this inner psychodrama is infused with

15. I am arguing here for an inscription of the "social" that would take place exclusively at the metaphoric level, quite in distinction to the kind of dialectic that has been proposed by Terdiman's reading of Proust. To make a "community" of the self is to indulge, I think, in more than paradox, and one is struck by the displacement of "neighborliness" and concern which become internalized virtues in Proust.

a gentleness and good will that one looks for in vain in the "real" world (one need merely think of the doctors surrounding the dying grandmother, the vicious jockeying for position in society, the Guermantes' callousness in face of the dying Swann). Here is the volume of an exquisitely literalizing imagination, one that not only allegorizes our states of mind into various people, but then lovingly nurtures refined intercourse between its creations. The silken threads of concern and community that bind these imagined personages delicately but firmly give the lie to Proust's own assertion: "Ce n'est pas parce que les autres sont morts que notre affection pour eux s'affaiblit, c'est parce que nous mourons nous-mêmes" (It is not because others are dead that our feeling for them weakens, it is because we ourselves die). We change, yes, but some residual self oversees the changes that occur, not only takes a census of the people we have been, but posits affection and kindness between this motley group, sets about chronicling these inner histories, showing how the death of one leads to the birth of another.

Swann, we may recall, repeatedly puts his hand to his forehead when confronted by arduous intellectual or moral challenges, and it is fair to assume that most of us resemble Swann in this way. But, Proust wrestles with the specter of human change, and his unswerving, almost maniacal focus on this elusive fact of life delivers some of the strangest results in literature. Has the ceasing of love ever been imaged more finely than in Proust's theater of the mind? As we hurt less, we stop being exclusively the weeping widower, and we tend to become *also* the friend who greets the guests at the wake; as we "heal" from loving, we gradually move from pure feeling to distanced reflection, luminously imaged as the teller of the tale becoming the listener to the tale, thereby retaining all the nuances while losing the urgency. The very awkwardness of my own discursive prose says something about the economy and elegance of Proust's new figurative language, the boldness of a fictive venture that finds words for the innermost facts of our lives, for the tiny but crucial transactions that mark the course of human feeling.

It may well be that the natural state of the human mind is amnesia and disjointedness, that countless corpses reside within us, unknown and unconnected. But Proust's novel celebrates and restores the bonds of inner continuity and community, and thereby gives us a picture of decorous transition rather than anarchy within the self. *Through such writing*, our multiplicity is transcended as well as demonstrated; the ellipses and lapses that Time creates are filled in and unified, even communalized. Rather than extending outward, synchronically, to the disparate individuals who live with us in the same society, the Proustian thrust toward knowledge and touch extends inwardly, diachronically, to the disparate selves who live within us, whose society we are. All of the "moi successifs" are still there, inside us, and the book calls them forth, much like some kind of Last Judgment where the dead arise but there is no judgment.

A la Recherche du temps perdu may be the most complete record we have (and its length is significant here) of the versions of self that a human being plays out over a lifetime. The metaphors used to designate this teeming inner life are persistently social. Beyond the task of illuminating this inner realm, Proust is bent on having us come to know—in the most elemental social and neighborly sense—what we are like within. The most charming image of this inner domain comes to us through the figure of Ali Baba and his cave; he is first mentioned, appropriately enough, in context of the unsuspected multiple life led by Swann, a life that would have so astounded the great-aunt that it would have been as if Ali Baba had been her dinner guest, "lequel, quand il se saura seul, pénètrera dans la caverne éblouissante de trésors insoupçonnés" (who, when he is certain he is alone, will penetrate into the cave, resplendent with its unsuspected treasures [*Recherche*, I, 18]). This great space with its hidden riches stands for the largeness and preciousness of the inner life, a magic place in which we fashion our own community. What would be sensation or feeling in another writer comes out as social metaphor in Proust; hence, Marcel experiences a delayed pleasure in terms of a surprise visitor:

> il était de ces visiteurs qui attendent, pour nous faire savoir qu'ils sont là, que les autres nous aient quittés, que nous soyons seuls. Alors nous les apercevons, nous pouvons leur dire: je suis tout à vous, et les écouter. Quelquefois entre le moment où ces plaisirs sont entrés en nous et le moment où nous pouvons y rentrer nous-mêmes, il s'est écoulé tant d'heures, nous avons vu tant de gens dans l'intervalle que nous craignons qu'ils ne nous aient pas attendus. Mais ils sont patients, ils ne se lassent pas, et dès que tout le monde est parti, nous les trouvons en face de nous. Quelquefois c'est nous alors qui sommes si fatigués qu'il nous semble que nous n'aurons plus dans notre pensée défaillante assez de force pour retenir ces souvenirs, ces impressions pour qui

> notre moi fragile est le seul lieu habitable, l'unique mode de réalisation. [*Recherche*, I, 865]
>
> [it was like one of those visitors who, before informing us that they are there, wait until the others have left, until we are alone. Only then do we perceive them; we can tell them: "I am at your service," and we can hear what they have to say. Sometimes between the moment when these pleasures come to us and the moment when we ourselves "come in," there have been so many hours gone by, so many people whom we've seen in the interval, that we fear they may not have stayed. But they are patient, they do not weary, and as soon as everyone has gone, we find them there ready for us. Sometimes, then, it is we who are so tired that it seems we will not have enough strength left in our exhausted mind to retain these memories, these impressions for whom our fragile self is the one habitable place, the sole means of realization.]

One recalls the polemic against friendship in the *Recherche*, the tough-minded conviction that friends can only be a distraction for the artist, an escape from the arduous discoveries that are to be made within. However, this tender friend—more loving than Saint-Loup, more faithful than Albertine—who bides his time, who tarries and waits for his rendezvous, so that we may fully possess the pleasure that is ours, this friend behaves with a generosity wholly lacking in "real" relationships. Note also the fine use of "entrer" and "rentrer" in this passage: our pleasures, like all our feelings, come "into" us, but life so engages us at the surface that we may fail to come "into" ourselves, to "return" to ourselves, much as one "returns" home; the fragile self is pointedly called a residence, a "lieu habitable," the "locus" of reality. Frequently, we are meant to assess the contrast between the social life within and without; a final instance of such domestic metaphors assigned to the soul can be seen in the depiction of the grandmother's illness, especially at the onset where Proust rigorously expresses her malady as a "housing" issue:

> Mais il est rare que ces grandes maladies, telle que celle qui venait enfin de la frapper en plein visage, n'élisent pas pendant longtemps domicile chez le malade avant de le tuer, et durant cette période ne se fassent pas assez vite, comme un voisin ou un locataire "liant," connaître de lui. C'est une terrible connais-

sance, moins par les souffrances qu'elle cause que par l'étrange nouveauté des restrictions définitives qu'elle impose à la vie. On se voit mourir, dans ce cas, non pas à l'instant même de la mort, mais des mois, quelquefois des années auparavant, depuis qu'elle est hideusement venue habiter chez nous. La malade fait la connaissance de l'Étranger qu'elle entend aller et venir dans son cerveau. Certes elle ne le connait pas de vue, mais des bruits qu'elle entend régulièrement faire elle déduit ses habitudes. Est-ce un malfaiteur? Un matin, elle ne l'entend plus. Il est parti. Ah! si c'était pour toujours! Le soir, il est revenu. Quels sont ses desseins? Le médecin consultant, soumis à la question, comme une maîtresse adorée, répond par des serments tel jour crus, tel jour mis en doute. Au reste, plutôt que celui de la maîtresse, le médecin joue le rôle des serviteurs interrogés. Ils ne sont que des tiers. Celle que nous pressons, dont nous soupçonnons qu'elle est sur le point de nous trahir, c'est la vie elle-même, et malgré que nous ne la sentions plus la même, nous croyons en elle, nous demeurons en tous cas dans le doute jusqu'au jour qu'elle nous a enfin abandonnés. [*Recherche*, II, 316–17]

[But it rarely happens that great illnesses, such as the one that had just struck her squarely in the face, do not set up house in the sick person for a long time before killing him, and do not, much like a neighbor or a "sociable" lodger, introduce themselves to him. It is a terrible acquaintance, less for the pain it causes than for the strange novelty of the definitive restrictions it imposes on life. One sees oneself die, in such cases, not at the exact instant of death, but for months, sometimes even years, ever since it has insidiously come to live with us. The sick person comes to know the Stranger whom she hears coming and going in her brain. Of course she does not know what he looks like, but from the noises she hears him regularly make, she can deduce his habits. Is he an evildoer? One morning she no longer hears him. He has gone. Ah, if only it were forever! That evening, he is back. What is he planning? The doctor in charge, put to the question, like an adored mistress, replies with assurances that seem believable on some days and dubious on others. Moreover, it is not so much the role of the mistress as that of the interrogated servants that the doctor plays. They are all only third parties. The person whom we press for an answer, who we suspect may be on the point of betraying us, is life itself, and even though we no longer feel it to be the same, we still believe in it, at least we remain undecided, up to the day when it finally throws us over.]

Quoted in its entirely, this passage fully displays the inversion that Proust has operated on his material. His long novel is filled with people trying to make the right acquaintances: Marcel himself "lodges" in the Guermantes' hotel, and he is anxious to benefit from such proximity. But death is the subject of this passage, not snobbism, and death comes to us as the lodger within, the stranger who comes and goes within our body. Marcel seeks to embrace Albertine, but he is never to achieve the degree of intimacy felt by the grandmother as she starts to die. The social players are brought in, all of them, doctor, mistress, servants, but they are there to frame a drama that is forbiddingly internal; after all, what could be more domestic than our death?

The Proustian self is a cosmos, equipped with its special terrain, society, and cast of characters, subsuming the so-called phenomenal world and replacing it with a unique constellation of its own. It is only as artist that one can embrace the multiplicity and mobility of people and things; as lover or snob, dependent on straight paths and single truths, one is undone. The self that begins to take its measure in *Moll Flanders* has now found out that the only thing worth measuring is its own career, a career that "passes show" in the social world. Each life has the startling cogency of a work of art, but only a prodigious effort of translation and assimilation will bring it to the surface. Each day adds to the "work": Moll needed seventy years for her careers in England and America; Marcel has lived long, but he must live longer still if there is to be time for the voyage within:

> Je savais très bien que mon cerveau était un riche bassin minier, où il y avait une étendue immense et fort diverse de gisements précieux. Mais aurais-je le temps de les exploiter? J'étais la seule personne capable de le faire. Pour deux raisons: avec ma mort eût disparu non seulement le seul ouvrier mineur capable d'extraire ces minerais, mais encore le gisement lui-même. [*Recherche*, III, 1037]

> [I knew quite well that my brain was a rich mineral basin, where there was a vast and varied expanse of precious ores. But would I have time to mine them? I was the only person capable of

> doing it. For two reasons: with my death would disappear not merely the only miner capable of extracting these minerals, but indeed, the geological formation itself.]

This rich ore deep within him is his only treasure. The mining imagery tells us unmistakably that he is Ali Baba, but, rather than hoarding his gold within his cave, he will dedicate his remaining days to a higher altruism: transforming his private realm, via art, into a public space.

3

There was a time when the name of Robbe-Grillet figured on the reading list of any self-respecting course on modernism. His groundbreaking work in both fiction and film, and the seriousness with which French intellectuals such as Blanchot, Barthes, and Genette elucidated his efforts as humanism's long-awaited bell-toller, all this made him a figure one could hardly ignore.[16] The 1970s and 80s have been less kind to him, partly because interest in modern theory and its dazzling practitioners has eclipsed interest in the novel, and also because his own later work has increasingly revealed the obsessive nature of his concerns. Hence, the earlier claim put forth by Barthes and Blanchot that we have, at last, a neutral "objectal" style, suited to depict a cleansed, untainted, non-anthropocentric world, is hardly compatible with the fantasms and hallucinations and persistent pornography of texts such as *Projet pour une révolution à New York*. Nonetheless, his extremist position in modern literature makes him a very apt concluding figure for the development of memory and multiplicity that I have charted in Defoe and Proust.

Robbe-Grillet's initial position seems to be a radical return to De-

16. See Maurice Blanchot's brief but seminal essay on *Le Voyeur* in *Le Livre à venir* (Paris: Gallimard, 1959), pp. 195–201; with characteristic lucidity, Roland Barthes also recognized, early on, what Robbe-Grillet was up to in his attack on the conventions of narrative, and his essay "Littérature objective," in *Essais critiques* (Paris: Seuil, 1964), was to provide Robbe-Grillet with much of the critical vocabulary for future manifestoes; Gérard Genette's "Vertige fixé" appeared as a *postface* to the 10/18 edition of *Dans le labyrinthe* (Paris, 1964) and, along with his earlier piece on Robbe-Grillet in *Tel Quel* 8 (Winter 1962), provided still another illuminating and influential account of the "Young Turk's" work (for he was known as such in those days).

foe's world of Things, seen, it is true, exclusively in terms of geometry and measurement, and visibly *disconnected* from their traditional obligations of "background" and "meaning." Occupying center-stage, defying any effort to co-opt them into a plot, the Things seem to rule supreme: erasers, banana plants, pieces of string, centipedes on walls, lampposts in streets. To be sure, "humanist" critics were quick to point out that these things were hardly innocent or "self-supporting," but were, instead, pawns put forth by the author intended to draw the reader into the fiction-making process; this, of course, is what the purists were waiting for, and with considerable glee, they claimed that Robbe-Grillet had exposed the nefarious addictions of traditional readers, exposed their total inability to do without "plot," their diseased reliance on the old humanist scripts. The later texts, on the other hand, appeared to retrieve the old subjective, humanist optic with a vengeance, for, no matter how you read or saw them, they displayed a world where lurid psychodrama and hallucination function supreme, where Things are flagrantly used as vehicles and "supports" for free-floating creations of the world and the mind.[17] In these texts, we witness a kind of kaleidoscopic tumbling of forms, a dizzying sense of all things being interchangeable: whereas Moll realized her multiplicity and Marcel inventories his, Robbe-Grillet's characters are ceaselessly transformed and altered, so much so that his work would seem to constitute a fierce denial of that self over time which Defoe (primitively) and Proust (sovereignly) sought to depict and impose.

How much, it may well be asked, does Robbe-Grillet actually deal with relationship? In the first mature novels, such as *Les Gommes*, *Le Voyeur*, *La Jalousie*, and *Dans le labyrinthe*, all encounters between characters are cunningly derealized by a series of techniques: characters disappear or merge with look-alikes; perspectives are altered or reversed; scenes yield to paintings or photographs, or vice versa; personal exchanges are enacted at such a "reduced," often dazed level, that the real gist of the encounter seems enigmatic or muffled (people seem amnesiac, do not understand what is being said to them, where they are, who they are, etc.). In the novels beginning with *La Maison de rendez-vous* and including *Projet pour une révolution à New York*, the

17. Bruce Morrissette wrote the first (and probably definitive) psychological account of Robbe-Grillet in *Les Romans de Robbe-Grillet* (Paris: Editions de Minuit, 1965), which he shrewdly had "introduced" by none other than Roland Barthes.

technique has evolved still further, featuring scenes where characters "alter" in front of our eyes, become someone else, either through a "merging" device or by being literally unmasked, even unskinned. In these latter two fictions, we can hardly speak of character anyway, for the protagonists are meant to be seen as two-dimensional, extended clichés or comic-book figures: international drug dealers, alluring Oriental prostitutes, etc. Robbe-Grillet's description of these figures is rigorously generic, especially concerning the women: all have the same exposed flesh, and the author's insistent, prurient focus on legs, breasts, and genitalia erases all sense of differentiation or identity. In these books, we begin to perceive reality as a *carnaval*, a kind of extended Mardi Gras taken, as it were, from the second to the fourth dimension (totally bypassing the third), so that characters change and dissolve at will, not their own but that of the novelist. At a characteristically charged moment in *Projet* one sees the deflowering of a murdered woman by a short, bald locksmith; but, once the sexual act is completed, there appears a bizarre kind of transmission of energy, resembling a sneeze or a seizure, and culminating in a paroxysm of rearranged particles, causing the prior givens, "short" and "bald" and "locksmith," to metamorphose:

> Au bout d'un temps assez long, occupé à violenter sans hâte le cadavre docile et tiède, le petit homme se redresse, rajuste le désordre de son costume, se passe les mains sur le visage, comme si quelque chose le démangeait en haut du cou. Il se gratte longuement des côtés; puis, n'y tenant plus, il enlève le masque chauve de serrurier qui recouvrait sa tête et sa figure, décollant progressivement la couche de matière plastique et laissant, peu à peu, apercevoir à la place les traits du vrai Ben Saïd.[18]

> [After a rather long period of time, steadily at work violating the warm and docile corpse, the little man gets up, straightens out his clothes, puts his hands on his face, as if something were itching him at the top of his neck. He scratches himself extensively on both sides. Finally, no longer able to restrain himself, he removes the mask of the bald locksmith that covered his face and

18. Alain Robbe-Grillet, *Projet pour une révolution à New York* (Paris: Editions de Minuit, 1970), p. 198. Subsequent quotations will be taken from this edition and noted parenthetically in the body of the text.

head, progressively peeling off the layer of plastic material and exposing, gradually, in its place the features of the real Ben Saïd.]

At another point in this novel, a character is desperately trying to get rid of his mask, because he fears that the morals squad may be coming on the scene; in his frenzy, "[il] tire au hasard sur les divers bords ou saillies qui peuvent offrir une prise, et se met à déchirer par lambeaux ses oreilles, son cou, ses tempes, ses paupières, sans même s'apercevoir qu'il est en train d'arracher dans sa hâte des grands morceaux de sa propre chair" ([he] pulls off at random the various edges or protrusions where he can get a grip, and begins to tear into pieces his ears, his neck, his temples, his eyelids, without even realizing that he is actually ripping off, in his haste, large segments of his own skin [61]). As post-Joyceans who have grown up with Blephen and Stoom, we know that characters in books are assemblages of letters, that their so-called identity and integrity are fictive, and that they can therefore be fused or dismantled on the spot. Nonetheless, it is hard not to assess such events, at least in part, in a representational or mimetic fashion; doing so, one would conclude that the self is a fragile, perhaps artificial cluster, that it can fall apart under stress, that it alters when subjected to great erotic or horrific strain. This view would lead to a notion of self as something momentary and precarious, calling to mind the tentativeness and fictiveness about which Borges wrote in his tale of the memorious Funes, whom it "bothered . . . that the dog at three fourteen (seen from the side) should have the same name as the dog at three fifteen (seen from the front)."

What is under attack here is the myth of continuity, the belief in an invisible but proprietary self over time that periodically plumbs his or her own depths and can be counted on finishing the story with the same name and the same face that he or she started with. As we have seen, Robbe-Grillet's encounters range from hazy and elliptic on to lurid and metamorphic, and although they are disturbingly mobile, there does not seem to be any compelling reason why they should stand still. The way one has to stand still if one makes a pair. However, there is one Robbe-Grillet work where relationship is at the heart of the matter, even though the setting is as much of a funhouse as we have come to expect from such a writer: I am referring to his film (and *ciné-roman*) *L'Année dernière à Marienbad*. *Marienbad* is, in the author's own words, "l'histoire d'une persuasion: il s'agit d'une réalité que le héros crée par sa propre vision, par sa propre parole" (the story of a persuasion: it is concerned with a reality that the hero creates through his own vision, through his own language).[19] The generic protagonist X is to *create*, in the mind of the woman he desires, A, their common past, their liaison "last year at Marienbad." Robbe-Grillet claims that the film knows only one tense, the *present,* and that our repertory of past, future, might-have-been, and the like are all equally present when depicted on the screen; so too, he goes on to argue, is the mode of the imagination a ceaseless present tense. If language and image and thought are all, ultimately, perceived as NOW, then it follows that the past is no longer an autonomous thing in its own right, a given thing, but—and this is crucial—a made thing. You make it by thinking it. Someone else can make it for you.

Marienbad is doubly intriguing: on the one hand, it displays the drama and ethics of coercion that one finds everywhere in Robbe-Grillet, where some form of rape or violation is always at hand; in addition to this, however, there is the novelty of the arena where coercion is played out: the making of the past. To see X invent last year for A implies something profoundly disturbing about the "softness" and malleability of one's inner space and private time. It is in this light that the imperialist ventures of Defoe and Proust are brought to a close. One's life over time, available only to oneself, visible to none, has always been regarded as a private topography, a set of vistas and echoes chartable only by a party of one, a universe at once immense and unique. This is the ultimate estate that Moll Flanders comes into, and it is the second womb to which Marcel returns. *L'Année dernière à Marienbad* auctions off that particular piece of property, showing it to be dislodgeable, an item on the open market that "le premier venu" with a strong mind can manufacture on his own. The echoing inner world of Defoe and Proust has become a nameless surface landscape. Relationship, in *Marienbad*, exquisitely "inverts" the Proustian dilemma of helplessness before the immensity of the other's past, the starkness of alterity itself; Robbe-Grillet, instead, posits the past as a controllable, producible fiction. Moll will try to make amends to her husband by what she does, make amends for that past which she sees and he does not; Marcel holds the finite body of Albertine and suffers its infinite extension in time and space. But X has all the trumps: he invents A's past and makes her see it; he provides her parameters in time and space; he sculpts her life. There

19. Alain Robbe-Grillet, *L'Année dernière à Marienbad* (Paris: Editions de Minuit, 1961), p. 125.

is something prodigious going on in Marienbad, but the mystery and richness of life, the reality of experience, have all been done away with. The present reigns supreme, as Robbe-Grillet deconstructs and spatializes that precious "vertical" world where the self journeyed across time.

Marienbad gives one pause. The emptiness of A and the ease with which X makes her past suggest that we have not come all that far from the ghostly or two-dimensional figures of Robbe-Grillet's other works. Should we, however, grant him his truth, that the past is a consumer item, then we come to see the realm of self adumbrated in Defoe and charted and chronicled in Proust as an essentially fictive realm. This, too, has its beauty, although it does make a difference who the artificer is. Whether it is seen as a human responsibility or an exploration or indeed a fabrication, the shaping of one's past creates the volume and stage of one's life. And it is on that stage that the play of relationship is enacted.

In turning his characters into figures, rendering them weightless and as maneuverable as figures on a chessboard, and in making them peculiarly dimensionless, deprived of time, of their own time, Robbe-Grillet has emptied "relationship" of whatever value it might be said to have in human life. Shorn of continuity, weaned from its own history, the self is indeed just a construct, and the encounter between two such constructs, two bodies without a past, would be an event without density, bereft of the resonance and echo that grace lives together with drama, beauty, and meaning. On the penultimate page of his long novel, Proust describes the human body as a precious, awesome container of time:

> Et c'est parce qu'ils contiennent ainsi les heures du passé que les corps humains peuvent faire tant de mal à ceux qui les aiment, parce qu'ils contiennent tant de souvenirs de joies et de désirs déjà effacés pour eux, mais si cruels pour celui qui contemple et prolonge dans l'ordre du temps le corps chéri dont il est jaloux, jaloux jusqu'à en souhaiter la destruction. [*Recherche*, III, 1047]

> [And it is because they contain in this way the hours of the past that human bodies can cause so much pain for those who love them, because they contain so many memories of joys and desires, already effaced for them, but so cruel for the person who contemplates and prolongs into the dimension of time the be-

> loved body of which he is jealous, jealous enough even to desire its destruction.]

Time creates the volume of a life, makes possible the multiple selves we play out as we live; to grasp the pattern of one's life, to see the figure in one's carpet, constitutes at once the making of a self and much of the basis for human connection. It is, as it were, the peculiar, ineluctable dowry brought by the self to the marriage(s) it enters. Like the plate Moll covets or the treasure in Ali Baba's cave, these are the riches that draw us out and draw us in; what is miraculous is that, in fiction and in relationship, these riches are shareable.

CHAPTER THREE

Body Control

On the face of it, Laclos' elegant eighteenth-century epistolary novel and Burroughs' obscene Beat Generation epic would seem to make an odd couple indeed. Yet, they enjoy an exemplary status in a study of relationship, for each of them may be seen as a *ne plus ultra* of the erotic novel; i.e. the erotic novel defined broadly as the text that focuses on the role of the body in culture: its peculiar needs, the uses to which it is and can be put, the authority it has, finally the spectrum of interactions that it either seeks or suffers. Now, it is well known that many, many writers toil in this vineyard, but Laclos and Burroughs are emblematic figures here, because they go further than the others in displaying the power dynamic of erotic fiction, that quintessential project of controlling someone else's body.

It is no secret that a very considerable body of major criticism, devoted precisely to issues of body control and the cultural sanctions behind it, has evolved over the past decades. In addition to the ground-breaking work of Foucault, one thinks especially of the contributions of feminist scholarship regarding these matters.[1] Doubtless the fundamental critical gauntlet that I am *not* taking up is the issue of gender itself. It has been intelligently argued that the body is always gendered, and that any "universalist" scheme for dealing with it is radically flawed. Moreover, Laclos' novel seems absolutely to demand a feminist perspective, since so very much of it consists of male plots and male fantasies, all geared toward the entrapment, penetration, and control of the woman's body. And, of course, there is the enormous issue of the gaze itself, the *regard* that positions and reifies the woman precisely as body, as spectacle; scholars working on ma-

1. See Michel Foucault, *Histoire de la sexualité* (Paris: Gallimard, 1976 and 1984) and, among others, Nancy J. Vickers, "Diana Described: Scattered Woman and Scattered Rhyme," *Critical Inquiry* (Winter 1981), and Laura Mulvey, "Visual Pleasure and Narrative Cinema," *Screen* 16 (Autumn 1975). I am grateful to Karen Newman for pointing out the Vickers and Mulvey material, in particular, and for discussing the possible bearing of feminist criticism on this chapter, in general.

terials from classical antiquity to film studies have opened our eyes to these matters and shown us how the woman's body has been, as it were, "manipulated" by the male artistic tradition ever since there was art.

Nonetheless, the vantage point of the following essay is universalist, and the body will be "treated" as ungendered. It will be seen, hopefully, that the themes of abuse and exploitation at the heart of Laclos and Burroughs actually cross gender lines, that they are oddly democratic in their victimization schemes. Laclos' Merteuil targets, manipulates, and undoes men with infinitely more zest and art than Lovelace displays with Clarissa; Burroughs' favorite object would seem to be the young male object, appropriately bound and offering its openings to the narrational gaze. The issue seems to be *generic*: the body, male or female, is charted and tracked in these books, and each manifests a heinous kind of scientism, an erudition in corporeal matters, involving "experts" in physiology and body language. Let it therefore be said at the outset that other perspectives are possible here, that a Foucault or a feminist reading would produce different results; but, for the purposes of the central argument of this chapter, the reduction of the other to that status of body, the books need to be assessed and linked in the ways that follow.

It is very much to the point that Laclos and Burroughs appear to be as different as day and night, and to link them together at all amounts to hurling a kind of critical gauntlet. So be it. The "fiction of relationship" is about *pairing*, and it is written out of the belief that we are oddly in the dark in this area, that literature has the capacity to illuminate our situation, our involvement with others, in ways that we are unequipped to see on our own; this book stems also, quite frankly, from the belief that traditional comparative criticism has not much aided us in assessing or imagining pairs, in seeing useful or salient connections between texts separated by history and culture. That particular claim is worth very little, unless it can be shown that such odd couples as *Les Liaisons dangereuses* and *Naked Lunch* teach us something special once we see them together, see them in terms of each other. This chapter is, then, about seeing, about what we are able to take in. It may even be that our ability to see is, in itself, a last bastion of freedom in the face of determinism and bondage, the freedom of recording in Laclos, the fragile freedom of patrolling in Burroughs.

Whereas Laclos' novel is classically outfitted with a seduce-and-abandon scenario, Burroughs takes the whole matter into quite another realm, one where sexual congress is merely part of a larger series of power plays centered on bodies. At their very core, both texts share the same preoccupations, not to say obsessions, with body control and human connection; each charts what might be called an "erotics of power."[2] Their staunch differences in design, language and "propriety" are illuminating differences, differences having to do with literary climate, differences that point us out of the anthropocentrism of an earlier age toward a nightmarish world of viral and chemical forces in which the human is no longer a privileged form. Yet, the drama of relationship, of connection, of merging the body with something, is central to each work. It will be seen, because we see them together, that each of these books is a *cas limite*: the classical virtues of reason, transparency, and control are pushed so far by Laclos that they explode; and the freewheeling vistas of metamorphosis and hallucination are so rigorously structured by Burroughs that they imprison. Ultimately, one may, on the far side of such an analysis, be able to conclude that Laclos tends to the surreal while Burroughs becomes strangely classical, that each sends us to the other, and that we are then able to refocus on their theme of body control with a valuable sense of double vision and echo.

1

"Conquérir est notre destin" (Conquering is our fate), announces Valmont at the outset of *Liaisons*, and no book ever embodied the control ethic more fully. In structure, conception, and style, Laclos renders a glittery, highly polished, confident world, a tone that is secular and refined. His fools and naive characters are bait for the strong and clairvoyant, the commanding Valmont and Merteuil who early on establish the authority of the novel. For there is authority here, and it is no less than the visible reign of coherence in human affairs: motives can be understood, reasons can be stated, behavior can be programmed, stories can be told. The classical novel reassures us most by its form; even when it is nasty, it is cogent, packaging its filth in untroubling ways. This, Laclos' book seeks to soothe on all

2. The phrase is taken from Eric Mottram's *William Burroughs: The Algebra of Need* (London: Marion & Boyars, 1977), p. 54. Mottram provides an exceptionally wide literary context for the work of Burroughs, but he does not mention Laclos.

fronts: all of its many projects—the erotic domination of the other, the making of intrigue, the relentless transformation of detail into plot, the dynamics of its own telling—involve the exercise of control.

The letter itself is doubtless the most privileged triumph of form. Whereas Richardson's novels are sometimes open to the charge that letter-writing is an awkward piece of narrative machinery, Laclos brilliantly dramatizes his vehicle. Letters, as Seylaz has shown in his well-known study of *Liaisons*, carry out the will's colonization of experience.[3] Written afterward, letters are the tools of organization and analysis, and they may be called in to offset the pressures of feeling. Thus, Valmont, off balance, writes. He does it, as he explains to Merteuil, for therapy: "J'ai besoin de me faire violence pour me distraire de l'impression qu'elle m'a faite; c'est même pour m'y aider que je me suis mis à vous écrire" (I must curb my feelings to distract me from the impact she made on me; it is with this in mind that I undertook to write to you).[4] Form and theme are inseparable in such instances, and it becomes clear that Laclos is offering us a meditation on writing itself as reprieve, power, and control, much as Rousseau was doing, at the same time, in his *Confessions*. Valmont's tools for victory are intelligence and analytic power, and the letter grants him respite, lets him retool, so that he can return to the charge. The letter protects against heat (although Valmont is going to learn that it has an indigenous heat of its own), provides a necessary distance. It is not going too far to state, straight out, that Valmont seduces as Laclos writes: with lucidity, by lucidity.

Lucidity, to see clear: is this not the one quality most enshrined by the French intellectual tradition, from Chrétien de Troyes on through the *moraliste* tradition and the psychological novel? It has been noted that other writers, such as Stendhal or Proust, were to offer richer, even more profound analyses of the human psyche, but no one has ever matched Laclos in displaying the power of analysis. Not so much the philosopher in his study or the scientist in his lab-

3. Jean-Luc Seylaz, *Les Liaisons dangereuses et la création romanesque chez Laclos* (Geneva and Paris: Droz, 1958). An interesting alternative to Seylaz's perhaps "overdetermined" reading is Keith Palka's "Chance as a Means of Balancing a Closed Ecological System," in *Laclos: Critical Approaches to* Les Liaisons dangereuses, ed. Lloyd Free (Madrid: Ediciones José Porrúa Turanzas, 1978), pp. 137–66.

4. Choderlos de Laclos, *Les Liaisons dangereuses* (Paris: Garnier Flammarion, 1964), p. 220. Subsequent quotations will be taken from this edition and noted parenthetically in the body of the text.

oratory, but rather the lover on the make, shows to the full just how knowledge becomes power. Lucidity, the great classic virtue, is used toward very unvirtuous ends in *Les Liaisons dangereuses*. Valmont seduces women by the same method Descartes outlined for the sciences: analyze the problem, break it down to its constituent parts, master each part, master the whole. In Laclos, lucidity is leverage; whereas the *moraliste* tradition foregrounds self-knowledge, Laclos' subject is the self-ignorance of the victim that is exploited by the knowledge of the controller. Here is the erotic dialectic in a nutshell: your ignorance is my power; my role is to know you better than you know yourself. And what is to be known in these situations is sharply defined: the human body and the affections that animate it.

Mastery seems possible in *Liaisons* because the body seems knowable. Indeed, the superiority of Valmont and Merteuil over their fellows and victims (it is not easy to separate these two groups) lies in superior knowledge, a confident sense that people are essentially bodies, and that bodies are essentially machines. They are specialists in pleasure, for they understand that it dictates all behavior. Confirmed hedonists, they expose the sham of ethical categories and moral cosmetics while paying careful attention to the sensorial code that alone matters. The descriptions of Valmont's encounters with Tourvel reek with didacticism, seem virtually lifted from some kind of behavioralist textbook on stimuli and response:

> Vous avez sûrement remarqué combien, dans cette situation, à mesure que la défense mollit, les demandes et les refus se passent de plus près; comment la tête se détourne et les regards se baissent, tandis que les discours, toujours prononcés d'une voix faible, deviennent rares et entrecoupés. Ces symptômes précieux annoncent, d'une manière non équivoque, le consentement de l'âme. [221]

> [You have surely noticed how, in this situation, the weakening of the defense is in proportion to the speed with which requests and denials are made; how the head wavers and the eyes are lowered, while the spoken words, pronounced always in a feeble voice, become rare and disjointed. These precious symptoms announce, in unequivocal fashion, the consent of the soul.]

There is no intrinsic interest whatsoever in the emotions or even in psychology; the real prey is the perfect experiment, the infallibility of the method itself. We see, in this passage, an anatomy lesson (replete with the unctuous, professorial tone that we all know: "Vous avez sûrement remarqué . . ."), an attention to physiology that is nothing if not professional. In fact, Valmont's tactics adumbrate an entire scientific paradigm. In the classical scientific model (and this is no less true of the classical literary model), the observer rigorously keeps his distance so that the object can be studied "untouched," intact; in the erotic version, the observer is to play a more active role, to "manipulate" his material in the strictest sense of the term, but he is still to maintain, at least inwardly, his precious distance. You recall ("Vous avez sûrement remarqué") the letter that Valmont had to write to preserve that distance. But, as is well known, in postmodern science, the Cartesian model of detached observer and objective experiment has been discredited in favor of a more ecological view, a crucial recognition that the scientist is, like it or not, part of the experiment. The erotic project of *Les Liaisons dangereuses* hinges precisely on whether the Cartesian "separatist" view can be maintained, whether, to put it more bluntly, the female object can continue to be viewed as a machine during and after intercourse (by the male scientist).

The text does have its candidate for machine status in the "person" of Cécile Volanges. With her, we come a far piece from the dreamy, adolescent, starry-eyed girl who figures so prominently in romance and the stock scenarios of playwrights such as Molière and Marivaux; Cécile is dreamy and starry-eyed enough, but Laclos has taken the extra step of outfitting his nubile maiden with senses, and her role in *Liaisons* is that of consummate tool, the transparent, utterly malleable figure who will be undone, dismantled, and reconstituted for the powerful. There is more than a little pathos here, since Cécile remains unknowing throughout, never once grasping what is happening to and with her (body). Merteuil, who toys with her even more sovereignly (and with more erotic zest) than Valmont, nonetheless finds Cécile disgustingly manipulable:

> . . . je ne connais rien de si plat que cette facilité de bêtise, qui se rend sans savoir ni comment ni pourquoi, uniquement parce qu'on l'attaque et qu'elle ne sait pas résister. Ces sortes de femmes ne sont absolument que des machines à plaisir.
>
> Vous me direz qu'il n'y a qu'à n'en faire que cela, et que c'est assez pour nos projets. À la bonne heure! mais, n'oublions pas que de ces machines-là, tout le monde parvient à en connaître les ressorts et les moteurs; ainsi, que pour se servir de celle-ci

> sans danger, il faut se dépêcher, s'arrêter de bonne heure, et la briser ensuite. [242]

> [. . . I know of nothing so banal as this idiotic complaisance of women who yield without knowing how or why, simply because they are attacked and do not know how to resist. These kind of women are absolutely nothing but pleasure-machines.
>
> You will say that we need merely treat them as such, and that will suffice for our needs. Well and good! but don't forget that everyone soon becomes familiar with the gears and components of these machines; so, if we are to use this one without danger, we must move quickly, stop in good time, and then break it.]

There is no clearer example of Laclos' New Science. Reduced to a "machine à plaisir," Cécile is entirely programmable, something for the grown-ups to tinker with at their leisure, a thing composed of "ressorts" and "moteurs" so elementary that there is not even any sport in the gambit. Burroughs himself does not present exploitation any more coldly than this. The power of Valmont and Merteuil rests entirely on the mechanistic premise at work here: the workings of the other are both knowable and manipulable. We shall see, in *Naked Lunch*, that this view of the creature spawns an entire subculture of parasites and power brokers, and we shall also see that their knowledge of body need and function is nothing short of erudite. In *Liaisons*, Cécile fills this slot all by herself, and the eighteenth-century setting—a time without junkies or genetic engineers—only underscores the vulnerability of her condition. While her mind continues to dally among rose-colored fantasies, her body is fornicated with by Valmont, impregnated, aborted, and then what is left is sent off to a convent. It is a grisly affair, every bit as ruthless as the antics of Burroughs' Dr. Benway with his Reconditioning Center.

In Laclos' elegant fiction, with its polite soul-talk and ceaseless body-pursuit, we gain a new perspective on the role of the human body in relationships. To be sure, the fiction of relationship is always fixated on the body. The initial drive for connection must be, in some sense, erotic, and the alterity of the desired body accounts for much of the mystery of a book such as *Manon Lescaut*; even the cerebral aura of *The Good Soldier* is inevitably counterpointed by bodies, by the odd mix of bad hearts and active genitals. And, as we saw in such books as *To the Lighthouse* and *L'Ecume des jours*, the fate of the loved one's body becomes the very horizon of relationship, especially when death visits. This corporeal vulnerability, the scandal of a body's mortality, can contribute a great deal to the pathos of the fiction of relationship; it can even give rise to fictions of great poetic power. But, it is nonetheless a dreadfully *material* issue. Just as Defoe often renders his things dimensionless, so too can the body appear exclusively as matter, as a corporeal system that need have no truck with emotion or mind. Let the writer cut or attenuate the connection between body and mind, and the fiction of relationship may become a course in anatomy and physiological signs; let the writer go one step further and show that the body constitutes the better part of "self," that it is the first and last authority of human behavior, and then we will see fictions that systematically background all talk of motive and thought and feeling (the very medium of a text such as Ford's), while they zero in on the "undiscovered country" of the body that has its own peculiar laws, customs, and tyrannies. The cliché of the "inner life" is once again literalized, not in the fantasy-like vein we saw in Boris Vian (lilies growing in chests), but in a more molecular, visceral sense; for the "inside" of a person does have a life of its own, a life of blood, organs, nerves, and absolute *wants* of its own. These wants can be known, both from "within" by the self, and from "without" by others. These wants can be programmed. In short, the body can be taken over, according to this scheme, and when this happens, the traditional humanist virtues of virtue and will power become shockingly powerless, exposed as obsolete relics from an older, more genteel age.

It is almost impossible to talk about love or relationship if one opts for a single, exclusive code of mind *or* body, because the love ethos of Western culture, from the troubadours to our time, has accustomed us to complex blends of the mental and the physical, allowing room for desire and need, but tempering them—often through the very writing itself—with consciousness and will. The great benefit that flows from a juxtaposition of Burroughs and Laclos is that Laclos acquires a ruthlessness and even a philosophical program that are somewhat concealed by eighteenth-century rhetoric. The old love language is still there (affection based on esteem, interest only of a high-minded sort, mutual admiration, etc.), but Laclos is out to discredit those notions forever, to show that the love story, even the polite love story, is always an affair of panting breath, stirred genitals, reddening faces, surging blood. This materialist view bathes the whole novel in irony, and its cutting edge goes beyond the events of this text; it does to the idealist love tradition pretty much what Cervantes did to the chivalric tales. Not that Laclos' characters are mindless, or that they do not think about their amorous activity—on the contrary, they think of little else—but, with the crucial exception of the two seducers, they are in the dark as to the operation and antics of their own bodies.

If Cécile Volanges is essentially a pushover for the team of Valmont-Merteuil, the Tourvel campaign is a considerably richer, murkier affair. On the one hand, Valmont's capacity to arouse sexual interest in Tourvel, and then to decipher, unerringly, the signs he arouses, is shown, in every one of their encounters, to be an unqualified success. Like a hunter stalking his prey, he corners Tourvel repeatedly, in parlors and meadows, at the dining table, and though she is as guarded and disciplined as a human can be, he never fails to detect her response to him, virtually to sniff out her emotional and sexual involvement. It is as if he carried a seismograph or a portable EKG or EEG machine with him: what is customarily hidden to human eyes is to Valmont's trained gaze as "clear and distinct" as it needs to be for the Cartesian observer. The eighteenth-century erotic novel is often stereotyped with isolated chateau, abducted maiden, chains and straps; but Laclos, unlike his contemporary Sade, is always decorous, and therefore considerably more disturbing. He shows us that the body is not protected anywhere in culture, neither in common rooms nor on walks with maiden aunts. Just as you can drown in a teaspoon of water, so can you announce sexual interest by a blush, a fast heartbeat, a tremble. Or rather, you cannot stop your body from making this announcement. Tourvel can deny Valmont her bed, but can she refuse a handshake? Can she forbid a peck on the cheek? Can she stop him, as he assists her in climbing over a ditch, from grazing her breast? Can she prevent her hands from trembling as he watches her sew? Valmont diagnoses Tourvel before she even knows she is sick. What is still dark and gestating for her is as legible as an X-ray for him. The language of the senses, what we today call "body language," is what Valmont and Merteuil are schooled in; it is, as Melville might have said, the Yale and Harvard that they attended, and within the world of this text they appear to be the only enlightened figures, the only cognoscenti. This language, so at odds with the words and concepts of the characters, is wholly reliable, and Valmont's time-tested premise is that the body never lies, and if he can prepare it for intercourse, the person has to follow.

To be sure, there is a discrete sociopolitical dimension to all this, since Valmont's strategy obviously depends on his presence (he is persistently resisted by Tourvel in his letter campaign), and if you could banish him, quarantine him, then there would be no danger. Indeed, Mme. Volanges would like to do exactly that, and she prophetically cautions Tourvel that it is not safe to be *near* this man. Laclos is showing that the refusal of polite society to ban its rakes and dissolutes (whatever their other credentials may be) carries real consequences. Yet, it is not easy to imagine a world so well policed that a Valmont could not slip in and ply his trade. Above all, Tourvel understandably feels that she can take care of herself, that she is, after all, a free agent. But Laclos is out to show that there are no free agents; in fact, he wants to show that the decorum, restraint, and discipline of civilized behavior are little more than a whimsical shadow-game, in contrast to the ongoing spectacle of interest and desire unwittingly staged by the body.

Valmont's tactics spring, as we have seen, from an utterly determinist view of the body's behavior, and the signs thus produced can be "read" with all the clarity of algebraic equation. However, Laclos has still more strings to his bow or, to keep with our mathematical figure, moves from the arithmetic to the exponential in the making of Valmont's partner, Merteuil. Whereas the male rake is merely analytic, schooled in the deciphering of the code, Merteuil rather grandly surpasses him by moving into the creative sphere. He decodes signs; she produces signs. The formerly automatic, servile expression of the body (an automatism on which, we must not forget, the entire analysis-and-seduction business depends) becomes something quite different with Merteuil, becomes transformed into art. Merteuil's body and face are her canvas, her marble, the medium of her shaping will. This mastery is the result of method, and Merteuil began early:

> . . . Ressentais-je quelque chagrin, je m'étudiais à prendre l'air de la sérénité, même celui de la joie; j'ai porté le zèle jusqu'à me causer des douleurs volontaires, pour chercher pendant ce temps l'expression du plaisir. Je me suis travaillée avec le même soin et plus de peine, pour réprimer les symptômes d'une joie inattendue. C'est ainsi que j'ai su prendre, sur ma physionomie, cette puissance dont je vous ai vu quelquefois si étonné. [172]

> [. . . when I felt some distress, I carefully put on an air of serenity, even of joy; I even went so far as to hurt myself voluntarily, so as to seek a simultaneous expression of pleasure. I labored

with the same care, and even more difficulty, to repress the symptoms of unexpected joy. This is how I achieved that mastery over my expressions at which I have sometimes seen you so astonished.]

In Merteuil we have the final, most arresting version of the body-machine: not the one that can be taken apart, like Cécile Volanges, but the one that can be assembled and reassembled at will. It is the control ethic in its purest form: Merteuil chooses her face, her body, her words. She speaks them, but they do not speak her. Merteuil is mad for assertion. Sexually, she tells us, she enjoys being a harem to the lover of her choice. She is equally multiple to the various characters of the novel, each one thinking that he (alone) knows her. Underlying all her operations is a prodigious freedom, a performance of pure signifiers, free-floating, nonbinding images that do not refer back to some kind of core or essential self. Unconstrained by any vulgar obedience to referent or truth, Merteuil's life is a ceaseless exercise of pure creativity. She is the total performance.

In the modus operandi of Merteuil, *Les Liaisons dangereuses* comes very close to exploding the classical frames. The newer criticism would not fail to see in her an instance of pure semiosis, a character freed from psychology, undetermined by origin—"je puis dire que je suis mon ouvrage" (I can say that I am my own creation [172]), she tells us—a genuinely free being. Impenetrable and unknowable—for which of her acts renders her?—she penetrates others and knows her own pleasure. Yet, her dream is that old classical one of free observer and knowable object, but with the characteristic erotic turn of the screw: unknowable therefore free controller and knowable therefore manipulable object. But the older truth of Laclos' novel turns out to be, indeed, a truth of origins and centers, an absolute certainty that the self is centered, and that it is that center which the controller must take over. Merteuil herself announces this strategy: "Descendue dans mon cœur, j'y ai étudié celui des autres. J'y ai vu qu'il n'est personne qui n'y conserve un secret qu'il lui importe qu'il ne soit point dévoilé" (From the depths of my own heart, I studied that of others. And I saw that there is nobody who does not hide a secret that can never be revealed [176]). These lines have not only the economy and rigor, but even the volume and poetry of Racinian verse. The body may be our currency and our language, but the heart is where we live; it is the place into which we "descend," much like a kind of pit or abyss, and it states, with absolute reliability, not only who we are, but who the others are as well, since they are modeled on the same lines. The fierce negatives of Laclos' prose bespeak crystalline certainty ("il n'est personne qui n'y conserve . . .") and also something resembling the prohibitive power of taboo ("un secret qu'il lui importe qu'il ne soit point dévoilé"). Merteuil's truth is that the heart can be taken, that, in our very depths, even to be seen is to be lost.[5] We have seen that self-creation is a prodigious display of freedom; we learn now that it is also a prodigious smoke screen, a relentless defense against being known, being taken.

At the end of Laclos' novel we begin to realize that the separatist ventures and body machines do not work. Valmont seduces Tourvel's body, but cannot procure her person until he appeals to her generosity; her generosity appeals to his. The controllers cannot keep their distances; the seducers find themselves seduced. Laclos' book turns out to be one with its title, *Les Liaisons dangereuses*: its subject is relationship, connection, ties. All his characters are destroyed because they are connected: mothers and daughters, aunts and nephews, especially lovers. The letters insidiously prove connection between parties, high-flying rhetoric that is exposed as "true," cynicism that is whistling in the dark, blood lines as well as ink lines between people.[6]

5. The most sophisticated and intriguing reading of Laclos in terms of structures of defense is Joan DeJean's chapter on *Liaisons* in her excellent volume, *Literary Fortifications: Rousseau, Laclos, Sade* (Princeton: Princeton University Press, 1984), pp. 191–262. DeJean argues that "fortifications" betoken multiple projects of defense and bellicosity, ranging from issues of literary inheritance to psychic structures of sanctuary and siege, and her reading constitutes one of the most interesting accounts of these eighteenth-century writers that we have.

6. As might be expected, there has been considerable criticism of *Liaisons* in terms of linguistic and semiotic systems. The most famous account is doubtless that of Tzvetan Todorov, appearing variously in his *Littérature et signification* (Paris: Larousse, 1967) and "Les Catégories du récit littéraire," *Communications*, 8 (1966): 125–51. Whereas Todorov works with speech-act theory, Ronald Rosbottom makes a very thorough case for the relevance of an "interactional" communicative model, involving the issue of "metacommunication": "Dangerous Connections: A Communicational Approach to *Les Liaisons dangereuses*," in *Critical Approaches*, pp. 183–221. Relying on the concepts of Gregory Bateson and the Palo Alto group, Rosbottom is able to extend his communicational argument to a critique of the culture at large: "Laclos documents the perversion of a system that was far from error-free. Social formulae, social classes are in an advanced stage of decay in *Les Liaisons dangereuses*, and there is a bankruptcy of words, of data transmission and

The murky ecological picture replaces the transparent Cartesian grids. The elegant frames will not hold against the affections set loose. At the end, the letters are dispersed everywhere, just as the bodies are, like a nuclear explosion.

Tourvel, dying and hallucinating, expresses Laclos' dark truth about the vulnerability of the self, and she does so with the associative logic of nightmare:

> Mais quoi! c'est lui . . . je ne me trompe pas; c'est lui que je revois. Oh! mon aimable ami! reçois-moi dans tes bras; cache-moi dans ton sein: oui, c'est toi, c'est bien toi! Quelle illusion funeste m'avait fait te méconnaître? combien j'ai souffert dans ton absence! Ne nous séparons plus, ne nous séparons jamais. Laisse-moi respirer. Sens mon cœur, comme il palpite! Ah! ce n'est plus de crainte, c'est la douce émotion de l'amour. Pourquoi te refuser à mes tendres caresses? Tourne vers moi tes doux regards. Quels sont ces liens que tu cherches à rompre? Pourquoi prépares-tu cet appareil de mort? Qui peut ainsi altérer tes traits? que fais-tu? Laisse-moi: je frémis! Dieu! c'est ce monstre encore! [355]

> [What! it is he . . . I am not deceived; it is he I see again. O, my sweet friend! take me in your arms, hide me in your embrace. Yes, it is you, it is indeed you! What dreadful delusion caused me to mistake you? how I've suffered in your absence! We must not separate again, we must never separate. Let me breathe. Feel my heart, how it beats! Ah, it is no longer from fear, but the sweet excitement of love. Why do you turn away from my caresses? Look gently upon me again. What are these chains you seek to break? Why are you preparing those instruments of death? How can your features be so changed? What are you doing? Let me go: I am trembling. God! it is the monster again.]

We see here, in spectacular fashion, the entire plot of the novel—Valmont's relentless pursuit, the metamorphosis of tenderness and lust, connection itself as fatal, as "appareil de mort"—removed from the leisurely pace of Laclos' ordinary prose and speeded up, issuing

---

collation, of relationships in this novel which, coincidentally or not, came perfectly in 1782, only seven years before the entire culture short-circuited" (pp. 220–21).

forth as a dizzying array of pure images. Note as well that the slippages and fissures displayed here (the shifting from "crainte" to "amour," the alteration of Valmont from lover to monster) multiply the threats to the self, show it open to siege from without and within, but—and this needs to be emphasized—they do not thereby fragment the heart. As cracked and pained consciousness, Tourvel registers the story of her life, the invasion and take-over that she has endured. This final testimony is essentially the self's farewell: its transactions with the other have not been survivable, but it is bent on narrating, with hallucinatory power, its Calvary before withdrawing from consciousness altogether. This final tale is a veritable distillation of the fiction of relationship: although physically alone, Tourvel is nonetheless joined by her lover, a lover who comes through walls in the form of dreams, who demonstrates the terrible ambivalence of human touch, the infinitesimal gap between caress and murder. Laclos seems to have many languages at his disposal, and all of them tell a story of dispossession and undoing.

Finally, Merteuil, the intact Merteuil who is the consummate mask, who cannot be penetrated, learns that her very medium of power and control—her body—is not exclusively hers. It belongs, has always belonged, to an alien system, and may be visited by smallpox. Merteuil, as we know, does not die, but she does go out of business. Her will remains intact, but everything else is broken, and her pockmarked face, said by the gossips to display her soul, also displays her ultimate impotence, her ultimate enslavement to the corporeal world she had thought she ruled. We finish where we began, with the body, but the seduce-and-abandon plot has yielded to a more composite picture of human affairs. The arrogance of knowledge as power has been punished, and the intact, enclosed individual is a dream of the past. Laclos' novel prophetically images relationship as invasion, as take-over, and it centralizes the body as the inevitable currency of human affairs. Modern literature will up the ante.

2

If *Les Liaisons dangereuses* moves from wit and elegance to death and disease, William Burroughs' *Naked Lunch* starts on the far side of things. It would be a postnuclear work, wise at the outset about the futility of reason and the sham of form. Appetite alone seems to exist in Burroughs' anarchic text, and the cherished underpinnings of classical art—lucidity, intellect, and will—have been banished from this New World. Yet, Burroughs, no less than Laclos, is writing about power and control, and he too envisions the human body as the raw material of all commerce. But Laclos' *ancien régime* pattern of selectivity—both social and verbal—is no longer operational, and therefore *Naked Lunch* can be inclusive, one might say "democratic," in ways that few other works of literature ever have been.[7] We would appear to move from the salon to the bazaar, from the privileged sanctity of aristocratic boudoirs to the wide-open arena of the marketplace:

> In the City Market is the Meet Café. Followers of obsolete, unthinkable trades doodling in Etruscan, addicts of drugs not yet synthesized, pushers of souped-up Hermaline, liquids to induce Latah, Tithonian longevity serums, black marketeers of World War III, excisors of telepathic sensitivity, osteopaths of the spirit, investigators of infractions denounced by bland paranoid chess players, servers of fragmentary warrants taken down in hebephrenic shorthand charging unspeakable mutilations of the spirit, bureaucrats of spectral departments, officials of unconstituted police states, a Lesbian dwarf who has perfected operation Bangutot, the lung erection that strangles a sleeping enemy, sellers of orgone tanks and relaxing machines, brokers of exquisite dreams and memories tested on the sensitized cells of junk sickness and bartered for raw materials of the will, doctors skilled in the treatment of diseases dormant in the black dust of ruined cities, gathering virulence in the white blood of eyeless worms feeling slowly to the surface and the human host, maladies of the ocean floor and the stratosphere, maladies of the laboratory and atomic war . . . A place where the unknown past and the emergent future meet in a vibrating soundless hum.[8]

7. Eric Mottram eloquently situates Burroughs' novel within an indigenous American tradition dealing with power: "The novel is a comic horror strip whose theme is those obsessions with power that lie well within a strong American literary tradition of power relationships—from Brockden Brown and Poe through Hawthorne to Henry James" (*William Burroughs*, p. 44).

8. William Burroughs, *Naked Lunch* (New York: Grove Press, 1959), pp.

This is Burroughs' team. It is a distinctly egalitarian outfit: the conceptual and perceptual grids of eighteenth-century mind have been drastically opened to include a mix of races, species, humans and not-so-humans. But this crew is no less coherent than the gathering at Mme. de Rosemonde's country estate: these are the parasites, the caterers to human need, and they are united in their marketplace relations and their commitment to the programmable wants of the human body. In contrast to the elegant confines of the eighteenth-century novel, where sexual exploitation is a refined activity of the leisure class, Burroughs opens onto an entire world of enslavement and exploitation, and he seems to be saying that the control of bodies is at the heart of all commerce and life.

Of course, a considerable distance has been traveled. Manipulation has become a big business, and it now permeates the international (and interstellar?) political scene as well. The erotic erudition of Valmont and Merteuil is no longer necessary to perform acts of manipulation and control, because there has been a knowledge explosion (along with, perhaps, other explosions), and there are now armies out there, whole populations trained in "take-over": pushers, black marketeers, osteopaths of the spirit, bureaucrats, sellers of orgone tanks and relaxing machines, doctors, professionals and amateurs alike. As Burroughs' list gathers intensity, we cannot fail to see how the players form one great family, that they are united under the heading of "virus," a panoramic display of parasites feeding on the human host. The exotica of the Meet Café reminds one of older, now unreadable icons and fantasies, such as are present in Bosch's *Garden of Earthly Delights*, especially when it comes to the torments of hell. Bosch, like Burroughs, focuses on where the action is, on orifices and genitals, our avenues of appetite, and he effects monstrous transformations there. In Bosch, too, we sense a dreadful *system* at work, as the manifold creatures of legend and Nature feast on genitals, batten on the human creature, punishing him (or her) for excesses, illuminate the real combat zones of the body, show that the organs of pleasure will be horribly privileged in the onslaught that follows death. But the scene at the Meet Café sends us, pointedly, forward as well as backward, into our space-age nightmares, replete with Star Wars scenarios (both the film and the weapons project) and the emergent forces of death and deformity arising from the ocean floor, the strat-

108–109. Subsequent quotations will be taken from this edition and noted parenthetically in the body of the text.

osphere, and the laboratory. Body control has been "upgraded" in Burroughs' hands, and the old love-story paradigm disappears forever, yielding instead a manic, multilevel tapestry of an entire world gone amuck.

Naked Lunch may appear chaotic in comparison to the clear lines of demarcation in Laclos, but Burroughs' universe is nothing if not coherent: his creatures coexist in a rigorous ecosystem, a system so powerful that interdependence and connectedness reign everywhere we look. Whereas Laclos connects his few players amorously, Burroughs posits need and addiction between his multitudes. For too long, this business of need and addiction has been regarded as a matter of syringes and junkies, as the peculiar province of an extravagant "druggie," and this has led to the great neglect of Burroughs as a serious writer. He is writing about the great theme of human connection, but in unheard-of ways; *Naked Lunch* marks the end of traditional narrative and the beginning of something so new, so unsettling, so unacknowledged by literary historians, that it remains a visionary work without followers. Burroughs shows, quite simply, that our commerce, our relations, our dependency are far more extensive than we had ever suspected. His cardinal truth is that we *traffic* in everything: bodies, drugs, food, oxygen, electronic waves, gadgets, weapons, print, media, ideology, telepathy. Just as the physicists have the dizzying choice of viewing light as either wave or particle, depending on what there is to prove, so too is Burroughs' view of human affairs a potent challenge to received notions. Western metaphysics is so accustomed to privileging actors and agents, so oversubscribed to the view that individuals initiate actions and that phenomena exist in discrete forms, that Burroughs' critique has been largely ignored. His is a view of endless take-over and usurpation, of a force field where the self enters a maelstrom. And he has acted on that view as a writer, not just as a thinker: hence, the sustaining structures of individualism and will power, notably the conventions of plot, character, even syntax, are mocked in *Naked Lunch*, as if to show that human gesture no longer commands the kind of credence it got in the old days. In such art, the customary boundaries between matter and spirit, real and imaginary, human and nonhuman are transgressed. A sentence of realist prose can be followed by something like this:

> The Sailor put a hand to the boy's eyes and pulled out a pink scrotal egg with one closed, pulsing eye. Black fur boiled inside

> translucent flesh of the egg. The Sailor caressed the egg with nakedly inhuman hands—black-pink, thick, fibrous, long white tendrils sprouting from abbreviated finger tips. [204]

It will not do, simply to label such writing "visionary" or "drug-induced"; Burroughs' scene is prodigiously expanded, making room for states of consciousness and types of phenomena that are either imperceptible or off-limits to the classical novelist. An entirely new kind of propriety becomes imaginable here, and this wide-angle view of experience makes for distinctly rough reading, since it refuses to play by the rules we are accustomed to. This breakthrough (or, perhaps, break-in) is perceptual, but it is also social, because an ecological fiction surrounds us with neighbors we never knew we had. Burroughs' menagerie causes Laclos' pristine demarcations to appear nostalgic in their primness, in the amount of traffic they keep out. Laclos' control rests on his anthropocentrism, his rigorous reduction of the world to human motive. Laclos knows we are linked to one another, but the fiction that his fiction tests is the degree to which we will our linkages. No such constraints are operative in Burroughs.

The carnival in *Naked Lunch* annihilates individual autonomy, single plots, and pristine forms, and it indeeds looks, at first glance, like a celebration of randomness and heterogeneity. Yet, as I mentioned earlier, Burroughs too possesses rigor and selectivity if we know how to look. Beneath its surface anarchy there is pattern: not the traditional plot and character paradigms of the classic text, but an indigenous structure of its own, a kind of *Urform* that is replicated throughout the text.[9] The structure may be played out in terms of drugs, sex, disease, or ideology, but the structure remains the same: the opening of the body by a foreign object. No less than Laclos' Merteuil, Burroughs starts with the premise that the opened, exposed self courts danger or destruction. However, he then goes on to chart the virtual geometry and geography of such openings: the syringe penetrates the skin and the junk hits the blood stream; the penis or its substitute enters the vagina or the rectum; the bacteria enter the body to grow; the scalpel or the rusty tin can cuts open the flesh; the genes are tam-

9. For another view of Burroughs' "pattern," see Michael Bliss, "The Orchestration of Chaos in William Burroughs' *Naked Lunch*," *enclitic* 1, 1 (1977): 59–69. Eric Mottram has described the effect of the novel as "one of controlled chaos, confusion close-hauled into art, arbitrary order and manic manipulation exposed through careful composition" (*William Burroughs*, p. 46); this essay is an attempt to give some specificity to such a claim.

pered with and "re-form"; the worm enters the egg; the pregnant woman carries "the little stranger"; the cells revolt through cancer and take over the body; the body's physiology is redesigned by doctors and scientists; the mind is altered by ideological and chemical programming. The actors may change, but the fable remains constant: the parasite enters the host to control it.[10] Burroughs thus demonstrates a rigor of his own, a repetitive pattern so fierce and reliable that it becomes Fate within the text and has, as well, the effect of endowing this apparently chaotic text with a grisly pattern, achieving a strangely modern classicism. Yet, the stage is not merely broadened; it is also deepened. Here is the very *form* of breaking and entering, which may range from physical rape to genetic engineering to psychological pillage. Beneath the shadow-play of characters and beds, this is literally the modus operandi of the erotic novel, the dialectic of freedom and control seen up close, at the end of your spoon, as Burroughs would say.

The integral self, previously armored in will and analytic method, is under siege in Burroughs just as he is in Laclos, but Burroughs adds considerably to the picture by stressing that the body desires *out* as much as *in*. Merteuil's walled-in self, fated to be altered if not opened in *Liaisons*, is countered by a view of the organism that craves violation and exodus. The flip side of Burroughs' parasitism is a theory of ecstasy, ecstasy in the literal sense of being put "out of place."

10. Swayed by the title of the book, Mottram has emphasized the theme of cannibalism in Burroughs, and passages depicting Mary devouring Johnny ("she bites away Johnny's lips and nose and sucks out his eyes with a pop . . . She tears off great hunks of cheek . . . Now she lunches on his prick"[97]) obviously support his claim. Nonetheless, the viral-parasitic paradigm seems far more central to Burroughs' view of relationships, and it is ultimately a much more disturbing concept than "mere" cannibalism. But an argument could indeed be made, in contrast to the exploitative pattern I am highlighting, that *Naked Lunch* proposes an odd form of equilibrium, a type of homeostasis in which what goes "in" is rigorously matched by what comes "out." In an unpublished paper, Fernanda Moore (Brown University, November 1986) has pointed to Burroughs' strange give-and-take: the needle that fills with blood as the heroin enters the body, ejaculation upon entry, plants growing out of genitals, the selling of used condoms, Greek boys bearing bowls of shit. In this light, the talking Asshole would epitomize Burroughs' economy, his fascination with the in's and out's of the body, indeed his paralleling of language and feces and semen as the equivalent currencies of the body.

Merteuil moves laterally, from lie to lie, mask to mask, never herself, always herself; the characters in *Naked Lunch* are headed out, traveling from the center, moving from the core. Burroughs is showing that ecstasy—at least chemically and sexually—is achievable only when something or someone enters us; ejaculating and mainlining are both trips; for Burroughs, they are more or less the same trip. That trip has replaced the plots, itineraries, and directionalities of prior narrative; hence we have the crude doctrine, "Gentle reader, we see God through our assholes in the flash bulb of orgasm . . . Through these orifices transmute your body . . . The way OUT is the way IN" (229).

This is the language of transcendence, and it gives a homely locus to the traveling and tripping of the text: the real frontiers of human life, the first as well as the last frontiers, are those of the body, its vital entries and exits. Burroughs depicts every possible form of penetration, and the homosexual preferences in the work are arguably structural as much as personal. His women puncture men by means of Steely Dan, his old junkies dream of tight young asses. The moments of ecstasy actually depicted in the book have great beauty, but their ferocity is properly metamorphic, destructive of the human form, bent on transfiguration:

> Johnny dowses Mary with gasoline from an obscene Chimu jar of white jade . . . He anoints his own body . . . They embrace, fall to the floor and roll under a great magnifying glass set in the roof . . . burst into flame with a cry that shatters the glass wall, roll into space, fucking and screaming through the air, burst in blood and flames and soot on brown rocks under a desert sun. [98–99]

Ecstasy is violent, and it rends as well as releases. Laclos had to reach for hallucination, in an epiphanic moment of truth, for Tourvel to see that desire and murder are related, that her connection with Valmont, her liaison leads ineluctably to a death-machine, an *appareil de mort*. Burroughs, on the other hand, has no need for a climactic deathbed scene, since he is routinely dealing with climaxes (of a sort), and for him, murder and pleasure are the most predictable of all bedfellows. Murder is doubtless the ultimate sexual high in the pecking order of *Naked Lunch*, and here we confront, once again, the issue of control. Consider, for instance, the following episode: "Two Arab women with bestial faces have pulled the shorts off a little blond French boy. They are screwing him with red rubber cocks. The boy snarls, bites, kicks, collapses in tears as his cock rises and ejaculates" (78). Here is the ultimate confounding of will power, and we can begin to measure how far we have come from Laclos. The boy's will is in play—he snarls, bites, kicks—but it counts for naught, as he is simultaneously raped and climaxing. The body is a machine, and others can turn it on, whether you like it or not. This is what the army of junkies, parasites, and power brokers in *Naked Lunch* know: how to harness the body. The two Arab women flaunt the body's frailty and its autonomous power at once.

Naked Lunch does full justice to its twin subjects: the splendor of ecstasy ("wouldn't you?") but also the heinous nature of addiction and exploitation ("wouldn't you?"). In a characteristic passage, Burroughs positions the American pleasure-seeker against the diseased backdrop of a culture gone wrong:

> A vast still harbor of iridescent water. Deserted gas well flares on the smoky horizon. Stink of oil and sewage. Sick sharks swim through the black water, belch sulphur from rotting livers, ignore a bloody, broken Icarus. Naked Mr. America, burning frantic with self bone love, screams out: "My asshole confounds the Louvre! I fart ambrosia and shit pure gold turds! My cock spurts soft diamonds in the morning sunlight!" He plummets from the eyeless lighthouse, kissing and jacking off in the face of the black mirror, glides oblique down to cryptic condoms and mosaic of a thousand newspapers through a drowned city of red brick to settle in black mud with tin cans and beer bottles, gangsters in concrete, pistols pounded flat and meaningless to avoid short-arm inspection of prurient ballistic experts. He waits the slow striptease of erosion with fossil loins. [75–76]

This scene has an apocalyptic flavor to it, and it displays the manifold failures of modern civilization: pollution, decay, filth, a whole city drowned, its violence and crimes building up like sludge, undecomposable, as the environmentalists would say. This degraded external world is counterpointed by the insanely narcissist brilliance of the "inner world," the organs and productions of the human body rivaling with precious stones and perfumes, "confounding the Louvre," showing us with great power the kind of reversal that Burroughs has effected. With God at the lower end of the intestinal tract, we achieve a distinctly new view of things, one that relegates all reality to the happenings within our own organism, especially its complex neural circuitry, the countless nerve-endings that dot the body at all its major articulations, the brain, the intestines, the genitals, the orifices.

Here, too, in a sense, Laclos precedes us. Merteuil was also wise about the whereabouts of pleasure, and in one of her letters to Valmont, she ridiculed the deluded women of her time who think that

> la nature a placé leurs sens dans leur tête; qui, n'ayant jamais réfléchi, confondent sans cesse l'amour et l'amant; qui, dans leur folle illusion, croient que celui-là seul avec qui elles ont cherché le plaisir, en est l'unique dépositaire, et vraies superstitieuses, ont pour le prêtre, le respect et la foi qui n'est dû qu'à la divinité. [171]

> [nature has placed their senses in their heads; who, never having thought about it, constantly confuse love with the lover; who, in their senseless illusion, believe that the man with whom they have found pleasure is pleasure's only source, and, in true superstitious fashion, have for the priest the respect and faith that are owed only to the divinity.]

All of Laclos' wit and impudence are in this passage, as it systematically makes a religion out of pleasure, and marvelously adapts the Enlightenment anti-church rhetoric to its own hedonist ends. In separating the pleasure she receives from the lover who "occasions" it, however, Merteuil is already pointing toward the body constellation that is to reign in Burroughs. Ecstasy and orgasm are impersonal, located within our own bodies.

One can hardly go further from the notion of mutuality as the cornerstone of relationship; yet, all the narcissism and cynicism notwithstanding, one is nonetheless entirely dependent on others for servicing one's needs, and one still cannot avoid opening, as it were, one's entries and exits for the work that is required. In *Naked Lunch*, the procuring of ecstasy is totally front-and-center, and there is no longer even any pretense of relationship, no longer even the rhetoric of meaningful connection. Thus, we encounter vignettes such as the following:

> "Ever make sex in no gravity? Your jism just floats out in the air like lovely ectoplasm, and female guests are subject to immaculate or at least indirect conception . . . Reminds me of an old friend of mine, one of the handsomest men I have ever known

and one of the maddest and absolutely ruined by wealth. He used to go about with a water pistol shooting jism up career women at parties. Won all his paternity suits hands down. Never use his own jism you understand." [111–112]

It is a remarkable passage. Much of it could be lifted from traditional storytelling of the moralizing type ("one of the handsomest men I have ever known and . . . absolutely ruined by wealth"), but it is so stamped with infantilism and misogyny that it ultimately offers a quintessential Burroughs image of intercourse: disconnected, anonymous, turned literally into a form of "shooting up."

Even though Burroughs' world is profoundly narcissist and locked into its private pleasure syndrome, his creatures are nonetheless driven by their wants into the hands (or syringes or other props) of that caterer society depicted at the Meet Café. Indifferent to others, capable of staring at his shoelaces for eight hours straight, the Burroughs character is still one of the most enmeshed, interconnected characters in fiction. He may be locked into his own world, but he has no illusions about self-sufficiency; and he knows full well that he is enterable, porous, and permeable, and that he craves such invasion. This is more than a question of drugs or sex. In the unforgettable person of Dr. Benway, we see the full ramifications of the ideological and philosophical underpinnings of *Naked Lunch*; the doctor is a control specialist, and his views hark back precisely to the body-machine assumptions of Valmont and Merteuil, this time taken to drastic lengths. The days of dalliance and casual conquest are over; Benway is a professional: "a manipulator and coordinator of symbol systems, an expert on all phases of interrogation, brainwashing and control" (21). Benway defines his mission as "assault on the subject's personal identity" (25), and he is possessed of countless anecdotes to illustrate his war against the self:

"The case of a female agent who forgot her real identity and merged with her cover story—she is still a fricoteuse in Annexia—put me onto another gimmick. An agent is trained to deny his agent identity by asserting his cover story. So why not use psychic jiu-jitsu and go along with him? Suggest that his cover story is his identity and that he has no other. His agent identity becomes unconscious, that is, out of control, and you can dig it with drugs and hypnosis. You can make a square heterosex citizen queer with the angle . . . that is, reinforce and second his rejection of normally latent homosexual trends—at the

> same time depriving him of cunt and subjecting him to homosex stimulation. Then drugs, hypnosis, and—" Benway flipped a limp wrist. [27]

In Benway's Reconditioning Center the kind of work done to Cécile Volanges has become standardized, outfitted with state-of-the-art equipment. The old-fashioned erotic project of controlling the body of the other has turned into a full-fledged dismantling operation.

Burroughs' program for psychic engineering seems much less futurist at the end of the century than it must have in 1959. As they say, we now have the science for it. But, the writer deals ultimately in imagination, not hard facts, and Burroughs thus outruns even today's science in his experiments with cloning, cloning now seen as an inevitable follow-up to his view of the manipulable subject. On the one hand, in *Naked Lunch* we find replicas, clones that individuals make in apparently different forms (blacks producing blond, blue-eyed replicas, etc.), and, true to his narcissist principles, Burroughs then imagines people coupling with their replicas. We are even treated to the topography of such a society: "Bars subject to be inundated by low class replica lovers put up signs in ditto marks: ' ' ' ' 's Will Not Be Served Here" (166). On the other hand, perhaps even more intriguing, one finds the Latah, a kind of living shadow that does not always behave, as the following story suggests:

> "This citizen have a Latah he import from Indo-China. He figure to hang the latah and send a Xmas TV short to his friends. So he fix up two ropes—one gimmicked to stretch, the other the real McCoy. But that Latah get up in feud state and put on his Santa Claus suit and make with the switcheroo. Come the dawning. The citizen put one rope on and the Latah, going along the ways Latahs will, put on the other. When the traps are down the citizen hang for real and the Latah stand with the carny-rubber stretch rope. Well, the Latah imitate every twitch and spasm. Come three times. . . ." [79–80]

How does one even begin to assess such a passage? One notes in it the sharp verbal pungency that Allen Ginsberg appreciated when he referred to Burroughs' "fantastic gamut of speech rhythms, diction and still-life style."[11] But the language is fully in the service of a grotesque, homosexual fantasy, one attuned with hangings as sexual come-on's and homocidal con games as the funniest show in town.

11. Allen Ginsberg, "*Naked Lunch* on Trial," in *Naked Lunch*, p. xxxiii.

Such an episode stretches our notion of "relationship" beyond any recognizable form; this intercourse "with" one's shadow displays the masturbatory (and doubtless racist) energies of an egomaniacal pleasure cult, but it also stages something of the demonism in Burroughs' scheme, the kinds of things that can happen to your body.

Latahs excepted, most of the damage done to the body in *Naked Lunch* is carried out by recognizable human agents with a profit to make. Benway is the mad scientist who reprograms the body, changes its sexual preferences, domesticates it to his own purposes. But he does not stand alone, and we begin to grasp the ambitiousness of Burroughs' undertaking, the perverse cogency of his view, as we see that all of history and culture is nothing but a great meta-theater of Control. Benway's cohorts include the great religious leaders, Christ, Buddha, Mohammed, and Confucius, each one paraded forth as a carnival con man, bent on manipulating the public. Here is the Christ of *Naked Lunch*:

> "Step right up, Marquesses and Marks, and bring the little Marks too. Good for young and old, man and beast. . . . The one and only legit *Son of Man* will cure a young boy's clap with one hand—by contact alone, folks—create marijuana with the other, whilst walking on water and squirting wine out his ass. . . . Now keep your distance, folks, you is subject to be irradiated by the sheer charge of this character." [113]

The figure of the Ancient Mariner who accosts the Wedding Guest with his unsolicited "wisdom" appears frequently in this book; sometimes his goods are spiritual, sometimes intellectual, but always he is conceived of as a threat, a vampirish figure who battens on the subject and takes him over. When the venerable philosopher speaks (expressed by Burroughs as "some old white-haired fuck" staggering "out to give us the benefits of his ripe idiocy"), we invariably encounter the imagery of pollution or diarrhea (the "Word Hoard" is to be "unlocked" and more or less spill onto the innocent bystanders). In short, language is also an assault, and its victim is persistently presented as subjected to something akin to sexual violence and radioactive contamination: "I tell you when I leave the Wise Man I don't even feel like a human. He converting my live orgones into dead bullshit" (116). There are no innocent exchanges or interactions in *Naked Lunch*. The Male Hustler speaks of the violation he suffers, in words that recall the plight of the Wise Man's victim:

> "What a boy hasta put up with in this business. Gawd! The propositions I get you wouldn't believe it. . . . They wanta play Latah, they wanta merge with my protoplasm, they want a replica cutting, they wanta suck my orgones, they wanta take over my past experience and leave me old memories that disgust me. . . ." [125]

Burroughs' vision is astonishingly integral, of a piece. The control ethos informs all human activity, and he obliges us to see, close up, what is on the edge of our spoon: the panoramic scope of our vulnerability. Sexual exploitation, genetic engineering, psychological manipulation, emotional connection, verbal communication, they are all, either literally or figuratively, invasive. The human subject in Burroughs is incessantly victimized, entered and emptied. The audaciousness of *Naked Lunch* lies in its fusions, its insistence that takeover is happening all the time and in manifold ways. But we who have been trained to distinguish between sex, drugs, language, and politics, cannot see the awesome pattern at hand. At one point, Burroughs writes, "Man contracts a series of diseases which spell out a code message" (66), but the code is readable only when we align the diseases, recognize that the sexual, the verbal, the chemical, and the political are faces of each other, have the same story to tell.

That story, as we have repeatedly noted, is about the targeting of the human body, about how enmeshed it is within nets and systems that prey on it. His book is shot through with parasitism, with ghostly and bodily take-overs. But, because the subject is entered all the time, it is crucial to distinguish between controlled, one-way traffic and mutual intercourse. The greatest warning of *Naked Lunch* extends beyond the addictions of drugs and sex; it embraces the generic threat of biocontrol: "The logical extension of encephalographic research is biocontrol: that is control of physical movement, mental processes, emotional reactions and *apparent* sensory impressions by means of bioelectric signals injected into the nervous system of the subject." The mythic figure of Evil behind the biocontrol threat is appropriately called the Sender:

> The Sender will be defined by negatives. A low pressure area, a sucking emptiness. He will be portentously anonymous, faceless, colorless. He will—probably—be born with smooth disks of skin instead of eyes. He always knows where he is going like a virus knows. He doesn't need eyes. . . . Some maudlin citizens

> will think they can send something edifying, not realizing that sending *is* evil. Scientists will say, "Sending is like atomic power. . . . If properly harnessed . . ." Philosophers will bat around the ends and means hassle not knowing that *sending can never* be a means to anything but more sending, like Junk . . . The Sender is not a human individual . . . It is the Human Virus . . . The broken image of Man moves in minute by minute and cell by cell . . . Poverty, hatred, war, police-criminals, bureaucracy, insanity, all symptoms of the Human Virus. [168–69]

The Sender exists as a malevolent force behind the entire ecosystem, the figure who enmeshes the self in its webs, takes on the individual in order to take him over. In a viral world there are no protective walls of defense, no lines that can be drawn: this far, and no farther. Viral take-over is as revolutionary as the events of 1789, and Burroughs' surrealist art enables him to depict a panorama of freedom and control, of desire for connection and cost of connection, that affords us a strange new view of the erotic novel: *Les Liaisons dangereuses* under the microscope, as it were, with all its living organisms on display. The decorous stasis of *Liaisons*, a stasis that respects individual posture and relegates action to the realm of will and control, is shown by Burroughs to be what it probably always was: traffic, interconnection, linkage. As a threat to human integrity, to the intact self, the bonding between people may be viral, telepathic, or erotic; Burroughs' brand of fiction writes large the relational mesh in which we are all caught.

Laclos' novel ends, we may recall, on a bleak note, with letters scattered and hidden, bodies strewn, lives destroyed or dismantled. The venerable Mme. de Rosemonde who is left to ponder these events can find no consoling wisdom, nothing on which to build. Burroughs, to one's surprise, adumbrates a homely but appealing solution to the catastrophic threats of invasion that he has charted: his answer is "patrolling." The subject must be vigilant in his self-defense, in his self-maintenance, even while fully acknowledging the appeal of other-level experience, the temptations of ecstasy:

> Patrolling is, in fact, my principle [*sic*] occupation . . . No matter how tight Security, I am always somewhere *Outside* giving orders and *Inside* this straight jacket of jelly that gives and stretches but always reforms ahead of every movement, thought, impulse, stamped with the seal of alien inspection . . . [221]

Mutuality and love remain beyond the pale, unreachable, unimaginable; but at least there is an effort to keep the self together, to grant the body a measure of peace and respect. We return, once more, to the issue of control, but it is at last exercised by the subject in his battle for self-preservation. Given the carnage and wastage of *Naked Lunch*, this lesson has a ring of well-earned truth.

3

It may be fairly asked, What has been gained by reading *Les Liaisons dangereuses* and *Naked Lunch* "together"? No systematic conflation of texts has been attempted, nor will it be. Yet, Burroughs' book is filled with salutary truths for the literary critic, especially for the comparatist. To "follow" the eighteenth-century epistolary novel with the iconoclastic modernist text is to acquire special lenses for rereading *Liaisons*. His control ethic and the widespread abuses of power that he depicts help us to highlight those matters in the earlier novel, help us to see that the body-machine philosophy of Valmont-Merteuil is to be found, alive and well, in the 1950s drug scene.

Yet, these are only the most obvious gains of such a comparison. There is more that *Naked Lunch* teaches us, insights and warnings of much broader import. To understand the dazzling "cogency" of Burroughs' novel, to see that its various "fields" (sex, drugs, language, politics) are rigorously unified by a single code message—viral takeover—is to rethink the very notion of categorization, of difference. *Naked Lunch* was granted, at the outset of this essay, status as a modern "classic" because it boldly establishes a formal harmony of its own, what has been called the *Urform* of breaking and entering. Like modern paintings and modern music whose harmonies and patterns are no longer to be found in the space where they used to be located, so too does *Naked Lunch* oblige us to discern a new kind of propriety, a propriety that we cannot possibly gauge until we let go of the old proprieties, see beyond the old rubrics and categories. Reading this text requires something of a conceptual revolution, a change in our ways of seeing, and this change is far more significant than our possible reaction to Burroughs' obscene or excessive materials. To move beyond established categories of experience, established rubrics for the marshaling of data, is no simple matter, but it lies at the very pulse of *comparison* as a mode of discovery, as a vehicle of knowledge. To compare discrete things, to make each of them a reference for the other, to remove each from its established "home" in order to create a larger context and thereby see them better, see what they portend, has been the fundamental rationale of this book. It is also the goal of this book: namely, that the act of juxtaposing carefully selected materials is an exercise of critical freedom, an open-ended way of attending to the richness and significance of one's subject(s).

Understanding *Naked Lunch* amounts to rethinking how things fit together. The most immediate example of such "understanding" is the project of this chapter: a study of how Laclos and Burroughs might fit together. Both writers tell the story of the body in culture; they both recognize manipulation as evil, and that connection—liaison—portends the transcendence and loss of self. Each book helps us to read the other. The refined social and verbal frame of Laclos' text enables us to measure the seriousness as well as the anarchy and bestiality of *Naked Lunch*. In turn, *Naked Lunch* enables us to take a much closer look at desire itself, to see how and why we open ourselves to the world. Burroughs' surrealist presentation announces the collapse of the *ancien régime*—politically, verbally, conceptually; the person and the letter are shorn of their privileged status, analysis is to no avail, the self wants "out" as well as "in," and the detached observer is part of the scene.

An old world has gone, and another one has emerged, one that we are still unused to seeing; for, despite our so-called knowledge of quantum mechanics, ecology, the systemic nature of language, and the like, we are still accustomed (addicted?) to a literature of the past, a literature that confirms precisely our sense of Control. This kind of literature trucks in merchandise that we, unknowingly, crave: plot, character, story. This literature endows the self with integrity and will, endows him or her with an indigenous shape, sets him or her "against" the world and then measures the contest; this literature treats us to meaningful segments of experience, tied up and packaged as episodes, handsomely arranged among one another to spell out "education" or "success" or "tragedy." This literature respects form: the human form, the form of phenomena. We require authors to outfit their books with these desiderata, or else we deem their books "unreadable." Many people consider *Naked Lunch* "unreadable." It more or less dismantles (or discredits) plot, character, and story. Ever since Cervantes and Sterne, novelists have been turning conventions upside down, but Burroughs is not so much inverting as he is challenging the old ways of perception and organization. In his scheme the self is not privileged: it is merely an element in the field, and it is open or opened constantly, under attack virally by all the forces that have been discussed. Will power is a myth ("wouldn't you?"), and the old regime of individuals (each having a separate form) is blown sky-high, leaving only traffic, indiscriminate, endless traffic. It moves everywhere: in the body, in the atmosphere, in the words, on wires and screens, in molecules and genes. This is not some sci-fi background: it is the foreground, it is the only ground. For too long, *Naked Lunch* has been read as a diseased, fantasized self-portrait; we should start reading it as a text for our time.

Let me repeat: understanding *Naked Lunch* amounts to rethinking how things fit together. It is therefore a central text for this study, because it alters our notion of relationship. It makes us see how imperial, not to say imperialist, our notions have been. Relationship is customarily construed as the fit between two people or things, and we invest it with choice, value, and design. We have spoken of relationship as the figural drama of life, the connections and linkages either desired or chosen by individuals. Implicit in all this is the arrogance of thinking we know, the hubris of thinking we are doing the steering, entering the marriage, making the fit, assessing the bond. In fact, do we ever see or know so much? One recalls Joyce's sibylline remarks that accompany Bloom crawling into his marriage bed, redolent with the warmth of his present wife, still bearing the imprint of the absent lover:

> If he had smiled why would he have smiled?
>
> To reflect that each one who enters imagines himself to be the first to enter whereas he is always the last term of a preceding series even if the first term of a succeeding one, each imagining himself to be first, last, only and alone, whereas he is neither first nor last nor only nor alone in a series originating in and repeated to infinity. [*Ulysses*, 731]

Joyce destroys the myth of individualist primacy, but the infinite serial chain he proposes seems quite orderly, in contrast to the dreadful democracy of Burroughs' universe. The individual is the target in Burroughs: from within and without. He is shown to be permeable and scattered, pillaged and spilling as he goes.

There would seem to be slight grounds for celebration in reading Burroughs, and the frailties of the human have rarely been expounded on to such effect. But, there is one tonic effect that may come from such a reading. We may be helped toward a view of connection, a view of our place in the larger scheme, conceivably even a view of our possible responsibilities in this ecosystem which we do not rule. The hubris involved in our habitual view of relationship comes from a failure of heart as well as a failure of intellect or vision. One imagines the world small because one construes it as appendage, construes the others in it as ghosts at best, pawns at worst. In this light, "relationship"would designate the chosen and willed arrangements we think we control, the kinships we deign to recognize, the family we acknowledge. Our maneuvering room and our right to choose are rarely questioned; whose life is it anyway? It is here that Burroughs jolts us, makes us expand the picture of our connectedness. *Naked Lunch*, for all its bestiality and heartlessness, situates us unmistakably *in* the world, and radically challenges any sense we might have of hegemony. Burroughs' ecological scheme has a peculiar generosity in it, even though private appetite rules everywhere you look; it is the generosity of a mind that has moved beyond the elitisms of the past, those conceptual hierarchies and categories which roped off phenomena from one another and kept the whole consort away from the career of the self, except in the palatable form of arm's-length encounters. The Terror has come, the ropes no longer hold, the self is part of the consort, the body is under siege. Burroughs is instructive, and it makes sense to read *Les Liaisons dangereuses* and *Naked Lunch* together, for we gain thereby a sharper awareness, a more stereophonic sense of human fragility and human relation.

CHAPTER FOUR

Metamorphosis

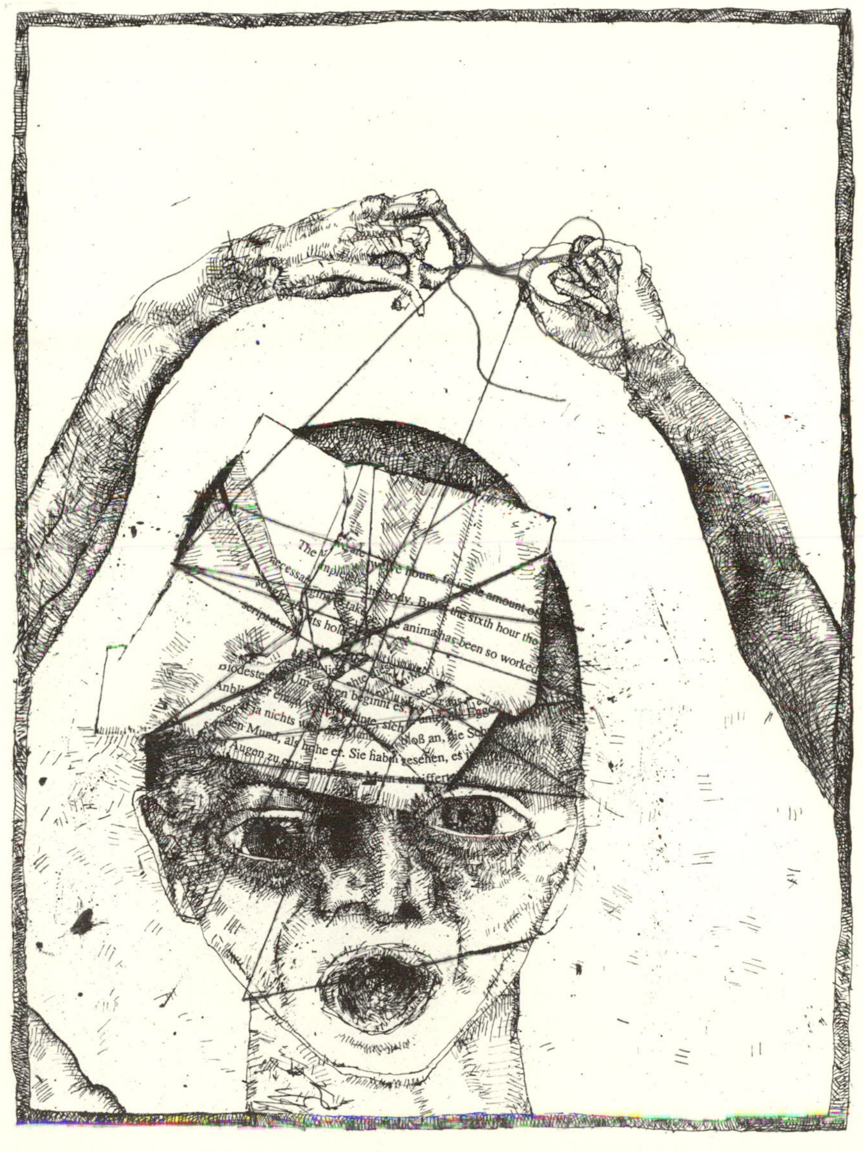

Becoming other, becoming another, becoming the other, these three models of transformation run the gamut from personal change to empathy to fusion. The darker variants of such activity shade off into paranoia and dementia, but such "stretching" of the self, such alteration is usually thought of as a good thing, a way of bridging the distance that separates all living creatures. This distance is not a matter of coldness or indifference, but rather the landlocked condition of the individual mind, a mind that can know, firsthand, only what is happening to itself. How does one approach the other? Earlier studies in this book have dealt with the issues of blindness and solipsism, or else the essential mystery of the other, even the tactical gambit of appropriating the other's body. The motive power for relationship, and for the fiction of relationship, has been shown to be at once mental and physical, imaginative and sexual, and every text studied thus far tells us something about merging, about fusion. Fusion and merging will be at the heart of this chapter as well, but we will be examining much more closely just how such fusion takes place, how it can be that one person merges with another.

The overtly sexual dimension of coupling has been examined already, in Laclos, Burroughs, even in Proust, Prévost, Ford, and others, but the imaginative journey that is undertaken has been less central. We have, of course, had a good look at the obstacles that prevent fusion, but, at issue here is the trajectory itself, the complex and sometimes frightening ways in which "I" approaches, knows, or becomes "you." These matters are by no means restricted to the subject of love or desire, and we shall have occasion to see that they are close to the foundation of knowledge itself; i.e., knowledge of the other. It can be argued that social and political knowledge are crucially predicated upon this prior and enabling exercise of generosity and imagination; the fundamental awareness of alterity is what brings the self out of its habitual precincts and instigates the "voyage" to the other. "Voyage" hardly seems excessive as a metaphor here, and it is used to underline the distances involved, the space between people and the inherent inertia of the individual mind. It is in this light that true knowledge is arduous and experiential, usually gained by the startling discovery that the other—socially distinct, politically apart—is *real*. And the bottom line of such a theory is radical: the other becomes real, only to the extent that we become the other. That is why metamorphosis appeals to the political imagination: the greatest obstacle to social justice is not human cruelty but human blindness, the incapacity to see the other as real; but the metamorphic text operates a devastating breakthrough in this area, precisely by swapping skins. And even this extreme view softens and understates the case, because it seems to imply that we choose such transactions, that we willingly enter into metamorphosis, like some virtuous masquerade where we agree to wear another's mask for a stint, so as to "know" what he or she is like. But, in fact, the radical knowledge imparted by metamorphosis is rarely chosen or consented; more often, it is suffered and undergone, wrecking one's habitual frame, fissuring one's "own" identity, welding the self to the other, operating somewhat like a surprise mind-transplant. These are doubtless melodramatic, extremist terms for assessing the dynamic and displacement so evident in the works to be studied, but hyperbole is sometimes necessary if we are to get a fix on the kinds of violent wrenching and trauma that make up what we call love and knowledge.

We cannot fail to see that literature itself is a prime party in this arrangement. To read is to enter another's field of vision, to see the world through another's eyes. We are not equipped to do this on our own. (The entire institution of literature owes a very great deal to this basic human lack.) To go one step further with this logic, one can legitimately view reading as a form of empathetic bonding, a way of "endorsing" lives or entering perspectives that are not one's own. It might be argued that all artistic perception is similarly "interested," "situated," perspectival, but novels especially owe much of their popular appeal to this generic promise of "another" view. An entire voyeurist theory might be elaborated along these lines, but my concern is more with the power dialectic that is adumbrated here. By choosing to read, we open ourselves to the writer's control. For the writer's power resides squarely in his capacity to mold the vision of his reader, to touch the sensibilities and shape the values of his reader. Surely this is one of the reasons why one writes. To rephrase this only slightly, one could say that all writers desire, at some level, to alter their readers via their art, to mobilize the reader's energies with such force that the reader "enters" the work (and irony is merely another mode of entry), gives the work a life of its own, a borrowed life, the reader's life.

To describe the workings of literature in such vampirish terms is to suggest that the peculiar exchanges that take place in reading, knowing, and loving can be dangerous as well as enriching, lethal as well as sustaining, crippling as well as enabling. In the studies that follow—a full analysis of Kafka's "In der Strafkolonie" as emblematic metamorphic text displaying all the varieties of transformation and exchange that have been mentioned; and then briefer discussions of Melville's "Benito Cereno" and selected works of Faulkner—we shall see that "becoming the other" is at once the goal and the trap of fiction. We shall also see that the writer turns to such extreme tactics when no other bridge will do, when the distance between people is all too forbidding, and the barriers of time or social rank or epidermis can be overcome in no other way. These are all crisis-fictions, works that dramatize the conflicts of caste and race, and it follows that their concern with imagining the other is a profoundly moral and political concern, a desperate, end-game meditation about alterity. It will be seen, as well, that these books are also meditations about the whereabouts of power: as it is displaced from color to rank to imagination to language, we will be witnessing the very play of metamorphosis.

Such fictions customarily make arduous demands on readers, sometimes directly as in the narrative poetics of Faulkner, sometimes indirectly as in the maddeningly veiled narrative of Melville's Good Captain, and sometimes through surrogates as in the allegory of reading, writing, and understanding that Kafka images in his tale of the Machine. Examining these texts together should enable us to begin seeing something of the larger picture: the extent to which all narrative literature seeks to alter its readers, and the extent to which love and understanding are always costly, transformative affairs, entered into at the risk of one's skin.

1

Like all of Kafka's best stories, "In der Strafkolonie" is maddeningly rife with multiple and contradictory interpretations. Some have made it announce Auschwitz and Dachau; others have seen in it a grim reminder of harsher Old Testament values, according to which our modern liberal world stands either condemned or threatened; given the context of our own inquiry, Kafka's bizarre story of penetration and invasion is obviously akin to the fictions of body control we examined in Laclos and Burroughs. The plurality of meanings that have been grafted onto it reflect no mere critical dilemma or impasse that would somehow be external to the material itself: the story is about interpretation, about the process of coming to understand, about the dynamic of bringing someone over to a point of view that is not his own. Hence, the explorer's response to the penal colony, his response to the officer, are at the very center of things, and the fact that the story has been interpreted so variously serves as a special warning: just how hard it is to do the very thing that would seem crucial here, and seems to be happening everywhere in Kafka; i.e., to pronounce judgment. The only way to move beyond this impasse is to give it the total emphasis it deserves: by focusing on communication and language, on the joint issues of understanding/interpretation/judgment, we may begin to perceive the remarkable coherence of Kafka's materials, the disturbing, echoing analogies between the narrative frame, the nature of the Machine, and the purposes of art.

"Es ist ein eigentümlicher Apparat" (It is a special Machine).[1] Kafka's genius in mixing understatement and prophecy—so often in evidence in the first lines of his stories—is fully displayed here.[2] Just how "eigentümlich," just how special this machine is, is something the explorer and, indeed, the reader must gradually come to understand. The entire story may, in fact, be seen as a gloss on those lines: can the officer make the explorer adequately comprehend the Machine? The critical debate concerning the story suggests that its readers have been equally perplexed, equally stymied in their grasp of these strange events. As well they might be. There is considerable desperation and passion in this tale, but they lie not so much in the events themselves as in the urgent project of the officer, his efforts to reach the explorer, to persuade the outsider. One might even go so far as to say that the officer's enterprise is more essentially rhetorical than it is judgmental: to persuade the explorer counts ultimately more

1. Franz Kafka, "In der Strafkolonie," in *Franz Kafka: Sämtliche Erzählungen*, ed. Paul Raabe (Hamburg: Fischer, 1970), p. 100. Subsequent quotations will be taken from this edition and noted parenthetically in the body of the text.

2. One need merely consider the opening sentence of "Die Verwandlung": "Als Gregor Samsa eines Morgens aus unrühigen Träumen erwachte, fand er sich in seinem Bett zu einem ungeheueren Ungeziefer verwandelt" (*Sämtliche Erzählungen*, p. 56). The first line of *Der Prozeß* could also be cited.

than to punish the prisoner. One even has the sense that the justice of the entire System (that of the Old Commander, to be sure) is strangely dependent on the explorer's verdict: to succeed in conveying (to the officer, to the reader) the special nature of the Machine would restore truth and clarity to a world riddled with doubt and equivocation. This mutual drama of understanding is, as it were, the hidden script of the story, and Kafka shows, if I may extend his pertinent metaphor, just how thick our skin is.

There was a time, we are told, when the validity of the Machine did not require such special pleading. The spectacle of justice being done was an occasion of civic and spiritual celebration, a time of community. Crowds came from far and near, and children were given preferential treatment in seating arrangements, in order to miss nothing of these formidable executions. At issue was no less than the revelation of truth, the dazzling "exteriorization" of one's inner soul, made visible and legible for all. These were halcyon days, epistemologically as well as morally, illuminating for all parties involved:

> "Wie war die Exekution anders in früherer Zeit! Schon einen Tag vor der Hinrichtung war das ganze Tal von Menschen überfüllt; alle kamen nur um zu sehen; . . . Vor hunderten Augen—alle Zuschauer standen auf den Fußspitzen bis dort zu den Anhöhen—wurde der Verurteilte vom Kommandanten selbst unter die Egge gelegt . . . Und nun begann die Exekution! Kein Mißton störte die Arbeit der Maschine. Manche sahen nun gar nicht mehr zu, sondern lagen mit geschlossenen Augen im Sande; alle wußten: Jetzt geschieht Gerechtigkeit. . . . oft hockte ich dort, zwei kleine Kinder rechts und links in meinen Armen. Wie nahmen wir alle den Ausdruck der Verklärung von dem gemarterten Gesicht, wie hielten wir unsere Wangen in den Schein dieser endlich erreichten und schon vergehenden Gerechtigkeit! Was für Zeiten, mein Kamerad!" Der Offizier hatte offenbar vergessen, wer vor ihm stand; er hatte den Reisenden umarmt und den Kopf auf seine Schulter gelegt. Der Reisende war in großer Verlegenheit, ungeduldig sah er über den Offizier hinweg. [111–12]

> ["How different the executions were in the old days! A full day before the ceremony the whole valley was crowded with people; they all came just in order to look on . . . In front of hundreds of eyes—all the spectators standing on tiptoe right up to the

> heights there—the condemned man was placed by the Commander himself under the harrow . . . And now began the execution! No discordant noise distracted from the work of the Machine. Many chose not even to look directly on, but lay in the sand with closed eyes. Everyone knew: Now justice is being done . . . Often I would be squatting there, holding a small child in either arm. How we all took on the look of transfiguration from the tortured face, how we bathed our cheeks in the radiance of that justice, finally achieved and already fading. What times those were, comrade!" The officer had obviously forgotten whom he was addressing; he had embraced the explorer and laid his head on his shoulder. The explorer was extremely embarrassed, and he stared impatiently past the officer's head.]

This passage deserves to be borne in mind when Kafka's story is "rejected" out of hand as an exercise in torture and butchery. Whatever one ultimately makes of the old system of justice or the role of the Machine, we are struck by the insistence on communal harmony. The moment of truth and justice is unmistakably a moment of bonding and sharing. Moreover, Kafka has pointedly "replayed" the scenario by having the officer embrace the explorer, as a natural extension of those brotherly days, but he finds, instead, coolness, objectivity, and embarrassment. There is much to note here: not only were the old executions celebrations of community spirit, but their *telling* is also communal, or at least might be communal. Narration seems to be all that is left of the old tradition, and Kafka wants to test whether such storytelling can be efficacious or not, can restore the communal bonds celebrated by the old rituals. It is therefore highly significant that the officer seeks, throughout the entire story, to "touch" the explorer; the explorer, man from another realm, keeps his distance.[3] I am less interested in assessing the explorer's character than in underscoring his detachment, his quasi-professional sense of noninvolvement. Because, as we shall see, distanced judgment counts for very little in Kafka; "understanding" something comes, sooner or later, to mean "entering" into it, and in this story such an entry will

3. Although the title does not suggest it, James Rolleston's *Kafka's Narrative Theater* (University Park: Pennsylvania State University Press, 1974) contains some very close analyses of Kafkan point-of-view narrative; in particular, Rolleston does an interesting job on the complex maneuvering of the explorer in this text.

be literally enacted at the close. In Kafka's work, filled as it is with endless corridors, closed doors, secret chambers, and labyrinthine passages, contact with the Other, sought, feared, or enacted at every level of the narrative, is both the ultimate hunger and the ultimate taboo.

*

From our vantage point in the latter part of the twentieth century, "In der Strafkolonie" can hardly be viewed as anything other than a horror story, a torture story. The grotesque disproportion between crime and punishment, the radical assumption of guilt, the heinous nature of the sentence, the powerfully symbolic dysfunction of the Machine, all this seems to constitute an irreversible indictment of the officer and his penal system. Finally, the Machine itself appears to be on trial: technical know-how, mechanical expertise, and scientific engineering have, as we today know better than Kafka could have suspected in 1914, a will and impetus of their own, determining rather than serving the uses to which they are put. The Machine may then also be "eigentümlich," in that it is the most seductive and potent agent of the story, the ultimate winner in the modernist game of persuasion, the forerunner not only of Dachau and Auschwitz, but of all the technological nightmares of our own nuclear age.

And yet . . . Kafka's story refuses to fit this scenario. There is something great as well as something disturbing in Kafka's Machine. Technical craft, fine-tuning, and scientific precision must have a special ("eigentümlich") appeal to any artist. Given what we know of Kafka's self-discipline as a writer, his severe and torturous sense that what he had written would not quite do, we are compelled to feel that this complex, harmonious, (up to now) perfectly functioning Machine—with its complete adequation of ends and means—cannot be simply dismissed as evil. Finally, our post-1914 history, with its well-known atrocities, has, it is true, enabled us to read Kafka's story in a grimly prescient manner; but it has undeniably also led us to *mis*read Kafka's story, to see in it the precursor of concentration camps, but to be tone-deaf to the echoes of Flaubertian aesthetics, the Flaubertian mystique of a *mot juste* that would miraculously wed language to reality. The most painstaking of stylists, the most scrupulous of craftsmen, Kafka knew all too well that words veil as well as disclose, that they can only name, never be. How can he not have yearned for that Edenic realm where language and substance are united, that special writerly *Heimat* whose uniform the officer still wears, in poignant contrast to the homelessness of the explorer who is afloat in the relativism of his age and is rooted nowhere? Finding a potent, magic language is, then, the unifying thread of Kafka's story: in this light, the Machine's special power perfectly images the drama of understanding and contact at the heart of the tale.

Understanding one another is, to some extent, the cornerstone of all community, for it shows that mutuality is possible, that the self can "read" the other. Language has, since the beginning of human society, played a crucial bridge-making role in the transactions between men and their gods, between men and their peers. Much of Kafka's work seems polarized by two dominant, antithetical modes of such relationships, definable as the Old Law versus the New Law, the injunctions of authority versus the openness of love. This familiar Kafkaesque conflict receives historical coloration in this story, thereby giving us, on the one hand, the memory of a time when truth was known and despotically enforced (with the Machine as a central player), versus our modern period of liberal relativism with its bureaucratic procedures.

The written word, as Kafka well knew, has long been central to the traditional transmission of truth; the German term for "writing" is "Schrift," and Kafka significantly noted that it also stands for "Scriptures," for holy books. A number of critics have been drawn to this connection, and they have sketched elaborate parallels between the religiously guarded, hieroglyphic instructions for the Machine and the sacred books of the past.[4] Such texts would constitute the corpus of belief; it would only (!) be necessary to decipher them (one thinks of the exegetical discussion of the Law in *Der Prozeß*, of the endless interpretive haggling that fills Kafka's books). In this story, however, no matter how one labels the mysterious hieroglyph—Old Testament, New Testament, Torah, or Talmud—it is abundantly clear that the written document is, at least for the modern explorer/observer, illegible; to put it another way, the holy book fails to create its community of believers. But that is only the beginning of Kafka's meditation on language. If we take the notion of "Schrift" in its broadest acceptation, not reducing it to the page of instructions for the Machine, but extending it to the larger spectrum of communicative acts

4. The most detailed case for holy books has been made by Erwin Steinberg, "Die zwei Kommandanten in Kafkas 'In der Strafkolonie,'" in *Franz Kafka*, ed. Maria Luise Caputo-Mayr (Berlin: Agora Verlag, 1978).

that make up the form and meaning of the tale, we see two distinct alternatives to the written word: the Machine and the spoken word. It would seem, to return to our historical paradigm, that Kafka is showing us the collapse (or, at the least, the deterioration) of the old, absolute code, while still retaining its vehicle, the Machine; and, of course, he retains the spoken word too, makes it indeed the central currency of his story. Will either vehicle promote understanding? make the soul legible? bring the self to the other?

In the secular age that has come, the time of the New Commander and the time of the explorer, literature itself may be called on to regenerate the interactions between men and their gods, men and their peers. Kafka's story, his own writing, whatever its claims on knowledge and truth, can at least be true to the bridge-making requirements of community. Written words—the writing of literature, not the sacred texts of Scripture—and spoken language are the last remaining agents of connection. They are civilization's vehicle for understanding, and if they can no longer peremptorily command assent, they can perhaps strive for a still nobler goal: to invite response, to incite love. Understanding and love are those "voyages" that enable mutuality in a world that contains only individuals. Understanding and love are modes of entry, promises of reciprocity. The writer, more than most, plays a role in this drama, because his is the medium that bonds and connects. It was only in the old days that the Machine made truth visible, enabled all to understand, together, effortlessly, at once. How can it be done today? That is the echoing question of Kafka's tale. How is one to achieve the knowledge that is commonality, not the scientific knowledge of logic or system, but the more biblical form of knowing, of knowledge as experience, as entry into things? Without this kind of understanding, human beings are reduced to dreadful extremes, to being either logical robots or animals of instinct, each trapped in its own self-enclosed system, each bereft of mutuality. In either of these degraded forms—and these are the forms that Kafka finds current—there is no knowledge worth having, either of the self or of the other. "In der Strafkolonie" is about the glaring inadequacy of these two extremes, and it is in the creation of his macabre but mesmerizing Machine that we may find Kafka's strange, disturbing remedy.

The distance maintained by the explorer has already been mentioned. Vaguely an emissary of "our" humanist society, he is perplexed by the conflict between judgment and action; he disapproves, but does not want to meddle. He leaves the island apparently unchanged in his views, preventing the soldier and the prisoner from following him. He threatens them with a heavy, knotted rope, as if they were subhuman. And, indeed, as Kafka has presented them, that is what they are. The prisoner is described as "ein stumpfsinniger, breitmäuliger Mensch mit verwahrlostem Haar und Gesicht" (a crude-featured, thick-lipped man with hair and face in disarray), whose passivity is termed "hündisch ergeben" (doglike and submissive [100]). His crime is strictly one of instinct: when whipped in the face by his superior, "Statt nun aufzustehen und um Verzeihung zu bitten, faßte der Mann seinen Herrn bei den Beinen, schüttelte ihn und rief: 'Wirf die Peitsche weg, oder ich fresse dich' " (Instead of standing up and begging pardon, the man grabbed his superior by the legs, shook him and cried: "Throw away the whip or I'll eat you alive" [105]). As the story proceeds, the soldier and the prisoner, squatting in dirt and vomit, reveal something of the abyss between matter and language as they listen uncomprehendingly to the officer's explanation—in French no less, to point up still further the alienation that is language—of the Machine to the explorer. The prisoner strains mightily, but Kafka images his very confusion in terms of thick skin, blubbery lips, organs that have no access to meaning: "er hielt den Kopf gesenkt und schien alle Kraft des Gehörs anzuspannen, um etwas zu erfahren. Aber die Bewegungen seiner wulstig aneinander gedrückten Lippen zeigten offenbar, daß er nichts verstehen konnte" (he lowered his head and concentrated, all ears, in order to learn something. But the movements of his blubbery, thick-pressed lips showed clearly enough that he could understand nothing [104]).

The prisoner's animality notwithstanding, the explorer remains true to the modern legal code he has brought with him to the island, and he therefore asks the fundamental question underlying all matters of justice and equity: does the prisoner know what his crime is? That code is predicated not only on the presumption of innocence, but also on the possibility of self-knowledge, a self-knowledge implemented by language, both written and spoken. These are, however, precisely the assumptions that are up for grabs in Kafka's story, and the response of the officer is shattering in its announcement of a new regime, a new schema for knowledge and language: "Es wäre nutzlos, es ihm zu verkünden. Er erfährt es ja auf seinem Leibe" (It would be useless to tell him. He will know it in his flesh [104]). Kafka critics have been much exercised with the glaring injustice of such a procedure, the calm assuredness that guilt need not be proven—"Die Schuld ist immer zweifellos" (Guilt is always indubitable [104])—since it appears concomitant with existence, but what has gone largely uncommented is Kafka's radical view of communication itself. For now we see the awesome mediation that the Machine is to provide: to make good on language. And we see, at once, how perfectly at home the Machine is, in this story of failed communication: words, both spoken and written, in French or any other tongue, on diagrams or in texts, including the full exchange between the officer and the explorer, including the story itself, the exchange between author and reader, fail to deliver their meaning, to bridge the gap, to penetrate the other, to get through the other's skin, to make an entry, to effect intercourse or discourse, to transform animals into men.

Yes, the piercing Machine turns animals into men, makes their thick skin into its luminous script, brings the soul to the surface; but one has to strain a great deal, stretch and maneuver with one's concepts, before it can be seen this way, because the savagery of the procedure is not only terrifying, but also bestial in itself, a sharp writing beak that rends the flesh, a toothed pen that writes in blood. We may recall the bloody projects of *Naked Lunch*, its persistent pillage of human flesh, its monstrous scenarios of penetrating the body. Nonetheless, this is a writing machine. Kafka's fable is astounding, because it seems to reach back to the most primitive reaches of human culture in order to find its shimmering metaphor for language itself. Kafka is dealing here with the most elemental dilemma known to verbal creatures: language cannot *be* what it says. And men's skins are thick. This story depicts a search for a language that would be immediate, rather than mediated, and it comes up with a terrible solution: we must learn viscerally, not verbally; the script must be in us, not in front of us. Like a savage geneticist, knowing that our very chemistry and cells perform linguistic operations, Kafka seems to be saying that the verbal message can achieve a magic oneness with its referent, only if it is encoded in our flesh. His writing machine actualizes and vitalizes all our limp clichés about knowledge: "deep" or "profound" awareness, "to scratch the surface," to have "inner" certainty. There is an entire organicist mythology here, emergent from the belief in an inner core and the suspicion of surface, that Kafka is inserting into his parable on language and understanding. The Machine is to provide deep knowledge (for thick-skinned, "thick-lipped" humans need no less), as the prisoners acquire a visceral understanding of their crimes, as the needles invade and imprint.

The full performance takes, we are told, twelve hours, for this is the amount of time necessary to write the crime completely into the body. But around the sixth hour the sought-after metamorphosis begins to take place: the animal flesh has been so worked into script that it begins to relinquish its hold on life:

> Erst um die sechste Stunde verliert er das Vergnügen am Essen. Ich knie dann gewöhnlich hier nieder und beobachte diese Erscheinung. Der Mann schluckt den letzten Bissen selten, er dreht ihn nur im Mund und speit ihn in die Grube. . . . Wie still wird dann aber der Mann um die sechste Stunde! Verstand geht dem Blödesten auf. Um die Augen beginnt es. Von hier aus verbreitet es sich. Ein Anblick, der einen verführen könnte, sich mit unter die Egge zu legen. Es geschieht ja nichts weiter, der Mann fängt bloß an, die Schrift zu entziffern, er spitzt den Mund, als horche er. Sie haben gesehen, es ist nicht leicht, die Schrift mit den Augen zu entziffern; unser Mann entziffert sie aber mit seinen Wunden. [108]
>
> [Only around the sixth hour does he lose all desire to eat. Usually I get down on my knees at this point and observe what happens. Rarely does the man swallow the last mouthful, he merely rolls it around in his mouth and spits it out in the pit. . . . But how still the man becomes around the sixth hour! Understanding comes over even the thickest of them. It starts around the eyes. From there, it spreads. A sight that could tempt you to get under the harrow with him. Nothing actually happens beyond this, the man simply begins to decipher the script, he purses his mouth as if he were listening. You have seen that it is not easy to decipher the script with one's eyes; our man deciphers it with his wounds.]

Let there be no mistake about the double miracle at work here. It is a miracle of knowledge, but it is no less a miracle of art. The spectacle of understanding, of finally (fatally) deciphering the script that must elude us in life and on paper, is a magic fusion of spirit and matter, words and things, and this moment of transfiguration is itself so seductive that those who witness it yearn to be themselves initiated into its mystery.

*

Such knowledge and such language are fatal. Even Laclos' Merteuil knew that the self requires closure, "qu'il n'est personne qui n'y conserve un secret qu'il lui importe qu'il ne soit point dévoilé"; in Burroughs, the opening of the self is literalized, and his narrative is one of endless take-over and enslavement. In Kafka, at last, we encounter the perfect paradox: the body is fatally opened, so that the soul may be "liberated," the animal human, the words reality. Here we may measure the abyss between the figurative and the literal: to "open" the self is regarded as laudable, so long as we are in the realm of metaphor, but to "open" the body is quite another matter, akin to rape, always invasive. Kafka is drawn to these opposing sets of meanings. He knows that the individual is, physically, an integral, enclosed system, which will not stand too much opening; but he also knows about apertures and orifices, the kind of traffic necessary to maintain the body's closed system. The body takes in food and then puts out what it cannot assimilate; the species cannot continue if the male does not enter his seed into the female's womb. Thus we are hardly surprised that food and sex—the most basic modes of entry into the closed body—are portrayed in starkly ambivalent ways in Kafka's fiction: K. and Frieda lick and nuzzle each other like dogs; Gregor Samsa starves to death, while sensing in the music of his sister that impossibly refined nourishment which might keep him alive; the hunger artist's rarefied art—his professional refusal of the body—is replaced by the solid appetites of the panther. The prisoner, at the sixth hour, spits out the food so that he can attend to the new body language he is receiving in his flesh. Kafka seems to feel horror at the body, but he nonetheless reveres the human longing for sustenance and contact. This yearning is viscerally experienced by many of his characters, appearing almost as a generic form of hunger, but gratification does not appear to be fully imaginable, much less achievable. This is why his are the most searching, questing, ungratified characters in modern literature. This is also why he has bequeathed to us the most thorough iconography of the enclosures of modernity, and he has given us, as well, the pitiable creature who lives inside them: the hungry, yet walled-in, bureaucratized, reified functionary. Kafka's world is one of "Beamte" (functionaries), because functions have replaced relationships; mutuality, concern, and reciprocity are cut off at every turn. Demarcation is everywhere, preserving distances, making character into cipher. The macabre story, "Der Bau" (The Burrow) is merely an extreme instance of that fear of contact and violation, of being broken and entered, which is everywhere operative in his work.

We must, then, look to literature for the possibilities of finer intercourse, an unthreatening commerce between selves, a penetration that gratifies but does not maim. If nourishment and love cannot come through the flesh, then perhaps the mind and its agency of language can provide them. Thus, we return to the notions of understanding and knowledge as modes of contact, modes of entry. Language is doubtless the most privileged vehicle of figurative contact; it renders possible a very special type of exchange, wherein the self remains physically intact but nonetheless entered. The beauty and horror of Kafka's story lie in the creation of a physical language. With the advent of the Machine, the hermeneutic circle is broken, and interpretation is no longer necessary; communication at last happens, and truth can be known. The enclosed nature of the self and the thickness of its heart, mind, and skin can finally be cut through. But this language kills. "In der Strafkolonie" presents a nightmarish version of the *open* self as the *opened* self, with the attendant horror of violation and mutilation fully enacted. The flesh itself must be rent, before understanding is achieved.

Such, at least, is the theory. In fact, as all readers know, these multiple projects fail, and we see, everywhere, dysfunction and distance, incomprehension and murder. "In der Strafkolonie" depicts the failure of love and the failure of understanding. Language falls short. The prisoner's ignorance of his "crime" is only one phase of the breakdown. The main thrust of the tale, informed by the narrative strategy and endowing the material with a muted urgency, lies in the officer's declaration. His efforts to "touch" the explorer, to explain what is special about the Machine, to bring the past to life, are essentially an attempt at seduction. All fails. The prisoner is left untouched. The skeptical explorer does not respond to the officer's passion, the only real emotion in the story. The pleas are received but unmet. The explorer leaves, perhaps to explore other places. Has he understood the Machine? Has the reader understood the story?

*

In the end, as we know, the Machine acts. When the explorer fatefully denies the officer his help, when the effort to explain the Machine has been seen to fail, the exemplary, illuminating reversal finally takes place. The officer frees the prisoner and takes his place. The Machine butchers him and self-destructs. Here, I think, we are at the heart of Kafka's world. Many critics have understandably focused on the behavior of the Machine, suggesting either that it is a travesty of justice (the officer is not "saved"), or that it is proper poetic justice (the officer gets what he deserves). But the most eloquent act of the tale is not that of the Machine; it is the *geste* of the officer. For he enacts the major transformation of the work: *the officer becomes the prisoner*. His mission is no longer to supervise or command or explain; he will encounter the Machine himself, but from the inside, this time.

No more lessons. Explanations and instructions—whether deriving from holy books or design plans or as the modus operandi of modern life—are no more than a fruitless kind of verbal Ping-Pong, a futile, doomed mode of exchange. There is only one way to understand the Machine: that is to become the prisoner. There is only one way to understand: that is to become. In becoming the prisoner, the officer breaks out of his role in the hierarchy and achieves, briefly, grotesquely, the experience of the other. The machine breaks down because, in some profound way, its writerly work has been done, achieved by the eloquent *geste* of the officer; only the cutting work remains, and the Machine carries out its job in that department. The officer is butchered, I think, because he has never once concerned himself with what truth or justice look like—from the other side. To win the explorer, he has huffed and puffed, courted and pleaded; the prisoner has been little more than a workout for the Machine. It has never occurred to him that there might be a view there. At the end, he has reached the vantage point of the other, made the "voyage" of understanding, through his small but epic journey into the Machine. Even though there is no sign of redemption on his face, there is no sign of torture either; he has had his encounter with truth, his experience with justice, and they are synonymous with his move toward the other, culminating in the fateful "inside" view that is required, if one is actually to judge or understand.

We know that Kafka remained dissatisfied with the last pages of the story, those that depict the explorer's visit to the teahouse and final departure.[5] The fragments that he wrote in 1917 suggest that the

5. See Richard Thieberger, "The Botched Ending of 'In the Penal Colony,' " in *The Kafka Debate*, ed. Angel Flores (New York: Gordian Press, 1977).

explorer was ultimately more implicated, more drawn in, than appears at first glance. Not only has the officer moved fatally toward the prisoner, but the explorer now feels the power of the bond that links him to the officer, even to the extent of seeing the dead man in his imagination, with a spike protruding from his forehead. Asked if his appearance is magic, the ghost officer replies, "A mistake on your part; I was executed on your command."[6] I think it fair to say that this fragment of a finale makes good on the communicative act that was left incomplete, in the story proper; moreover, it restates the story's central truth: to understand the other is to become the other, to be so involved with his life and death that they become one's own.

In becoming the prisoner, the officer undergoes the fundamental Kafkaesque metamorphosis, the one that haunts his best work. To become the other is the recurring spiritual and structural drama of Kafka's stories: its twin faces are love and metamorphosis, understanding and trauma, transcendence of the flesh and rending of the flesh. The officer "becomes" the prisoner no less than Gregor Samsa becomes an insect. Kafka's country doctor experiences the same elemental upheaval: he projects, easily enough, onto the boy's wound the sexual drama at home; but he is made to lie, naked, on the bed with the boy, thereby revealing his manifold impotence, showing his own malady, becoming the patient. The officer, placing himself within the Machine, illuminates Kafka's classic procedure: rational discourse, logical explanation, all interpretation, are rife with futility, doomed to failure, attempts at bridges that do not connect; knowledge comes only through personal transformation, and it must be "am eigenen Leibe erfahren," known in the flesh.

Thick-skinned humans come to knowledge of others by an act of violent metamorphosis. *In* Kafka's story, or, as they say, "intradiegetically," this transformation is frequently literal and monstrous, for the language-bridge does not hold, and discourse remains sterile, short of understanding. But, *through* Kafka's stories (and this is not "extradiegetic," but is the very result of the narrative, what it is aiming for), even that metamorphosis may be a figurative one of great beauty. Through art, and perhaps only through art, we are able, without being dismembered, to become another, to extend our first

6. I am indebted to Heinz Politzer's treatment of this issue and to his reference to Kafka's diaries (*Franz Kafka: Parable and Paradox* [Ithaca: Cornell University Press, 1966], p. 112. Politzer's overall commentary on this story has been influential in my own reading of it.

person onto the lives and events we read about. Narrative is the reader's entry into other lives, and that entry constitutes its greatest claim to "knowledge." Kafka's painstaking narrative art, perhaps more than that of most other twentieth-century writers, demands that extension of its readers, requiring that we experience, vicariously, the limits and sensations of a bug, the yearning of the hungry artist, the powerlessness of the doctor, the mazelike quandaries of K. and Joseph K., the fascination of the Machine. Kafka's very narrative techniques, his skillful control of point of view, his intensely (maniacally) myopic realism, his courage to be literal, his fearless presentation of an enigmatic world whose authority can never be known or avoided—all these features are also features of his craft, his own writing machine, which are manifestly intended to *open* us to the world of the other.

There is the metamorphosis, and there is the Machine. Kafka's writing Machine is a demonic, fascinating figure for the role of art and understanding in a world of impenetrable flesh and empty signs. How can signs and flesh be connected, the thickness of matter be penetrated by the logos of spirit? The Word of the past, the Word that spoke truth and commanded assent, is gone. But the writer remains. Kafka's Machine depicts the need that every writer has felt for a language so potent and searing that it would *become* the reality whereof it speaks. The writing Machine is to succeed where all else fails: to remedy the absence of understanding in a degraded world, to grant the animal body access to its soul by making them both legible, to bridge the gulf between individuals. The Machine is indeed intolerable in its flagrant violation of the body and its tyrannical control of the subject, but it functions as a sublime symbol of Kafka's—and all artists'—aspirations: to read his work is to be penetrated by it; his words are to be inscribed in the reader's flesh; the reader's understanding of the story, of the other, is to be visceral, even transformative. The text is the Machine; the metamorphosis is in the reader.

2

Many find "In der Strafkolonie" a grisly, brutal story. Like the story of the exodus from the Garden, it is about the cost of knowledge. We are so accustomed to defining knowledge as information (rather than experience), so habituated to language as explanatory (rather than initiatory), that the high stakes of Kafka's parable seem melodramatic or Gothic. Kafka's story seems, when one looks at it from a certain distance, to embody in virtually archetypal fashion some of the central underlying issues of narrative literature. The fable of the Machine encompasses both the search for truth and also the writer's desire for a magic, unmediated language. No less striking is the interplay between the officer and the explorer, that framing drama of love and understanding which recasts precisely those issues of truth and language which were to be clarified by the Machine. These notions are, I think, at the forefront of the story, and no interpretation can fail to take them into account. Less overt, but equally crucial is that metamorphic *geste* which climaxes the story. I have suggested that the challenge of becoming the other is found in a good deal of Kafka's fiction, that it offers both threat and promise, and that it betokens an experiential form of knowledge that has authority in Kafka's scheme of things. That knowledge is quite simply the knowledge of connection, the scandalous, ultimately killing connection between officer and prisoner, controller and controlled. Whereas we can never know what final insight the officer may have achieved, what we can see—indeed, what the story flaunts through its plot—is the forbidding metamorphosis of officer into prisoner.

Metamorphosis intrigues and frightens because it denotes a radical instability of self, a capacity to become definitively other. One speaks popularly of changes in life, thresholds, passages, and the like, and we know, of course, that time alters living beings in its special ways. But, such changes are almost always envisioned as inner or figurative; and where they are external or corporal, they are seen as gradual if they are seen at all. Finally, all such changes are viewed as "one's own," never fully challenging the self's proprietary scheme; the body alters, perhaps the stage of life is different, but the person inside the changes is not displaced. Metamorphosis means becoming not only other, but, more crucially, *another*. It is hard to maintain a literal conception of such change, since most of us—even knowing full well that our cells change entirely every seven years, etc.—presume to live and die as essentially the same, relatively stable mind-and-body set. But the absolute alterity of metamorphosis constitutes its real challenge and interest as a figure of relationship. Only in this extreme perspective can it truly function as a symbol for understanding or love. And, by now it should be evident that "becoming the other"—far from being some titillating experience of empathy—must mean, at least at some level, disrupting or destroying the self. It is here that Kafka's story serves as paradigm: not only does its context of torture indicate that true understanding maims and kills, but it unequivocally shows (if not tells) us that the only way of reaching the other is the suicidal one of metamorphosis.

We have had occasion to note that the *vicarious* experience of the other is generally esteemed to be an unqualified good, and that it is frequently posited as one of the ultimate humanist goals of reading fiction. These are weighty matters, and they have long been debated by aestheticians, theorists, and artists. One could effectively argue that the chief virtue of literature is precisely its virtuality, its status as vehicle for vicarious experiences; such a view is argued as far back as Aristotle's *Poetics*, and the central doctrine of catharsis, as a form of release engendered in the public by dint of its "involvement" in the events on stage, points to the therapeutic values traditionally ascribed to vicarious experience. Particular literary tropes such as simile and metaphor also perform this kind of imaginative "work," in that they open up figurative realms, make possible certain displacements that are not feasible in the ordinary world. Much could be (and has been) said about the self being valuably exercised through the play of imagination and feeling that must arise from reading; in its more intense phase, this play of imagination and feeling moves toward empathy, the identification with the other through art.

Nonetheless, Kafka's forbidding text gives one pause; the fateful yoking of one character into the position of another—or, to be more precise, the man-in-power's experience as prisoner—may not be survivable. Why? There can be no easy answers to such a question, since we have no way of measuring just how far the self may extend itself with impunity. And much doubtless depends on what is being imagined. Kafka's tale certainly suggests that the powerful cannot afford to experience impotence. Just how the writer illuminates his peculiar type of tolerance is an intriguing literary issue, since the field of action for such a conflict is not easily charted or viewable. "In der Strafkolonie" spends most of its time in preparations, in depicting a seduction that fails, in articulating a meditation about the nature of language and understanding; only at the end does it leave this terrain and move into the realm of pure gesture, of actual substitution and sacrifice. Might there be works of literature that begin where Kafka ends, that take as their complete subject the suicidal project of becoming another? With such a goal in mind, how would the writer best proceed? In a transformational fiction, whose story would you tell?

Borges, in his fine essay, "Kafka and His Precursors," suggests that great art creates new constellations, that we see, as critics, both backward and forward in our efforts to discern intellectual or spiritual kinship between authors. The resulting alignments produced by such criticism are rather more cubistic than linear or historical; "influence" and "reception" are reconceived, even inverted, as the critic enjoys the peculiar freedom inherent in this new dispensation. This study has, up to now, made extensive use of such critical freedom, and, using Kafka's own tale as a base, it will do so again. Once again, the subject is the metamorphic text, and I would like now to explore, by looping backward and forward in time, a number of texts that leave us with the same dark knowledge. Melville's tortured tale, "Benito Cereno," depends entirely on point-of-view narrative, thereby showing that the perfectly innocent mind cannot see evil. But the underside of Melville's story is a muffled narrative of displacement and metamorphosis. After Melville, we will move squarely into modern fiction by examining the work of Faulkner, the novelist who has devised the most extensive and radical array of writerly strategems for moving self to other, both within the text and by means of the text.

3

On the face of it, "Benito Cereno" does not quite fit our description; "Bartleby" would seem the more likely tale of obsessive empathy. But the story of the American captain's experience on the strange Spanish vessel is one of the most amazing narrative constructions in all of prose fiction, and underneath its bravura performance of point-of-view imprisonment one finds a still darker fable of power and play and metamorphosis. There has been, in general, astonishingly little attention given to this story, outside of Melville criticism,[7] and most

7. But, among the Melvilleans, this story has received considerable attention. For quite some time the shorter fiction was only grudgingly acknowledged, but "Benito Cereno" has become something of a *locus classicus* in Melville studies over the past twenty-five years. Melville's dependency on a "real" Delano source was discovered by Harold Scudder as far back as 1928, but the source-emphasis was challenged by a counter-focus on the career of Charles v and the significance that his abdication held for Melville at the time of writing "Cereno." From Charles v to a contemporary political reading is a small step, and there is little doubt that Melville is making a complex, perhaps sibylline statement about race relations in the United States in the 1850s. Harold Beaver in his introduction to the Penguin edition of the story

serious analysis has understandably remained with the story of the captain, the elaborate spectacle of a blindness that is at once cultural and personal. Delano misconstrued everything, and Melville has diabolically entrusted the narrative to him. Hence, the American consistently mistrusts the Spaniards while regarding the blacks as innocent menials, not fully human, rather like Newfoundland dogs.

Melville is able to achieve dazzling effects by juxtaposing a kind of cinematic rendering of the scene and its skewed interpretation by Delano. Much depends on what we see in what we see; consider the following description of the Spanish deck, as Delano takes it in:

> The quarter-deck rose into an ample elevated poop, upon the forward verge of which, lifted, like the oakum-pickers, some eight feet above the general throng, sat along in a row, separated by regular spaces, the cross-legged figures of six other blacks; each with a rusty hatchet in his hand, which, with a bit of brick and a rag, he was engaged like a scullion in scouring; while between each two was a small stack of hatchets, their rusted edges turned forward awaiting a like operation. Though occasionally the four oakum-pickers would briefly address some person or persons in the crowd below, yet the six hatchet-polishers neither spoke to others, nor breathed a whisper among themselves, but sat intent upon their task, except at intervals, when, with the peculiar love in negroes of uniting industry with pastime, two and two they sideways clashed their hatchets together, like cymbals, with a barbarous din. All six, unlike the generality, had the raw aspect of unsophisticated Africans.[8]

---

gives a succinct articulation of this view: "Thus, far from being a tale of Yankee innocence, or idealism, or even naïveté, this is Melville's veiled but uncompromising attack on Yankee gullibility due to corrosive double standards and a self-deluding hypocrisy—an awful warning of the dangers of the complacency, the ignorance, the sheer intellectual limitations of gentlemen from Duxbury, Massachusetts, blankly incomprehensive of a larger world beyond the grasp of their patrician joviality with coloured seamen, valets and barbers, whose ground may be 'mined with honey-combs' under them" (*Billy Budd, Sailor and Other Stories* [Harmondsworth, Eng.: Penguin, 1967], p. 36).

8. Herman Melville, "Benito Cereno," in *Billy Budd, Sailor and Other Stories*, ed. Harold Beaver (Harmondsworth, Eng.: Penguin, 1967), p. 222. Subsequent quotations will be taken from this edition and noted parenthetically in the body of the text.

This passage itself is something of a graphic marvel, especially its lengthy, cameralike, exploratory first sentence, in which Melville has found a perfect use for the tortured, baroque, richly articulated syntax that seemed to come so easily to him. This material is larded with information that Delano does not recognize as such, and soon enough we see the interpretive smoke screen being erected ("the peculiar love in negroes of uniting industry with pastime"), the cultural script that impairs (rather than enables) vision. Immediately following this passage, we have a moment of impatience as the American captain seeks out his counterpart: "But that first comprehensive glance which took in those ten figures, with scores less conspicuous, rested but an instant upon them, as, impatient of the hubbub of voices, the visitor turned in quest of whomsoever it might be that commanded the ship" (222–23). Coming to this passage the second time around, the reader knows full well that he has had an eyeful, that he has been looking at "whomsoever it might be that commanded the ship," but so strong is the tug of the Delano perspective, indeed of all narrative perspective, that it is a rare and perspicacious reader who sorts it out at the beginning.

"Benito Cereno" is a text punctuated by blind spots, telling a story drastically at odds with its narrator's view of things. One finds countless references such as the following, "a privileged spot, no one being near but the servant," and it is up to the reader to savor the delicious irony of such assertions. Melville's pyrotechnics would be of little interest if his goal were merely to mock and expose Delano; he is, instead, after larger fish, as it were, and he is bent on revealing something about the general operation of vision, not just that of his American captain, but also that of his American readers. Delano is indeed looking for the right thing (i.e., who commands the ship), but he persistently and grotesquely misreads the signs of the power play he witnesses. At the end of the story, as we know, his "long-benighted mind" finally receives a "flash of revelation," and, to cap it off, Melville then includes portions of the real Delano's recorded deposition, which served as a factual basis for the story. The narrative would seem to be operating in the classic manner of mystery stories, whereby light is shed on the residual nooks and crannies, and the reader can put down the book, reassured by the triumph of reason and analytic acumen. In putting actual historical material into his narrative, Melville seems to go as far as one can go, in replacing the blindness of illusion with the veracity of fact. There is, regrettably, darkness, but at least we know it to be followed by the light, and thus it makes good sense that the "enlightened" Delano should remonstrate with Cereno at the close, exhorting him to optimism, now that the trial and torture are at last over:

> "You are saved," cried Captain Delano, more and more astonished and pained; "you are saved: what has cast such a shadow upon you?" [306]

"The Negro" is Cereno's tragic and cryptic answer, and with that utterance, at the very end of the narrative, we begin to glimpse the depths of the story, those reaches of life and death which have nothing to do with Massachusetts naiveté or guessing games.

*

It is possible to regard the narrated, ironic Delano story as a foil to the untold, tragic story of Benito Cereno, a story that Melville could not directly narrate—much as he could not directly narrate the experience of Bartleby or articulate the innocence of Billy—but, in essence, the unnarrated story is the deep psycho-cultural drama that powers the narrative. Cereno's experience is the black one of empathy unto death, the Spanish captain's forced, ritualistic, ultimately fatal apprenticeship as slave. The rules on board require, of course, that this experience be unstated; at best, it can only be hinted: "Oh, my God! rather than pass through what I have, with joy I would have hailed the most terrible gales; but—" Even the thick Delano senses that there is something dreadful happening in the Spaniard which passes show: "He is like one flayed alive, thought Captain Delano; where may one touch him without causing a shrink?" (276). To be sure, it is the plot which requires that Cereno's story be untold; but there are poetic reasons for silencing this "subtext" that are still more compelling: unstated, veiled in secrecy, experienced as fatal, Cereno's agony exists on the far side of language, infused with a terrible purity, seen only afterward, seen only through Delano's tissue of errors. This story is one of psychic displacement, of being flayed alive precisely through play.

Once the prosaic screen of Delano's inanities is removed, the poetry and ritual of the story begin to appear. One is especially struck by the strange excesses of the blacks. The elaborate false spectacle of Atufal in chains, ritually asking forgiveness of Cereno; the sublime shaving sequence, replete with Spanish flag as apron, with castration echoes, with Babo's utterly gratuitous self- inflicted wound to match the one he gave Cereno—these theatrical sequences can hardly be said to be necessary. The conspiracy does not require such frills, nor indeed does the simple mind of Delano. Why are the blacks indulging in such histrionics?

We can perhaps better understand the value of such *play* by considering the work of Jean Genet who seems to have continued, in *Le Balcon* and *Les Nègres*, pretty much where Melville left off. In the former play, Genet dramatizes the potency and power that are invested in imagery itself; he effectively demonstrates that sexual and political authority are imaginative constructs, dependent on image and mask. *Les Nègres* takes such views even further, making extraordinary use of double and triple disguise, of cover-story theater and in-the-wings action, of ritualistic violence being the only—and perhaps the best—arena of action for those in chains. What is uncanny is that all these devices are already present in Melville's story, even the cover story versus the in-the-wings action that corresponds to the Delano and Cereno experiences. Genet is intrigued with virtuality, because he knows that the theater is built on nothing else. His view of the world is profoundly conservative, because the hierarchy, the nomenclature is to be found encoded in the minds and viscera of ordinary people, rather than lodged in some potentially destroyable court or palace. Such a dramaturgy resembles the practice of voodoo, the pure spectacle of power through fetish and icon, the radical displacement of energy over time and space; when the needle in the dolls can cause bleeding across the water, then one would behold the final triumph of virtuality, of the peculiar authority of appearances. Finally, such a dramaturgy is perfectly suited for political scenarios of exploitation and revenge, because it has seized on the cardinal truth that the imagination is a free, open field for action even when all avenues are closed; and the still cannier truth which follows in its wake is that such imaginative, virtual gestures are not merely a *pis-aller*, but rather the only truly unfettered realm where endless potency is possible. In Genet, this pattern is quite visible. In Melville, we have not thought to look for it.

I think we now are better able to assess the artist metaphors contained in the text. In particular, Babo, the ringleader of the mutiny, is described in the crucial shaving scene as a "Nubian sculptor finishing off a white statue-head" (269). Later, the deposition shows us Babo again in his true colors, as *metteur-en-scène*: "in every particular he [Babo] informed the deponent [Cereno] what part he was expected to enact in every device, and what story he was to tell on every occasion, always threatening him with instant death if he varied in the least" (297). Sculptor and statue-head, director and actor, always the same artistic team; critics have not missed the theatrical and artistic references here, but they seem not to have noticed just how deadly the game is.[9] Melville wants to illuminate a set of power relations, those of history and those of art, and he makes us see that each set is equally grisly: sculptor's shaping is statue's maiming, director's control is actor's death.

Artistry is not an alternative to political power; the domain of illusion and play is shown to be the place where we live, the place where desire and revenge can find their fullest enactment. One is reminded of the comment made at the time of the Eichmann trial, that the man did not have enough blood in him to begin to compensate for the blood he spilled. The blacks on board that Spanish ship are answering centuries of systematic enslavement and debasement, and no concrete act, no finite gesture could be remotely commensurate with their hate. The violence and atrocities that creep forth at the end of the narrative, the unmitigated and wordless murdering and maiming between blacks and whites, the limitless cruelty inflicted on the Spanish noblemen by the mutineers, these are the reservoirs of hatred and resentment that run very deep, darker than language, inexpressible by conventional means. What narrative line is equal to the violence that fuels genocide? This is the twisted but profound affective material that Melville is tapping, and he has audaciously solved the problem of venting these powerful feelings. Unable to find a "black country," they *invent* a world of their own, a ghastly but free alternative to the bankrupt worlds of history, not only the Old World but also the New, a bankruptcy repeatedly imaged in the anchoritic retirement of Charles V.

Melville was drawn again and again to the sealed-off world-within-

9. The temptation to read "Benito Cereno" as a superior who-done-it is very strong, and this has led to a more benign view of the text, a more Delano-view of the text than is warranted. William Dillingham's chapter on the story in his *Melville's Short Fiction, 1853–1856* (Athens: University of Georgia Press, 1977), pp. 227–70, is a striking exception to this pattern, however, and he takes the same dark view of these materials that I do. He ultimately favors a more "equivalent" and balanced reading than I am arguing for here, in that he feels Melville is offering a kind of round-robin in his depiction of mastery and slavery; hence, Babo, who has been a slave in his native land, rules over Cereno and also Atufal (the former king) on the boat, but is himself ruled by the very scenario he devises, etc.

a-world created on a ship at sea, but only in "Benito Cereno" did he fully dramatize its ludic potential. When reread, this story looks downright operatic: the music and dance, the hatchet-polishers and oakum-pickers, the women singing their men on to butchery. Only in such creative, overdone, gratuitous play could the blacks strike back. Atufal in false chains is a triumph that is at once theatrical and political: the slave's sweetest freedom is to *play* the slave. In carrying out their dazzling charade, the blacks transform Melville's material from the spectacle of power to the power of spectacle, and in so doing, they chart the lines of force that connect these two spheres: politics and theater.

To play the slave is to experience freedom. Schiller long ago defined the play instinct as the most advanced phase of civilized behavior. Melville has discovered the unique freedom afforded by play, the extent to which play actualizes desires and needs for which no outlet can be found, the extent to which play is a giddy, unceasing, yet disciplined exercise of control and shaping power. Playing the slave is particularly delicious, since the very operation itself inverts the condition, is a triumphant solution to the condition.

But, what about playing the captain? To play the captain is, quite simply, to become the slave. Taking orders from Babo, witnessing the elaborate masquerade on board, gauging the circus that his life and station have become, Benito Cereno's "play" is understandably tough medicine.[10] It will kill him. Play caps the life of Cereno no less than it does that of the blacks, but it does so in reverse. He discovers and experiences bondage. He is obliged to drain the cup, right down to the dregs, to participate in his personal and even his generic undoing. This is more than the isolated case of Cereno and Babo and company; *play* scandalously introduces an element of creativity, of malleability, of "what if?" into a script he thought eternal, unchanging, as firm as the heavens and the earth. Cereno moves into Genet's world, collides into the discovery that there are no essences, only roles. And it is only on rereading (or, at the very least, rethinking)

10. Dillingham makes a very interesting parallel here with the modern phenomenon of "brainwashing," and he points out that Cereno has suffered from the same kinds of duress: removal of familiar props and support systems, humiliation, revilement (*Melville's Short Fiction*, pp. 256–59). But Dillingham does not go the extra step and gauge what kind of political scheme is required for brainwashing to exist: a view of norms and controls that have been thought universal and are revealed to be moveable.

that we begin to measure the enormity of Cereno's Calvary. We must invert the story, actually see that every single posture is an imposture, that the gaudy spectacle violates Cereno at every turn. Consider the following passage in light of our final knowledge:

> Meantime his servant knelt before him, with a large fan of feathers. And Francesco coming in on tiptoes, handed the negro a little cup of aromatic waters, with which at intervals, he chafed his master's brow; smoothing the hair along the temples as a nurse does a child's. He spoke no word. He only rested his eye on his master's, as if, amid all Don Benito's distress, a little to refresh his spirit by the silent sight of fidelity. [274]

How poisonous and eloquent this little scene looks, when one views it "in reverse." The kneeling, the tiptoes, the chafing of the master's brow, the insidious nurse simile, this entire cluster of images now illuminates its colonialist, imperialist origins, shining viciously backward, making us see just how invisible the institutions of slavery and servitude remain, until the lighting is changed. These are the accouterments of "captain," and the ostensible solicitude, love, and obedience they are supposed to signify go up in smoke, as we realize they can be imitated, "aped." Those intimacies which are the very terrain of masters and servants—feeding, soothing, clothing, shaving—are revealed as terrible, threatening intimacies, occasions of insufferable physical closeness and vulnerability that are not diagnosed as such only because we do not see them, because we follow, like the good American captain, the script of convention rather than our own eyes.

Cereno knows better. He suffers every minute of this text while Delano is trotting out his various fancies and fantasies. Benito Cereno has been obliged to taste, to savor his own undoing with remarkable thoroughness. There is, as it were, no inch of his authority that has not been travestied. Even his scabbard, we are told at the end, was empty and artificially stiffened. The most gruesome feature of the story is its economy. Cereno dies, I think, because his undoing is self-inflicted. Like a man obliged to disembowel himself by walking, he has had to act out his shame by acting a sham. Power, he learns to his horror, is a performance; he will not survive the cost of such a performance. And we surmise that imagination can be a truly magic force, liberating or enslaving, endlessly generative or endlessly corrosive, depending on its focus. Cereno is dismantled before our eyes, although we see it only on second reading. His power reduced to play, he is effectually one of the living dead, much like the skeleton of Don Alexandro, prepared "in a way the negroes afterwards told the deponent, but which he, so long as reason is left him, can never divulge" (300–301).[11] The formula for keeping the dead alive (for a while), like the secret of keeping the scabbard stiff, is "artificial," is perhaps Art itself, the elaborate art of Melville, who has elected to tell the story of Cereno's crucifixion by entrusting it to the guileless Amasa Delano.

"Play," in the context of "Benito Cereno" has nothing light or frivolous about it. The theatrics of this story carry its deepest meaning, but that meaning has little to do with aesthetics. As I have said, Melville and Genet knew that power resided in image. They also knew that power is a binary concept, that it cannot exist unless and until there is a pair. You cannot have a captain unless you have slaves. The myth that Melville wants to explode and expose is the myth of "independence," the illusion that either of these terms could exist by itself, that the captain would be all authority and the slave all bondage. This essentialist view undergirds both the prison-house of the slaves and the certitude of the captain. Through play and theatrics, Melville deals a deathblow to such a view, and he is then able to demonstrate the necessary umbilical cord between these notions, these poles, these roles, Cereno and the blacks. They experience, ecstatically for the blacks, devastatingly for Cereno, their connection. Each becomes, through imagination, the other. Cereno suffers the horrible, relational reality of his role, and it destroys him. It is as if Melville, a half-century before Kafka wrote "In der Strafkolonie," *started* with the moment the captain enters the Machine and becomes the prisoner, the moment where Kafka closes his story, and then devised a bold strategy for actually telling the story of metamorphosis. Cereno's answer to Delano's bewildered question, "what has cast such a shadow upon you?" is, as we saw, "the Negro." But there is no enigma at all when we adequately grasp the fact that Melville's world *has shadows*, that nothing stands alone, that we are connected all the

11. Dillingham makes a strong argument for cannibalism here as the ultimate unmentionable deed carried out by the blacks. He invokes Melville's well-known terror of cannibalism, and he enlists a number of images from the text to support this view. Yet, "eating" the body would appear less heinous in this particular story than killing and preserving it at once, such as has been done to Don Arando and is being carried out with Cereno before our (unseeing) eyes.

more powerfully, all the more powerful we think we are. The play on the Spanish ship illuminates those connections.

4

Whereas Melville's story of metamorphosis and role-change explores "the power of blackness" even more thoroughly than Kafka's text, the final author I want to examine, Faulkner, would appear to take a much more positive, benign view of empathy and its workings. It is well known that the American modernist creates an entire narrative ethos out of empathy, obliging his reader, in ways that few novelists before or since have done, to "enter" into the world of the fiction; this may entail endorsing the first-person perspective of an idiot or a suicide, or coping with the delayed disclosures of Faulknerian mysteries and the baroque eccentricities of Faulknerian rhetoric, trying out "might-have-been" versions of events, moving ceaselessly between regular print and italics, past and present, event and motive. Whereas a modernist text such as *Ulysses* appears not to know that it is diabolically hard to read, Faulkner cunningly foregrounds and highlights his own difficulties, revels in the obstacles to interpretation, thrusts the epistemological horrors directly into the minds and laps of his readers. Trauma appears to be his favorite mind-set, and he is especially partial to stories of outsiders breaking into communities (*Absalom, The Hamlet*, even Christmas in *Light in August*) or to insiders behaving in bizarre, unsettling ways (the Bundren pilgrimage in *As I Lay Dying*), such interpretive crises providing him with the dosage of shock and incomprehension on which he thrives. It may, of course, be possible to regard all narrative in hermeneutic terms, as more or less elaborate forms of who-done-it (and why). But Faulkner occupies a space all to himself regarding the urgency of these queries. By specializing in characters who are off-balance, enraged by events, at once bruised and musing, fixated on the scene and locked into themselves, Faulkner has invested the dilemma of interpretation with remarkable power; he has focused, unswervingly, on the project of understanding, building his stories on it and passing it on, "live," to his readers, via his arsenal of narrative devices.

His novels obviously differ in tone and theme, and there is a clear evolution from the raw trauma of the early works (*Sanctuary, The Sound and the Fury*, even *As I Lay Dying*) to the more speculative, expansive, and baroque fictions of the later years, with their increasing (and redemptive) emphasis on storytelling as reprieve, as maneuvering room. But one is tempted to say that amid all the changes that are rung, the value of empathy remains constant. His relentless experimentation with forms of storytelling, his recourse to interior monologue, his suspicion of what Walter Slatoff has called "mind's reasons,"[12] those countless abstractions and conceptual "sanctuaries"[13] in which we seek shelter from the onslaught of experience, these features of Faulkner's art constitute a veritable affective technique, a persistent foregrounding of feeling as mode of knowledge. His characters come to know what they know, in their viscera, and, insofar as books can afford visceral knowledge, Faulkner's books do so. The challenge of understanding or knowing or becoming the other is the quintessential Faulknerian challenge, found at the heart of the major fictions, encountered in especially keen ways by all his readers. But the significance of these empathetic ventures is by no means easy to assess. Faulkner, just because he regards this drama of entering into the other as the central event of his work, has given this issue more thought, has worked it through in more hues and colors, than any other figure of this century, and he is, therefore, a particularly rewarding figure to examine in the context of Kafka's and Melville's versions of metamorphosis.

*

A book-length study could be written about the role of empathy and fusion in Faulkner, so the following discussion is offered as a sampling of those issues. My remarks will be limited to three novels—*As I Lay Dying*, *Light in August*, and *Absalom, Absalom!*—and my focus will be, at least initially, on specific figures. *As I Lay Dying* is an excellent jumping-off place for us, because its stereophonic use of point

12. Walter Slatoff has made what still seems to me the best and most sustained case for the rationale of Faulknerian rhetoric and style, namely the effort to reach a kind of visceral immediacy that orthodox narrative cannot attain. See both "The Edge of Order: The Pattern of Faulkner's Rhetoric," in *William Faulkner: Three Decades of Criticism*, eds. Daniel Hoffman and Olga Vickery (New York: Harcourt, Brace & World, 1960) and his *Quest for Failure: A Study of William Faulkner* (Ithaca: Cornell University Press, 1960).

13. For a penetrating discussion of the notion of "sanctuary" in Faulkner, see Philip Weinstein, "Precarious Sanctuaries: Protection and Exposure in Faulkner's Fiction," *Studies in American Fiction* 6 (1978): 173–91.

of view enables (and requires) the reader to endorse multiple and incompatible perspectives, not only between the Bundrens and the townspeople, but, perhaps especially, among the Bundrens themselves as they undertake their pilgrimage to bury the dead mother. By creating a panoramic spectrum of private optics, Faulkner indeed achieves a global picture, but his composite makes all the more visible to us the discord, blindness, incomprehension, and violent conflict of the principal parties. The interior monologue itself may be regarded as a kind of structural enclosure, sealing off a living self like some kind of jelly, conferring on it a set of limits and edges and windows, but irredeemably narcissist in its self-reflection, its unalterably privatist agenda. One need merely think of the first three monologues of *The Sound and the Fury* to measure the kind of solipsism that such a technique is geared to render; *As I Lay Dying* has, by and large, the same view of the subject: walled off, frequently raging within, alien to the world. Here, as elsewhere in Faulkner's cosmos, the reader finds himself, crucially and disturbingly, centralized, privy to what no one else can see, immersed in each character's dark inner conflicts which must remain imperceptible to others, called on to sort out and refract the lines of both public opinion and private bias, assigned the role of bridge-maker.

For all these reasons, Darl Bundren is an intriguing case, recognizably Faulknerian in many of his tics and proclivities, yet strangely an odd-man-out in terms of empathy. Up until now, we have considered empathy as a "voyage," an arduous approach to the other that may end up as fusion with the other; or, conversely, we have noted the wrenching drama of metamorphosis, the unhinging discovery of alteration, the fateful experience of transformation that is unchosen, suffered rather than willed. In Darl we witness the precariousness and threat to the self that empathy entails; he does not *strive* to become the other, and he is not trapped into alterity either. Instead, his very mode of being entails slippage, poaching, moving into other's territory, moving into others. "Empathy" seems too mild, too limited a term to account for Darl's "ubiquity," his ability(?) to penetrate others, to peer into their thoughts, to narrate key events at which he is not present (e.g., the death of his mother), to see what others seek to hide, such as the pregnancy of his sister or the illegitimacy of his brother Jewel. Thus, where other Faulkner characters are held in, choked, Darl is drastically loose, flowing, spreading, available. Darl is the brother to the swollen waters, the man who knows that he may "unravel," "as though the clotting which is you had dissolved into the myriad original motion."[14] We can see in him a perverse portrait of the artist, the man who knows others "from the inside," the man who tells it all, the invading angel who presses too close. In Darl, Faulkner illustrates the invasive, unbearable character of the imagination, and it is fitting that Darl speaks of what others hide, that he makes all people uneasy and makes some people enraged, especially Dewey Dell and Jewel, who show him how they feel at the end of their journey. Coming to know the other seems worthy enough, certainly seems to be what the writer does, worthy or not, but with Darl Bundren we can begin to measure the social, even the moral scandal of such knowledge.

But the damage to others is nothing compared to the damage to the self, and Faulkner's portrait of the artist is all the more harrowing in that it offers us a dreadful kind of algebra, a rigorous (inverse) proportionality between solidity of self and knowledge of the other. Darl's modus operandi seems like a kind of psychic hemorrhaging, a merging and spreading that neither he nor anyone else can control, an entry into others that betokens neither love nor understanding. Throughout the novel, Darl's manner of being, his intuitive knowledge of others' secrets, seems more a curse than anything else; he yearns precisely for the kind of solidity and finiteness that Jewel and Cash have, the psychic grounding of which Addie has willfully deprived him. Little is more indicative of his fated fluidity than the famous passage where he "empties" himself for sleep:

> In a strange room you must empty yourself for sleep. And before you are emptied for sleep, what are you. And when you are emptied for sleep, you are not. And when you are filled with sleep, you never were. I dont know what I am. I dont know if I am or not. Jewel knows he is, because he does not know that he does not know whether he is or not. He cannot empty himself for sleep because he is not what he is and he is what he is not. Beyond the unlamped wall I can hear the rain shaping the wagon that is ours, the load that is no longer theirs that felled and sawed it, nor yet theirs that bought it and which is not ours either, lie on our wagon though it does, since only the wind and the rain shape it only to Jewel and me, that are not asleep. And since sleep is is-not and rain and wind are *was*, it is not. Yet the

14. William Faulkner, *As I Lay Dying* (New York: Vintage Books, 1957), p. 156. Subsequent quotations will be taken from this edition and noted parenthetically in the body of the text.

> wagon *is*, because when the wagon is *was*, Addie Bundren will not be. And Jewel *is*, so Addie Bundren must be. And then I must be, or I could not empty myself for sleep in a strange room. And so if I am not emptied yet, I am *is*.
>
> How often have I lain beneath rain on a strange roof, thinking of home. [p. 76]

This is what the flow feels like, from the inside. Utterly precarious, Darl plays out his chess match with existence, trying to nail himself down by verbal fiat, like someone putting rocks in his pocket so the wind will not sweep him away. Much is being expressed here: envy of Jewel, erosion by consciousness, fixation with Addie's death, fascination with not being, estrangement that is total, (pitiable) need for some frame to "instance" him (figured in the wagon shaped by the rain, in the urgent possessive pronouns that are being emptied, dispossessed in front of our eyes). Only a very fine writer would cap this dazzling metaphysical exercise with the poignant, limpid summation "thinking of home." Darl does, as we know, unravel, unclot, at the close of the novel, in an eery, quite graphic coming apart of the self. The fissuring of identity that closes Darl's career stems unmistakably from his "availability," his ceaseless and helpless forays into others; and Faulkner gives us thereby a haunting picture of knowledge as loss, of connection as erosion, of entry and exit being one and the same thing, for we can move into the other only by leaving ourselves.

*

Becoming the other can also be comic. Fans of Woody Allen hardly need to be told that simulation and "modeling" have a profound appeal for the "little person," and traditional comedy has always been drawn to the spectacle of servants aping their betters. Such outright role-shifting and social swapping are the sort of thing we find in Twain rather than Faulkner, but he does give us, in the person of Byron Bunch, a portrayal of metamorphosis without metaphysics, a character as far from Darl Bundren as one could be, yet nonetheless altered in front of our eyes, and funny to boot. Faulkner seems to be drawing on Bergson's view of comedy in his depiction of Byron in *Light in August*, because the character is, at least initially, a virtual automaton, functioning exclusively in terms of work at the mill (where he puts in enough hours to be paying rent) and routinized spiritual sessions with Hightower and the choir. This meek figure remains in low profile right on through the novel, and he can hardly compete, for our interest, with the larger-than-life figures of Christmas, Lena, Hightower, and Joanna Burden; but, as Dilsey put it, "I've knowed de Lawd to use cuiser tools dan dat," and the author has some very special plans for this little fellow. Byron is to play his part in the spectacular goings-on of *Light in August*, and it is worth attending to. Byron must make the tiny but miraculous journey from Bu*n*ch to Bu*r*ch.[15]

Verbally, as we can see, Bunch and Burch are so alike as to be taken for one another, and indeed Lena Grove is, at the outset, misled by this similarity, coming to Byron Bunch, thinking he is Lucas Burch. Yet, the poetic logic of this novel is such that Byron Bunch will, in a crucial sense, become Lucas Burch, become the missing husband and father. Or at least try to. Brought accidentally into Lena Grove's orbit, Byron is altered, yoked into the world of feelings, made to participate in the rhythms of life, as personified in the birth of Lena's child. This will entail providing for the child and pledging his faith to the mother; it will also require something more arduous still: he must fully confront Lucas Burch, both in the flesh and in the still-more-difficult-to-accept presence as sire to the child and lover to the woman. Byron Bunch, who knows that he "*weeded another man's laidby crop*,"[16] must go the whole route and become that other man. Byron will play Joseph in Faulkner's tale of immaculate conception, but the author has added a turn of the screw by having the surrogate husband seek to take on, to assume the reality of the figure he stands in for. To put it graphically—for it is indeed carried out *graphically* in the novel—Byron grows into the man whom he resembled, at the outset, only by name.

It is here that we move into the heart of things. At some critical moment in Faulkner's novels, words must be overpassed, so that the frontiers imposed by names can at last be crossed. Names either bind or confuse. *The Sound and the Fury* has too many Jasons and Quentins, but at a certain point the confusion stops, and the dead brother

15. This reading of *Light in August* is part of a larger study, "Fusion and Confusion in *Light in August*," appearing in *The Faulkner Journal* 2 (1986): 2–16.

16. William Faulkner, *Light in August* (New York: Modern Library, 1950), p. 365. Subsequent quotations will be taken from this edition and noted parenthetically in the body of the text.

can never be confounded with the rebellious niece. In *Absalom*, when enough heat has been generated and leaves raked up, the two roommates begin to understand one another *à demi mot*, no longer stymied by the "he's" and "she's" of their furious dialogue. Now, Byron must also go beyond the words to see what they conceal and contain:

> *I'll have to tell him now. I'll have to tell Lucas Burch.* It was not unsurprise now. It was something like the terrible and irremediable despair of adolescence *why, I didn't even believe until now that he was so. It was like me, and her, and all the other folks that I had to get mixed up in it, were just a lot of words that never even stood for anything, were not even us, while all the time what was us was going on and going on without even missing the lack of words. Yes. It aint until now that I ever believed that he is Lucas Burch. That there ever was a Lucas Burch.* [352]

Something roughly akin to fission is taking place in these lines, as we see Byron burst through the word-shell, the word-fence that everywhere encloses and imprisons meaning: to crash this barrier is, as Faulkner would say, to "abrupt" onto a new realm, to encounter difference, to experience a rupture of self that must be close to the elemental "opening out" that characterizes the birth of a child. Byron must go beyond the enclosed linguistic system, break free into a kind of no man's land where all is immediate, and we have no defenses. Names fall away. Such is the metamorphosis of Byron Bunch:

> The hill rises, cresting. He has never seen the sea, and so he thinks. "It is like the edge of nothing. Like once I passed it I would just ride right off into nothing. Where trees would look like and be called by something else except trees, and men would look like and be called by something else except folks. And Byron Bunch he wouldn't even have to be or not be Byron Bunch Byron Bunch and his mule not anything with falling fast, until they would take fire like the Reverend Hightower says about them rocks running so fast in space that they take fire and burn up and there aint even a cinder to have to hit the ground." [371–72]

This is a moment that many writers doubtless strive for, when the words become incandescent, shed their tired name-skins and reveal their true mysteries. Faulkner images this "overpass" in terms of weightlessness and utter estrangement, an event in outer space where the meteoric return and disintegration hauntingly point to and complete the "black blast," "the rush of sparks from a rising rocket" of Joe Christmas' death. In this moment of self-eclipse, the prison of individuation is broken, and the elements, freed from their old labels, may now regroup and find new ones. Here, Bunch may become Burch.

*

There can be little doubt that the fullest, richest treatment of the nature, costs, and rewards of empathy is to be found in *Absalom, Absalom!* In the figure of Thomas Sutpen, Faulkner has given us his most arresting portrait of the walled-in type, but he has wrought some interesting changes in the model. There is no rage, no brimming-over inner life, no personal life whatsoever, to speak of; but the principle of self-sufficiency, of the impregnable self, has been extravagantly heightened, so much so that Sutpen stands as an embodiment of autogenesis.[17] No one knows where he or his plantation came from; they seem, at least in Rosa Coldfield's imagination, to have appeared from nowhere, Sutpen and his "band of wild niggers," "creating the Sutpen's Hundred, the *Be Sutpen's Hundred* like the oldentime *Be Light*."[18] Sutpen is the self-made man, in all senses of the term, ontologically as well as socially and financially. The cornerstone to Sutpen's view of life and of others is calculation, a kind of ratiocinative sickness unto death that Faulkner calls "innocence," "that innocence which believed that the ingredients of morality were like the ingredients of pie or cake and once you had measured them and balanced them and mixed them and put them into the oven it was all finished and nothing but pie or cake could come out" (263). This mechanistic scheme leads him to treat everyone he deals with—his first wife, Ellen, Rosa, the architect, his children (both legitimate and illegitimate)—as so many pawns, as measurable and predictable ciphers. His highly Latinate language is pure legalese, but it effectively expresses his reified, functionalist view of others: "I found that she was not and could never be, through no fault of her own, adjunctive

17. Cleanth Brooks' reading of *Absalom* as, among other things, the quintessentially American story of a self-made man, remains the base study for an interpretation of Sutpen along these lines. See *William Faulkner: The Yoknapatawpha Country* (New Haven: Yale University Press, 1963).

18. William Faulkner, *Absalom, Absalom!* (New York: Modern Library, 1951), p. 9. Subsequent quotations will be taken from this edition and noted parenthetically in the body of the text.

or incremental to the design which I had in mind, so I provided for her and put her aside" (240).

This view is egregiously flawed. The world, in Faulkner, is not just a discrete set of people-things, but a living ecology, a tentacular arrangement that is relational at every turn, revealing the individual to be embedded in a network that thwarts and mocks his individual will. Judith gives the classic image for this state of being:

> You get born and you try this and you dont know why only you keep on trying it and you are born at the same time with a lot of other people, all mixed up with them, like trying to, having to, move your arms and legs with strings only the same strings are hitched to all the other arms and legs and the others all trying and they dont know why either except that the strings are all in one another's way like five or six people all trying to make a rug on the same loom only each wants to weave his own pattern into the rug; [127]

A good deal of Faulkner's art is mirrored in this passage; the loom metaphor is fleshed out by the peculiarly "lateral" syntax of the piece, the tentative, groping, annexing prose that keeps moving out, flaunting interconnectedness, exposing the sham of closure and private design. But Sutpen's intellectual shortcomings are the least of his problems; he is defective in the realm of the heart and the imagination, and this will kill him. Sutpen's innocence is, at bottom, a colossal lack of imagination, a total incapacity to grasp the emotions, the human reality of others. He is the complete individualist, the imperial self, and *Absalom* recounts his fall.

The relational mesh makes itself known to us by the most elemental communication code known to the species, through *touch*. "Touch" is the very language of connection: "Im gonna tech you," is how Wash Jones informs Sutpen of his relatedness and his impending death (and it hardly matters whether we read "tech" as "touch" or "teach," since they come down to the same thing, thanks to the scythe). It could be shown that the entire baroque aesthetic of *Absalom*—its circling prose, its fractured narrative, its delayed disclosures—is in the service of "touch," is meant to draw the reader into Faulkner's loom-text, to oblige him to enter the fabric and weave his pattern. It is given to Rosa Coldfield to spell out the significance of this ethos, and her paean to touch speaks not only for the Faulknerian world, but beyond it to the issues raised throughout this chapter:

> *Because there is something in the touch of flesh with flesh which abrogates, cuts sharp and straight across the devious intricate channels of decorous ordering, which enemies as well as lovers know because it makes them both—touch and touch of that which is the citadel of the central I-Am's private own: not spirit, soul; the liquorish and ungirdled soul is anyone's to take in any darkened hallway of this earthly tenement. But let flesh touch with flesh, and watch the fall of all the eggshell shiboleth of caste and color too.* [139]

Faulknerian "touch" is seen to be as devastating, as "cutting," as Kafka's Machine, and there is something distinctly murderous in the "mugging" scenario that Faulkner offers as metaphor for contact, the soul that is violated in the "darkened hallway of this earthly tenement." It is for the virginal Rosa Coldfield to express, throughout the lush dithyrambic prose of the fifth chapter of *Absalom*, the explicitly sexual dimension of such fear and desire; and her celebration of physical bonding—born of the denial she suffered forty-three years earlier—establishes the authority of Faulkner's text, creates the code against which Sutpen and his design are to be measured. Sutpen lives in "the citadel of the central I-Am's private own," and it will be blown sky-high. Wash Jones' "touch" with the scythe is the literal cause of his death, but the deeper cause is that old innocence of his, the failure to acknowledge human connection. The issue is generic, but it is also sociopolitical, just as it was in Kafka and Melville: Sutpen's inability to perceive the humanity of the other makes us understand that fratricidal wars are possible; his "innocence" is emblematic of a caste system that walls off others, sorts them out according to gentlemen and "wild niggers," measures blood with an eye to 1/32 blackness, relegates daughters to stables, proposes trying it like dogs to see if it works, cannot say "son" to "the forlorn nameless and homeless lost child" who shows up at his door.

Faulkner, like Kafka, presents bonding through language as the other face of bonding through flesh, but, on that front, he goes beyond the failed love story of "In der Strafkolonie"; in poignant contrast to the breakdown of communication that informs Kafka's tale, Faulkner's narrators, his two college roommates, "earn," by dint of their highly visible labors, the understanding they arrive at. In a brilliantly structured fiction we see them enact the bonds of kinship and intimacy that Sutpen denied. They themselves, the Northerner and the Southerner, enter into a "marriage of speaking and hearing" that clearly images a might-have-been alternative to the war which is at the center of the book and of Faulkner's mind. In a memorable sequence, Faulkner refers to that special act of bonding and imagining as an "overpass to love," and he is thereby telling us something very old, yet very startling: the medium of fiction is love; the imagination comes to its knowledge of others, be they dead or living, by an act of love, not by an act of language or logic, or any comparable measuring of ingredients.

One of the most gripping passages of the novel actually shows us this overpass, this voyage from here to there, from now to then, from us to them. One can hardly conceive of a more perfect paradigm of empathy, as the roommates "become" Henry Sutpen and Charles Bon in Mississippi at the time of the war:

> It did not matter to them anyway, who could without moving, as free now of flesh as the father who decreed and forbade, the son who denied and repudiated, the lover who acquiesced, the beloved who was not bereaved, and with no tedious transition from hearth and garden to saddle, who could be already clattering over the frozen ruts of that December night and that Christmas dawn, that day of peace and cheer, of holly and goodwill and logs on the hearth; not two of them there and then either but four of them riding the two horses through the iron darkness, and that not mattering either: what faces and what names they called themselves and were called by so long as the blood coursed—the blood, the immortal brief recent intransient blood which could hold honor above slothy unregret and love above fat and easy shame. [295]

The more one considers this passage, the more curious it becomes. At first, it is, of course, the overpowering rhetoric that takes you in, the stunning metamorphosis and the ringing tribute to the blood. But there is more to it. There is something almost algebraic in its trade-off dimension as an equation, virtually a contract, establishing what is hard and what is easy, what is particular and what is generic, what you gain and what you lose. What is easy is the voyage itself ("no tedious transition"), but more arduous is perhaps the price of identity and particularity that must be paid, if one is to become another. Faulkner assures us that "it did not matter," but we cannot fail to be struck by the cost of the transformation: we see, in sharp focus, the scene of the past to which the roommates are transported, the frozen ruts, the Christmas dawn, the holly and logs; but Quentin and Shreve enter that past namelessly and, as it were, selflessly, as four boys on two horses. They are generic now, having sloughed off all accessories, such as faces and names, constituted only by the coursing blood that vitally links them to Henry and Charles, like an umbilical cord. This flowing blood is the very emblem of unmediated connection, the kind that Addie Bundren experienced for a while when she whipped her school children. The flowing blood, like the flowing river, has the kind of urgency and binding power in Faulkner that it had for Blake in "London," where the charter'd Thames *becomes* the soldier's blood that flows down palace walls. One is tempted to say that Faulkner's great fictions actually navigate this waterway, this bloodstream: genealogy and history are names for this moving, binding force that contains and meshes all individuals. In certain ecstatic moments—the Bundrens crossing the swollen waters, the old man coping with the flood, the black congregation listening to the Easter sermon, the spectacle of Joe Christmas' black blood spurting into the heavens—the Faulknerian individual either relinquishes or transcends his private markings and becomes one with the flow. This is what Quentin and Shreve do here, and they do so at the cost of their identity.

It is not easy to gauge with any finality the value of their gesture. Their act of generosity and empathy stands in direct contrast to the closed nature of Sutpen's "central I-Am" and his failure to recognize the humanity of others, of his own blood. But, at the same time, this overpass to love is not without peril. Shreve retreats from it with dispatch at the book's close, and he has little qualms about taunting Quentin at the end. He will return to Canada, where he came from, to practice medicine; we do not know what he brought with him from Harvard. About Quentin, however, there is considerably more evidence in, and it gives one pause. Quentin will commit suicide before the year is up, and although we can ascribe his death to "sister problems" by consulting *The Sound and the Fury*, we would also do well to take account of the problematic at hand here.[19] Among the

19. It should be rather obvious that this reading of Quentin's quandary in *Absalom* focuses on the issues and dynamics of *Absalom* itself, which is to say that even such a brilliant book as John Irwin's *Doubling and Incest, Repetition and Revenge: A Speculative Reading of Faulkner* (Baltimore: Johns Hopkins University Press, 1975) sheds as much darkness as it does light. By creating a meta-text and interpreting Quentin's situation in terms of the psychic issues of *The Sound and the Fury*, Irwin does a beautiful job establishing commonality between the texts, but he effectively denies himself even the possibility of illuminating the trauma and the narrational drama of *Absalom* itself.

many things that *Absalom* shows us is also the sight of Quentin Compson becoming a ghost. He has early referred to himself as a barracks, a kind of echo chamber where the old stories reverberate. His father has spoken of Southern women already as ghosts, and Rosa Coldfield has been living dead for some time now. It seems to be a regional hazard.

Coming to be a ghost in Faulkner is not so much a matter of spooks or horror; it is, instead, the condition of life when one inhabits the loom-world described by Judith Sutpen. It is the dawning realization that one is part of something serial, something that began before one was born and that will continue after one's death. At a certain point there are no lines, no contours left, only the blood, only the flow; Quentin speaks to us much like a man whose edges are being erased:

> *Maybe we are both Father. Maybe nothing ever happens once and is finished. Maybe happen is never once but like ripples maybe on water after the pebble sinks, the ripples moving on, spreading, the pool attached by a narrow umbilical water-cord to the next pool which the first pool feeds, has fed, did feed . . .* thinking *Yes, we are both Father. Or maybe Father and I are both Shreve, maybe it took Father and me both to make Shreve or Shreve and me both to make Father or maybe Thomas Sutpen to make all of us.* [261–62]

The vertical uprights of genealogy, history, and narrativity no longer hold; their structuring power has been displaced, and the new arrangement is concentric, spherical, ubiquitous, cubistic. The clear-cut directionality of fathering and narrating is dazzlingly imploded into a *carnaval* of connection and linkage, a demonic new constellation without origin or end. The sons create the father, and the story makes its tellers, and each party can become the other in this new dispensation.

It is as a ghost that Quentin understands that "it took Thomas Sutpen to make us all." This awareness of relation as something that may come from any angle, any vantage point in time or space, spells the end of autonomy. The self is eroding in Quentin, much as it was in Darl. Here, then, is the flip side of the cathartic imaginative gesture that caps the novel, for we are obliged to see that the imaginative extension of self exacts a special price. There seems to be almost a Faustian contract at work here, except that no one is free to choose his dealings and arrangements; instead, one is doomed to be a ghost, to experience one's terrible, unchosen linkages. This may appear, in some sense, to be a peculiarly Southern malady, the plight of the imagination in the Old South, a paralyzing sense of relatedness. As a Southern mind-set, this condition is, of course, neither lethal nor very interesting. But, when taken to the ecstatic extremes to which Faulkner brings it, it says something very sobering about the working of the imagination: namely, that empathy can be corrosive as well as liberating, leading to suicide as well as community. Ultimately, this double-edged posture illuminates the psychic disposition of the writer; to imagine the other is what the writer does as a way of life and, Faulkner appears to be saying, as a way of death.

CHAPTER FIVE

Heaven and Hell

Is anything more ambivalent than human connection? About "touch" Faulkner observed, in *Absalom*, that "enemies as well as lovers know" it "because it makes them both." Seventy-five years earlier, Baudelaire, in his poem "Duellum," imaged love-making as a duel, a fight to the death. The linkage of bodies can signify murder or pleasure, not merely because the other's intent is unknowable, but because all *contact* with others is, inherently, an awesome widening of experience, even, in some sense, a matter of eclipse.

That is the physical side of it. Mentally, imaginatively, the issue is conceivably of even greater import. The physical outcome of pleasure or death is fully matched by the drama of connection as "completion" or "invasion." At the risk of being arithmetic, does relationship betoken addition or subtraction? Is the self expanded, or diminished, when it encounters linkage? In the work of Borges and Strindberg we may see the fuller reach of these issues, because each of them views the self as so wholly inscribed, so limitlessly enmeshed, that something on the order of a new metaphysic, a reshaping of the cosmos is at hand. So wide are these vistas, so extended in time and space is the career of the self, that it does not seem exaggerated to term these provinces of relationship "heaven" and "hell."

1

Who is Borges? To know who you are is the central enigma and the central challenge of Borges' art: his "fictive" characters (and it is not easy to ascertain who is fictive, and who is not) find themselves "completed" and their identities "revealed" through the strangest kinds of adventures, often involving forays into the world of dreams or else entailing bold leaps in both time and space. Hence a nineteenth-century Englishman, Edward FitzGerald, finds not only his calling, but indeed his spiritual identity by the translation of a work by the eleventh-century Persian poet Omar ben Ibrāhīm al-Khayyāmī, and Borges is struck by how unalike they were, and how necessary they were to each other: "la muerte y las vicisitudes y el tiempo sirvieron para que uno supiera del otro y fueran un solo poeta" (death and vicissitudes and time caused one to know of the other and made them into a single poet).[1] This bizarre type of "pairing" over time and space is a persistent motif in Borges' tales, and he unfailingly presents it as the achievement of form, as the unveiling of identity, a composite whose lines are not visible to the fragmentary individual who is a part of it. Others of his characters are not actually paired, but nonetheless go through their lives, as it were, in the dark, waiting to be "revealed" to themselves; Borges imagines Shakespeare in such terms, and in the haunting "Borges y yo" we see that the identity of the author is equally fissured, equally at the far side of some revelatory act, possibly death.

Yet, we are doubtless justified in seeing an ideal portrait of the artist in the handsome tribute Borges wrote for Paul Valéry; the piece itself is entitled "Valéry como símbolo," and we may regard the French poet as a symbol of the Argentine writer himself, in that each of them, "en un siglo que adora los caóticos ídolos de la sangre, de la tierra y de la pasión, prefirió siempre los lúcidos placeres del pensamiento y las secretas aventuras del orden [107]" (in an age that worships the chaotic idols of blood, earth and passion, preferred always the lucid pleasures of thought and the secret adventures of order [74]). Borges himself is caught in these admirable lines, and they give us a sharp sense of his artistic agenda: the quest for order, but conceived as cerebral, hedonistic, and adventuresome at once. That exercise of thought and the narrative forms it inhabits are invariably committed to the project of identity, the articulation of who you are; but in the hands of Borges, this project is remarkably expansive and generative, showing over and over that "you" are a far greater sum than was ever suspected, that "you" are twinned and replicated and secretly consummated in ways that mock or explode individualist thinking. The self becomes a huge, open-ended item in Borges' repertory, but it never ultimately goes hungry or frustrated, for all his stories end up gratifying its need for form and closure, even if they do so at cost of death or annihilation. But, in the process of experi-

1. Jorge Luis Borges, *Otras inquisiciones*, in *Obras completas* (Buenos Aires: Emecé Editores, 1957–1960), VII, p. 113; the English translation that follows the Spanish is taken from *Other Inquisitions: 1937–1952*, trans. Ruth L. C. Simms (New York: Simon & Schuster, 1968), p. 198. Subsequent quotations from Borges' essays will be drawn from these two editions and noted parenthetically in the body of the text.

encing the fullness of its identity, the self comes to understand that apparent conflict and distance are secret linkage and kinship. It is this serene confidence that life is ultimately orderly, that one ultimately achieves a "fix" on the larger shape of one's life, that makes relationship an angelic theme in Borges, a heavenly mode of vision (of that larger "picture") that used to be regarded as the exclusive province of the gods.[2]

In this light, Borges stands as a cheerful antidote to the darker visions of most of the writers we have studied. Erotic connection is not very central to his scheme, and the depictions of entrapment or asphyxiation registered in Laclos or Flaubert or Ford or Burroughs are not to be found in these spare tales; but Borges has nothing to learn from anyone about the meshes in which individuals live and fall, and therefore he would understand the "loom view" of life expressed by Faulkner's Judith Sutpen:

> Because you make so little impression, you see. You get born and you try this and you dont know why only you keep on trying it and you are born at the same time with a lot of other people, all mixed up with them, like trying to, having to, move your arms and legs with strings only the same strings are hitched to all the other arms and legs and the others all trying and they dont know why either except that the strings are all in one another's way like five or six people all trying to make a rug on the same loom only each one wants to weave his own pattern into the rug; and it cant matter, you know that, or the Ones that set up the loom would have arranged things a little better.[3]

2. This entire essay is intended to offset the "minimalist" interpretations of Borges that abound among English-speaking critics. One thinks of the otherwise admirable monograph by J. M. Cohen (*Jorge Luis Borges* [New York: Harper & Row, 1974]), which concludes with the following charge (stemming from the Marxist critics) of manipulation and narrowness: "It is true that the characters in his stories have 'neither soul nor body' that they are no more than chessmen on a metaphysical board. They are his pawns in a game he is playing without human opponent. He makes all the moves. The two parties may be labelled gaucho and soldier, police and robber, the 'Company' and the individual, the Minotaur and his slayer, the spy and the professor. Always one will stand for death, the other for a possible life, one for dream and the other for a dubious reality" (p. 110).

3. William Faulkner, *Absalom, Absalom!* (New York: Modern Library, 1951), p. 127.

Borges would have understood these sentiments, but Faulkner's text shows just how far we are from the "lucid pleasures of thought" and the "secret adventures of order." Judith Sutpen's loom parable expresses the fatigue and nihilism of a mind that experiences entrapment, not order, and the Faulknerian syntax ("like trying to, having to") conveys the very feel of imprisonment and frustration. There is not to be a grand vista in *Absalom*; Quentin and Shreve will doubtless achieve an overview that goes beyond the contingent perspective of Judith, but they too will experience anguish and muddle, so much so that Quentin will, at least in some sense, die of it. People die in Borges as well, but most of them die happily, illuminated, beyond contingency at last. All of the varieties of connection that we have seen—political, imaginative, emotional, even sexual—are recast in the work of Borges as manifestations of order, of unsuspected, perhaps scandalous, even murderous order, but order just the same. The question, of course, is: Whose?

It is a question that Borges does not beg. The distant gods who arranged things in the past, the "Ones" who set up Judith's loom, come into the stories of Borges, sometimes as discreet presences behind the scenes, sometimes as central players. Hence, in "Three Versions of Judas," we are treated to the astounding view that God became Judas:

> Dios totalmente se hizo hombre pero hombre hasta la infamia, hombre hasta la reprobación y el abismo. Para salvarnos, pudo elegir *cualquiera* de los destinos que traman la perpleja red de la historia; pudo ser Alejandro o Pitágoras o Rurik o Jesús; eligió un ínfimo destino: fué Judas.
>
> [God made Himself totally a man but a man to the point of infamy, a man to the point of reprobation and the abyss. To save us, He could have chosen *any* of the destinies which make up the complex web of history; He could have been Alexander or Pythagoras or Rurik or Jesus; He chose the vilest destiny of all: He was Judas.][4]

4. Jorge Luis Borges, "Tres versiones de Judas," in *Borges: Sus mejores páginas* (Englewood Cliffs: Prentice-Hall, 1970), p. 110. The English version is taken from *Labyrinths: Selected Stories and Other Writings*, eds. Donald Yates and James Irby (New York: New Directions, 1964), p. 99; subsequent English versions of all the "fictions" will be drawn from this edition and noted parenthetically in the body of the text.

A good deal can be learned about Borgesian "economy" by considering this turn of events. God became Judas for reasons that are every bit as much aesthetic as religious: in becoming Judas, he turns the Passion into a harmonious unfurling of events, moving like clockwork, each person playing out his appointed role. There is no longer any betrayal, or, rather, the betrayal itself comes to be seen as the enabling climax of the prearranged story. God-as-Judas erases all dissonance, alters apparent conflict into secret service. There is something sublime in this effort to replace the crude betrayal scenario with a finer motive, a motive altogether more appealing to the imagination because it endows the whole sequence of events with purpose, yielding an unsuspected fit, where we had been accustomed to seeing treachery and anarchy.

Equally unsuspected is the reversal played out in "La casa de Asterión." Here we have a retelling of the Minotaur story from the Minotaur's point of view, and Borges offers us a monster who yearns for completion, one who knows that the figure of his life involves an other, the "other" Asterion who will endow him with the form that he awaits. It is a strange love story, filled with longing for the redemption that will establish his final identity. With consummate coolness, Borges closes this brief tale by giving the last, laconic word to Theseus: "—¿Lo creerás, Ariadna?—dijo Teseo—. El minotauro apenas se defendió" ("Would you believe it, Ariadne?" said Theseus. "The Minotaur scarcely defended himself" [140]).[5] An entire mythic construct has been reassembled here, but done with an elegance and a deftness that we have not encountered in any other writer of this study. Once more, Borges has given us a parable about harmony, about the unsuspected harmony that may underlie the bloodiest of events, if only one knows how to look at them, or how to retell them. The legendary antagonism between the monster and the heroes has been transformed into a lifelong courtship, one that was gratefully consummated with the arrival of Theseus.

It is tempting to regard the machinations of Borges as the result of a profoundly conservative vision that denies process and freedom at every turn, in order to celebrate the final pattern. Borges himself uses, more than once, the term "teleology" to designate the a priori nature of the design that emerges through his tales, and it would seem that

5. *Obras completas* (Buenos Aires: Emecé, 1957–1960), VII, p. 70. Subsequent quotations from this edition will be noted parenthetically in the body of the text.

the role of the individual in such an unfurling can be little more than passive acceptance. This issue is presented in its starkest terms in the story, "Deutsches Requiem," where the protagonist, Otto Dietrich zur Linde, waiting for his death, muses on his past role as subdirector of a concentration camp. Zur Linde's view of his own life minimizes his individuality, his possibility for choice or change of direction: on the one hand, he is the member of a long line of German military figures, and has as such a serial rather than a private identity; on the other hand, however, his acts derive less from himself as source than from the needs of history, which are the imperious first cause in all human gesture. This leads him to the astonishing conclusion that his own will, far from being submerged and eclipsed by prior forces, is in fact sovereign and authoritative, privy to the will of the gods and history, secretly shaping its destiny at every moment:

> Así, toda negligencia es deliberada, todo casual encuentro una cita, toda humillación una penitencia, todo fracaso una misteriosa victoria, toda muerte un suicidio. No hay consuelo más hábil que el pensamiento de que hemos elegido nuestras desdichas; esa teleología individual nos revela un orden secreto y prodigiosamente nos confunde con la divinidad. [*Obras completas*, p. 84]

> [Thus, every negligence is deliberate, every chance encounter an appointment, every humiliation a penitence, every failure a mysterious victory, every death a suicide. There is no more skillful consolation than the idea that we have chosen our own misfortunes; this individual teleology reveals a secret order and prodigiously confounds us with the divinity. (143)]

Borges has written other tales that are more speculative and overtly philosophical than this one, but none raises quite so many questions about its own assumptions. The angelic disposition (which Sophocles would have doubtless termed "hubris") that serenely believes in the harmony of the pattern that is being unveiled by one's life is, willy-nilly, situated in history; moreover, Borges goes on to show us that this teleological article of faith, far from ensuring passivity, may mobilize great energy and passion, as indeed it does in the life of Zur Linde, since it authorizes the most extreme actions while dispensing the actor from judgment. More precisely, the actor is enjoined to dismiss any "local" moral categories for assessing what he does, and to throw himself wholly and uncritically into the contest arranged by history; thus, Zur Linde tells us of the particular encounter, at the prison camp, with the Jewish poet David Jerusalem with whom he identified but whom he implacably tortured to death. If one contrasts this dark encounter with the metamorphic strategies of Kafka, Melville, and Faulkner, one can measure what it is Borges is and is not doing. Unlike the fateful "inside" knowledge of the other that finally characterizes the officer's experience of the prisoner, the captain's experience of the slaves, or the two Harvard roommates who "become" Henry Sutpen and Charles Bon, Zur Linde becomes, magisterially, *himself*, using David Jerusalem largely as a phase of his development. One surmises that, in the hands of Borges, the Oedipus story would be altered so that the two fateful transgressions—the murder of one's father at the crossroads, and the fornication with one's mother—would be recast as necessary stages in Oedipus' "progress." It is important to see that something is both lost and gained in these transactions, for the equilibrium he achieves, the final poise of character, event, and history, displays a mind for whom all things ultimately "even out." Who else could claim that a new cure for cancer had been found: human flesh?

Zur Linde's endorsement of his role as vehicle of history should, however, be counterpointed by the attitude and behavior of another of Borges' figures under stress: Emma Zunz. The tale of Emma's revenge on the man who caused the suicide of her father is a brilliant illustration of just how far Borgesian "aggressivity" can go. Emma elaborately contrives to "make" history, rather than suffer or embody it, and her enlistment of others as unwitting participants in her scheme constitutes a rare tribute to the shaping powers of the self. But Borges remains Borges, and Emma too must essentially perform an act of self-annihilation if she is to impose her grand design on the world of the living. In this instance, Borges has given us just enough clues to realize that the sexual nature of Emma's "plot" works precisely as much against her as for her: in order to assassinate Aaron Loewenthal, she who has "un temor casi patológico" (an almost pathological fear) of men must have sex with an anonymous sailor in order to sustain her case of alleged sexual abuse. Nor is Borges content with only this: in the moment of fornication with the sailor, Emma is made to discover, with revulsion, the obscene nature of her own origin, and it is not going too far to suggest that Emma's murder of Loewenthal is a desperate effort at self-erasure, as much as it is a dazzling implementation of personal will and form. Once again we see the enactment of a pattern, and once again we realize the high cost it demands.

*

Borges is willing to go to great lengths to find and celebrate harmony, because he has no stomach for chaos. The carnage of history and the ever-present reality of conflict lead him to search for his peculiar form of overpass, that "northwest passage to the intellectual world" which Sterne managed to chart in *Tristram Shandy*. Yet, disorder is hardly limited to the moral or the political sphere; one encounters it in the flesh, but one encounters it in the mind as well. Who ever said that the intellectual world was a haven? In a number of his most provocative stories, Borges offers ample evidence that the mind is unrivaled in its capacity for chaos. The old suspicion that fantasy and imagination are ways to "escape" reality is a suspicion that dogs Borges criticism, although Borges is usually credited with a peculiarly scholarly form of escape: notably, he uses his erudition to reinvent history and thereby gloss over the messiness. This attitude presupposes, of course, that mental operations are a form of cover-up, a way of gaining control over events. There may be some truth in that proposition, but it is a deeply vexed matter for Borges, since the mind itself is a suspicious beast, and it will not endorse facile "rewrites." In some extreme cases, the mind is so scrupulous in its devious and intricate operations that no pattern is even thinkable.

The most interesting tale, from this point of view, is the remarkable story of "Funes el memorioso." Here is what must be the Borgesian nightmare: a world of infinite, discrete nuances, utterly atomized, unconnected. Funes, paralyzed, blessed (or cursed) with a prodigious memory—hauntingly reminiscent of the near-blind Borges who seems to carry the entirety of the tradition with him, portably, at all times, in his head, ready for instant and perfect quotation—shows us the appalling results of pure, unmediated, "untampered" perception. He sees the world in its manifold variety, and for him there can be no imaginable pattern or scheme, no significant relationships at all:

> Éste, no le olvidemos, era casi incapaz de ideas generales, platónicas. No sólo le costaba comprender que el símbolo genérico *perro* abarcara tantos individuos dispares de diversos tamaños y diversa forma; le molestaba que el perro de las tres y catorce

(visto de perfil) tuviera el mismo nombre que el perro de las tres y quarto (visto de frente). Su propria cara en el espejo, sus propias manos, lo sorprendían cada vez. . . . Era el solitario y lúcido espectador de un mundo multiforme, instantáneo y casi intolerablemente preciso.[6]

[He was, let us not forget, almost incapable of ideas of a general, Platonic sort. Not only was it difficult for him to comprehend that the generic symbol *dog* embraces so many unlike individuals of diverse size and form; it bothered him that the dog at three fourteen (seen from the side) should have the same name as the dog at three fifteen (seen from the front). His own face in the mirror, his own hands, surprised him every time he saw them. . . . He was the solitary and lucid spectator of a multiform, instantaneous and almost intolerably precise world. (65)]

It would be hard to imagine a more extreme suspicion of mental shortcuts or facile patterns than we see in this tale. For Funes, the world has incredible scope and variety, composed exclusively of momentary perceptions that are utterly anarchic in their assertiveness. This is a scene of intolerable richness and purity, prior to all human acts of arrangement and selection that would screen out most of it and thereby make it palatable, and this perception of totality returns, like a bad dream, in the work of Borges—sometimes called the Zahir, at others the Aleph, present always as the elusive goal of the quest, the ultimate "total book" in the Library of Babel. The discovery of this totality, the initiation into the wholeness of time and space, exacts a heavy price: Funes is paralyzed, the Zahir tyrannizes the thought of its finders, the contemplation of the Aleph brings dizziness and tears. The disenfranchised Funes is a sobering figure of the cost involved in Borgesian vision; there is, as Michel Foucault has eloquently argued, something properly monstrous in such a vision, because it testifies to a world beyond order, a conflation of items that defy commonality by constituting what he calls a "hétérotopie" (as opposed to the harmonious term "utopie," which Genette accorded to Borges).[7]

6. *Borges: Narraciones* (Madrid: Cátedra, 1981), p. 119. Subsequent quotations from this edition will be noted parenthetically in the body of the text.

7. As is well known, Foucault attributes to Borges nothing less than the origin of *Les Mots et les choses*, and his commentary is among the richest and

The totality of the universe defies grids of thought and language, but the Borgesian hero never ceases to pursue it, to make it somehow amenable to just those grids of thought and language. Through the agency of thought and language, the fullness of the world can be miraculously focused and apprehended: a stone, a small iridescent

---

most suggestive that Borges has received, especially concerning the heterogeneity of Borges' world and the consequent impossibility of connection. Foucault is worth quoting at length here: "Ce texte de Borges [the 'disparate' list of animals in 'The Analytical Language of John Wilkins,' in *Other Inquisitions*] m'a fait rire longtemps, non sans un malaise certain et difficile à vaincre. Peut-être parce que dans son sillage naissait le soupçon qu'il y a pire désordre que celui de l'*incongru* et du rapprochement de ce qui ne convient pas; ce serait le désordre qui fait scintiller les fragments d'un grand nombre d'ordres possibles dans la dimension, sans loi ni géométrie, de l'*hétéroclite*; et il faut entendre ce mot au plus près de son étymologie: les choses y sont 'couchées', 'posées', 'disposées' dans des sites à ce point différents qu'il est impossible de trouver pour eux un espace d'accueil, de définir au-dessous des uns et des autres un *lieu commun*. Les *utopies* consolent: c'est que si elles n'ont pas de lieu réel, elles s'épanouissent pourtant dans un espace merveilleux et lisse; elles ouvrent des cités aux vastes avenues, des jardins bien plantés, des pays faciles, même si leur accès est chimérique. Les *hétérotopies* inquiètent, sans doute parce qu'elles minent secrètement le langage, parce qu'elles empêchent de nommer ceci *et* cela, parce qu'elles brisent les noms communs ou les enchevêtrent, parce qu'elles ruinent d'avance la 'syntaxe', et pas seulement celle qui construit les phrases,—celle moins manifeste qui fait 'tenir ensemble' (à côté et en face les uns des autres) les mots et les choses. C'est pourquoi les utopies permettent les fables et les discours: elles sont dans le droit fil du langage, dans la dimension fondamentale de la *fabula*; les hétérotopies (comme on en trouve si fréquemment chez Borges) dessèchent le propos, arrêtent les mots sur eux-mêmes, contestent, dès sa racine, toute possibilité de grammaire; elles dénouent les mythes et frappent de stérilité le lyrisme des phrases" (*Les Mots et les choses* [Paris: Gallimard, 1966], pp. 9–10). Borges finds himself enlisted here in a kind of radically dissociative project that is ultimately more proper to the French critic than to the Argentine writer; it seems likely that Foucault is countering the overly serene reading of Borges offered by Gérard Genette ("l'Utopie littéraire" in *Figures* [Paris: Seuil, 1966]), wherein the autonomy of spirit (which Genette quickly turns into something approaching the autonomy of literature) is celebrated and shown to be "instanced" in specific manifestations over time. Whereas Genette minimizes the particular, I think that Foucault tends to overstate the conceptual anarchy in Borges' work, and the burden of my essay has been to take a kind of middle ground, but to insist on the humanist drama of identity and coherence that ultimately emerges from Borges' strange pairings.

sphere, a book, a script. Here, then, is the task that Borges sets himself: to translate the infinite into pattern (riddle, labyrinth, loops and symmetries and concatenations beyond the constraints of time and space), but to do so in ways that command credence; this, in turn, entails precisely that strange celebration of achieved harmony already noted. It is not an accident that most of these revelations come at the expense of the seer's life. The old saying that one's entire life passes in review at the moment of death is vitalized in the art of Borges, except that he does not hesitate to expand the picture, to pass in review an incredible assortment of events and to make you see that this is your life, that its parameters are wider than you had thought; but death still follows. And one feels that this death is, in some sense, more an intellectual and perceptual matter than an organic one: the widening of the view is so extreme that it breaks the lense. To discover the riddle of the universe is to be annihilated in one's selfhood. That is precisely the lesson of "La escritura del Dios" (The God's Script): the questing, broken, dying magician Tzinacán perceives, in an ecstatic moment, infinity, and he is initiated into that larger mystery in which his own small life is a part:

> Yo vi una Rueda altísima, que no estaba delante de mis ojos, ni detrás, ni a los lados, sino en todas partes, a un tiempo. Esa Rueda estaba hecha de agua, pero también de fuego, y era (aunque se veía el borde) infinita. Entretejidas, la formaban todas las cosas que serán, que son y que fueron, y yo era una de las hebras de esa trama total, y Pedro de Alvarado, que me dió tormento, era otra. Ahí estaban las causas y los efectos y me bastaba ver esa Rueda para entenderlo todo, sin fin. ¡Oh dicha de entender, mayor que la de imaginar o la de sentir! Vi el universo y vi los íntimos designios del universo. Vi los orígenes que narra el Libro del Común. Vi las montañas que surgieron del agua, vi los primeros hombres de palo, vi las tinajas que se volvieron contra los hombres, vi los perros que les destrozaron las caras. Vi el dios sin cara que hay detrás de los dioses. [*Obras completas*, p. 120]

> [I saw an exceedingly high Wheel, which was not before my eyes, nor behind me, nor to the sides, but every place at one time. That Wheel was made of water, but also of fire, and it was (although the edge could be seen) infinite. Interlinked, all things that are, were and shall be formed it, and I was one of the fibers

> of that total fabric and Pedro de Alvarado who tortured me was another. There lay revealed the causes and the effects and it sufficed me to see that Wheel in order to understand it all, without end. O bliss of understanding, greater than the bliss of imagining or feeling. I saw the universe and I saw the intimate designs of the universe. I saw the origins narrated in the Book of the Common. I saw the mountains that rose out of the water, I saw the first men of wood, the cisterns that turned against the men, the dogs that ravaged their faces. I saw the faceless god concealed behind the other gods. (172–73)]

Here is the vision of plenitude, but it differs crucially from the fragmented perception of Funes; Tzinacán sees the luminous spectacle of truth, a dazzling moment of blinding light and clarity, a view of origins and ends. He himself is a part of the tableau he perceives, as is his torturer, but his private bearings have been imploded by what he has seen, and the individualist frame can no longer hold:

> Quien ha entrevisto el universo, quien ha entrevisto los ardientes designios del universo, no puede pensar en un hombre, en sus triviales dichas o desventuras, aunque ese hombre sea él. Ese hombre *ha sido él* y ahora no le importa. [*Obras completas*, p. 121]

> [Whoever has seen the universe, whoever has beheld the fiery designs of the universe, cannot think in terms of one man, of that man's trivial fortunes or misfortunes, though he be that very man. That man *has been he* and now matters no more to him. (173)]

*

Full disclosure, in Borges, is frequently a death sentence. One recalls the story of Jaromir Hladik, in "El milagro secreto" (The Secret Miracle), who is granted that extra year to finish his manuscript while waiting for the fatal bullet to come from the firing squad; the extra year and the poetic inspiration are unquestionably part of a death-bargain. But, for the most part, the grand illumination is a kind of fourth-dimensional portraiture, a final setting forth of the figure one has cut against the backdrop of all time and space. This essay began with the observation that the quest for self-identity occupies center-stage in the stories of Borges. The most interesting of these quest-narratives are possessed of a quite remarkable dynamic: they are like the Polaroid instant photograph that comes into focus as you watch it. The impersonal revelation of the universe's design would not make for interesting fiction, and the free operation of the protagonist is inconceivable, given Borges' larger aims; what we have, instead, is the fascinating interplay of these two forces—the will of history or the gods, on the one hand, and the antics of the hero on the other—and it is the prodigious mixture of light and darkness, of a gradually emerging pattern that no one could have foreseen, that makes his best stories both angelic and moving.

Consider, for instance, "La muerte y la brújula" (Death and the Compass). In this urban narrative of a detective seeking to solve a crime involving the Name of God, we may discern a variant of the Oedipal story. Detective Lönnrot has followed all the erudite clues concerning the mystery of God's Name, but he has failed to consider the mystery of his own, failed to realize that this labyrinthine pursuit leads inward as well as throughout the city; in particular, he has missed the linguistic connection between himself and the criminal, Red Scharlach, and he has failed, even more crucially, to see that this linguistic linkage points to a darker, more substantial linkage, involving pain and personal revenge. The abandoned villa where the trap is sprung is appropriately called "Triste-le-roi," and it is not fanciful to see in this sad king an echo of the ruler of Thebes who also failed to see that the source of the crime was shockingly personal. Above all, Borges is telling a tale of connection, of widening vision, so that one understands that Lönnrot and Red Scharlach are destined to be a single figure, as are Theseus and the Minotaur, or Jesus and Judas. And it is thus fair to say that Borges finishes his murder story on a happy note, because marriages are happy affairs, and there is an undeniable tone of satisfaction in the close of this narrative, the satisfaction one feels in seeing the endless and harmonious patterns made in a kaleidoscope. The fundamental terror of Sophocles' story lies in its repudiation of knowledge, its revelation that one is connected in ways that are unknowable and unavowable; in Borges, on the other hand, the doomed detective spends his last moment collaborating with his killer on the geometric niceties of their odd *pas de deux*, making suggestions for how it might be laid out the next time around, visibly at peace with a world that has such elegance. Death must follow exposure, yes, but the "lucid pleasures of thought and the secret adventures of order" sweeten its taste very considerably.

By using the term "adventures," Borges would seem to indicate a measure of narrative complexity and temporal sweep that no mere curtain-raising scenario could embody. "Borges" runs headlong into the Zahir and the Aleph, and Emma Zunz carries out her transactions with dispatch; others simply wait for their illuminating fate: Zur Linde, the Minotaur, Jaromir Hladik. But, in some of the most intriguing stories, we find an intricate process of uncovering and development, a series of true and false leads, an endless process of evaluation and re-evaluation. It is possible to assign "La muerte y la brújula" to this category, but the detective work in that story is still tame, in comparison to the more full-blown quest-narratives that take larger leaps and attempt bolder fusions. Here is where the heavenly mode is most perfectly realized: the individual stumbles into a mystery or puzzle of vast proportions (frequently reaching back into history) whose working-out holds the key to his own identity. In such art the fiction of relationship reaches an apex, for it makes entirely good on its claim that the individual is not only inscribed in a larger configuration, but there is no "loomlike" anarchy at all; we see, instead, a prodigious conferring of identity that is simultaneous with the eclipse of the self.

"El jardín de senderos que se bifurcan" (The Garden of Forking Paths) constitutes Borges' classic rendering of this theme. In this convoluted and glittering tale of espionage, Borges achieves his most condensed and provocative meditation on the enigmas of identity and the uses of art. The whole story functions as a flashback that is to account for a mysterious five-day delay in the attack against the Serre-Montauban line; from this modest point of departure, Borges leaps out and back into the reaches of Chinese history and philosophy, by offering us, as a protagonist, Dr. Yu Tsun, English professor, spy, and also great-grandson of Ts'ui Pên, who was governor of Yunnan and who supposedly renounced worldly power in order to write a novel that might be even more "populous" than the *Hung Lu Meng* and "para edificar un laberinto en el que se perdieran todos los hombres" (to construct a labyrinth in which all men would become lost [22]).[8] Ts'ui Pên's novel was deemed incoherent, his labyrinth was never found, and he was murdered by a stranger. Racing to complete his mission (which is never elucidated for the reader), Yu Tsun wonders about that "laberinto perdido":

8. *La muerte y la brújula* (Buenos Aires: Emecé, 1951), p. 100. Subsequent quotations from this collection will be noted parenthetically in the body of the text.

lo imaginé inviolado y perfecto en la cumbre secreta de una montaña, lo imaginé borrado por arrozales o debajo del agua, lo imaginé infinito, no ya de quioscos ochavados y de sendas que vuelven, sino de ríos y provincias y reinos . . . Pensé en el laberinto de laberintos, en el sinuoso laberinto creciente que abaracara el pasado y el porvenir y que implicara de algún modo los astros. Absorto en esas ilusorias imágenes, olvidé mi destino de perseguido. Me sentí, por un tiempo indeterminado, percibidor abstracto del mundo. [100]

[I imagined it inviolate and perfect at the secret crest of a mountain; I imagined it erased by rice fields or beneath the water; I imagined it infinite, no longer composed of octagonal kiosks and returning paths, but of rivers and provinces and kingdoms . . . I thought of a labyrinth of labyrinths, of one sinuous spreading labyrinth that would encompass the past and the future and in some way involve the stars. Absorbed in these illusory images, I forgot my destiny of one pursued. I felt myself to be, for an unknown period of time, an abstract perceiver of the world. (23)]

Each of these images of the labyrinth both poses and removes it, as if its "secret" could not be "violated," as if "saying" it were complemented by "erasing" it. Quickly enough, we see the labyrinth grow, move through negations ("no ya de . . . sino de") and out into space, encompassing now "ríos y provincias y reinos" (rivers and provinces and kingdoms), moving still further out, in time, containing "el pasado y el porvenir" (the past and the future) and, as grand climax, involving ("implicating," says the Spanish) the stars. These vast expanses are both contained and ordered by Ts'ui Pên's labyrinth, and we realize that this figure has the same exploratory and imperialist powers that Wallace Stevens ascribed to poetry itself:

> The maker's rage to order words of the sea,
> Words of the fragrant portals, dimly-starred,
> And of ourselves and of our origins,
> In ghostly demarcations, keener sounds.[9]

9. Wallace Stevens, "The Idea of Order at Key West," in *The Palm at the End of the Mind* (New York: Vintage Books, 1972), pp. 98–99.

Our art moves into the spheres, and patterns the waves; but Stevens, no less than Joyce, insists that the "longest way around is the shortest way home," that the "territory ahead" is always an extension of the person behind. These are the portals as well as the words "of ourselves," and we are led to see that the exploration is simultaneously personal as well as cosmic; likewise, Yu Tsun's belief that he is a "percibidor abstracto" (an abstract perceiver) of the world is illusory, for the perceiver of the world is ineluctably part of the world, and Yu Tsun's part is precisely that of a "perseguido." A profound Borgesian note is struck here, in this dual sense of visionary freedom and political contingency. Yet, this virtually schizoid apprehension of separate realms will give way to that peculiar oneness which is the author's trademark. Running from Richard Madden, Yu Tsun is also running toward him; reflecting on his ancestor's labyrinth, he will find that he inhabits it.

Yu Tsun is to learn, of course, that the novel and the labyrinth are one and the same, and that the beautifully penned phrase on the manuscript, "*Dejo a los varios porvenires (no a todos) mi jardín de senderos que se bifurcan* [*Muerte*, p. 105]" (*I leave to the various futures [not to all] my garden of forking paths* [25])," is the key phrase, to be interpreted temporally, not spatially, a forking in time, not space. These precious insights are offered to him by the man he pursues, the Sinologist Stephen Albert. At this point, both Yu Tsun and the reader begin to understand that something is nascent and emergent here, that an entire destiny has been gestating and is now to be born. But it requires expanding one's view of the parameters of a life, and this is accomplished easily enough when one realizes that life does not proceed in a straight line, but rather in a forking path. Nothing is ever over, because the path can still fork again, loop once more and disclose the pattern that was hidden up to now. The novel and the labyrinth are one and the same; this structure "en el que se perdieran todos los hombres" (in which all men would become lost) is the one being enacted here and now, and its players are, of course, Yu Tsun and Stephen Albert.

Ts'ui Pên's novel was thought to be incoherent, because impossible things "happened" in it:

> En todas las ficciones, cada vez que un hombre se enfrente con diversas alternativas, opta por una y elimina las otras; en la del casi inextricable Ts'ui Pên, opta—simultáneamente—por todas.

> *Crea*, así, diversos porvenires, diversos tiempos, que también proliferan y se bifurcan. [*Muerte*, p. 106]

> [In all fictional works, each time a man is confronted with several alternatives, he chooses one and eliminates the others; in the fiction of Ts'ui Pên, he chooses—simultaneously—all of them. *He creates*, in this way, diverse futures, diverse times which themselves also proliferate and fork. (26)]

There is a prodigious freedom in Ts'ui Pên's project, because he is bent on replacing "either/or" with "both/and." Here is the formula for a novel that need never be over, and the proof is, ever so elegantly, in the pudding: the novel of Ts'ui Pên *is* still "alive," since it is being enacted by players many generations later.

More than closure is at stake here. Ts'ui Pên's text accommodates many futures, because no single paradigm governs it. Borges is attacking all of Western logic here, especially its logocentrism which operates according to binary arrangements and defines its repertory by means of difference. That total universe which has seized the mind of Funes and the prisoner Tzinacán is never far from Borges' concerns, and once again he is celebrating multiplicity at the expense of coherence. "Consistency is the hobgoblin of little minds," said Emerson, and Borges is committed to large minds; here we see him attacking the very notion of consistency as human attribute, by imagining a fiction in which it loses all authority:

> En la obra de Ts'ui Pên, todos los desenlaces ocurren; cada uno es el punto de partida de otras bifurcaciones. Alguna vez, los senderos de ese laberinto convergen: por ejemplo, usted llega a esta casa, pero en uno de los pasados posibles usted es mi enemigo, en otro mi amigo. [*Muerte*, pp. 106–107]

> [In the work of Ts'ui Pên, all possible outcomes occur; each one is the point of departure for other forkings. Sometimes, the paths of this labyrinth converge: for example, you arrive at this house, but in one of the possible pasts you are my enemy, in another, my friend. (26)]

By including time in his work, Borges has attained a kind of plasticity of character that is rare in literature, and over which traditional coherence has no hold. All the materials of the story have been heated up by this point, and one realizes that the abstruse discussion of literary form is becoming wildly significant, indicating its enduring hold as pattern precisely by molding itself to real events. With enviable economy, Borges makes full political use of his storytellers, and reminds us that this leisurely philosophical tale is set in a context of war and urgency, that Yu Tsun is being pursued by Richard Madden and that he has his own designs on Stephen Albert that have little to do with literary forms. But the forking path is infinitely assimilative, absorbs all the strands and twists unto itself.

The contingencies of politics and war are inhuman in their dictates, and we have known since Homer and the Greek tragedians what a coercive, fateful role they play in human life, especially insofar as they deprive it of choice or maneuvering room. On the face of it, Borges' protagonist is in a comparable *huis clos*, and he will indeed assassinate Stephen Albert in order to accomplish his mission. But this brutal deed acquires a kind of ritualized status, as we observe its harmonious fit in the scheme of things, its obvious propriety as a modern replay of the ancestor's old scenario: "*Así combatieron los héroes, tranquilo el admirable corazón, violenta la espada, resignados a matar y a morir* [*Muerte*, p. 107]" (*Thus fought the heroes, tranquil their admirable hearts, violent their swords, resigned to kill and to die* [27]). Reminiscent once again of the Minotaur's attitude toward Theseus, or that of Judas concerning Christ, these words breathe linkage, not hate; decorous interplay, not murderous sundering.

Let us return to the central moment of Ts'ui Pên's text, that moment where time enters it and it becomes narratively incoherent:

> Alguna vez, los senderos de ese laberinto se convergen: por ejemplo, usted llega a esta casa, pero en uno de los pasados posibles usted es mi enemigo, en otro mi amigo.
>
> [Sometimes, the paths of this labyrinth converge: for example, you arrive at this house, but in one of the possible pasts you are my enemy, in another, my friend.]

It is especially here that Borges is reaching for freedom, for a kind of malleability that would militate against the past's most dreadful power: its *pastness*, its being over and done. Equally abhorrent to Borges is the proposition that any single quality is binding, any single characteristic constraining; instead, he wants to maintain the integrity of these qualities—friend, enemy—but to loosen them, to transcend their vulgar antinomy, to display their polarity as the slave of logic but also as the sovereign sport of literature and of life which may "overpass" such binds. The binary chains of Western thought—presence/absence, here/there, is/was, this/that, either/or—are being shrugged off in this brief story which celebrates simultaneity and multiplicity.

This is no escape into fantasy. Yu Tsun will murder Stephen Albert. Borges cannot change the facts. In "deed" he will be both a friend and an enemy to the man at whose house he has arrived; but in his heart, he will always regard Stephen Albert as a man "que para mí no es menos que Goethe" (who for me is no less great than Goethe), and he will twice assure him of his gratitude and friendship, a feeling of reverence that accompanies him right into the act of murder and beyond it. This is not incoherent, and although it is dreadful, it also possesses a rare human dignity.

The paths of a labyrinth converge and two men meet. In one scenario they are enemies, in another friends. Borges presents them as both at once. There is a crossroads; two men meet. In one scenario they have a murderous altercation, in another they are father and son. A man and a woman find that they are at once son and mother, husband and wife. Sophocles has plumbed the horror of "both/and," and he has shown what happens when roles and qualities do not bind. Oedipus discovers the ambivalence principle, the field of double-sowing, and he is unhinged. Borges has taken the Oedipal story and given it a cubist rendering: he too has proposed a field of double-sowing, a field where enemy and friend are both opposites and the same, but he has done so in the name of freedom, not scandal. "El jardín de senderos que se bifurcan" acknowledges the entrapment of history, that nightmare from which Stephen Dedalus is trying to awake; and like Joyce and Faulkner, Borges too ponders the might-have-been's, the repertory of possibilities that have been "impossibilized" by event. But, unlike the ludic treatment of Joyce or the tragic desperation of Faulkner, Borges fashions a peculiar blend of freedom and determinism. In his work the individual comes in possession of his age-old pedigree, the long shadow that has preceded him and about which he has known nothing. Yu Tsun is the victim of circumstance, if you will, but he also comes into his real estate, assesses and plays out his role as Chinese great-grandson to Ts'ui Pên and heir to the labyrinth. He comes to realize that nothing is discrete and unconnected in the world he inhabits, that the past is not over, and that the future is something he makes as well as endures.[10]

*

It seems fitting to close a discussion of Borges by focusing briefly on "Tema del traidor y del héroe" (Theme of the Traitor and the Hero), which may be read as a coda for "El jardín de senderos que se bifurcan" because it does for traitor/hero what has already been done for enemy/friend. Time and history have been brought into the fabric of this tale as well, and it would seem to continue the meditation on literary form that was initiated in the conception of Ts'ui Pên's labyrinth fiction; this time, however, Borges has worked out something close to the modern view of intertextuality, but his embedded texts are predictably surprising in their working, ultimately unlimited in their effects.

The parallels with the setting of "El jardín de senderos que se bifurcan" are unmistakable: the narrator, Ryan, is the great-grandson of the Irish revolutionary hero Fergus Kilpatrick, who was mysteriously assassinated. Ryan is writing a biography of his ancestor, but is troubled not only by the enigmatic circumstances of his death but also by the overtly literary coloration of those events: the story seems lifted from *Julius Caesar*, replete with omens and warnings; and Kilpatrick's friend, Nolan, had not only translated Shakespeare into Gaelic, but had conceived of a type of meta-theater "que requieren miles de actores y que reiteran episodios históricos en las mismas cuidades y montañas donde ocurrieron" [*Narraciones*, p. 122]" (which would require thousands of actors and repeat historical episodes in the very cities and mountains where they took place [74]). The lines between literature and life are increasingly blurred, as Ryan learns that a traitor was discovered at the time of Kilpatrick's murder, and gradually he pieces it all together: Kilpatrick was the traitor, and his guilt was found out by Nolan, who then had the sublime idea of

10. Once again, I would like to take issue with J. M. Cohen's view of Borges as a writer who "waffles" on every important issue and simply capitalizes on ambiguity. Cohen claims, "Even on the metaphysical side, he avoids issues. He thinks no problem to its conclusion, always stepping back to shelter behind a dry irony. He is the supreme example of the escapist, who fails to make good his escape" (*Jorge Luis Borges*, p. 110).

punishing the hero by assassinating him, thereby establishing him permanently as a hero of Irish political rebellion. The so-called events were entirely rehearsed:

> El condenado entró en Dublin, discutió, obró, rezó, reprobó, pronunció palabaras patéticas y cada uno de esos actos que reflejaría la gloria, había sido prefijado por Nolan. Centenares de actores colaboraron con el protagonista; el rol de algunos fue complejo; el de otros, momentáneo. Las cosas que dijeron e hicieron perduran en los libros históricos, en la memoria apasionada de Irlanda. [*Narraciones*, p. 125]

> [The condemned man entered Dublin, discussed, acted, prayed, reproved, uttered words of pathos, and each of these gestures, to be reflected in his glory, had been pre-established by Nolan. Hundreds of actors collaborated with the protagonist; the role of some was complex; that of others momentary. The things they did and said endure in the history books, in the impassioned memory of Ireland. (75)]

The unfurling of history is revealed to be the elaboration of a text, the secret enactment of a pattern. Shakespeare (the "English enemy") contributes passages and scenes from *Julius Caesar* and *Macbeth*, not only because Nolan is short on time and takes whatever material he can find, but perhaps even more crucially as a way of signaling the artistry of the entire construct, a way of saying that the form-impulse, the *Kunstwille* can have the upper hand, even in the realm of political passion and historical revolution.

What, then, is Kilpatrick? Once again, we realize that traitor/hero are imprisoning terms, that Kilpatrick is neither and both, that the forking narrative which "delivers" him shows him to be "both/and." And it is perhaps this forking narrative which most deserves commentary. Ryan, like Yu Tsun before him, understands that he is part of what he has uncovered, that his own life is implicated in Nolan's narrative of Kilpatrick. He decides not to expose Kilpatrick as a traitor, and he thus joins the conspiracy, the conspiracy of silence and also of readers who are on the "inside," behind the scenes. He even goes a step further, publishing a book dedicated to the glory of his ancestor, and he realizes that this, too, was foreseen. The ultimate verdict on Kilpatrick is less significant than the fascinating dynamic uncovered in this tale: the "text" is protean, endowed with endless lives, potent to effect real change, to change real lives. No longer the God's script, it is now the human script that shapes the lives of those who encounter it, orders (in all senses of the word) the world of its readers within its own pattern, creates a community of players who discover—and then decide—that they are bound together over time and space.[11] Borges' gambit is no less than a *défi*: he challenges the world to live up to the promise of intelligence, and he is ready to help it do so.

2

In the work of Borges, the self comes to recognize its place in a larger network, and that operation has been termed heavenly or angelic because it is profoundly beneficent, even when it is lethal; i.e., beneficent in that it satisfies the mind that order is real, that what seemed fragmentary or jagged is, in fact, a necessary part of a harmonious whole. But the loom-view of the self expressed in *Absalom* can also be experienced as darkening rather than lightening, an increasing sense of asphyxiation rather than epiphany, a feeling of dreadful en-

11. Emir Rodríguez Monegal, in *Borges, Hacia una lectura poética* (Madrid: Ediciones Guadarrama, 1976), devotes his last chapter to the vital French criticism of Borges that started with Blanchot, was continued by several of the *nouveaux romanciers*, and was completed by Foucault. In particular, Rodríguez Monegal refers to the work of Claude Ollier on the "Theme of the Traitor and the Hero," especially the notion of successive versions of the "same" story; Ollier argues that in this story "Borges monte et démonte sous nos yeux les rouages de la machine, montre comment les mots l'alimentent et assurent sa bonne marche, secrétant *une histoire* et secrétant *l'Histoire*" (quoted by Rodríguez Monegal, p. 114). The Uruguayan critic goes on to argue that the concatenation is even more far-flung than Ollier has recognized: "Pero es, a su vez, víctima de un error de interpretación. No advierte que el cuento de Borges no sólo indica las semejanzas entre el destino de Kilpatrick y el de Julio César, y entre los textos de Nolan y de Shakespeare, pero también entre el destino de Kilpatrick y el futuro de Lincoln, así como alude, en su entrelínea a otro famoso Héroe y otro famoso relato: Jesús en los Evangelios. Para establecer el vínculo secreto entre la interpretación del 'Tema del traidor y del héroe' con la historia evangélica sólo hay que releer cuidadosamente el penúltimo párrafo del cuento a la luz de lo que dice Borges en otro relato, 'Tres versiones de Judas', que se encuentra en el mismo volumen de *Ficciones*, apenas separado de aquél por otros dos cuentos" (p. 114).

croachment rather than liberation. Many writers, including Faulkner himself, have dealt with this dimension of relationship, but no one has charted the infernal character of relationship more memorably than Strindberg. His swollen ego, his misogyny, his posturing, his violence, all contribute to a world view in which the self is endlessly under siege, discovering its enmeshed condition at every turn.

The Strindberg most known outside of Sweden is the dramatist, especially the analyst and anatomist of modern love in such plays as *The Father, Miss Julie*, and *The Dance of Death*. This body of work rings a new note in European literature, makes visible a kind of ferocity in relations between the sexes that was unheard-of in polite literature, a view of coupling that is essentially Darwinian and to the death. In particular, the two earlier plays present man and woman locked in a kind of primitive *agon* that is peculiarly figural. To be sure, both plays are charged with intellectual and social overtones, involving the riddle of paternity, on the one hand, and the seesaw of attraction/repulsion that fatally unites the aristocratic woman and the servant on the make, on the other hand. But, beyond and, as it were, beneath these cultural scenarios is a recurring fable of intolerable connection, as despotic as the one caused by the love potion in the Tristan-Isolde story where sexual connection is fate. *The Father* opens as civilized nineteenth-century marital disagreement, and by the time it is over, the Captain has been systematically dismantled from a proud scientist to an infantile form in a straitjacket. *Miss Julie* is structured by a kind of recurring *huis clos* mechanism: Jean is trapped in the elegant outhouse and discovers his love for Julie as he makes his way through feces; Julie is trapped in Jean's bedroom as the revelers enter the kitchen; finally, Julie's suicide ritualistically closes the play, much like the final gesture in a *corrida*, as she commands Jean to command her to die, a splendid paradigm of dispossession and transferral. *The Dance of Death* would appear to be less grim in its depiction of coupling, but the comic view of marriage as eternal repetition merely adds to the case I am trying to make for Strindberg: namely, that he sees the couple as a new configuration, a *single* figure imbued with the kind of barbaric power that we discern in Shakespeare's "beast that makes two backs." Union with the other, whether it be the chains of marriage or the impulse of passion, confers a new shape on the life of the self, and the placing of the Captain in the straitjacket at the end of *The Father* is emblematic of Strindberg's view. There is a ferocity of pure conflict in these plays which may not exist anywhere else in the nineteenth century: Ibsen's Nora can walk out, even

Hedda Gabler does herself in as a proud, integral self, whereas the unfurling of Strindberg's plays is one of rigorous entrapment, a shrinking of space or maneuvering room.

The view of human relations as poisonous entrapment is equally present in the later, more experimental plays. *A Dream Play* appears to break out of the claustrophobic frame of the naturalist plays, given its inclusion of myth and fantasy and its episodic structure, but in its depiction of the union of Indra's daughter and the lawyer, it puts forth the same corrosive picture of relationship as repetition and asphyxiation; if anything, the picture of marriage in this play is even more sobering, since there is no malice involved, merely the quasi-structuralist certitude that people living together make a hell-on-earth for each other. "One person's pleasure is another's pain," as the lawyer sorrowfully informs his wife, and Strindberg illustrates both the sadism and the economy of this bind with the poise of a choreographer:

> LAWYER: . . . By the way, where is the paper?
> DAUGHTER (*embarrassed*): Which paper?
> LAWYER (*harshly*): Do I get more than one paper?
> DAUGHTER: Try to smile, and don't speak harshly . . . I started the fire with your paper.
> LAWYER (*violently*): Goddamn it!
> DAUGHTER: Remember, smile! . . . I burned it because it ridiculed the things I believe in . . .
> LAWYER: And that I don't believe in. Well! . . . (*smashes his fist in his hand furiously*) Oh, I'll smile. I'll smile so hard every tooth will show . . . I'll be considerate and keep my opinions to myself, and be evasive and hypocritical. So, you've burned up my newspaper! Well! (*adjusts the hanging on the bedpost*) You see! Here I am tidying up again, and making you angry! . . . Agnes, this is simply impossible!
> DAUGHTER: Of course it is!
> LAWYER: And yet we must put up with it, not because of our vows, but for the sake of the child.
> DAUGHTER: That's true. For the child. Oh!—Oh! . . . We must put up with it!
> LAWYER: I have to go out to my clients. Listen to them buzzing impatiently! They can't wait to tear at each other, to have each other fined and imprisoned . . . lost souls.

DAUGHTER: Poor, poor people! And this pasting! (*she bows her head in silent despair.*)

KRISTINE: I'm pasting. I'm pasting. (*The* LAWYER *stands at the door twisting the doorknob nervously.*)

DAUGHTER: Oh, how the doorknob screeches. It's as if you were twisting a knife in my heart . . .

LAWYER: I'm twisting, I'm twisting . . .

DAUGHTER: Please, don't!

LAWYER: I'm twisting . . .

DAUGHTER: No!

LAWYER: I'm . . .[12]

It is all dreadfully of a piece—the marriage, the lawyer's practice, the stage directions, the intolerable pasting and twisting—a strangely melodious concert of misery, a multilevel depiction of encroachment. The central icon of the play is a magic door, because the central event of Strindbergian drama is enclosure, suffocation; and Kristine's manic "I'm pasting, I'm pasting," perfectly caps the *huis clos* drama of the couple, but never before had it seemed quite so musical, quite so much of a ballet as it does here.

The most celebrated text in the Strindberg repertory, the one that has had the most potent impact on modern theater, is doubtless *The Ghost Sonata*, and its surrealist dramaturgy—mummies in closets, on-the-spot transformations, events on stage that are visible to some and invisible to others—gives a final hallucinatory power to the relationship theme. To compare this virulent, brief play with Ibsen's classic counterpart about ghosts, is to measure the prodigious quantum leap made by Strindberg in his exploration of theatrical possibility. Ibsen announces his truths about the living dead, but Strindberg puts them on the stage, in all their living horror. He takes the polite world of

12. August Strindberg, *A Dream Play*, in *Strindberg: Five Plays*, trans. Harry G. Carlson (New York: New American Library, 1984), pp. 234–35. This scene is, if anything, even sharper in the Swedish. "Le nu," the Swedish says, "smile now," rather than "try to smile." Carlson has taken an interesting liberty with his "twisting a knife in my heart" and "twisting . . . twisting," because the Swedish reads "som om du kramade mitt hjärtas fjädrar," or "as if you squeezed [hugged, embraced] the springs of my heart," which is followed by "jag kramar, jag kramar," or "I squeeze, I squeeze." "Twisting a knife" is more sinister (and more conventional) than squeezing the heart's springs, but it loses the "kramar . . . kramar" overtones of squeezing to death, of an embrace becoming intolerable.

upper-class decorum and reveals it to be a snakepit, concealing baseness, crime, and betrayal. To expose this muck is to demonstrate a new picture of relations: illegitimate children, adultery, murder, abandonment. Ibsen (and Dickens) had done this sort of thing already, but their pace was leisurely and their setting capacious; Strindberg achieves his effects with startling economy, limits himself to a single building, shows that its doomed inhabitants are endlessly twisted and tied in each other's strings and nets. In a letter to his German translator, Strindberg wrote:

> It is *schauderhaft* like life, when the veil falls from our eyes and we see *Das Ding an sich*. It has shape and content, the wisdom that comes with age, as our knowledge increases and we learn to understand. This is how "The Weaver" weaves men's destinies; secrets like these are to be found in *every* home.[13]

In addition to the expected network of liaisons, betrayals, and rivalries that "unite" the principals, Strindberg adds new ingredients of his own: he posits a kind of generalized vampirism at work in human affairs, a broad canvas of bloodsuckers and victims, some "interested," others, like the cook who drinks the juices from the meat and the wine from the bottles, simply parasites by vocation, nothing personal intended. But the chief vampire of the play is the unforgettable Mr. Hummel, its central character, the man who essentially devours others by exposing their lies and sham. He is the man who goes through walls:

> He looks at houses, tears them down, widens streets, builds over public squares. But he also breaks into houses, crawls through windows, destroys people's lives, kills his enemies, and forgives nothing.[14]

Hummel moles his way into secrets, invades this apartment house pretty much like the plague, revealing and infecting as he goes. He is an audacious creation, a kind of monstrous portrait of the artist as garbage collector. But the filth he brings is a match for what he uncovers, as if you could not know disease without being diseased; every crime he reveals is also a crime he has committed, and in him

13. Quoted in Michael Meyer's introduction to *The Ghost Sonata*, in *The Plays of Strindberg*, ed. Meyer (New York: Vintage Books, 1964), I, p. 420.
14. August Strindberg, *The Ghost Sonata*, in *Strindberg: Five Plays*, p. 287.

Strindberg has taken the already tarnished truth-seeker of Ibsen's *Wild Duck* and contaminated him beyond recognition.

All of these plays present a dark view of human connectedness, and the radical experiments of the latter plays may be seen as efforts to widen the picture, to get onto the stage that tentacular structure which would finally show the range of venomous liaisons that humans weave and excrete about themselves. This view of the enmeshed self goes beyond the erotic. It announces a program of paranoia and entrapment that extends to every phase of human activity, and it is dubious whether any art form—regardless of one's genius for innovation—could adequately mirror Strindberg's tortured sense of relationship.[15] How would you give form to the kind of virulent bondage expressed in this anecdote told by the painter Edvard Munch to a friend:

> "Strindberg lived next door until yesterday," said Munch. "But now he has gone quite mad. Look what he has written to me: 'Everybody knows that it is physically possible to extinguish a light through a thick wall. I am sure you want to kill me. But I'll prevent it. You are not to become my murderer.' "[16]

15. See Karl Jaspers' famous *Strindberg und Van Gogh: Versuch einer pathographischen Analyse unter vergleichender Heranziehung von Swedenborg und Hölderlin* (Munich: Piper, 1950), for a systematic interpretation of Strindberg's "testing" mania along lines of neurosis and persecution mania. Jaspers is particularly drawn to Strindberg's astounding "lucidity" in matters of his own psychic disturbances.

16. This anecdote comes from Max Dauthendy, who had it from Munch; it is quoted by Werner Timm in his *The Graphic Art of Edvard Munch*, trans. Ruth Michaelis-Jena (London: Studio Vista, 1969), p. 41. In reading about Strindberg's life (and Munch's as well, but that is another matter), one is struck over and over by his sense of persecution and resurrection. Consider the following letter written by Strindberg to Adolf Paul in 1894: "They [Lidforss and Przybyszewski] will destroy themselves, for they know that he who touches me dies, as when one carelessly fingers an electric accumulator. But without my needing to raise my hand . . . They attack me in Stockholm and I am dead one day, then pop up in Karlstad; they kill me in Christiania and I pop up in Paris . . . I fell in Rome, was whistled in Naples, rose like a sun in Copenhagen; was hissed in Berlin by Aspasia [Dagny Juel] and the cuckolds, and popped up at once in Moscow . . . No, they won't extirpate me, but I can extirpate my enemies . . . Today my wife has presented me with a daughter" (Michael Meyer, *Strindberg: A Biography* [New York: Random House, 1985], pp. 295–96). It should be added that Meyer's new biography

Here is a world of liberated desire that has become omnipotent. Time and space neither bind nor protect. You can be struck down from afar. The universe becomes an extended network of power, an energy system, and it is quite possible to regard Strindberg's major work as an exploration of that system, a new kind of mapping that reconceives the whereabouts of the individual.

*

The single most remarkable Strindberg text, from this point of view, is the novel, *Inferno*, a seminal account of Strindberg's bout with near-madness in the mid 1890s. Although Swedish criticism has always regarded this text as a central item for understanding Strindberg, it is strangely unread outside of Scandinavia.[17] The title *Inferno* announces Strindberg's debt to Dante, but it also indicates the tone of this strange fiction: the larger map of one's connections will be nothing less than hell, a world where linkage is experienced entirely as suffering. We reach, here, the antipodes of the Borgesian celebration of pattern and light. In *Inferno*, the larger picture is endlessly encroaching and punitive. Finally, it is worth insisting that we are dealing here with a work of art. The few Swedish critics who speak of artistry in this text do so as a way of branding Strindberg a liar, flouting his inventions as evidence precisely of bad faith; on the contrary, *Inferno* is most fascinating as literature, especially when one focuses on the brilliant iconography Strindberg devises for human relationship, an iconography which is so coherent that it, much like the imagery of *Naked Lunch*, unifies all the material around it, and

---

is crammed full of these kinds of disclosures, whereas the more balanced (and more discerning) Swedish biography written by Olof Lagercrantz, *August Strindberg* (Stockholm: Wahlström & Widstrand, 1979), ascribes a great deal of such invective to Strindberg's conscious theatricality; Evert Spinchorn takes pretty much the same "reasoned" view of Strindberg in the "guinea pig" thesis he presents in his reading of the plays, *Strindberg as Dramatist* (New Haven: Yale University Press, 1982).

17. The standard work on *Inferno* is Gunnar Brandell's *Strindberg in Inferno*, trans. Barry Jacobs (Cambridge: Harvard University Press, 1974); beyond that there is the 1936 ground-breaking study by Martin Lamm, *Strindberg och makterna* (Uppsala: Svenska Kyrkans Diakonistryrelses Bokförlag). I am indebted to both these scholars and also to Mary Sandbach for her lengthy and informative introduction to *Strindberg: Inferno, From an Occult Diary* (Harmondsworth, Eng.: Penguin, 1979), pp. 7–90.

thereby makes of this confessional text a haunting, obsessive, tragically overdetermined work of art.

What seems particularly striking about *Inferno* is its relentless pursuit of "energy," of the forces that move both the material and the moral world. Strindberg is delivering a picture of things where everything is suddenly alive, where the ordinarily discrete realms of physics and religion are seen to coexist in the same force field. Sensory perceptions are doubled by a strange spiritual aura; the phenomenal world is bristling with pattern for the person who knows how to read; the individual is (wittingly or not, like it or not) attuned to forces and powers ranging from cyclones of hatred to full-fledged *Doppelgänger* who appear in cafés and bars, implicating the protagonist's life in a strange relational mesh that mocks empirical logic. One could say that Strindberg is forging a new kind of grammar here, in that he refuses (is unable) to abide by the Western divisive notions of here versus there, spirit versus matter, now versus then, and instead is at pains to reconstruct his perceptual apparatus into a massive NOW, a new composite of forces and energies. Consider, in that light, a letter written to Torsten Hedlund during the height of the *Inferno* crisis:

> . . . Hallucinations, fantasies, dreams, seems to me to possess a high degree of reality. If I see my pillow assume human shapes those shapes are there, and if any one says they are only (!) created by my imagination, I answer—you say only? What my inner eye sees means more to me! And what I see in my pillow, which is made of birds' feathers, once bearers of life, and of flax, in whose fibres vitality has traveled, is soul, creative power, and reality, as I can draw those shapes, show them to others.
>
> And I hear a sound in my pillow, sometimes like a cricket. The noise that grasshoppers make in the grass has always seemed magic to me. Like a ventriloquist, for I have always fancied that the sound came from an empty hall under the earth. Suppose that the grasshopper has sung in a field of flax, don't you think that Nature or the creator can make a phonograph from its fibres, so that his song resounds for my inner ear when, by suffering, self-denial, and prayer, this has been prepared to receive more distant sounds than it normally does? But this is where your "natural explanations" fail us, and I abandon them forthwith.[18]

18. Sandbach, "Introduction," p. 56.

There is something splendid in this ecology which Strindberg depicts, and on the face of it, we do not seem all that far from the "heavenly" constructs devised by Borges; but—and this is crucial—one is struck by the insistence that suffering is what initiates us into this new cosmos. We see a kind of affective "tracking" in these lines, an uncanny apprehension of energy and life in all its guises, and a generous sense of opened channels and strange new thoroughfares.

To be sure, there is an unmistakable religious cast to *Inferno*. With the aid of Dante and Swedenborg, Strindberg comes to view his trials and travails as a living hell, and some fifty years before Sartre proclaimed, "l'Enfer, c'est les autres," Strindberg defined hell precisely as a relational straitjacket:

> It is earth itself that is Hell, the prison constructed for us by an intelligence superior to our own, in which I could not take a step without injuring the happiness of others, and in which my fellow creatures could not enjoy their own happiness without causing me pain. [211]

There is but a short step to take from this view of hell to its "privatist" ethical corollary—that we live in a hell of our own devising, that we are paying for our transgressions throughout our lives. Strindberg himself often took this step, and so too does much Strindberg criticism; and where the moral explanation does not cover, then a medical one is introduced, establishing a more acceptable causal relationship between our deeds and our visions. Hence, theories abound as to what *actually* was producing the hallucinations chronicled in *Inferno*, and we have been treated to a series of explanations ranging from schizophrenia, persecution complex, toxic poisoning (through alcohol and absinthe) on to downright lying (on the part of Strindberg).[19] Even Gunnar Brandell's carefully reasoned and exhaustive study of *Inferno*, to which we are indebted for the fullest picture available of what went "into" the text, leads ultimately to a thesis of sublimated guilt, and once again one feels that more attention should be given to the actual topography of Strindberg's "dreamscapes" and less to the so-called causes of which they are the so-called symptoms.

But my real argument is that the beauty and significance of *Inferno* lie on the far side of any explanatory myth, beyond all notions of causality, delivering a new world of utter immediacy. In this new dispensation, nothing remains discrete or indifferent; every detail, all

19. Ibid., p. 38.

of the "choses vues," fit into a privatist teleology, are the reified, external markers of a life that has gone strangely public. The tone of this text is therefore alarmingly suspicious, on the lookout for congruences and correspondences. Two stark, amazing theses emerge from *Inferno*: (1) matter and spirit are inseparable; (2) explanations fail. Let us examine both these premises in more detail, beginning with the latter. As Strindberg and his friend, the American painter (suspected, naturally enough, to be a *Doppelgänger* for the faith healer Francis Schlatter), compare their respective visionary encounters, commenting on the strange human shapes formed by pansies in the window or the cupola of the Hôtel des Invalides, the sculptor asks the inevitable rationalist question: "How are you going to explain these phenomena?" (149). Strindberg's answer is arguably the most modern statement in his book, but it is also of a piece with the poetic truth of the book: "Explain it? Has anyone ever explained anything except by paraphrasing one set of words by another set?" (149). Not only are visions more compelling than explanations (and this cannot fail to count for the writer), but explanations themselves are never more than a sleight of hand, a form of translation, a shuffling from one set of signifiers to another, an effort to deny the bold unitary logic of vision by breaking it up and down into a cause-and-effect paradigm. The world of Strindberg, especially the connections he experiences with that world, is far more interesting in terms of effects than of causes. *Inferno* is fascinating because it initiates the reader into the bizarre landscape of its protagonist, and no amount of reasoning will help us out:

> Enter your room alone at night-time and you will find that someone has got there before you. You will not see him, but you will sense his presence. Go to the lunatic asylum and consult the psychiatrist. He will talk to you of neurasthenia, paranoia, angina pectoris, and the like, but he will never cure you.
>
> Where will you go, then, all you who suffer from sleeplessness, and you who walk the streets waiting for the sun to rise?
>
> The Mills of the Universe, the Mills of God, these are the two expressions that are often used.
>
> Have you had in your ears the humming that resembles the noise of a water-mill? Have you noticed, in the stillness of the night, or even in broad daylight, how memories of your past life stir and are resurrected, one by one or two by two? All the mistakes you have made, all your crimes, all your follies, that make

> you blush to your very ear-tips, bring a cold sweat to your brow and send shivers down your spine.
>
> You relive the life you have lived, from your birth to the day that is. You suffer again all the sufferings you have endured, you drink again all the cups of bitterness you have so often drained. You crucify your skeleton, as there is no longer any flesh to mortify. You send your spirit to the stake, as your heart is already burned to ashes.
>
> Do you recognize the truth of all this?
>
> These are the Mills of God, that grind slow but grind exceeding small—and black. You are ground to powder and you think it is all over. But no, it will begin again and you will be put through the mill once more. [263–64]

Much of the force of *Inferno* is caught in these harrowing lines. In his direct address to the reader, Strindberg claims common cause with humanity. All of us, he seems to be saying, are afflicted with symptoms and signs that cannot be accommodated by medical explanations. To be sure, one's own past is held accountable for these manifestations, but even the past is shown to be anything but past or over; rather, one's deeds and—perhaps more important—one's desires are endlessly alive and potent, shaping one's environment long after they are presumably over or forgotten. The humming and the water mill also suggest the fluidity of energy itself, seen in the pulsating life of our past, seen earlier in the shapes and sounds discovered in one's pillow. The dominant image, of course, is the Mills of God, and Strindberg takes care to emphasize its status as image, expression, metaphor. Traditional though the image is, it recovers some of its disturbing power in the use Strindberg makes of it: we see not only the crushing punishment and annihilation meted out by the gods, but, equally important, we are struck by the actual image itself, the mill as generator, as producer of energy and power. Strindberg invites us to see in the humming and the water mill the very origin of the memories and symptoms that are to come. The human psyche is here defined as a power system, a network of channels and circuits through and over which energy flows.[20]

20. Much of the criticism of *Inferno* has understandably focused on the religious elements of the text, and the "conversion" Strindberg presumably experienced when he finally read Swedenborg (as well as his lifelong wrestling with religious doctrine and principles). Göran Stockenström has interpreted this imagery along traditional religious lines in his *Ismael i Öknen:*

This cluster of images can be "unpacked" still further, if we examine the later poem, "Street Scenes III (Gatubilder III)" which leads us yet closer to Strindberg's "power station."

Dark is the hill, dark the house—
but darkest is its cellar—
subterranean, windowless—
and the staircase serves as door and window—
and down there deepest in the darkness
stands a humming dynamo,
sparks flying around its wheels:
black and horrifying, hidden,
it grinds light for the entire neighborhood.

[Mörk är backen, mörkt är huset—
mörkast dock dess källarvåning—
underjordisk, inga gluggar—
källarhalsen är båd' dörr och fönster—
och därnere längst i mörkret
syns en dynamo som surrar,
så det gnistrar omkring hjulen:
svart och hemsk, i det fördolda
mal han ljus åt hela trakten.][21]

The poet Lars Gustafsson has offered one of the most eloquent commentaries on this poem, emphasizing both the Freudian and the linguistic features of the piece.[22] The humming generator that works in the dark, while producing light for the entire area, is an apt figure for the sublimated sexual energy that produces art. One is also struck by the remarkable metaphor of *grinding light* ("mal han ljus"), an old verb in a new role. Our metaphors speak our evolving history, and Strindberg has intentionally mixed his registers, giving us an agrarian verb for an electrical phenomenon. One is not too far here from the logic of Thomas Kuhn's conceptual revolutions, the shifting of paradigms from one age to another. Here, too, it behooves us to recognize that this tortured mind-set is at once personal and representa-

Strindberg som mystiker (Uppsala: Acta Universitatis Upsaliensis, 1972), p. 192.

21. August Strindberg, "Gatubilder III," quoted in Lars Gustafsson, *Strandhugg i Svensk Poesi* (Kristianstad: F.I.B., 1977), p. 23.

22. Gustafsson, *Strandhugg i Svensk Poesi*, p. 25.

tive, even emblematic; Strindberg wants us to see that a new era is at hand, that the power from this dark room makes our light, unseen though it is, accustomed though we are to fearing the dark. Freud seems close here, but not only Freud, for the poem centralizes the shift in the *production* and *dispersal* of energy, leaving us ultimately with an image of the human mind as "public utility" in the most rigorous sense of the term.

But if the poem shows the mind-generator as the producer of current, we see, in *Inferno*, a drastic picture of things the other way around. The mills that grind exceeding fine, that purify the subject into black dust, seem to have eroded all the defenses and barriers that usually keep the world at bay. Instead, it rushes in, unstoppable, on currents and in channels against which there is no defense: the ears hum, the heart palpitates, the objects and the people you see are the figures of your past, of your dreams. Here is the imperious new ecosystem that Strindberg has depicted, a view of psychic entrapment that is infinitely more fascinating in its workings than it might be in terms of any critical explanation offered for it. Critics have pointed out Strindberg's interest in figures such as Rochas and Guaïta, both of whom advanced theories of telepathy and invisible currents, and indeed, one could find figures all over Europe in the 1890s evincing interest in mesmerism, hypnotism, suggestion psychology, hysteria, and the like. But it would not be easy to find any major artist who transformed these materials in quite the way Strindberg did. *Inferno* is a nodal text because it offers us a radically new picture of man's place in his world. Opened and invaded, coextensive with the world, the Strindberg self resembles nothing quite so much as the prodigious creature drawn by Munch in "The Scream," a figure of pure victimization, a medium in the most literal sense of the word. The nineteenth century is coming to an end in these texts, and a new world view is being adumbrated, one considerably closer to our own Einsteinian scheme of things. It is now time to take a closer look at how Strindberg does it.

Early on, *Inferno* informs us of a potent spirit world. We are made to realize that the alchemist enterprise is a punishable invasion into God's secrets, and we learn that the protagonist is committed to "witchcraft and telepathy" (128). Above all, we see a world of energized signs: street names seem annunciatory, portentous initials (such as A. S.) and numbers or letters denoting crucial chemical compounds appear at dramatic moments, "chance" accidents are quickly seen as tailor-made humiliations and punishments. The outside world increasingly loses its randomness and alterity, as it becomes increasingly yoked into some preordained scenario, some mysterious teleology where everything fits, is locked into a damning pattern.[23] There is precious little freedom in such a realm, and we can anticipate that each and every event will be gruesomely overdetermined, calling into play some earlier misdeed or vice on Strindberg's part. At a certain point, however, the pace and the density of these episodes begin to alter, and this is initially signaled by the entry of "doubles" onto the stage. The following passage shows us what Strindberg is able to do with these "bristling" situations:

> Disquieting things happened in the hotel. The day after my arrival I found, on the board in the vestibule upon which the keys of the rooms were hung, a letter addressed to a Mr X, a student whose name was the same as my wife's. The stamp bore the postmark Dornach, the name of the Austrian village where my wife and child were living. This was mysterious, as I was quite certain that Dornach had no post office.
>
> This letter, displayed in a way that was obviously intended to attract attention, was followed by several more. The next one was addressed to Dr Bitter and postmarked Vienna. A third bore an assumed Polish name, Schmulachowsky.
>
> Clearly the Devil now had a finger in the pie, for that name was pure fabrication. I realized where my thoughts were being

23. Needless to say, this kind of mindset can cause a number of practical problems, leading its "holder" to make some strange assumptions about the significance of ordinary events, often transforming "innocent" details into portentous messages. It seems that Strindberg's friends occasionally took advantage of this proclivity of his, as the following story recounted by Frederick Delius suggests: "His [Strindberg's] interest in spirits caused Leclerc [*sic*] and me to play a joke on him. I asked them both to my rooms one evening, and after dinner we had a spiritualist séance in the form of table rapping. The lights were turned down and we joined hands around a small table. After ten minutes' ominous silence the table began to rap and Leclerc asked it what message the spirits had for us. The first letter rapped out was M, and with each letter Strindberg's interest and excitement seemed to increase, and slowly came the momentous letters 'MERDE.' I do not think he ever quite forgave us for this . . . He was extraordinarily superstitious, for often on our walks he would suddenly refuse to go up a certain street on the pretext that some accident or misfortune was awaiting him there" (quoted in Meyer, *Strindberg*, p. 335).

> directed, namely to one of my mortal enemies who lived in Berlin.
>
> Yet another that arrived had on it a Swedish name that reminded me of an enemy in my native land. Finally came a letter posted in Vienna, on which was printed the face of Dr Eder's firm of analytical chemists. In fact, someone was spying on my synthesis of gold.
>
> I had no doubts left. This was a plot, but the Devil himself must have shuffled the cards for the tricksters. No ordinary mortal could have hit on the idea of sending my suspicions roaming to the four quarters of the globe; it was altogether too contrived.
>
> When I asked the waiter to tell me about Mr X he artlessly replied that he was an Alsatian. I could get nothing more out of him. Once, when I returned from my morning walk, there was a card in the rack just by my key. For one moment I was tempted to solve the riddle by having a look at it, but my good angel immobilized my hand at the very instant that a young man appeared from his hiding place behind the door.
>
> I looked at his face. He was like my wife. We bowed to each other without uttering a word, and walked off in opposite directions.
>
> I have never been able to get to the bottom of this plot and still do not know who the conspirators were, as my wife has neither brothers nor male cousins.
>
> This state of suspense and the perpetual threat of vengeance was torment and enough for half a year. I bore this, like everything else, as a punishment for sins known and unknown.[24]

Quoted in its entirety, this episode displays the elaborateness and the fastidiousness with which Strindberg "re-scripts" the events that befall him, thrusting them all into a private psychodrama, drenched with intentionality: disguised names, devil's control, plots, hiding-places, and the like. The fine sense of certainty that is conveyed by Strindberg's authoritative tone—"quite certain," "obviously intended," "assumed Polish name," "Clearly," "In fact," "no doubts left," "altogether too contrived[!]"—must give the reader pause, for there is something unsettling in any narrative voice that is so oddly and intuitively sure of its findings. It is also worth noting the special

24. August Strindberg, *Inferno*, trans. Mary Sandbach, pp. 177–78. Subsequent quotations will be taken from this edition and noted parenthetically in the body of the text.

role accorded to language: letters, names of villages and people, these are the harbingers of that newer vision which *Inferno* announces, a vision of supreme coherence, since nothing can be random or innocuous in such a scheme. This peculiar type of "feathering one's nest" borders on comedy in the passage just quoted, as we see Strindberg reaching far and wide in his interpretations, yet remaining significantly untouched by it all, bowing wordlessly to the mysterious Mr. X, as safe and distant in his speculations as a character in a tale by Henry James (whose later work such passages resemble).

Somewhat like a cautionary *algebraic* tale, however, the blank spots, the "unknowns," the Mr. X's all become filled in, take on the specificity of doom itself. It all begins with the sound of a piano:

> I straightened my back, drew a deep breath, my whole self metamorphosized. It was Schumann's *Aufschwung*. And what was more, I was sure that it was *he* who was playing it. My friend the Russian, my pupil who had called me "Father" because I had taught him all he knew, my *famulus* who had called me "Master" and had kissed my hands because his life had begun where mine had ended. He had come from Berlin to Paris to kill me, just as he had killed me in Berlin, and for what reason? Because Fate had decreed that the woman who was now his wife had been my mistress before he had known her? [151–52]

Thus begins the saga of Strindberg haunted by the Pole Stanislav Przybyszewski, called Popoffsky in the text, already hinted at in the "assumed Polish name, Schmulachowsky" and obscurely lurking behind Mr. X, now rendered increasingly and pathologically present within the narrative. Strindberg persistently interprets these unsettling experiences as some personal punishment meted out for his past sins, both "known and unknown," and a good deal is known about the relations between Strindberg, Przybyszewski, Dagny Juel, and Munch in the tumultuous Berlin adventures that preceded his arrival in Paris. But, once again, one needs to distinguish sharply between the harrowing psychic phenomena depicted in *Inferno* and all explanatory theses that might account for them, including Strindberg's own hypotheses. What is rendered indelibly in *Inferno* is the transcendent power of spirit, the agonizing discovery that the world is filled with ghosts, avenging angels that speak in countless tongues and signs. Where they come from counts less than the fact that they are there. They cannot be explained (away):

> Enter your room alone at night-time and you will find that someone has got there before you. You will not see him, but you will sense his presence. Go to the lunatic asylum and consult the psychiatrist. He will talk to you of neurasthenia, paranoia, angina pectoris, and the like, but he will never cure you. [263]

In the haunting, lurking presence of Popoffsky, we may discern the beginning of a veritable psychic invasion. The external signs pile up: spilled absinthe, filth in his glass, being taken for a beggar, unaccountably striking terror into Munch, staring at Munch's portrait of Przybyszewski where the head seems cut off (just as Strindberg had dreamed it), encountering the written words "marten" and "vulture" (bringing to mind the Pole and his wife), hearing that the Pole has poisoned his wife and children (*sic*) and fearing that he has come to Paris to do the same to Strindberg. This sense of vampirism and encroachment is expressed in a crucial image that is central to this entire essay: "the Russian's hatred is causing me pain such as one might feel from the current of an electric machine" (163).

We have already seen the "humming" and the water wheel and the mill; these images can be said to constitute a coherent iconography of power and energy, and they invariably appear as conduits for the visitations Strindberg is to receive. But the dominant metaphor (if it is a metaphor) is electricity, and as the poem "Gatubilder III" makes evident, electricity betokens the energy of the mind, the flowing current between poet and community, a current that can insidiously flow upstream as well as downstream. Hence, it comes as no surprise that the stranger who kept his distance as Mr. X now reappears in a far more invasive fashion:

> At the beginning of July all the students left for their holidays and the hotel was unoccupied. My curiosity was therefore aroused by the arrival of a stranger, who was put into the room adjacent to my writing desk. This unknown man never uttered a word; he seemed to be occupied in writing something behind the wooden partition that separated us. All the same, it was odd that he should push back his chair every time I moved mine. He repeated my every movement in a way that suggested that he wanted to annoy me by imitating me.
>
> This went on for three days. On the fourth I made the following observation. When I went to bed the man in the room next to my desk went to bed too, but in the room on the other side, next to my bed. As I lay in bed I could hear him lying there,

> stretched out parallel to me. I could hear him turning the pages of a book, putting out the lamp, breathing deeply, turning over and falling asleep.
>
> Complete silence then reigned in the room adjacent to my writing desk. This would only mean that he was occupying both rooms. How unpleasant to be besieged on both sides at once! [172–73]

Although the passage stresses physical separation (wooden partition, other side of the wall), a form of ghostly, wordless intercourse is clearly taking place. Whoever or whatever is there is beginning to fuse with Strindberg, through repetititon of movements and gestures. Once again, we cannot fail to see that this fusion is intricately related to *writing* (he is next to the writing desk, he is writing something, he is reading a book), and writing itself seems linked to sleeping or dreaming, as if all these activities were privileged modes of communication. We see, ultimately, two men going to bed together ("besieged on both sides at once" has a disturbing ring to it), but this intimacy is soon to become pure pain. Strindberg now speaks of being "subjected to an electric current, passing between the two rooms," and he shrieks, "Someone is killing me! I will not be killed!" (175).

Strindberg leaves the fateful Hôtel Orfila in all haste, but the famous chase is now on. In the next hotel, near the Jardin des Plantes, strange lodgers again appear, the servant girl looks at him with pity, and he knows that the execution has been decreed. But why?

> In the room above mine they had set up a wheel that went round and round all day. Condemned to death! I was convinced of it. But by whom? By the Russians? By the devout, by the Catholics, the Jesuits, the theosophists? For what reason? As a sorcerer or a practitioner of the black arts? Perhaps it was by the police, as an anarchist? [178]

Note, once more, the folly of explanations. The "powers" that have been offended are legion, and one's crimes are endless, but the punishment never varies. That night, after Strindberg has ceremoniously made his adieus and prepared himself for death, that wheel which goes round and round, hums and grinds, goes again into action:

> I awoke. A clock in the house struck two, a door was shut, and I was drawn from my bed as if by a vacuum pump that was sucking at my heart.

> Hardly had my feet touched the floor than a stream of electricity was discharged upon the nape of my neck, pressing me to the ground. I struggled up, grabbed my clothes, and tore out into the garden, a prey to the most horrible palpitations. [182]

He flees Paris for Dieppe and is again waylaid:

> But now a discharge like a cyclone fell upon me and tore me from my bed. The hunt was on once more. I hid behind walls, I lay close to doorways, in front of fireplaces. Wherever I went, the furies sought me out. [186]

Then, in Ystad, he seeks asylum at the home of his friend, Dr. Eliassin, and once again the fateful icons reappear, regrouped:

> My attention was immediately attracted to an American bedstead of iron, whose four uprights were surmounted by brass knobs that resembled the conductors of an electric machine. In addition there was a flexible mattress, the springs of which were made of copper wire, twisted into spirals like those of a Ruhmkorff induction coil. [189]

The grand finale orchestrates all these "elements" into the most spectacular alchemist performance of the novel, a moment of pure transformational energy, pure metamorphosis, in which all the disparate images and forces fuse together, and the locus of their fusion is the besieged self:

> I was also much disturbed by what sounded like the steady roar of a machine. As it happened, I had been plagued by a buzzing in my ears ever since I left the Hôtel Orfila, a noise that resembled the pounding of a water-wheel. I was therefore doubtful whether the roaring noise I heard was real or not, and inquired about it.
>
> "The press in the printing house next door."
>
> There was a simple and natural explanation for everything, but it was just this simplicity in the means employed that so much alarmed me and drove me mad.
>
> Then came night with its terrors. The sky was overcast, the air heavy; there was thunder about. I did not dare to go to bed and spent two hours writing letters. Annihilated by weariness, I undressed and crept between the sheets. An awful silence reigned over the house as I put out the lamp. In the gloom I could feel

> someone watching me, someone who now touched me lightly, groped for my heart and sucked. [190]

The author never explains the possible connections between these electrical disturbances and writing; indeed, the printing press seems to him an innocuous source of the roaring noise. But the reader can hardly mistake the bold logic of this text, a principle of linkage and connection that is so imperious that the protagonist even puts his ear to a telegraph post whose humming noise intrigues him, and listens "as if bewitched." On the one hand, the writhing, buffeted figure who is hurtled out of bed by massive jolts of current is undergoing what every modern reader recognizes as electrocution, or at the very least, an epileptic seizure, which is also an electrical overload in the brain. But the presence of generators, printing presses, writing, and dreaming indicates a communications network of extraordinary proportions, and we sense that these two systems are faces of each other: electric current is the neural conduit for human thought, not only one's own thoughts, but—and this is frightening—the thoughts of others as well; writing, too, we see, is a flowing current, a channel that connects minds divided by time and space, a circuit not only of energy, but also of power: psychic power, moral power, sexual power.

Power is everywhere imaged in terms of language and electricity in Strindberg's work. Olof Lagercrantz has demonstrated, in his biography of Strindberg, the Swede's extraordinary interest in language studies at the very end of his life, but one can find evidence throughout his work of the peculiar potency with which language and its vehicles can be vested. Everyone remembers the Count's boots in *Miss Julie*, but the speaking tube is perhaps more intriguing still as an icon of authority, invested with the kind of energy that fetishes and sacraments possess; it is here that the voice of the gods is to be heard, and, at a critical moment, it will be heard, at least by Jean if not by the spectator, and we realize that we are seeing a nineteenth-century "hi-tech" version of the Oracle. In some strange way, "language" is always entering the world of Strindberg's protagonists, and we may view the post office in *To Damascus* in a similar light, for there too the protagonist receives fateful messages, containing either money or humiliation, functioning almost like the classical messenger in Greek tragedy. *The Dance of Death* offers a similarly magic apparatus in its telegraph, that system of communication which Alice is forbidden to use, the visible network that links this enclosed tower-prison to a larger world. Things *flow* in Strindberg, and he obliges us to see the etymological purity of our dry term "influence," which comes to mean precisely "flowing into"; this flow is easily sexualized as well, so that he can refer to the impact of Nietzche's writings on him in terms of a seed that has entered the uterus of his mind and impregnated it. Indeed, for such a mind, jealousy is tantamount to a fear of invasion, since the woman's intercourse with another man is experienced as one's own sexual defilement.[25] The flip side of Strindberg's well-known egomania is a paranoid logic that decenters and displaces power, thinks in terms of conspiracy because it knows itself to be vulnerable and permeable and fundamentally passive in the face of the potent machinations of others. Little is more revealing, on this heading, than the remarkable passages in Strindberg's *Occult Diary* where he recounts the frequent nightly visitations of Harriet Bosse, who was living estranged from him, sexual encounters experienced alone and quite helplessly. What does one make of these "encounters," these strangely moving experiences that simply do not conform

25. Once again, the correspondence is revealing, and it says something about the fearful circularity of Strindberg's thinking. Meyer quotes a letter written by Strindberg to Lidforss in 1894: "Do you know what *sansclou* are? Buffon writes that fructified eggs have been found in men's penises. *Sansclou* are a *Dröppel*. A *Dröppel* is a heap of male semen found in a vagina. Now, if one mounts a woman over-filled with semen, a man can get another man's semen in his penis or testicles, and so the seeds grow and the *sanscloued* man finds himself in a perverse state of pregnancy which, however, is stopped by the lowering of temperature (ice-bags!) . . . Everything is in everything, and everything moves, even semen. Wombs are only birds' nests in which the cock lays his eggs" (*Strindberg*, pp. 288–89). Even here, there is a bold poetic vision at work, an imperious sense of multidirectionality that makes all channels and circuits "two-way" in nature and therefore threatening, since the so-called originator may find himself to be the recipient. One thinks of the fine passage that Joyce ascribes to Bloom at the end of his ventures: "If he had smiled why would he have smiled? To reflect that each one who enters imagines himself to be the first to enter whereas he is always the last term of a preceding series even if the first term of a succeeding one, each imagining himself to be first, last, only and alone, whereas he is neither first nor last nor only nor alone in a series originating in and repeated to infinity" (*Ulysses*, p. 731). These arrangements do not cause Strindberg to smile, but it is well to remember that Bloom encounters merely the imprint of his wife's lover in his bed, whereas Strindberg may be receiving actual seed unto himself; it is a rather more compromising turn of events, possessing a kind of intimacy and invasiveness altogether typical of the Strindbergian dilemma.

to any notion of masturbation or even dream, as we usually conceive it?

It is essential to bear in mind this strange "availability" which characterized Strindberg when one tries to assess his notion of "self." We then perceive the radical defensiveness of his project, and the following passage from *Inferno* acquires the resonance it deserves:

> All that I know, little as that may be, springs from one central point, my Ego. It is not the cult but the cultivation of this which seems to me to be the supreme and final goal of existence. . . . to kill the Ego is to commit suicide. [168]

Strindberg criticism has perhaps been too taken up with the all-too-available biographical data provided by the man himself, or with his formulations regarding "the Powers," and too inattentive to the audacious redefinition of "power as language" which informs so much of his work. Not only did he experience the writing of others as infectious, but he clearly regarded his own readers as "pregnant with the seed of my soul."[26] The combination of Strindberg's monistic beliefs and his peculiar temperament led to the making of an artistic universe that is astonishingly unified by channels and circuits of psychic and spiritual energy. Whereas most critics seem to feel that *To Damascus* and *A Dream Play* are the fullest, most successful artistic embodiments of these beliefs, it is nonetheless *Inferno* that most provocatively and succinctly makes the prophetic link between energy and writing, between power and language. Yet, "language as power" is a profoundly troubling proposition, and it by no means elevates or empowers the artist who uses it, no matter how much Strindberg desired such verbal clout; on the contrary, it leads to a radically decentered view of verbal energy, as if the humming wires and grinding mills and neural circuits themselves somehow pre-existed, antedated the fated individuals who become the helpless receivers. That is why the electricity metaphor is so apt. Electricity revolutionizes the older concepts of cause-and-effect and Newtonian force; electricity is a force field where contacts and connections are instantaneous and immediate, where the individual receiver suffers the power of the system. Seen in human terms, electricity connotes a universe that is literally charged and flowing, where those who are cursed with vision must record the violent frequencies of which the world is made. Choice does not exist in such a scheme. Nor is protection possible,

26. Quoted in Sandbach, "Introduction," p. 23.

since one comes to know the world in one's flesh, through the shocks one has received. Finally, such a view is, strangely enough, more anthropocentric than one might suspect, because it sees Mind itself as the great wheel, the mill, the generator, the origin of these forces.

3

Two great wheels of destiny: the one that operates an invasive power system in Strindberg, the other epiphanically glimpsed in a moment of "allness," just before his extinction as a self, by Borges' quester, Tzinacán. The Strindbergian drama of asphyxiation tells us that connection with others is intimate and immediate, that it usurps not only the maneuvering room, but even the breathing space of the self. There are no forking paths in Strindberg, no twelve-month reprieves to finish a play, no unfurling patterns of history to confer shape to experience. Instead, all is happening simultaneously, and the self is subject to take-overs every bit as brutal as we saw in Burroughs. But, there are no marketeers or junkies out there to do the taking-over, not even any Popoffsky's—despite Strindberg's paranoid certainty to the contrary. Rather, the landscape is filled with one's own ghosts, those living dead whom Ibsen located in the past and whom Proust brought home to the self, and these self-extensions make life into a minefield far more perilous than the terrain drawn up by Joyce for his creature Bloom.

More than any figure in this study, Strindberg lives in a world of intolerable connection: everyone he has ever known, every deed he has ever done or even thought of doing, is alive still, active out there, busily converting the most trivial experiences—a walk down the street, a drink in a bar—into a personalized manhunt. He is, as we saw, hooked up, and there is no longer any outside world at all, since the world can at any moment pulsate into him on neural channels and electrical frequencies against which there is no protection. At the risk of muddying and mixing one's metaphors, one might claim that Strindberg is being *crucified electrically*: the immediacy of crucifixion, the nails driven into the flesh, the piercing penetration of the body itself, hardly seems much of an exaggeration as a figure for the sensorial invasion depicted in *Inferno*.

How leisurely and civilized the Borgesian labyrinth appears, by contrast. Strindberg flees Paris for Dieppe, and he finds that he has gone nowhere, that the infernal machinery—like the ever-repeating furnishings of modern hotels—is always the same. In Borges, it all moves, mercifully, the other way. The asphyxiation caused by encroachment, by repetition, by shrinkage of one's living space, is wonderfully altered in the work of Borges, transformed into the wider reaches of time and space. A man in a cell finds a new world; a monster meets his death as ecstatic union; a tortured quester has seen the God's script; a tracked spy enacts and completes his ancestor's labyrinth; Judas partakes of divinity. Borges expands, moves *out* instead of *in*, and offers thereby a picture of relationship as salvation, as harmonious extension of the private life and the private view. The Strindbergian vision turns the manifold world into a private torture-chamber of one's own; in Borges, the garret where you live—be it a prison of stones or the body that dies—opens out into the universe.

CHAPTER SIX

Art and Seeing Clear

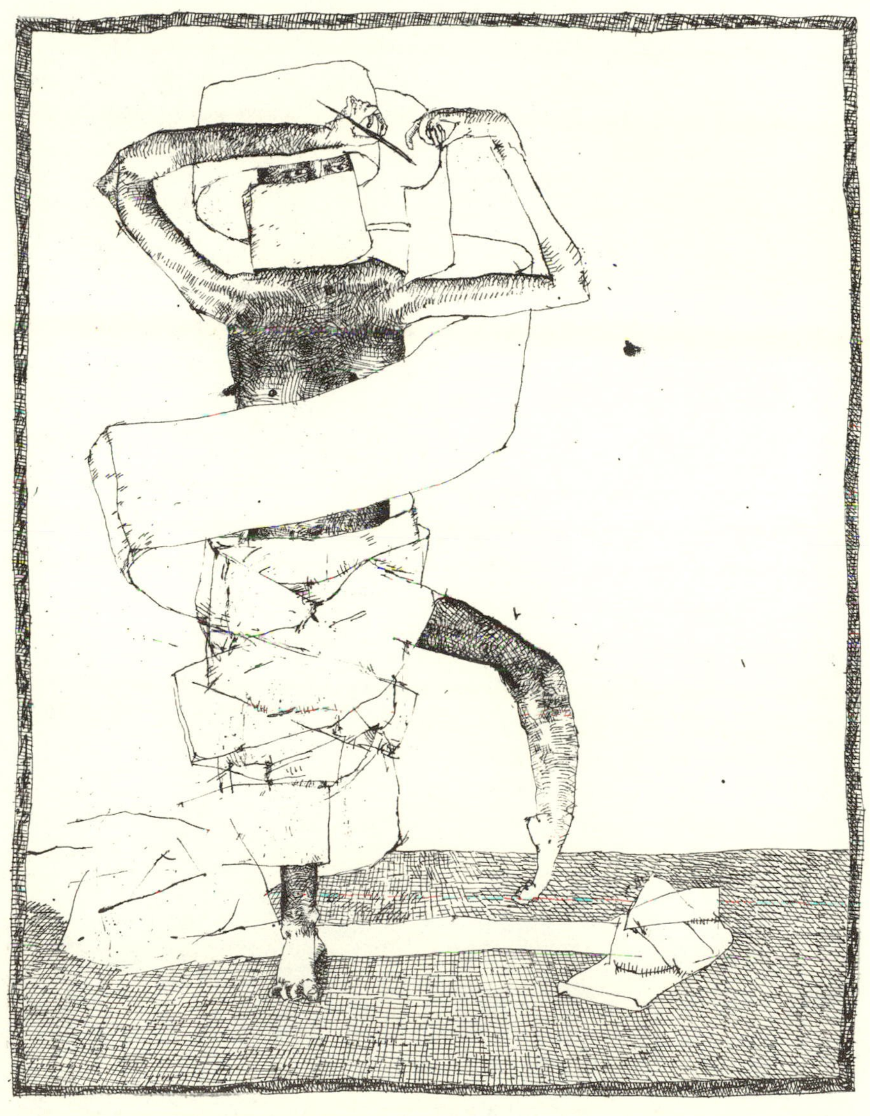

One of the oldest stories of our culture has to do with the discovery of relationship as fate. Oedipus comes to understand that nothing in his life has been either discrete or the way he has imagined it to be: the parents he thought were his were not his, the deformed ankles tell a story, the act of violence at the crossroads was itself a crossroads, he has lain with his mother and killed his father. As Teiresias angrily points out, Oedipus is a blind man in the most crucial areas of life:

> You have your eyes but see not where you are
> in sin, nor where you live, nor whom you live with.
> Do you know who your parents are? Unknowing
> you are an enemy to kith and kin
> in death, beneath the earth, and in this life.
> A deadly footed, double striking curse,
> from father and mother both, shall drive you forth
> out of this land, with darkness on your eyes,
> that now have such straight vision.[1]

Oedipus' hubris is significantly expressed by Sophocles in terms of "straight vision," a deluded sense of clarity and oneness, whereas the dreadful truths to be revealed are "double," a doubleness memorably expressed by Jocasta as she

> . . . groaned and cursed the bed in which
> she brought forth husband by her husband, children
> by her own child, an infamous double bond. [66]

Oedipus himself points madly to the same ontological scandal of doubleness that destroys single figures by twinning them, as he seeks

> to find this wife no wife, this mother's womb,
> this field of double sowing whence I sprang
> and where I sowed my children! [66]

1. Sophocles, *Oedipus the King*, trans. David Grene, in *The Complete Greek Tragedies*, eds. Grene and Richmond Lattimore (Chicago: University of Chi-

We sense, obscurely, that the scandal expressed here is also semiological, a terrible excess of meaning, a dissemination of seed and significance that transgresses single counters or fixed roles.[2] The Sophoclean doubleness is endlessly erosive and, as it were, plastic, showing the procedures of naming and seeding to be multidirectional, creating in Oedipus a hybrid every bit as monstrous as the sphinx: son-lover-murderer-father-brother. Oedipus must lose his "straight vision" and enter the darker realm of echoes and shadows, cancerously active signs, a realm where single things are multiple, a field not unlike that of Jocasta's womb, a "field of double sowing."

There is hardly any feature of Sophocles' play that is not central to our inquiry. The hidden crime is not conceived as some inner secret, some locked-in nugget of evil. On the contrary, the quest for self-knowledge leads *outward* rather than *inward*.[3] Oedipus discovers relation; it is the fact of his life. He is part of a field-picture, a field of double-sowing, and he learns the extent to which he is circumscribed, hideously bound, actively "networked." This is not only his private truth; it would seem to be the truth of the play, namely that

---

cago Press, 1959), p. 28. Subsequent quotations will be taken from this edition and noted parenthetically in the body of the text.

2. James Schroeter has argued, in his well-known essay "The Four Fathers: Symbolism in *Oedipus Rex*," that the "multiple" parentage of Oedipus is to be understood symbolically as well, including the figures of Teiresias, Creon, the Messenger, and the Herdsman, and he makes the telling point that numerous myths and religions "outfit" the birth of a special child with plural parents: King Arthur, Moses, Mohammed, Christ (article excerpted in Albert Cook, *Oedipus Rex: A Mirror for Greek Drama* [Prospect Heights, Ill.: Waveland Press, 1982], pp. 130–31). My own treatment of these matters entails a semiotic and epistemological look at essentially the same issues.

3. Alister Cameron deals at length with this central issue of self-knowledge in *The Identity of Oedipus the King* (New York: New York University Press, 1968), and the point is made that self-knowledge in this play has a profound *public* dimension to it, unlike modern works which would call "for an entry into a private world, sometimes a world of fantasy" (p. 55). Cameron goes on to account for the Sophoclean insistence that self-enactment takes place "in the world," quoting the marvelous line of Heraclitus, which might stand as an epigraph for a number of the chapters in this study: "The limits of the soul you could not go and find though you traversed every road, so deep is its *logos*" (p. 55). Surprisingly, Cameron does not assess the "situational" importance of incest and parricide in this discussion of "self-discovery in action," and hence there is no real interest in what is so central to my aims, namely the consequences of relationship.

"private" truths are illusory, that one is always inscribed and "active" beyond one's ken, that the figure of a life is always composite, eluding our understanding, not subject to our will. It is in this sense that the play moves outward, goes back in time, includes the whole city in its nets, opposes Oedipus' rash self-centeredness and straight vision with its unfurling, ecological, tentacular, pluralist and new dispensation.[4] As the play moves relentlessly toward the global and the revelatory, we sense a great energy at work, the seductive, irresistible power of pattern itself, of pieces falling into place, of a whole life falling into place among other lives, of a relational mesh that at once mocks individual control and celebrates the awesome order of things.

Oedipus enters into this realm at the play's close, as we know, and he does so through self-blinding. Modern analysis has focused a good deal on this enactment of the Law, especially in light of Freudian insights as to the nature of his sexual crime and the symbolic castration that is self-inflicted. Of equal significance for our purposes, however, is the relentless, vital unveiling of the play, an unveiling that goes into and even through blindness itself. The play does not close with the death of Oedipus; it closes with him being led from the city, a monster perhaps, but a living monster, one who has drained the full cup of horrors, has discovered the full extent of who he is. The revelatory ethos is very pure here: Jocasta takes her life, but Oedipus goes to the end of things. He is thereby of a piece with the play's deepest impulse, its relentless though circular pursuit of truth, and it matters little whether we "explain" this systematic revelation of horrors by

4. I am not trying to resurrect some version of tragic flaw or *hamartia*, since I fully agree with the well-known critique of that traditional concept expressed by William Arrowsmith in his essay "The Criticism of Greek Tragedy," reprinted in Cook, *Oedipus Rex*, pp. 154–69. Yet, Arrowsmith's spirited defense of Oedipus raises as many questions as it answers: "Thus it has always seemed to me that the single most pertinent fact of the *Oedipus* was not the hero's flaw, but his refusal to accept a readymade fate: he wants his own fate, not the gods', and though his personal fate may be cut short by his doom, Oedipus at the close of the play insists upon distinguishing his own responsibility by blinding himself. It is the magnificence of his own declaration of responsibility that makes him so heroic: his fate is *his* and no one else's" (pp. 164–65). It is hard not to see in Arrowsmith's very defense of Oedipus the origins of his hubris, and it is in this sense that the insistent twinning and coupling strategies of the play make a mockery of any notion of "*his*," since that particular kind of proprietary or straight vision is just what is being annihilated.

referring to catharsis or more modern accounts of the purposes of tragedy. What is unmistakable is the revelatory rhythm of the play, the inexorable peeling-away of the façade, the unswerving commitment to light.[5] The self-blinding of Oedipus in no way puts out the light, and although Jocasta urges her husband "Best to live lightly, as one can, unthinkingly," the entire play moves in the other direction, the illumination of that larger, relational mesh that we see at the close. We are supposed to know.

Sophocles seems to ask, How much light can we bear? And yet the question is profoundly rhetorical. This is not merely a matter of reader/spectator "knowledge" versus the "pain" of Oedipus. In some inexplicable way, all knowledge gratifies, even when it is dark knowledge, even when it is fatal. Art has always had common cause with this revelatory mission, for the obvious didactic reasons (art announces the truth, etc.) but also for the less obvious pact that all writing has with light, the quasi-instinctual certainty that spectating and reading *please* because they move toward revelation. Ophelia dies from what she sees, but Shakespeare enlists her death as an index of Hamlet's transformation, an altering of such proportions that it unhinges the mind that takes it in, much as Desdemona is mentally undone by the altered Othello well before he takes her life; but these two shattered lives give rare testimony to the unfurling madness that is at the heart of these plays, and the audience would not gauge or truly "see" what is at hand if it did not also see these key "spectators" destroyed by what they see. Jocasta and the Greek chorus may understandably prefer darkness, incuriosity, and low profiles, but those

5. This revelatory view of *Oedipus* should not be taken in the strictly determinist sense that Schiller articulated many centuries ago in his letter to Goethe: "The Oedipus is, as it were, only a tragic analysis. Everything is already in existence, and has only to be unravelled" (quoted in Cook, *Oedipus Rex*, p. 86). Karl Reinhardt has convincingly criticized this view of the play: "For Sophocles, as for Greeks of an earlier period, fate is, generally speaking, never deterministic, but is instead a spontaneous revelation of the power of the demonic. This is equally true when it has been foretold, and true even when it is brought about through an order immanent in events and their cosmic movement" ("*Oedipus Tyrannus*: Appearance and Truth," in *Twentieth Century Interpretations of* Oedipus Rex, ed. Michael J. O'Brien [Englewood Cliffs: Prentice Hall, 1968], p. 49). For an interesting recent view of "time" in *Oedipus* as something that both expands and contracts, see Charles Segal's "Time, Theater, and Knowledge in the Tragedy of Oedipus," in *Edipo: Il teatro greco e la cultura europea* (Rome: Ateneo, 1986), pp. 459–84.

are very rarely the choices made by authors or desired by reader/spectators. That is why *denial* of truth is so bizarre in literature. Brecht's Galileo knows how irresistible knowledge is, knows it to be as seductive as food and pleasure, and this endows his famous recantation at the end of the play with much pathos, with a disturbing sense of things run amok (quite in keeping with Brechtian dramaturgy). Proust's Marcel repeatedly discovers horrors regarding Albertine, but he finds a strange comfort, indeed a strange dignity, even in the worst of his discoveries. This is the secret pleasure and pride that are endemic to understanding, the gratification that assuages us, no matter how damning the pattern we discover. Pascal had, in his severe way, such a quality in mind when he characterized man as a *roseau pensant*, a thinking reed, and he did not hesitate to regard such rational, interpretive powers as a vestige of kingship, insisting that the only power we possess is the power to see and to understand. (In Pascal's Jansenist scheme, of course, this power is to be focused on the endless spectacle of human abjection and misery.)

The imperative to "see clear" grounds much of our thinking about art and knowledge. As an ethical postulate, such an injunction has been with us since the days of Renaissance humanism. But it is obvious that we can go further back still, can see in the working of Greek tragedy a comparable tribute to understanding, to the shedding of light, even when it annihilates one's most precious beliefs and assumptions. Finally, the very modus operandi of the artwork—the watching of the play, the reading of the book—is, in some crucial sense, developmental, an itinerary with an endpoint, an instructional project for all parties involved, a sequential enterprise of exploration and assimilation, an unfurling pattern. Authorial attitudes toward knowledge and exposure doubtless vary from temperament to temperament, from culture to culture, but there is something "institutional" in literature's abiding concern with revelation. As I have suggested, there may be prurient as well as philosophical interests here, a kind of itching to know that corresponds to the itching to tell. Part of this appeal doubtless has to do with voyeurism, with the pleasures of vicariousness offered to us by literature, the peculiar pleasure of adding to our experience via art. But, it must also be the case that discoveries and secrets and revelations fascinate us in art, precisely because we are so benighted in life. Revelatory art gratifies us most because it confers pattern on our muddle, offers us truth in a world of appearances and riddles. Hence, part of the enduring beauty of *Oedipus the King* lies in the magnificent "full disclosure" it provides on a human life, that final act of portraiture which sets forth the subject in all its hues and colors, follows the radii of a life as far as they go, showing the ultimate circle in which one's works and days—from seed to death, from prophesy to memory—are at last illuminated by the light of truth.[6] Such disclosure belongs only to God or the artist. It proclaims both the nullity and the awesomeness of the individual life, the comedy of errors one lived and the tragedy of connection one suffered. The hubris that Sophocles is punishing is the hubris of individuation, the arrogance of control, the naiveté of thinking that one *knows*; his play is profoundly ecological, and its revelatory strategy discloses a new picture of the subject: enmeshed, linked, mirrored, multiple.

1

Although the Sophoclean formula flourishes throughout literary history as a timeless strategy for exposing the limits of knowledge and the interconnectedness of individuals, it may be said to reach its heyday in the nineteenth century. One thinks especially of two concurrent forms of writing that achieve great prominence at this time: the detective story and the story of denied kinships. Much has been written about the relation between the detective novel and the modern urban setting, and it is true that the detective is a mythic figure, one who applies rationality to the opaque cityscape, one who knows what happens in the remote corners of the urban maze, how the disparate individuals are linked together by crime and fate. Poe begins the tra-

6. Richmond Lattimore has suggestively shifted the meaning from *fate* to *pattern* in his study of Greek tragedy: "As Perdita is lost, so she can be found; so the Sphinx is there for Oedipus to answer. To say he was 'fated' is to overstate it with prejudice toward the grand designs of heaven; but it is a part of his pattern of story-*tyche*, which in Greek does not mean 'fate,' 'chance,' or 'fortune' so strictly as it means 'contact,' or, say, 'coincidence,' the way things are put together" (reprinted in *Twentieth Century Interpretations*, ed. O'Brien, p. 111). This view of "the way things are put together" seems very much in line with the "relational" perspective I have been emphasizing. In that light, the doubleness and ambiguity announce a world view where unitary knowledge is no longer conceivable, and although this spells tragedy for protagonists, it would appear to be an inexhaustible resource for writers, having common cause, as it does, with the very processes of language and signification.

dition with Gothic and garish colors, but when it reaches Conan Doyle we see just how fruitful the notion of *readability* can be (Holmes' marvelous confidence that sufficient analytic prowess will make the world give up its secrets), and by the time we get to James, the sleuthing has become distinctly psychological in tone, that gradual piecing together of motive which stamps all his work and relates it back to our Sophoclean model. The novel of denied kinships has less of a formal history, but it ineluctably emerges in a bourgeois culture of social pretension and hypocrisy, a culture where human bonds are severed and replaced by the connectives of money or rank. At its most metaphysical, this art form will produce books with mysterious doubles, such as we see in texts by Dostoevsky and Conrad, books of bizarre linkages and twinnings. But the genre is no less fascinating in its earlier manifestations, its more literal treatment of fissured and denied relations, the kind of thing that is at the core of Dickens and Balzac. Both these novelists deal with the fractured family, the orphan, the coming of a cash ethos that erodes love or fidelity; in their most famous texts, these writers are profoundly *familial*, obsessed with finding fictive fathers for their lost sons, binding Pip to Magwitch, Rastignac to Goriot, disclosing blood connections everywhere, illuminating the illegitimate children, the abandoned partners, all those "relations" which cannot be denied. Once again, the Oedipal story comes to mind, as a kind of spare, almost formulaic ancestor for the dense, picturesque, quasi-sociological investigations undertaken by these novelists.

*

It is hardly happenstance that Sophocles' archetypal revelatory text is a dramatic work. Theater is peculiarly suited for surprising exposure, for peeling away of externals, for displaying the larger network in which the subject is meshed. "Curtain-lifting" tells us, as a metaphor, something about the importance of revelation in theater, the role played by the (either gradual or shocking) disclosure of truth in a web of appearances, the thrust toward exposure and knowledge that characterizes the movement of much dramatic art. For these reasons, it will be desirable to stay a while with dramatic literature, if we want to get a fix on the art of seeing clear, on the revelatory process at work. As a kind of *summa* of nineteenth-century concerns, the work of Ibsen seems ideally constituted for an investigation of this kind: it picks up both the strands mentioned, the sleuthing approach to mystery as well as the story of denied kinships; moreover, it consciously looks back to Sophocles, as it makes of the pursuit of truth its grand subject, and the exposure of deceit its modus operandi.

The "whole" of Ibsen is rather too large for the considerations at hand, but it will be possible to gain a sense of the revelatory dynamic and its surprising consequences by considering, as a special composite, three of his most famous works: *Ghosts, The Wild Duck*, and *The Master Builder*. Although *A Doll's House* is the first mature Ibsen work to bring him international recognition (and it remains a staple item in any feminist repertory), it is in *Ghosts*, written two years later in 1881, that we may encounter the sleuthing plot in its most perfect form. Profoundly shocking at the time, *Ghosts* remains one of Ibsen's most virulent and pure indictments of moral hypocrisy, and the Norwegian public's indignation at the play's defense of hedonism, free love, and even incest is not so hard to fathom, even today. Here is Ibsen's most scathing critique of Scandinavian pieties, his exposure of middle-class traditions and legacy as the traditions and legacy of disease.[7] The French doctor uses the appropriate term for Oswald's condition: *vermoulu*. Oswald is worm-eaten, a living specimen of decay, of the diseases of the father visited upon the son. Like a surgeon, Ibsen opens up the encrusted past and probes with his scalpel, exposing the thickness and oppressiveness of the lies and deceit: Mrs. Alving's cover-up regarding her husband, Pastor Manders' mealy-mouthed pieties and cowardice, Captain Alving's own excesses and repressed *joie de vivre*. *Ghosts* appears, at the outset, to be a Freudian exercise in rememoration; Mrs. Alving has, at last, the courage to speak the truth to Oswald about the family past, to let in light and air, to repudiate the stifling and fearful conventionality that surrounds her. Ibsen's gambit would seem to be therapeutical: by exposing the sins and lies of the past, one might be cured, find the will to live in the present and face the future. But nothing works as it should. Oswald cannot be salvaged, Regina is bitter and wants out, Manders abets the cunning Engstrom out of fear and stupidity, Mrs. Alving presides over the dissolving of her son. Sophocles had exposed the dreadful doubleness of Oedipus' relations; Ibsen, too, displays multiplicity: the honored father is shown to be the depraved father, who then is revealed as the repressed father; Oswald is both

7. Probably the most sustained reading of Ibsen as rebel is to be found in Robert Brustein's spirited chapter on him in *The Theater of Revolt* (Boston: Little, Brown, 1964), pp. 35–83.

the prodigal son and the doomed child; Captain Alving's home is virtually pirouetted in the play, exposed for the duplicitous place it always was, and as the orphanage burns, we see in its wake the final "Captain Alving's home," the whorehouse to be run by Engstrom, with Regina as vedette inhabitant.

Ultimately, Ibsen's tidings are not unlike those of Sophocles: no one is free in this world, and the liberated son comes to understand the fatal web of which he was and is a part. As the light of truth is shed on the dark circumstances of the Alving family, we see the fearsomeness of revelatory theater: the living are shown to be dying, the free are shown to be enslaved, the ghosts are everywhere. In her famous conversation with Pastor Manders, Mrs. Alving beautifully sums up Ibsen's philosophy of usurpation (of the living by the dead):

> . . . When I heard Regina and Oswald in there, it was as if I saw ghosts. I almost think we are all ghosts—all of us, Pastor Manders. It isn't just what we have inherited from our father and mother that walks in us. It is all kinds of dead ideas and all sorts of old and obsolete beliefs. They are not alive in us; but they remain in us none the less, and we can never rid ourselves of them. I only have to take a newspaper and read it, and I see ghosts between the lines. There must be ghosts all over the country. They lie as thick as grains of sand. And we're all so horribly afraid of the light.[8]

8. Henrik Ibsen, *Ghosts*, in *Ibsen: Plays*, trans. Michael Meyer (London: Eyre Methuen, 1980), I, p. 62. The Norwegian term for ghosts is "gengangere," which, like the French "revenants" suggests "returnees," the living dead. The full passage in Norwegian has a kind of nuance, colloquialism, and eloquence that are missing in the spare English of Michael Meyer: "Da jeg hørte Regine og Osvald derinde, var det some jeg så gengangere for mig. Men jeg tror naesten, vi er gengangere allesammen, pastor Manders. Det er ikke bare det, vi har arvet fra far og mor, som går igen i os. Det er alleslags gamle afdøde meninger og alskens gammel afdød tro og sligt noget. Det er ikke levende i os; men det sidder i allegevel og vi kan ikke bli det kvit. Bare jeg tar en avis og laeser i, er det ligesom jeg så gengangere smyge imellem linjerne. Der må leve gengangere hele landet udover. Der må vaere så tykt af dem som sand, synes jeg. Og så er vi så gudsjammerlig lysraedde allesammen" (*Samlede Vaerker* [Kristiania: Gyldendalske Boghandel, 1908], IV, p. 107). Ibsen insistently uses present participles such as "levende" where Meyer gives us "alive," and in Norwegian the ghosts "live" all over the country, rather than merely "being" there. Ibsen's ghosts "sneak in" between the lines of the newspaper, unlike Meyer's who are merely positioned there.

It is the living who are exposed here as mummers, shadow-figures of a play that has already taken place. Oswald and Regina are performing an old charade, but only Mrs. Alving knows it. The awareness of ubiquitous shadows and echoes heralds in a terrible vision, one where nothing stands alone as it seems to, but is, instead, bathed and encrusted with ghosts, with relics and vestiges of the past, "as thick as grains of sand." This crowded world is shot full of half-beings, real ghouls in effect, a nightmarish picture of never dying, something on the order of nuclear waste, matter that has a lifetime of centuries; it is the very opposite of the entropic scheme to which we are accustomed, the merciful passing away of people and the beliefs they held. To see such a realm of phantoms is to lose, at once, innocence and hope, and Ibsen stresses the issue of vision, of actually seeing the living past. It is as heavy and poisonous as the rottenness in Denmark or the polluted skies at the close of Racine's *Phèdre*.

All this accounts for the most remarkable line of all: "And we're all so horribly afraid of the light." Ibsen has seized on the age-old, childlike fear of the dark that lives on in all adults, and he has prophetically inverted it, even coining a term of his own—*lysraedde*—to make his modern point.[9] Light is what is unbearable; reality, as Conrad tells us in *The Secret Agent*, will not bear much looking into. It is precisely at this juncture that Ibsen's theater acquires a kind of resonance and poetry; he has discovered that the stage is an echo chamber, and that to write for it, one needs to write a palimpsest language; he has also begun to take the measure of his own dramaturgy, to see that the Light which haunts all his work, the final Revelation that would at last banish deceit and hypocrisy, is a fearsome matter. The exposure of truth, he begins to realize, does not have to be the conventional ending of his plays, but may be the more intriguing, more problematic beginning of the newer drama he wants to write.

9. In his introduction to *Ibsen and the Theater* (New York: New York University Press, 1980), Errol Durbach has offered an illuminating analysis of Ibsen's line: "Og så er vi så gudsjammerlig lysraedde allesammen." He has shown the poverty of existing English translations, especially regarding "gudsjammerlig" which Meyer renders lamely as "horribly," and he has argued, with regard to "lysraedde" [light-afraid], that "Ibsen is *coining* a concept here, inventing a term for the inversion of a child's fear of the dark into an adult's fear of the light and the horrors it may (and in this play *does*) reveal" (p. 10).

*

When *The Wild Duck* was first staged in the 1880s and 90s throughout Scandinavia and Europe, the general reaction was one of bewilderment. At the Paris premiere at the Théâtre Libre, some of the spectators actually went so far as to quack like ducks. Why?

The answer is not hard to find. Given Ibsen's reputation in 1894 as the man who fearlessly exposed hypocrisy and bogus institutions, ranging from marriage to religious values and town government, audiences and readers were anxious to see who was being exposed this time. They were understandably surprised to see the truth-seeker himself turned on his head, and they must have had trouble discerning this play's political agenda. By casting Gregers Werle as a parasitic, diseased figure, scarred by the loveless marriage of his parents, spitting his truth-venom into an uncomprehending world, Ibsen seems to be repudiating the very ideas and pursuits for which he was known throughout Europe. The exposure scenario that Ibsen always handled with such poise is still there in *The Wild Duck*, but it is in real trouble. One might say that it is in its death throes.

It all starts well enough. Gregers Werle plays the sleuth, and we know, soon enough, that there is considerable murkiness and irregularity to be cleaned up here, both in his own family and in that of his friend, Hjalmar Ekdal; but Gregers' detective work becomes more and more peripheral, as we encounter the human center of the play: the Ekdal family, the House of Ekdal (as one would say, the House of Atreus). Ibsen has reported how the Ekdals grew on him, especially as he revised this play, prior to sending it off. The child going blind, the old man living in the past, the former servant girl with child, the photographer nursing his Great Invention: these are the walking wounded whom Ibsen has taken into his heart. He has begun to realize that the kinds of truths which most matter to him are to be located at the far side of politics and ideology, are perhaps to be found lodged in those very fortresses he has always attacked. What comes to be known in this play as the "life-lie" is seen now as an enabling deception, an illusion that makes life and belief possible. Ibsen may know Hjalmar Ekdal to be puffed-up, but he also knows that the man is idolized by his daughter, and that that hero worship endows each of their small lives with whatever beauty they are to have. The Ekdals are all refugees from the world of reality, and Ibsen has discovered their poetry, much as O'Neill was drawn to the pipe dreams of his down-and-outers in *The Iceman Cometh*. No ideological program can give the measure of the maimed Ekdals, but Gregers' relentless exposure of their deceptions—just the sort of thing Ibsen earlier specialized in—is shown as chilling, diseased and, finally, fatal. Without the necessary illusions and lies, the marriage cannot survive, the inventor realizes his nullity, the child is disowned and dies. The light of exposure comes to resemble, in this play, the fearsome and lethal light of an explosion, that nuclear blast of energy which illuminates us to death.

Seeing clear has been the Ibsen call-to-action, but this is a profoundly cautionary play, peopled by personages with "bad eyes," with defective vision, raising severe doubts about the meaning of truth, the cost of discovery. Gregers claims to bring light to the dark Ekdal household, to tell Hjalmar the "truth" about the origin of his daughter Hedwig. But we will never know whose child it is. Is it known where children come from? The wild child, like the wild duck, can be tracked but never certifiably known in its origins; "getting to the bottom" will only bring maiming and death, not knowledge. The only way to know human beings is to attend to them, to love them; "look at the child," is Gina's futile warning, but Gregers and Hjalmar are too busy with their schemes and categories to see the living child. Every person in the audience sees Hedwig to be Hjalmar's daughter in the only sense that counts—a bond of love unites them—but Hjalmar is searching for Truth.

During our own century, Ibsen has often been accused of being old hat, of writing "was-drama" instead of "is-drama." His focus is always, so the claim goes, backward-looking, sorting out the events of the past; everything, we are assured, has already happened. It is time to explode this critical myth; such a view butchers most of the plays, but it is blatantly inadequate to *The Wild Duck*. It is all unfurling in front of our eyes, and that is what is so monstrous and myopic about the truth-seeker: on the prowl for proofs and disclosures, he cannot make out life itself. (One understands why Henry James was such an Ibsen fan, especially the James of "The Beast in the Jungle.") The Ekdals live on the stage, as very few families in theater do. Their little routines, their small talk, their fudgings and deceptions: this is the very stuff of life, although its measurable truth-coefficient is doubtless unimpressive. The hidden data of their past—was Gina pregnant with Old Werle's child when she married Hjalmar?—comes to seem trivial, even absurd, in contrast with the living tissue of their life at home.

Had Ibsen merely rendered this, he would have created a memorable play. But he has done more. The Ekdals are alive in still other ways, and it is the haunting rendition of that "other" life which makes *The Wild Duck* such a masterpiece. Virginia Woolf once claimed that, in Ibsen, "the paraphernalia of reality have at certain moments to become the veil through which we see infinity."[10] And that description leads us to the true terrain of this play, the Attic of the Ekdals. This is the place of travel books, folklore, giants, fairies, trolls, and all those magic denizens who are never to be found in drawing rooms or on street corners, but who exist nonetheless. The Attic is a place of paintboxes and books and pictures of churches, the home of the Flying Dutchman as well as the wild duck. It is where the Ekdals *live*. Here is where their illusions, even their life-lies, become their private truths. It is here that Old Ekdal's lost forest still lives and has its revenge, where the "vasty deep" reclaims its own, where Hjalmar and his father and his daughter finally have their fill of mystery, fantasy, dream, and belief. "Truth" has no purchase here. This is a world of darkness as much as light, and if the detective or the geometrician or the torchbearer enters this realm to take its measure, he will either find nothing to measure or he will destroy what he finds. Ibsen's achievement was to show in this play, indeed in its very stage-set, that we live in our Attics, that our life-lie is the very place where we carry out our most precious transactions. In doing this, Ibsen achieves one of the great breakthroughs of modern theater: the stage now becomes a privileged place, to be found on no map, a realm far beyond Norway; and the actions which transpire there, far from expressing a dead past, give the very shape and form of our living experience.

*

Two of Ibsen's greatest plays, *Rosmersholm* (1886) and *Hedda Gabler* (1890) follow *The Wild Duck*, but we must wait until 1892, for *The Master Builder*, if we are to bring the meditation about revelatory drama to the spectacular conclusion that Ibsen is to give it. At first glance, *The Master Builder* appears to rework the themes of *Ghosts*: it too is about the sins of the fathers, but, in this case, the father is on stage, haunted by the corpses and misadventures on his hands and

10. The Woolf quotation is cited by M. C. Bradbook in her immensely readable *Ibsen the Norwegian: A Revaluation* (London: Chatto & Windus, 1948), p. 98.

conscience. As Freud said of *Lear*, this play is about the necessity of accepting age and making friends with death; in Solness, Ibsen has given us an unforgettable picture of a man who fears youth knocking at the door. Finally, this play hinges on the status of past events, the fateful contract entered into by Solness and Hilde some ten years before the action begins, a crucial event of the past that has the same kind of potency and centrality as hidden truth about Captain Alving, or the siring of Hedwig. The revelatory thrust of *The Master Builder* is meant to illuminate this seminal encounter, because everything that follows derives logically from it, because without it, Hilde would appear to be deranged and the entire play cockeyed.

But, what really happened ten years ago? Did Solness bend Hilde over backward, kiss her many, many times? Why does Solness not remember? Is he amnesiac? Is she mad? In *Ghosts* nothing whatsoever remains hazy or dubious, after the light of truth has settled on it: the nature of the Alving marriage is known *sub specie eternitatiss*. It is wonderfully different here: Solness toys with the notion that he did not *really* kiss Hilde, merely that he wanted to, wanted to with such force that it became reality for her. Those events of ten years ago could thus be accounted for: it would be a case of telepathy and hypnotism, something a little *outré* for Ibsen perhaps, more in the line of Strindberg's crazed figures, but nonetheless explanatory.[11] The magnificent thing about *The Master Builder* is that even this theory will not wash.

We are very, very close here to Robbe-Grillet's *Marienbad*. It may even be recalled that a performance of Ibsen's *Rosmersholm* is taking place in the French text, and one could make a strong case for Ibsen's long shadow in Robbe-Grillet's cubist film (even though the Frenchman has covered his tracks by referring to the wrong play). The parallels are unmistakable: each work is ostensibly about the past, about pledges made last year or ten years ago, about a debt come due, about origins; but, if we look closer, each work is entirely about the present, about persuasion, about desire, about a love affair that is taking place in front of our eyes, right now, on the screen and on the stage.

The Master Builder, more than any other Ibsen play, is about the portentous discovery that human desire and theatrical performance

11. This is not to say that hypnosis and telepathy do not interest Ibsen in other plays as well; one need merely think of *Rosmersholm* and *The Lady from the Sea* as other instances where this notion is significant. Even in those works, however, it never reaches the virtually homicidal dimension that one finds throughout Strindberg.

know only one tense: the present. "Make way! make way!" is the imperious message that Solness knows he must heed. "Gi plads!" says the Norwegian: give space. This need not be understood temporally, as Solness himself understands it; it is a spatial directive, even a theatrical directive, and it demands that a new realm come about. Solness questions Hilde about her dreams, because the oneiric might be the necessary place, the realm where time and space do not bind. But, even dreams are too tame a vehicle for what is transpiring here. When the door opens early in the play, and Hilde enters the scene, bringing her dirty underwear, her "memories" of Solness's intimacy, her intense desire to be taken sexually, as the Viking women were taken, her propensity to trance, her talk of giddiness and towers, we know that the very medium of the play is erotic, that the relationship between this older man and this younger woman is "taking place" right now, and that it is a powerful sexual attraction. There is no past in this play: Solness' putative flirtation with Hilde is a gesture to the realists, a rational alibi that is utterly unnecessary, blown to the winds by the actual forces of the play; whatever kissing went on ten years ago is being enacted on the stage now, just as the Viking lust is shown to be timeless, reenacted on the stage as well.

Nothing could be clearer. Solness is initially a man with guilt on his mind, fearful of the young, a man who "willed" the death of his own children and the burning of his wife's ancestral home in order to succeed in his art; he is entirely ghost-ridden, presiding over empty nurseries and a loveless marriage. The introduction of Hilde into the play changes all that. The special properties of desire and the stage make it possible for Solness finally to *build* something, to make a space and a time of his own, to move into the saga world and to erect a castle in the air. He will do it with her. Together, Solness and Hilde, in what seems more and more like a duet, rewrite the master builder's past, alter every single item on his list, transform it entirely into the here-and-now:

SOLNESS (*more earnestly, leans closer to her, with his arms on the table*): What does it look like, this castle of yours, Hilde?

HILDE (*slowly*): My castle must stand high up. High above everything. Open and free on every side. So that I can see for miles around.

SOLNESS: It's got a tower, I suppose?

HILDE: A frightfully high tower. And right up on the top of the tower there'll be a balcony. And that's where I shall stand—

SOLNESS (*involuntarily clutches his head*): How can you want to stand so high? Doesn't it make you giddy—?

HILDE: I want to stand up there and look down at the others—the ones who build the churches. And homes for mothers and fathers and children. And you can come up there and look down too.

SOLNESS (*humbly*): Has the master builder leave to climb up to the princess?

HILDE: If the master builder wishes.

SOLNESS (*whispers*): Then—I think the master builder will come.

HILDE (*nods*): The master builder—he will come.

SOLNESS: But he will never build again. Poor master builder!

HILDE (*alive*): Oh, yes he will! We'll do it together! And we'll build the most beautiful thing—the most beautiful thing in the world!

SOLNESS: Hilde—tell me. What is that?

HILDE (*looks at him with a smile, gives a little shake of her head, pouts and says, as though to a child*): Master builders—they are vewy—vewy stupid people.

SOLNESS: Yes, they're stupid, I know. But tell me—what is the most beautiful thing in the world? The thing we two are going to build together?

HILDE (*is silent for a moment, then says, with the enigmatic expression in her eyes*): A castle in the air.[12]

It is a magic moment. High above the others, having overcome his fear, Solness can, through desire, achieve his freedom. All the roles have been redistributed: Solness is at last as he wishes himself to be, and he attains that state through his love for Hilde; Hilde has rid the stage of its ghosts by becoming the children Solness has lost, by filling up his empty nurseries, above all by becoming the wife he has lost. What, indeed, is the most beautiful thing that two people can do together? What is it that they will build together? The text says, marvelously, "a castle in the air," but every reader and spectator must

12. Henrik Ibsen, *The Master Builder*, in *Ibsen: Plays*, I, pp. 307–308. One must acknowledge that the "vewy—vewy stupid" is all of Michael Meyer's doing, but I think he errs in the right direction. All that Hilde says in the original is that "master builders are really, really stupid folks": "Bygmesterne,—de er nogen svaert—svaert dumme mennesker" (*Samlede Vaerker*, V, p. 224).

supply a different answer: the act of love, the creation of a child. This scene is properly ecstatic, because it transports Solness from his ghost-ridden world into a timeless present, a moment where the old contracts are denied and the new dispensation is achieved. This moment cannot be sustained, and Solness will fall to his death; the dues to reality must be paid, and the spectators allowed to go home. But it is nonetheless a moment of magic and splendor, and it climaxes the courtship between Solness and Hilde that is the proper subject of the play, the poetic and affective matter that is in front of the reader/spectator almost from the moment the curtain rises. Solness falls, and the spectators go home; but the theater is real, and so too is that realm of desire for which no temporal or rational constraints exist. The world of the past is finally past, deader than the lost children, more completely gone than the burned house, brought at last off the stage, beyond revelation.

Ibsen has grasped the essential truth of the theater: it is a place of creation, not revelation; its scenario is always of the present, never of the past; if it stages ghosts, they are living ghosts, freed from their origins, playing out their lives.[13] The dramaturgy of *Ghosts* has undergone a sea change, and the Sophoclean revelatory model comes to seem increasingly remote, tied down to a truth-scenario that is more and more irrelevant to the story the playwright wants to tell. That story is still one of relationship, but it has moved beyond the curtain-lifting exposure of the earlier work, and it now conceives of relationship in radically different terms—not as a given to be uncovered, but as a connection to be created, a coming together that might be virtual as well as provable, a construct of desire rather than evidence. The hardheaded might view such an itinerary as evasion into dream and inwardness, but hardheadedness is perhaps a narrow virtue, perhaps not the best virtue for the interpretation of art. Whatever one's moral verdict, one can hardly fail to see that Ibsen's new kind of theater moves cleanly in the direction of freedom and poetry.

13. Ultimately, I am proposing a view of Ibsen theater as "generative" rather than revelatory, and hence closer to the purely spontaneous, liberated model proposed by Antonin Artaud and admired by Derrida in his essays on Artaud. Needless to say, this flies in the face of most Ibsen criticism, but it seems a welcome antidote to the kind of put-down and charge of deadness one finds in Ronald Gray's ill-conceived *Ibsen: A Dissenting View* (Cambridge, Eng.: Cambridge University Press, 1977).

2

Revelatory art inevitably transforms the writer into a scribe, the Horatio who will record for posterity what is left after the curtain has finally been lifted, or the smoke cleared. And the writing itself may bring solace. Consider the remarks of Ford's narrator Dowell at the onset of his story; broken by the events he will narrate, Dowell too has suffered devastation-by-light, and writing is all there is left:

> You may well ask why I write. And yet my reasons are quite many. For it is not unusual in human beings who have witnessed the sack of a city or the falling to pieces of a people to desire to set down what they have witnessed for the benefit of unknown heirs or of generations infinitely remote; or, if you please, just to get the sight out of their heads. [5]

Dowell's metaphor brings us back to the plagued, dying city with which *Oedipus* began, and he posits writing as a double-edged response: to leave a record of the carnage, but also to *do* something, to transform passive suffering into active doing. The Ibsen itinerary from revealed horrors to a theater of presence also testifies to a tenacious belief in art as a possible rival to fate, the artist as demiurge rather than scribe.

Can we be surprised that the writer is, as it were, generically repelled (as well as attracted) by fateful revelations? To be sure, the revelatory process has its own inherent appeal, and the magnetism of a truth-to-be-revealed counts for a good deal, too. But there is always something of an affront in such art, a systematic humbling of individual sovereignty, a dissolving of the self, a denial of freedom. For some writers, this humbling may be just the chord they want to sound; but rarely is the writer so self-effacing that he nullifies, "sterilizes" his own medium, makes himself merely a passive vehicle for truth. Truth-based art, the text that exposes the workings of Higher Powers, is inherently deterministic and preordained. The artist of such texts finds himself presiding over the extinction of things that must matter: imagination, liberty, play. In revelatory art, the author is free only to stage the exposé, but the patterns that emerge are the very constituent parts of reality. Hence, the high seriousness of such art: through its workings, we are supposed to see the universe "as it is"; everyone has his blinders removed, even if the characters do so at the cost of their private dreams and integrity. The world that dawns in such texts has the fearful nakedness of unadorned truth, a place where all the illusions, deceits, and hiding-places have simply gone up in smoke. There are writers who will not live in such precincts.

Even the scribe, as we have seen, produces something that outlives the disaster, even if it is an account of the disaster. But there are also writers who challenge the very principles of revelation and exposure. Ibsen already begins to move in this direction when he creates the Attic of the Ekdals or the castle in the air in *The Master Builder*. One can go still further in this direction; one can fashion a language, a "doing" that asserts its own authority, all the while telling a story. In Proust's *Recherche* and Joyce's *Ulysses* we have spectacular examples of the poetics of revelation; at the same time, these monumental novels quixotically tilt at the determinist reality-principles that revelation depends on. What comes out of this is something like the revenge of the artist, the flaunting of a form-principle that makes its way as it goes, rather than lifting the curtain on the absolute.

*

Proust's great novel has such a suspiciously nineteenth-century look to it that it may well seem *outré* to make the claims for it that have been advanced here. Proust's view of his people seems anchored in causality and determinism, and there can be little doubt that he thrives on the revelatory technique. He does. When one considers the stunning reversals that he sets up throughout the novel—Françoise killing the chicken, Legrandin's snobbism, the lesbian scene at Montjouvain, the homosexual pendant to it in the Guermantes' courtyard, the final brothel scene in wartime Paris—it is clear that this author loves to have his character *stumble* onto the truth, onto startling new vistas of a world he thought he knew, much like the aging narrator stumbles on the uneven pavement in the last volume and "trips" into an ecstatic vision of his past. Overhearing, peeping into, falling asleep by the side of, and other forms of "curtain-lifting" are rampant in Proust, and generally the discovery is of the illicit and the aberrant, the unsuspected night side of the daytime people. Occasionally, when the surprises involve folks such as Françoise or Legrandin, people about whom Marcel is merely curious, the effects can be hilarious; when the discovery concerns Albertine, however, it is quite another matter. One of the high moments of revelatory trauma occurs when Albertine coyly informs the narrator that she is a close friend of Mlle. Vinteuil and her "accomplice":

> Albertine amie de Mlle. Vinteuil et de son amie, pratiquante professionnelle du saphisme, c'était, auprès de ce que j'avais imaginé dans les plus grands doutes, ce qu'est au petit acoustique de l'Exposition de 1889, dont on espérait à peine qu'il pourrait aller du bout d'une maison à une autre, les téléphones planant sur les rues, les villes, les champs, les mers, reliant les pays. C'était une *terra incognita* terrible où je venais d'atterrir, une phase nouvelle de souffrances insoupçonnées qui s'ouvrait. [*Recherche*, II, 1115]

> [Albertine: friend of Mlle. Vinteuil and of her accomplice, the professional and practicing sapphist, this was, in comparison to what I had suspected even with my wildest doubts, like comparing the little acousticon of the 1889 Exposition, which was expected, at most, to link one house with another, to the telephone which extends over streets, cities, fields, oceans, linking entire countries. It was a terrible *terra incognita* on which I had just landed, a new phase of unimagined sufferings that was opening up for me.]

The conventional "curtain-lifting" paradigm of discovery is altogether too limited and two-dimensional to account for what is happening in this passage; revelation in Proust is exploratory, but it is also transformative, in that the very terrain one inhabits is suddenly altered, becomes a dark new continent ("une *terra incognita* terrible où je venais d'atterrir") that defies orientation and promises pain. The Proustian breakthrough, strangely enough, has much in common with the cubist project, because it seeks to transcend the grids of time and space that constrain ordinary perception and art; but, unlike the celebratory mode of the cubists, Proust depicts this experience of simultaneity, this liberation from the here-and-now as pure trauma (which can become ecstasy only through the Olympian agency of art). We recall the incident of Marcel holding Albertine's body and of his feeling anguish at that body's infinite inner reach, its maddening and unplumbable depths in time and space which must remain closed to the lover; in like manner, this discovery of Albertine's lesbianism is rendered as a kind of dreadful space-time travel, a wrenching of the self out of its habitual ruts, comparable, perhaps, to the agonized realization of Oedipus that he is himself a figure of double-sowing, that he is part of an intolerable sexual circuitry.

The power of Proust's passage derives largely from its amazing metaphor, which compares this new suffering to the earlier suspicions in terms of the telephone versus the acousticon. The telephone erases the boundaries of space by transforming the world into a network; we "know" this, but it takes the imagination of a Proust to make us rediscover the revolutionary thrust of such an instrument. Thomas Kuhn has spoken of conceptual revolutions and shiftings of paradigms, and Marshall McLuhan has educated us as to the imaginative and communicative dimensions of our technology; Proust has a great deal to teach us as well, for his imagination is exquisitely sensitized to history, and his metaphors register the coming of the modern age. They do so, however, in his own peculiar way, by giving us the spiritual equivalence of these mechanical developments, showing us how our ways of feeling cannot only be expressed by technology, but how they, the feelings, have, somehow, got there first. Thus, McLuhan's systematic inquiry into the role of specific media as extensions of the human brain is brilliantly foreshadowed by Proust: the telephone is assessed here as a frightening extension of self, as a spatialization of the central nervous system that exponentially increases our vulnerability and captivity. The scientific and moral implications of such a view are staggering, for they imply a new world without personal sovereignty, a world where the nerves and their electronic ambassadors *lead* us, where the individual is reduced to being a receptacle of ever-widening stimuli. The *terra incognita* that Marcel lands on (or discovers that he has always been there, but has never known it) is, as it were, the province of relationship, relationship defined as neural and affective network, where supposedly distant and separate beings are connected, and suffer their linkage. It should be clear, by now, that Proustian revelation is peculiarly generative and transformative, that it operates on the known world a strange type of liberation, wrenching things from their habitual frames, pointing to new, unchartable constellations, disorienting.

The most famous instance of revelation in the entire *Recherche* is doubtless the great scene in the Guermantes' courtyard, where Marcel discovers the homosexuality of Charlus and Jupien. The turgid, breathless prose of this section, its syntactical overheatedness, makes it fairly luminous and bristling in the scheme of things, as if the writerly energies themselves were strained to the utmost, hard to corral within the frame of the narrative at hand. The far-reaching, systematic comparisons Proust draws here between the erotic life of plants, insects and humans, or the ongoing, often pathological parallels between homosexuals and Jews (as somehow equivalent forms of aberrant outsiders, figures so profoundly alienated that they become emblematic of the fissured self that can never avow its dark side), these features of the novel have been much discussed by Proustian criticism. Less noted, however, is the remarkable way in which this discovery points us toward an entirely new universe. The Renaissance topos of exploring new horizons, demonstrably connected with the settling of the New World, is vividly present in Proust, but it has become, appropriately enough, a perceptual matter. The Proustian new world is the one you have been living in for some time, but the blinders of habit and inertia have prevented you from seeing it. This is most sensationally true, of course, for the sexual revelations at hand. To put it crudely, Proust's novel seems, at a certain point, to flip on its back, to become "inverted," as he would say; and soon enough the reader comes to anticipate that every male character in the novel is going to be exposed as homosexual, and every female as lesbian.

It is easy—especially when more than half a century separates us from Proust, and when there has been a widespread liberalizing of sexual mores—to miss what Proust is doing here. There can be no doubt that the shock value of his revelations has shrunk considerably, and the issue of sexual preference is now widely discussed; homosexuality is certainly not the taboo it was then. Shock effect is indeed a risky aesthetic criterion, and a good number of older texts may seem outdated to the modern reader if they appear to depend on local prejudices or values that now appear quaint and of merely historical interest. But is that the case with *Sodome et Gomorrhe*? The central—and enduring—issue for Proust is the epistemological one, not the sociomoral one, and that issue—how well do we know what we know?—is a timeless one, something that no amount of "liberation" or enlightenment is going to do away with. In short, Proust moves from revelation to exploration, and he drastically redefines the issues of linkage, kinship and connection. By playing his homosexual card, Proust effectively re-creates the deck. Somewhat like Freud, perhaps still more like a botanist or morphologist, Proust makes us see a sexual link where we had not thought to look for one. This is an undertaking at once perceptual and structural, and, in its own dizzying fashion, it remakes the world. Hence, the new universe of homosexuals forms

> une franc-maçonnerie bien plus étendue, plus efficace et moins soupçonnée que celle des loges, car elle repose sur une identité

> de goûts, de besoins, d'habitudes, de dangers, d'apprentissage, de savoir, de trafic, de glossaire, et dans laquelle les membres mêmes qui souhaitent de ne pas se connaître, aussitôt se reconnaissent à des signes naturels ou de convention, involontaires ou voulus, qui signalent un de ses semblables au mendiant dans le grand seigneur à qui il ferme la portière de sa voiture, au père dans le fiancé de sa fille, à celui qui avait voulu se guérir, se confesser, qui avait à se défendre, dans le médecin, dans le prêtre, dans l'avocat qu'il est allé trouver; [*Recherche*, II, 617]
>
> [a freemasonry far more extensive, more efficient, and less suspected than that of the Lodges, because it is based on an identity of tastes, needs, customs, dangers, apprenticeship, knowledge, traffic, vocabulary, and one in which even those members who seek not to know one another, immediately recognize each other by natural or conventional signs, which disclose one of his kind to the beggar in the nobleman whose carriage door he is shutting, to the father in his daughter's fiancé, to the person in search of healing, confession, or protection in the doctor, priest, or lawyer whom he consults;]

The first thing one sees here is, of course, the sexual reversal, and it leads to new formations that are energized along channels we had not seen; the sexual connection is everywhere dominant, making any other link a mere pretense, a cover story for the uninitiated. This constitutes a sweeping reversal of function as it is thought to exist: the "grand seigneur" is assumed to be separate, both socially and careerwise, from the "mendiant" who closes the door of his coach; likewise, the father is designated by his name as linked to the daughter, not to her fiancé; the penitent who seeks confession, the sick person who seeks healing, the person needing protection find in the priest, the doctor, and the lawyer sexual intrigue rather than professional assistance. The cutting edge of these reversals lies in the insidious displacement that has occurred, a displacement of function that sounds the sexual note in arenas where it should not be operative. One notes as well that the initial relation of aid or support no longer obtains, and in its place is a mating game at best, or a sexual power scenario at worst. A loss of innocence is taking place in this passage, for the reader is obliged to reconsider alignments he had not even thought to be alignments.

This entire segment of the novel is studded with images of kinships, guilds, language affiliates, cognates of all kinds. Like an obsessive anthropologist, Proust finds patterns of bonding everywhere, but he surprises us in his findings, for we are not linked where we thought we were. Somewhat like a mock version of a professional convention, where the pediatric neurologists confer in one camp, the cardiologists in another, the divorce lawyers here and the tax specialists there, the early Shakespeareans in this room and the sci-fi deconstructionists in that, Proust makes us see what a specialist's world it really is, how particular groups share common words, tics, attitudes, perspectives, while others walk right past these codes, never even knowing they are there. We see, also, the odd pleasure that is special to specialization, the hermetic joys of the coterie, the sense of security and standing that are possible in such precincts. The obvious form of specialization at hand here is homosexuality, and Proust uses all these metaphors to characterize the scenes of recognition and denial that punctuate the homosexual life and go unnoticed by the others. But the most persistent analogy of kinship and sameness is that of speech, the human tool that is at once cultural and personal, generic and individual; Proust makes brilliant references to strangers abroad who discover themselves to be compatriots, who "speak the same language," even though they do not, in any other sense, "know" each other, and he widens our sense of what commonality really is, how impersonal it might be, how people belong to many, many "families," have allegiances and shared kinships that no Almanach de Gotha could hope to render.

Proust's very special form of palimpsest writing might be thought of as a mix of languages, of dialects and patois, and his greatest comic effects are earned when someone fails to translate properly, fails to realize that these are foreign languages, even though the words certainly look familiar enough. The phenomenon of jealousy derives from precisely the same "reading problems," the nascent awareness that the words one hears do not mean what the dictionary says they should, but have another signification, invariably that of betrayal. Proust termed, at the end of his long book, his mission as a writer to be that of *translator*, by which he meant that the artist finds a language for the originary impressions "written" in us by experience; he went on to say that his book would be a kind of magnifying glass for his readers, a device for reading into themselves. One is tempted to say that the Proust reader has almost as much translating to do as the author. For that is the manner in which the *Recherche* must be read, as a text to be translated, so that Charlus' so-called conversations with the narrator would then be "reconsidered" in the light of the new sexual *éclairage*, enabling us then to "see" them as charged though sublimated erotic encounters with the baron. Proust's novel, long though it is, needs even more than most to be reread, for it is then truly savored; only then do the subterranean levels of the seemingly innocuous and decorous events show for what they are.

Seeing clear is an arduous if not impossible task, given the "multilingual" nature of Proustian discourse. A particularly rich example of obfuscation and multivalence can be found at one of the Guermantes' dinner parties, as the homosexual motif snakes its way in, even in the midst of Oriane's celebrated wit. The passage begins with the claim that Robert de Saint-Loup's language has become mystifying, that he speaks Latin; thus, the Duchess explains to the Princess of Parma:

> —Mais comment, Madame, l'autre jour il a dit dans une seule phrase, d'un seul trait: "Je ne connais pas d'exemple de *Sic transit gloria mundi* plus touchant"; je dis la phrase à Votre Altesse parce qu'après vingt questions et en faisant appel à des *linguistes*, nous sommes arrivés à la reconstituer, mais Robert a jeté cela sans reprendre haleine, on pouvait à peine distinguer qu'il y avait du latin là-dedans, il avait l'air d'un personnage du *Malade Imaginaire*! Et tout ça s'appliquait à la mort de l'impératrice d'Autriche!
>
> —Pauvre femme! s'écria la princesse, quelle délicieuse créature c'était!
>
> —Oui, répondit la duchesse, un peu folle, un peu insensée, mais c'était une très bonne femme, une gentille folle très aimable, je n'ai seulement jamais compris pourquoi elle n'avait jamais acheté un râtelier qui tînt, le sien se décrochait toujours avant la fin de ses phrases et elle était obligée de les interrompre pour ne pas l'avaler. [*Recherche*, II, 509–510]
>
> ["But, Madame, he said the other day, in a single phrase, all at once, 'I don't know of any more touching example of *Sic transit gloria mundi*'; I can repeat the phrase to Your Highness because, after endless questions and by consulting *linguists*, we were able to reconstruct it, but Robert simply spit it out without pausing for breath, you could hardly make out that there was Latin in it, he seemed just like a character from the *Malade Imaginaire*! And the whole thing had to do with the death of the Empress of Austria!"

"Poor woman!" cried the Princess, "what a delicious creature she was!"

"Yes," replied the Duchess, "a bit mad, a bit extravagant, but she was indeed a good woman, a sweet, kindhearted lunatic, only I never understood why she never got a set of false teeth that fit; hers always came loose in the middle of her sentence, and she couldn't finish talking or she would have swallowed them."]

Early in this sequence it becomes apparent that "speaking Latin" is a trademark for Proustian characters, that their personal idiom requires decoding if we are to see what is concealed in their words. Linguistic sleuthwork is always necessary in Proust, and it is going to be necessary here as well. Oriane's wit is displayed in her description of the deceased Empress of Austria not only as a sweet madwoman, but most specifically as a person whose dentures interfered with her speech, who had to interrupt her sentences before their conclusion, for fear of swallowing her false teeth. But much more than Guermantes wit is unfurling here. Interrupting one's speech is just what the author does at this juncture, as another spoken phrase is cited, which the reader initially takes for the continued dinner conversation:

—Cette Rachel m'a parlé de vous, elle m'a dit que le petit Saint-Loup vous adorait, vous préférait même à elle, me dit le prince Von, tout en mangeant comme un ogre, le teint vermeil, et dont le rire perpétuel découvrait toutes les dents.

["That Rachel was telling me about you; she said that young Saint-Loup worships you, likes you even better than he likes her," Prince Von told me, while eating like an ogre, with his face scarlet and all his teeth bared by his perpetual laughter.]

Not only has the speaker suddenly changed, taking the narrator and the reader by surprise, but the language itself is not far from Latin, offering a statement that needs decoding. Still more arrestingly, Proust *retains* his crucial eating motif, showing us a character charged with bestiality and emotion, showing us especially all those teeth, hence recalling the "delicious" dead princess who was always on the verge of eating her own teeth. We are close to the figures of fable here, the red-faced ogre who exposes his teeth to the narrator, much as the wolf does to Little Red Riding Hood. The innocent little narrator seeks to decipher the words:

> — Mais alors elle doit être jalouse de moi et me détester, répondis-je.
>
> —Pas du tout, elle m'a dit beaucoup de bien de vous. La maîtresse du Prince de Foix serait peut-être jalouse s'il vous préférait à elle. Vous ne comprenez pas? Revenez avec moi, je vous expliquerai tout cela.
>
> ["But then she must be jealous of me, she must despise me," I answered.
>
> "Not at all, she spoke very highly of you. The mistress of the Prince de Foix would perhaps be jealous, if he liked you more than her. You don't get it? Come home with me, and I'll explain it all to you."]

The Latin becomes still more impenetrable here, as the narrator is told of jealousy games and power plays which hinge on sexual inversion, but which are mystifying so long as the "key" is not revealed. Prince Von infers that the Prince of Foix's homosexual taste would make any affection for the narrator sexually charged, that his mistress would take umbrage; with Saint-Loup there is no danger, but of course he can explain it more fully to the narrator if they go out together. But, Proust's delicious novel is inverting even this, since we are to learn, later, that Saint-Loup is also a homosexual, and we are also to learn, later—but to sense *now*, by means of the threatening, bestial images—that Prince Von is also homosexual, that he has designs on the narrator, wants indeed to devour him. The boy explains that he cannot come, little realizing that his other plans will lure him into deeper waters still:

> — Je ne peux pas, je vais chez M. de Charlus à onze heures.
>
> ["I can't; I am to see M. de Charlus at eleven."]

Since Charlus has not yet been "officially" exposed, the boy does not know that his rendezvous is with the supreme pederast of the novel. Nor does the first-time reader. But, Proust has succeeded in devising a language of innocence, much as Blake did; and, like the English poet, he makes it possible to see the ravages and ironies of experience in those same words that appear so limpid at first glance. We reread this passage to discover its remarkable beauties. Perhaps, the most perfect turn of events comes with the Prince's response to the boy:

> —Tiens, il m'a fait demander hier de venir dîner ce soir, mais de ne pas venir après onze heures moins le quart. Mais si vous tenez à aller chez lui, venez au moins avec moi jusqu'au Théâtre Français, vous serez dans la périphérie, dit le prince qui croyait sans doute que cela signifiait "à proximité" ou peut-être "le centre."
>
> Mais ses yeux dilatés dans sa grosse et belle figure rouge me firent peur . . .
>
> ["Why, he sent word to me yesterday to dine with him tonight, but not to come after a quarter before eleven. But if you insist on going to see him, come with me at least as far as the Théâtre Français; you'll be in the periphery," the Prince said, doubtless believing that that word meant "proximity" or perhaps "center."
>
> But the dilated eyes in his large though handsome red face frightened me . . .]

The dilated eyes and apoplectic look of the Prince make his language visibly double, just as one might say false teeth double real teeth; finally, the linguistic delusion of "périphérie" passing for "à proximité" or perhaps "le centre" underscores the sexual delusion at hand, the homosexual intrigue that is being woven in front of our eyes if we are willing to reread. The upshot of such a narrative practice is that it delivers a network of linkage and innuendo, a multilayer script which, like that Sophoclean field of double-sowing, defies "straight vision" or seeing clear.[14]

14. This facet of Proustian prose is what I understand Gérard Genette to be describing, in more theoretical terms, in his superb discussion of Proustian style, "Proust palimpseste," in *Figures* (Paris: Seuil, 1966), pp. 39–65. But there is scandal in Proustian doubleness, a kind of transgression comparable to the Sophoclean "double-sowing" of incest, wherein the proprieties that are ruptured are semantic as well as ethical. Consider, in this light, Barthes' commentary on the treatment of the family that one finds in Sade: "La Famille se définit à deux niveaux: son 'contenu' (liens affectifs, sociaux, reconnaissance, respect, etc.), dont le libertin se moque, et sa 'forme,' le réseau des liens nominatifs, et par là même combinatoires, dont le libertin se joue, qu'il reconnaît pour mieux les truquer et sur quoi il fait porter des opérations syntaxiques; c'est à ce second niveau que pour Sade s'accomplit la

Far from being curtain-openers, these revelations make the scene more mobile, less knowable than it was before. Proust, like Ibsen, may appear "nineteenth century," in that he is bent on removing veils and disclosing what has been concealed; but, if we look more closely, his work displays a distinctly modernist kind of freedom, a writerly playfulness that works through a prose which is rarely univalent or closed, yielding ultimately something quite dynamic: a language so empowered and energized as to resemble a perpetual-motion machine. When you come down to it, there is a curious contempt for Truth in Proust, an aristocratic preference for play and ambivalence, whatever the moral price for such an attitude might be. Thus, at special moments in the *Recherche*, the would-be revelation stalls, peters out, and the prose moves majestically into the sovereign motions of dissembling. Truth bows to the higher, giddier powers of fiction. One such incident is Legrandin's exposure. This passage has all the earmarks of a classic revelation: Legrandin's imposture is to be illuminated, and we are to see the snob underneath. But what actually happens is something quite different, and it testifies to a new order

---

transgression originale, celle qui suscite l'enivrement d'une invention continue, la jubilation de surprises incessantes: 'Il raconte qu'il a connu un homme qui a foutu trois enfants qu'il avait de sa mère, desquels il y avait une fille qu'il avait fait épouser à son fils, de façon qu'en foutant celle-là, il foutait sa sœur, sa fille et sa belle-fille et qu'il contraignait son fils à foutre sa sœur et sa belle-mère.' La transgression apparaît ainsi comme une surprise de nomination: poser que le fils sera l'épouse ou le mari (selon que le père, Noirceuil, sodomise sa progéniture ou en est sodomisé) suscite chez Sade ce même émerveillement qui saisit le narrateur proustien lorsqu'il découvre que le côté de Guermantes et le côté de chez Swann se rejoignent: l'inceste, comme le temps retrouvé, n'est qu'une surprise de vocabulaire" (Roland Barthes, *Sade, Fourier, Loyola* [Paris: Seuil, 1971], p. 142). Tanner has also cited this passage in his discussion of the family in Rousseau (*Adultery in the Novel*, p. 154), but he is uninterested in the connection with Proust. What is intriguing here is the way that Barthes seizes on the semantic transgression in Sade, but fails to follow all the way through with the Proustian spin-off; the juxtaposition of the two "côtés" is less apposite than the "doubling" that characterizes the sexual behavior of Proust's people. Finally, Barthes' claim that the Sadean figure is both "épouse" and "mari" is not borne out by the quotation itself, but would apply perfectly to the metamorphoses in the *Recherche*. As for the dazzling epigram that closes Barthes' commentary, "l'inceste, comme le temps retrouvé, n'est qu'une surprise de vocabulaire," wit seems to have the better part of meaning.

of reality; Legrandin fabricates a rainbow of passion, and he does it in the corner of his eye:

> Il passa contre nous, ne s'interrompit pas de parler à sa voisine, et nous fit du coin de son œil bleu un petit signe en quelque sorte intérieur aux paupières et qui, n'intéressant pas les muscles de son visage, put passer parfaitement inaperçu de son interlocutrice; mais, cherchant à compenser par l'intensité du sentiment le champ un peu étroit où il en circonscrivait l'expression, dans ce coin d'azur qui nous était affecté il fit pétiller tout l'entrain de la bonne grâce qui dépassa l'enjouement, frisa la malice; il subtilisa les finesses de l'amabilité jusqu'aux clignements de la connivence, aux demi-mots, aux sous-entendus, aux mystères de la complicité; et finalement exalta les assurances d'amitié jusqu'aux protestations de tendresse, jusqu'à la déclaration d'amour, illuminant alors pour nous seuls, d'une langueur secrète et invisible à la châtelaine, une prunelle énamourée dans un visage de glace. [*Recherche*, I, 125–26][15]

> [He passed by us, and did not interrupt what he was saying to his companion; but from the corner of his blue eye he gave us a little sign that somehow remained on the inside of his eyelids, and this sign, not involving the muscles of his face, managed to pass quite unnoticed by the lady; but, seeking to compensate by the intensity of his sentiments for the somewhat restricted field in which they were expressed, he made that corner of an eye set apart for us sparkle with all the zest of affability, which went beyond playfulness and bordered on roguery; he refined on the delicacies of amiability right to the point of winks of connivance, hints, innuendos, mysteries of complicity; finally, he exalted these assurances of friendship into protestations of affection, even a declaration of love, thereby illuminating for us alone, with a secret languor invisible to the chatelaine, an enamored pupil in a countenance of ice.

15. Once again, I refer to Genette's brilliant treatment of these matters, in the analysis of Legrandin found in "Proust et le langage indirect," in *Figures II* (Paris: Seuil, 1969), esp. pp. 287–91. I find the Proust essays in the first two volumes of *Figures* infinitely more deft and illuminating, less tendentious and barbaric, than the famous *Figures III*, which is devoted, at least ostensibly, entirely to the *Recherche*.

How does one assess this kind of thing? Not even "irony" will account for the performance here. The curtain raises, once again, not on any single truth, but rather on an abyss. What we see is the astounding energy of signs, the prodigious spectacle of semiosis. The fine humor derives from the tiny material stage where the miracle is taking place, and Proust wants us to realize that whatever moral judgments we might care to make here are probably irrelevant. Legrandin's charade bespeaks a world where truth is not a major category, where the engendering power of signs is celebrated for its own particular vitality. For this is vitality, health, in the Proustian scheme, and nowhere is that more evident than in the contrary spectacle of the grandmother's death. The grandmother is the very paragon of truth and rectitude, unquestionably the most admirable character in the entire work; unitary and integral, she is the very opposite of Legrandin's chameleon identity, and because she has only one life, she is fated to lose it, and to serve as a sad example of what happens to truth; consider her on her deathbed:

> Courbée en demi-cercle sur le lit, un autre être que ma grand'mère, une espèce de bête qui se serait affublée de ses cheveux et couchée dans ses draps, haletait, geignait, de ses convulsions secouait les couvertures. Les paupières étaient closes et c'est parce qu'elles fermaient mal plutôt que parce qu'elles s'ouvraient qu'elles laissaient voir un coin de prunelle, voilé, chassieux, reflétant l'obscurité d'une vision organique et d'une souffrance interne. Toute cette agitation ne s'adressait pas à nous qu'elle ne voyait pas, ni ne connaissait. Mais si ce n'était qu'une bête qui remuait là, ma grand'mère où était-elle? [*Recherche*, II, 336]
>
> [Bent in a half-circle on the bed, a creature other than my grandmother, some kind of beast that had put on her hair and crouched in her bedclothes, was panting, groaning, shaking the covers by its convulsions. The eyelids were closed, and it is because they didn't close right, not that they were open, that they revealed the corner of a pupil, blurred, rheumy, mirroring the dimness of an organic vision and an internal suffering. None of this agitation was addressed to us, whom she didn't see, didn't know. But, if it was only a beast stirring there, then where was my grandmother?]

Let us remember Legrandin. The spectacles are eerily comparable: a performance, a question of whether love and recognition are reflected in an eye. Once more, we see the Little Red Riding Hood fable, but this time the wolf does more than show his teeth; he has eaten up the grandmother entirely; "straight vision" is put out for good.

The unrivaled master of multiple vision is doubtless Elstir. In the dazzling pages that enunciate the painter's aesthetic practice, Proust gives us the fullest embodiment of the artist's revenge, the supreme image of a man who makes and remakes the world, rather than discovering or revealing it. Thus, Elstir majestically composes and recomposes his materials: he inverts land- and sea-motifs in his paintings, using the magic of his genius to force the natural world to its knees; in his painting of Odette as Miss Sacripant, he performs once again, suggesting sexual ambivalence everywhere, not so much as a sign of character (Odette's) but as evidence of his own prowess:

> Mais surtout on sentait qu'Elstir, insoucieux de ce que pouvait représenter d'immoral ce travesti d'une jeune actrice . . . s'était au contraire attaché à ces traits d'ambiguité comme à un élément esthétique qui valait d'être mis en relief et qu'il avait tout fait pour souligner. [*Recherche*, I, 849]

> [But above all one felt that Elstir, indifferent to what might be immoral in the young actress's disguise, had, on the contrary, focused on those features of ambiguity as if they were an aesthetic element that deserved to be highlighted, and what he had done all he could to emphasize.]

In his portraits, Elstir "de-creates" his subjects and then recomposes them, to their horror and to his pleasure. His work explodes the truth/illusion dichotomy, for it has no truck with the givens of the world, and with that, the revelatory principle goes out of business. In Elstir's creativity and power, we see the modern Proust, the artist who will not abide by the dreary limits of realism or contingency.[16]

16. There is, as one might expect, a good bit of respectful, even adoring, criticism of Proust's notion of art, and it therefore comes as quite a surprise to encounter the biting but interesting sarcasm that J. Theodore Johnson, Jr. expresses concerning the august figure of Elstir: "We first meet Elstir "Dieu-le-Père" in his darkened studio recreating the world through his mind, an

There is no single moment when Proust declares his break with causality and exposure. Instead, the novel as a whole expresses its nostalgia for the old dualist, illusion/reality world, for it knows that madness becomes possible if orientation is not. In the very opening pages of the novel, we encounter a cautionary parable about the human need for single truths:

> Quand nous dormons et qu'une rage de dents n'est encore perçue par nous que comme une jeune fille que nous nous efforçons deux cent fois de suite de tirer de l'eau ou que comme un vers de Molière que nous nous répétons sans arrêter, c'est un grand soulagement de nous réveiller et que notre intelligence puisse débarrasser l'idée de rage de dents de tout déguisement héroïque ou cadencé. [*Recherche*, I, 28]
>
> [When we are asleep, and a raging toothache is not yet perceivable to us other than as a young girl whom we seek over and over to rescue from drowning, or a line of Molière that we repeat again and again, it is a great relief when we wake up and our intellect is able to sort out the notion of a toothache from all heroic or metric disguises.]

The dream is the one arena where things cannot be pinned down or taken by the throat, where the multiple script flaunts its richness.[17]

---

indeed curious occupation for a painter who is supposed to be an Impressionist and who would deal with the outside world. But since Proust rejects the outside world, his homologue must also reject the world, and so he most definitely strains our credulity by presenting us with an Impressionist who is painting a sunset in the early afternoon and who turns to paint some flowers without benefit of live flowers as a model. What do we find in the Elstir scene but that same 'magic lantern' trope so dear to Proust" ("Against 'Saint' Proust," p. 126). This is a niggardly critique of Elstir, but it is eye-opening nonetheless, and thereby peculiarly worthy of its subject.

17. Although I am citing this passage as evidence of Proustian multiplicity, J.-Francis Reille finds it quite possible to pin it down in his book on desire in the *Recherche*. After quoting the passage, he says: "On ne voit pas très bien en quoi un 'déguisement héroïque' rendrait une douleur plus pénible. Par contre, on comprend que l'angoisse obsessionnelle le fasse, et que le réveil, libérant le rêveur de l'obligation de sauver la jeune fille sans cesse remise en péril, apporte le soulagement. Mais d'où vient cette angoisse? On a dit longtemps 'Mal de dents, mal d'amour' avant que la dent ait été définie

The work of art, too, Proust must have sensed, is strangely bottomless and egalitarian in its findings and its operation, as painful as that may be for the mind that seeks answers to its mysteries and wants to wake up. Elstir's freedom from the phenomenal world, his capacity to make things anew, these are the grand tributes to the power of the artist. They are also responsible for the bottomless neurosis of Proustian psychology, because they adumbrate a world without truth or authority, a world of endless effigies and proliferations, a field of double-sowing where the old imperative to see clear and face the facts seems both futile and prehistoric.

3

The challenge of seeing clear is one that all writers, in some sense, tackle. One writes because one has something to say, to make known about reality, and this something usually entails a process of *revision* for the reader/spectator for whom the world is just a bit altered because of the work of art. It is hard to imagine a writer whose goal is to be opaque, to muddy the world, to lose the reader, to make the reader understand (confusedly) just how lost he is. Even *Tristram Shandy* moves toward order. Confusion and murkiness are undeniable ingredients of the literary experience, but one thinks of them as somehow instrumental, as vehicles toward some desirable clarity, as phases of initiation, modes of entry, for which an achievable exit exists, on the far side of the book. One's willingness to encounter art, to invest one's energies and time and intelligence in it, must derive, at least in part, from the elementary confidence that there is light ahead, that a clarifying moment is on the way, that this whole business leads to something. Taken to such an extreme, this formula looks dreadfully utilitarian, but I do not think it can be dismissed out of hand, when one thinks about the purposes of art and the rationale for taking it seriously—or, to put it more crassly still, the reasons for finishing the books we start.

---

comme symbole sexuel, notamment dans la connotation de la chute—onanisme, castration—ce qui est loin d'être indifférent ici où la thématique du rêve est ouvertement érotique, mettant en scène une jeune fille, dans une circonstance de frustration—la séparation d'avec la mère. Freud a analysé ce type de rêve: 'Lorsqu'un homme rêve qu'il sauve une femme de l'eau, cela signifie: il la rend mère, ce qui, d'après les réflexions précédentes a le sens de: il en fait sa mère.' " (*Le Temps*, p. 58).

But we have had ample opportunity to see that this issue of seeing clear is by no means a straightforward issue. The curtain-lifting text is an imprisoning text, a text that systematically entraps (by dint of its own system-nature); the light comes, but it illuminates bondage, reveals the mesh in which the subject is caught. This exposure and this knowledge may be unbearable as in the case of Oedipus, who puts out his eyes after discovering the extent of his relation; in Ibsen's *Ghosts*, we see Oswald blindly, pathetically, seeking the sun, and this spectacle of a man becoming an infant in front of our eyes is so brutally regressive that it is as if time were turned around, turned backward, erasing any possibility of freedom. But the determinist text disturbs in still other ways, transforming the writer into scribe, ruling out any kind of reprieve, acknowledging no maneuvering room, dishing out its medicine to caught-up figures. There is, as I have tried to show, something of an affront here, and one can discern a strange rivalry between artist and fate in many of the texts we have discussed, a strange tug-of-war to determine just where authority is, just who has the last word. So, Ibsen moves into his Ekdal Attic and has Solness and Hilde fashion a castle in the air, because he has discovered a new freedom, a realm of desire and fantasy that is not constrained by truth or revelation, and thereby offers not so much a refuge as an entire new arena for life. In Proust we see further evidence of the artist's revenge, his refusal to abide by givens, and thus Proustian revelation becomes something infinitely open-ended, multiple, defying closure. It is indeed a matter of "having the last word," because words are of the essence here; the words of the writer can become energized and liberated, establishing an echo chamber of their own, multilayered in their palimpsest arrangement, part of a ludic scheme that inverts straight answers and mocks the truth.

I have called this "the artist's revenge"; what about the rest of us? Is the writer especially privileged in this cavalier handling of truth? What kind of maneuvering room or last word do ordinary people have, in their skirmishes with ugly truths, with indicting facts? "Facing the facts" is a time-honored expression for looking life in the eye, and although this discussion has perhaps seemed excessively abstract, we are actually touching on one of the central challenges in life, as well as in art. Does knowing about one help us to cope with the other? One of the often-repeated tenets of this study is that we are in the dark concerning the shape of our own experience, and that literature can play a privileged role here. Very few books show us as much about our daily skirmishes and transactions with home truths as Joyce's *Ulysses* does.

The sad irony, of course, is that *Ulysses is* a cultural luxury item, perhaps comparable to *foie gras a*nd truffles, and although it cuts a commanding figure in histories of literature and in graduate seminars, it is hardly read by the common man or woman. Yet, it is truly a book of life, a book of basics, in just the sense we have been discussing. In the person of Bloom, Joyce gives us an unforgettable portrait of a man who must negotiate his life, who knows that there are truths, pressures, ghosts, and issues which he cannot deal with, head-on; Bloom's escapades make him the perfect fit for Dickens' term, the artful dodger.[18] Much of *Ulysses*' most enjoyable writing has to do with the wily Bloom controlling his life, peering into the high drama that surrounds him but quickly diverting his gaze toward more palatable issues. Much in this man's life *could* take him under: the death of his son, the suicide of his father, the infidelity of his wife. Traditional fiction would treat us to a detailed, agonizing plumbing of those heady issues: Proust would offer exquisite discourses on guilt and memory; Faulkner would play it in terms of loss and rage. But Joyce does what most of us do: he treats these issues as impending pressures, spots where we cannot afford to dwell long or, worse still, to end up. One recalls the *père* Swann in Proust's *Recherche* who thinks about his dead wife often, but never very long, "souvent mais peu à la fois," much to the amusement of the narrator's father. Proust takes, on the whole, a dim view of artful dodging, but not so Joyce; he takes pleasure in ducking, makes us realize that there may be a good deal to be said for it, and therefore, much of *Ulysses* depicts the rich antics of evasion and maneuvering, as Bloom squirms through

18. In characterizing Bloom as "artful dodger," I would like to add a Dickensian flavor to the brilliant maneuvering gambits that Fritz Senn has discussed concerning *Ulysses*. Senn's view of the book as a "polytropic" text, and the fascinating ways in which its multiplicity informs character and plot as well as style and manner, establish a kind of base reading of Joyce's novel for me. But, just because Senn is so attuned to the tricks and recombinant strategies of *Ulysses*, he is also less inclined to read the book strategically; instead, his Olympian perspective causes him to emphasize Joyce's neutrality and indeterminacy, and to warn against any single-minded or "monotropic" interpretations. See "Book of Many Turns," in *Joyce's Dislocutions: Essays on Reading as Translation*, ed. John Paul Riquelme (Baltimore: Johns Hopkins University Press, 1984), pp. 121–37.

his plight-ridden day in Dublin.[19] To return to our metaphor of the sun, we could say that its light of truth is potentially fatal, as we see when it finally goes up in *Ghosts*, but we all know that we cannot look directly at the sun, that we can only squint at it now and then. The balancing act in *Ulysses* entails that Bloom look at the light just long enough for the reader to measure these existential crises which surround him, but that he then exercise the Odyssean virtues of shrewdness and cunning in his modern efforts to "navigate" around the shoals and reefs that Joyce has set out for him.

In one of the early Bloom chapters of the novel, corresponding to Homer's "lotus-eaters," we encounter the Bloomish evasion in its simplest, most direct form. Bloom recalls words of his father about Nathan and the poignancy of changing one's God, and Joyce moves directly from memory to musing:

> Every word is so deep, Leopold.
>
> Poor papa! Poor man! I'm glad I didn't go into the room to look at his face. That day! O dear! O dear! Ffoo! Well, perhaps it was best for him.[20]

So straightforward as to be almost childlike ("O dear! Ffoo!"), this expression of pain and the resultant turning away from the corpse and the memory will be handled in increasingly complex ways throughout the novel. Turning away from the facts comes to be a kind of lotus-solution, an opiate that serves to palliate or disguise the ugly truth. But even in this passage, Joyce is going to display his wiles: the text moves from Bloom's mind to the "outside" world, but it would seem that lotus is still high on the agenda: "Mr Bloom went round the corner and passed the drooping nags of the hazard. No use thinking of it anymore. Nosebag time. Wish I hadn't met that M'Coy fellow" (76). The "drooping nags" and their "nosebags" will be fully

19. There is something wonderfully natural, perhaps inevitable, in the sometimes evasive, sometimes rival-like character that language itself acquires in literature. There is a moment in Sterne's *Tristram Shandy* where the capacity of language to offset experience receives an almost paradigmatic formulation: "A blessing which tied up my father's tongue, and a misfortune which set it loose with good grace, were pretty equal" (*The Life and Opinions of Tristram Shandy, Gentleman*, ed. Ian Watt [Boston: Houghton Mifflin, 1965], p. 266).

20. James Joyce, *Ulysses* (New York: Vintage, 1961), p. 76. Subsequent quotations will be taken from this edition and noted parenthetically in the body of the text.

developed into a complex narrative cluster, coming to signify, at once, complacency, evasion, impotence, and bad faith; hence, the horses are doing considerable narrative business for Joyce: "Poor jugginses! Damn all they know or care about anything with their long noses stuck in nosebags. Too full for words. Still they get their feed all right and their doss. Gelded too: a stump of black guttapercha wagging limp between their haunches. Might be happy all the same that way" (77). Before Joyce is finished, this composite will come to represent evasion in still more forms: the appeal of organized religion and the Catholic Mass in particular, and of course, subsuming everything else, the evasion of none other than Leopold Bloom, who is doing the musing.

Bloom has been abundantly (and rightly) admired for his curiosity and his openness to the world, but these qualities are profoundly protectionist: they direct Bloom "outside" when the going is tough "inside." *Ulysses* is an astoundingly "strategic" novel, and in Joyce's hands, the novel form loses a good deal of its prior innocence: nothing is simply "given" or free or weightless or without context in this book, and we realize that the inner thoughts of a character are not random, that they can be a form of navigation, that we think about certain subjects to avoid others, that all the projects of the psyche have a tactical dimension. Hence, the behavior of this text is psychological to the core, but its psychology is everywhere, in the textual utterances, but also in the interstices, in the changing of venue or subject, in the actual dance of the mind rather than in single enunciations. Bloom turns away from his painful thoughts, yes, but the scene delivers the same message. Joyce's irony and artistry are especially visible at such moments, because we understand that "outside" is never all that far from "inside." The musings of the dodger lead away from trouble; they are virtually "street wise" in their security operation, taking Bloom out of danger, skirting pitfalls; but their exit is illusory, and their thrust outward is no more reliable than the motion of a boomerang which inevitably circles back, which returns with all-the-more-murderous intensity, all the harder you throw it.[21]

21. Hugh Kenner has offered a charming analysis of the first "Calypso" scene between Bloom and Molly (the distributing of the mail) in which he illustrates the kind of maneuvering that the wily Bloom engages in. Especially nice is Kenner's notation of that word "carefully" ("—A letter for me from Milly, he said carefully, and a card to you. And a letter for you."):

We are to read, many chapters later, the Joycean law of continuity: "So it returns. Think you're escaping and run into yourself. Longest way round is the shortest way home" (377). The entire project of the *Portrait* goes up in smoke here; nothing is ultimately "leavable": nationality, language, religion, family. Flying over nets is adolescent fantasy, and the Daedalus that Joyce admires may be the maker of the maze, instead of the man who constructed the wings to leave it. Portraiture itself is in trouble here, since you cannot depict an individual unless you know where he begins and where he ends; but, the subject is decentered in *Ulysses*, scattered a little all over the place, finding his figure as he goes, realizing that he is, in every sense of the term, a "made-up" person, one who is "composed" of the things he encounters. The old demarcation between self and world is so blurred here that the concept of evasion loses much of its meaning, since there is no longer any place that is sufficiently "not you" for you to go to. Not that Joyce ignores the so-called real world out there; on the contrary, few books do homage to the grittiness of the phenomenal world in as thoroughgoing a way as *Ulysses* does. But Joycean arrangement is cunning: it is happy to insert large chunks of "material" into the text, large slices of life; however, it then makes that inert material speak volumes, makes it mirror the personal and moral issues that have been, at least ostensibly, left.

Let us see how it works. We know that the item Bloom would most like to escape is, of course, Blazes Boylan, whom he is always running into. One of these "encounters" is staged when Bloom is in the coach going to Dignam's funeral. The paragraph begins with objective description, "They went past the bleak pulpit of Saint Mark's," and soon enough moves into Bloom's mind as he wonders whether Martin Cunningham could get him a pass for the Gaiety. Next paragraph is a one-liner:

> He's coming in the afternoon. Her songs. [92]

This is obviously thought, not spoken, and it is evasively thought by Bloom: "He" must be Boylan, whom (as the clever reader must figure out on his own) Bloom presumably has sighted, but the evasion lies in "Her songs," since Bloom is well aware that Boylan is coming for more than singing (although, again, the reader may not be aware of the game, at this stage). The next line is another one-liner:

"Bloom's way of negotiating minefields," says Kenner, and he is right (*Joyce's Voices* [Berkeley: University of California Press, 1978], p. 85).

> Plasto's. Sir Philip Crampton's memorial fountain bust. Who was he?

This is pure Joyce. Any other writer in the history of fiction would have pursued the line of Boylan and his coming rendezvous with Molly. Joyce has Bloom describe the street scene, even to the extent of musing, Who was Sir Philip Crampton? Or, indeed, can we call this "musing" at all? Bloom is escaping once again, although there is no way to "measure" the urgency or slackness of this turning away. Fatigue, terror, panic, indifference? The text will now belatedly verbalize what it has shown:

> —How do you do? Martin Cunningham said, raising his palm to his brow in salute.
>
> —He doesn't see us, Mr Power said. Yes, he does. How do you do?
>
> —Blazes Boylan, Mr Power said. There he is airing his quiff. [92]

Just as Boylan receives public notice, forcing Bloom to do at least something, the text gives us the bizarre line:

> Just that moment I was thinking.

Private once more, this line must reflect Bloom's thinking, but once again, it reflects his evasive thinking, since he is obviously telling himself what posture to assume, what air to put on as the others acknowledge Boylan. He, Bloom, will be lost in thought. It is a classic dodge. Boylan approaches still closer:

> Mr Dedalus bent across to salute. From the door of the Red Bank the white disc of a straw hat flashed reply: passed. [92]

In pithy shorthand Joyce delivers the menacing Boylan, and we can feel the relief in the colon and the consoling verb "passed" at the end. Now for Bloom's performance:

> Mr Bloom reviewed the nails of his left hand, then those of his right hand. The nails, yes. Is there anything more in him that they she sees? Fascination. Worst man in Dublin. That keeps him alive. They sometimes feel what a person is. Instinct. But a type like that. My nails. I am just looking at them: well pared. And after: thinking alone. Body getting a bit softy. I would notice that from remembering. What causes that I suppose the skin can't contract quickly enough when the flesh falls off. But the

> shape is there. The shape is there still. Shoulders. Hips. Plump. Night of the dance dressing. Shift stuck between the cheeks behind.
>
> He clasped his hands between his knees and, satisfied, sent his vacant glance over the faces. [92]

Nothing is ever simple in Joyce, and much is happening in these lines. We note first Bloom's disciplined charade, as he methodically progresses from the left hand to the right hand, conducting his review; "review" lends an air of public ritual to the phrase, and the deliberate, slow-but-steady pace of the prose and the gesture contribute enormously to the show of control that is affected here. What is Bloom reviewing, we might wonder: "The nails, yes." But the interior monologue blows that particular cover, at least for us if not for the people in the coach, and we see Boylan crash back into the picture, into the coach. Bloom deals head-on with Boylan here, wondering about his magnetism, and the run-on from "they" to "she" clearly signals the Molly-Boylan match. But discipline is not lost, and the troops are again rallied: "My nails. I am just looking at them: well pared." This emphasis on nails, for the perceptive reader, cannot fail to echo the earlier Bloomism equating I.N.R.I. with "iron nails ran in," and once again the Joycean text speaks its many tongues, since the Crucifixion reference is curiously apposite for the wedge-like, invading hurt caused by Boylan and Molly. Once again, we are witnessing the Joycean short circuit: "Think you're escaping and run into yourself." Evasion, in *Ulysses*, is rendered as a textual "from the frying pan into the fire," and things can neither be fled nor forgotten: "The shape is there still." The following line, "And after: thinking alone," also does double duty; "thinking alone" is Bloom's cover at this moment ("Just that moment I was thinking"), but "And after" entitles us to widen our reference: after what? after coitus? Certainly, the entire phrase, "And after: thinking alone," resonates for us here, achieves an emblematic status as figure of Bloom's life: the man who has ceased having sex with his wife and spends his time thinking alone. Thinking what? More than nails are being reviewed here. The body getting "softy" may refer, initially, to his fingers, but it soon enough pulls its true prey into the picture. Memory again hints at a lost sexual existence, and Bloom's mind closes its reverie on the subject it loves best, the remembered luscious body of Molly Bloom, a body that was his but will be Boylan's today at 4:00 P.M.

Joyce is more Proustian than has been realized, at least in passages like the one cited, or the famous memory of the seedcake passed between Molly and him on Howth Hill, but he is a reluctant Proustian, in that memories are obliged to get around the defenses of his character. The sequence closes ostensibly where it ostensibly began, with the nails that Bloom can one final time pass in review, then become satisfied (with what? his nails? his performance? his memory?) and then make his most sublime contribution to the conversation by sending a *vacant* glance over their faces, a glance that is vacant only for those in the coach since it is full indeed for Joyce's reader, to whom it is perhaps destined in the first place since it went, condescendingly, over the faces of the others.

As still another instance of Bloomish evasion, let us consider the saga of Pat the waiter. Bloom is sharing a table with Richie Goulding, and, true to form, he seeks to avoid unpleasant thoughts by letting his mind dawdle over Pat the waiter: "Car near there now. Talk. Talk. Pat! Doesn't. Settling those napkins. Lot of ground he must cover in the day. Paint face behind on him then he'd be two. Wish they'd sing more. Keep my mind off" (280). It is obvious that the first phrase refers to Boylan's impending rendezvous. "Talk. Talk." works doubly, describes perhaps the noise in the Ormond, but also has a hint of urgency in it, as if the "!" belonged to them rather than to "Pat!" and suggests the frantic need for cover. Only Pat is there to provide this service, and Bloom will make the best of it. "Doesn't" stands as a marvelous piece of unspecified verbal negation floating midair, a denial that is possible only in language since Bloom can stop nothing in reality. Watching Pat front and back, thinking perhaps in terms of front and back, Bloom "doubles" Pat, gives him two faces, struggles to put together something to ward off what is pressing in, and comes up with the following:

> Bald Pat who is bothered mitred the napkins. Pat is a waiter hard of his hearing. Pat is a waiter who waits while you wait. Hee hee hee hee. He waits while you wait. Hee hee. A waiter is he. Hee hee hee hee. He waits while you wait. While you wait if you wait he will wait while you wait. Hee hee hee hee. Hoh. Wait while you wait. [280]

Here is how one keeps one's mind off. The words repeat, roll over, and do somersaults, giving a kind of stuck-record effect that slows down psychological activity. The phrase becomes musical in front of our eyes, and its sonorities and grammatical skeleton are persistently foregrounded at the expense of its meaning. There is a certain Odyssean cunning at work here, a kind of verbal boycott, an effort to impede bad news, to create a linguistic filibuster, to put up a ludic roadblock. We cannot fail to see, however, that Joyce has once again "networked" Bloom, displayed Bloom's entrapment in the very midst of his sortie. Because *waiting* is of the very essence here, not the waiting of Pat but that of Bloom, waiting for Boylan to reach Molly. Hence, to play out "waiting" in every hue and color, to make it pirouette into "While you wait if you wait he will wait while you wait," does not so much evade Bloom's predicament as *flaunt* it, "spell it out" as it were. Joyce is again forcing Bloom to run into himself just as he thinks he is escaping. But that is not all. Joyce's prose is at once ludic and pathological. To repeat a word or phrase over and over leads, as everyone knows, to a predictable paradox: the word loses its meaning and becomes an empty shell; but, no less true, the incessant sounding of the word displays its hold on the mind, wildly energizes its signifying power, signifies obsession. Finally, we can hardly miss the most obvious ploy of this passage, the sound-game it plays: the transformation of "he" into "hee" and then into "hee hee hee hee" delivers unmistakably the sound of laughter, but it is manifestly the laughter of the creator toward his creature. The "Sirens" chapter where this occurs is, if anything, still far more complex than I have indicated, and in it Joyce is weaving together many different threads and sounds that "echo" Bloom's plight, that speak his secrets, make both public and musical his inner dilemma.

Henry James once said that the artist is the man for whom nothing is lost, and this retentiveness is the hallmark of Joyce's art. At the core of this richly conservative imagination lies a dark truth: "you cannot escape, you cannot get away." James Joyce of Trieste, Zurich, and Paris managed what his fictive surrogate Stephen could not pull off: he left Dublin; but as for flying past the nets of language, religion, and nationality, it is not a thing that can be done, partly because every act of repudiation is secretly an act of homage, partly because the "longest way round is the shortest way home." On the continent, steel pen in hand, ostensibly free, Joyce created two characters that are haunted by the ghosts of their dead, porous to their environment, threatened in their integrity. As if this were not enough, as if the writer's power could not be exercised without tyrannizing his creatures, Joyce went on to bind and invade them in still another terrible way, namely by dint of his writing. All writing is doubtless an assertion of power, and all characters are (ineluctably and deviously) coerced by the works they inhabit—for they have to negotiate a world not of their own making, but manifestly one devised by their creator—but Joycean writing binds and enmeshes his people, links them and exposes them in ways they can neither know nor control.

Much of the poignancy of *Ulysses* is to be found in the lovable, wily Bloom's efforts at concealment and balance as he negotiates the carnival world where Joyce has inserted him. Whereas Proust's Elstir is empowered to recompose the people and things he paints, in Joyce the world of the text is increasingly energized and encroaching, seemingly bent on exposure, making secrecy and sanctuary impossible. "Circe" is clearly the most ruthless display of the revelatory poetics. Let us remember the passages cited from "Lotus-eaters" and "Sirens," passages that depend entirely on the inner/outer dialectic which Joyce handles so brilliantly. In those instances, we saw what could not be seen, namely the private thoughts of Bloom, and we also saw just how "unsheltered" that private realm was, how persistently the external scene exposed Bloom, how difficult evasion proved to be; nonetheless, Bloom's mind was his own place, a place to practice his wit where none could see, a place to stage his private war with what life has done to him, and no one to be the wiser for it. In "Circe" those days are over. Joyce seems to have intuited Wallace Stevens' apocalyptic line (for it spells the death of poetry), "let be be the finale of seem," and his strong lamp now affixes its beam on Bloom, exposing him utterly and putting him endlessly on trial. All that has been protected up to now, by being thought rather than enacted, by being past rather than present, by being might-have-been rather than actuality, all this now receives voice and form, so that there are no secrets, no virtualities left. It is both hilarious and terrifying, since we depend a great deal on the kinds of distinctions and demarcations that Joyce is sovereignly erasing here. Everything that Bloom has ever kept to himself—whatever its status: deed, desire, fear—comes, like a boomerang, back, and publicly so. As Beaufoy says, "Why, look at the man's private life! Leading a quadruple existence! Street angel and house devil" (459–60). Bloom's erotic dalliances, his lusting for society women, his sexual proclivities, his "exchange" with Gertie on the beach, his past moments of masturbation and defecation, his entire psychic agenda, all this undergoes a miraculous ontological sea change and now tangibly occupies the stage. One would have to look far afield to find a comparable depiction of the self on trial, caught in a determinist web, victimized by its own inner life, an inner life that is no longer inner, but totally reified and bent on terrorizing its former host. Artful dodging is possible only when the self can still master its two environments, the inner one and the outer one: by sidestepping, staring at your nails, dawdling, putting on a charade. In "Circe" Bloom is pure artistic material, malleable even unto his sex, and thus his cunning evasions are at a close. The curtain has been raised on Bloom, and he is mired in his "truth."[22]

In order to expose Bloom so exhaustively, Joyce has had to break all the rules of realism: soap bars speak, ghosts appear, the past returns, the virtual becomes real. The character's freedom has quite simply been swapped for that of the author. In exercising his power, Joyce seems to have understood that his authorial freedom was potentially boundless, that it *could* be used to illuminate the "inner" Bloom, but that it was by no means restricted to the needs and vagaries of character. Hence, in "Ithaca" we have the spectacle of a style that no longer even pretends to be revelatory, but instead goes about its truest mission: to make a world of its own. Here is the artist's revenge, for the determinist nets can be flown over as long as one is willing to pay the price of turning the self into a cipher. Joyce pays it. The "bottom line" truth of Leopold Bloom is no longer to be found by exposure of past and ghosts; it is to be manufactured. Who is Bloom? Bloom is an assemblage of letters: Leopold Bloom, Ellpodbomool, Molldopeloob, Bollopedoom, Old Ollebo, M.P. The old-fashioned essentialist drama of a young man seeking a father and an older man seeking a son yields to the numbers game:

> What relation existed between their ages?
>
> 16 years before in 1888 when Bloom was of Stephen's present age Stephen was 6. 16 years after in 1920 when Stephen would be of Bloom's present age Bloom would be 54. In 1936 when Bloom would be 70 and Stephen 54 their ages initially in the ratio of 16 to 0 would be as 17½ to 13½, the proportion increasing and the disparity diminishing according as arbitrary fu-

22. It hardly needs to be emphasized that I am not speaking of "truth" here in some kind of demonstrable or provable sense. But I think we are expected to regard fabulous events of "Circe" as items on Bloom's psychic agenda, and the force of the chapter lies precisely in its erasure of those traditional distinctions between event and desire. For a very different, very interesting reading of Joyce's own strategies for handling issues that were high on his own personal psychic agenda, see Lionel Trilling's "James Joyce in His Letters," in *Joyce: A Collection of Critical Essays*, ed. William Chace (Englewood Cliffs: Prentice-Hall, 1974), pp. 143–65.

> ture years were added, for if the proportion existing in 1883 had continued immutable, conceiving that to be possible, till then 1904 when Stephen was 22 Bloom would be 374 and in 1920 when Stephen would be 38, as Bloom then was, Bloom would be 646 while in 1952 when Stephen would have attained the maximum postdiluvian age of 70 Bloom, being 1190 years alive having been born in the year 714, would have surpassed by 221 years the maximum antediluvian age, that of Methusalah 969 years, while, if Stephen would continue to live until he would attain that age in the year 3072 A.D., Bloom would have been obliged to have been alive 83,300 years, having been obliged to have been born in the year 81,396 B.C. [679]

This passage remains one of the most hysterical sequences that Joyce ever penned, and it stands as a sober (or dizzying) reminder of where the fiction of relationship might take you. Relationship is a construct, and in the realm of numbers, everything is possible, unlike in the realm of flesh. Joyce gently and beautifully fictionalizes here, proposing a respectful narrative frame for his outlandish reckonings, making the appropriate biblical references, obliging ever so sweetly his characters to play by his arithmetic rules. There is causality and necessity in this passage, but it is manifestly a causality of the artist's making, unconstrained by other forms of causality that flesh obeys; and in this arena Joyce is free to fling his characters back and forth like weightless tag-alongs, frisbees rather than boomerangs, docilely going exactly where he has decided they can be made to go. Sophocles exposed connection; Joyce invents his:

> Did they find their educational careers similar?
>
> Substituting Stephen for Bloom Stoom would have passed successively through a dame's school and the high school. Substituting Bloom for Stephen Blephen would have passed successively through the preparatory, junior, middle and senior grades of the intermediate and through the matriculation, first arts, second arts and arts degree course of the royal university. [682]

Blephen and Stoom have arrived at last. We may wish to regard them as a special pair, but their merging is manifestly achieved by authorial fiat, a marriage of names only, a linguistic tandem that has no truck with human relationship. Joyce's treatment of Bloom in "Ithaca" is perfectly expressed in the sense of power and control we find in these lines:

> Reduce Bloom by cross multiplication of reverses of fortune, from which these supports protected him, and by elimination of all positive values to a negligible negative irrational unreal quantity. [725]

Bloom is an integer, little more than the dot that closes the chapter; he is the material of the artist.[23] He is, of course, relatable to Stephen formally, wordwise, but his dodging days are over. In this new scheme, there are no truths to discover or avoid; but in their place we see a world of inebriating play, a world of rhyme but not reason, a world where writing is pure power, making its own rules, its own liaisons, its own logic. Joyce has left Ireland.

4

In the thirteenth stanza of his "Thirteen Ways of Looking at a Blackbird," Stevens proposes a paradox:

> It was evening all afternoon.
> It was snowing
> And it was going to snow.[24]

One can, as it were, "bend over backward" conceptually, and thereby ratify these lines: the darkness of the afternoon made it seem like evening; the snow was somehow discontinuous, intermittent; etc. But the full force of what Stevens is doing can be felt only when one allows him his contradiction, because then we see, very clearly, that words can enunciate propositions which are not logically possible. Stevens' poem is enough of a tribute to the generative powers of the imagination to warrant such an interpretation of these lines. At the close of a quite different text, *Molloy*, Beckett introduces a similar paradox:

23. Needless to say, most Joyceans do not take such a dim view of the happenings in "Ithaca," and it is customarily asserted that Bloom, like his legendary counterpart, returns "home" in some meaningful sense of the word. Perhaps he does. But how elastic are we to think him? At what point is the convention of character utterly discarded? For an appealing reading of Bloom's return as part of a larger Joycean strategy of enveloping the daytime, male principle within a larger nighttime, female order, see Fritz Senn's "Nausicaa," in *Joyce's Dislocutions*, esp. pp. 165–66.

24. Wallace Stevens, "Thirteen Ways of Looking at a Blackbird," in *The Palm at the End of the Mind* (New York: Vintage Books, 1972), p. 22.

> Alors je rentrai dans la maison et j'écrivis. Il est minuit. La pluie fouette les vitres. Il n'était pas minuit. Il ne pleuvait pas.[25]

> [Then I went into the house and I wrote. It is midnight. The rain is splashing the windows. It was not midnight. It was not raining.]

Once again we see the rivalry between language and its referent, between signifier and signified. These are perfectly innocuous sentences, but, taken together, they utterly undermine the narrative situation, since there is no credible truth scenario here, no real-life scene that could answer at once to both statements. Stevens closed his paradox with the figure of the poetic imagination: "The blackbird sat / In the cedar-limbs." Beckett behaves more like the post-Joycean that he is, showing us in the very language just how such a paradox is manageable: "Alors je rentrai dans la maison et j'écrivis" (I went into the house and I wrote). We could perhaps alter the period after "écrivis" into a colon, and then there would be no problem, since you can write whatever you care to, whether what the words say is "possible" or not; but, even if we do nothing to Beckett's sentence, he has nonetheless informed us of the writerly authority at work here, the designation of language itself as the source of the text, not its servile lackey.

These are curious matters, and they have much to do with how "readable" our world is, and how "readable" our texts are. Although the professional critic may be at ease with texts that assert the kind of language priority visible in Stevens and Beckett, the ordinary reader is understandably shocked by such procedures and legitimately feels that an article of faith has been flouted. The linguists and the post-structuralists never tire of explaining to us that language is far less controllable than the layman thinks—that it is, on the one hand, a closed linguistic system with a purely conventional relation to the things it names, but that it is, on the other hand, an astoundingly open system, freighted with ideological and cultural cargo that enters all enunciation, even though the speaking layman rarely takes it into account. Most of us have not come all that far from Molière's Monsieur Jourdain, who is flabbergasted to learn that he speaks "de la prose." Words, like colors, can appear as building blocks or constituent elements for edifices that do not or cannot exist. But when

25. Samuel Beckett, *Molloy* (Paris: 10/18, 1963), p. 234.

words are *used* (for orientation, explanation, even expression), when they are an operational currency, then we expect them, as it were, to "behave." Most readers would not venture very far into the texts they read if they felt that the language itself were inherently capricious and unreliable, that it was flexing its own muscles at the expense of its referents. It is not certain that a text written entirely in such a ludic vein could be read at all, and much of the criticism devoted to "hermetic" literature consists in "translating" it, showing that its referentiality is intact, but is located and indicated in ways we had not understood.

The novel has not generally been thought of as "unreadable," and the very appellation "prosaic" indicates something that is matter-of-fact, straightforward, whereas its counterpart, "poetic," warns us of metaphoric reaches, of meanings that may be at variance with the actual terms themselves. The sociological history of the novel teaches us that it was often looked down upon, just because of its artlessness, its all-too-easy commerce with the marketplace world. These are, of course, generalizations, and the novel has been a subject of verbal experimentation ever since Rabelais; and its dubious purchase on "reality," its dependence on paradigms that blind as well as illuminate, has been central to the genre ever since Cervantes. Even so, fictioneers, for the most part, have rarely highlighted their own medium—words—to such an extent as we saw in the selections by Stevens and Beckett, as indeed we saw adumbrated in the final chapters of *Ulysses*. In these passages there is something of a crisis, because the reader is no longer able to entertain the notion of a world "out there" which is consonant with the words of the text. It is at this point that we reach the end-phase of our inquiry into the status of "seeing clear." Seeing clear, and the revelatory poetics that embody or promote it, demand of language that it be a faithful, reliable guide, a self-effacing instrument of denotation. Although such a view of language may seem simplistic in today's critical climate, it seems to have been a normative one for several centuries of novel-writing, and it seems especially requisite for the literature of exposure. But, what happens in novels where this faith in verbal transparency is gone? Ever since the story of Babel we have known that such transparency was a fiction, but what does one make of texts that flaunt the autonomy of their medium, celebrate through their words vistas and constructs that have no possible counterpart in the world "out there"? Returning to our earlier examples, could you build an entire novel on the structures of paradox evident in Stevens and Beckett? What could you see clear there?

As is well known, some of the most interesting writers of this century proceed along just these lines. The remainder of this essay will be devoted to a passing glance at some of these books, with a special eye toward the problems of vision and orientation which occur in those precincts. One of the most notorious practitioners of verbal autonomy is Alain Robbe-Grillet, and although his work is suspect from a number of angles, it will continue to stand as a kind of brazen triumph of *écriture* at the expense of plot. Consider, for instance, the opening lines of *Dans le labyrinthe*:

> Je suis seul ici, maintenant, bien à l'abri. Dehors il pleut, dehors on marche sous la pluie en courbant la tête, s'abritant les yeux d'une main tout en regardant quand même devant soi, à quelques mètres devant soi, quelques mètres d'asphalte mouillé; dehors il fait froid, le vent souffle entre les branches noires dénudées; le vent souffle dans les feuilles, entraînant les rameaux entiers dans un balancement, dans un balancement, balancement, qui projette son ombre sur le crépi blanc des murs. Dehors il y a du soleil, il n'y a pas un arbre, ni un arbuste, pour donner de l'ombre, et l'on marche en plein soleil, s'abritant les yeux d'une main tout en regardant devant soi, à quelques mètres seulement devant soi, quelques mètres d'asphalte poussiéreux où le vent dessine des parallèles, des fourches, des spirales.[26]

> [I am alone here, now, well under cover. Outside, it is raining. Outside, someone (*on*) walks in the rain, with his head bent down, sheltering his eyes with his hands, nonetheless looking straight ahead, a few meters ahead, a few meters of wet asphalt; outside, it is cold, the wind is blowing through the black, bare branches; the wind blows through the leaves, rocking whole boughs, rocking them, rocking them, casting their shadows on the rough, white walls. Outside, the sun is shining, there is no tree, no bush, to give any shade, and someone walks in the hot sun, sheltering his eyes with his hand, looking straight ahead, only a few meters ahead, a few meters of dusty asphalt where the wind draws parallels, forks, spirals.]

26. Alain Robbe-Grillet, *Dans le labyrinthe* (Paris: 10/18, 1974), pp. 9–10.

This is hypnotic prose, and its sonorous cadences and insistent repetitions form a verbal construct of considerable harmony and poise. Once again we encounter the paradox: the language tells us of an "out there," a "dehors" that refuses to stay put: "Dehors il pleut, dehors on marche sous la pluie . . . dehors il fait froid, le vent souffle dans les feuilles. . . . Dehors il y a du soleil, il n'y a pas un arbre . . ." The transformations recorded here are proper to language, but not to landscape as we know it. What is most arresting about this opening gambit is the extent to which Robbe-Grillet puts his cards on the table; we have both the landscape and the writerly "source" of it: "Je suis seul ici, maintenant, bien à l'abri." There is a crying distinction between the "je" who is cozy inside, and the "on" who is outside, endlessly walking, having to deal with the peculiar weather pattern that either Robbe-Grillet or "je" has given him. The entire novel is caught in these lines, not only its fable of the displaced, wandering soldier, but more interestingly its verbal inventiveness, its metamorphic style that rings changes in the outside world as easily as putting words on the page. What is also sensed here is the murderous potential of such a writing strategy, for the characters in novels have to negotiate the "scene" that is laid out for them, and in this novel, the single greatest burden for the protagonist is to find his way, to get out of the moving labyrinth that is being constructed for him on every page. Imagine, for a second, a mobile London for Pip or a moving Paris for Rastignac; Dickens and Balzac are committed to seeing clear, and they are not about to move their setting, since their goal is to open up the eyes of their young protagonists to that setting, to its moral configuration. We have something quite different here, and it is essential to see that the innovation is more than belletristic, more than a new style. The rigorous propriety of the writing, the firm control and the regulated changes it displays, these features of authority not only contrast with the helplessness and homelessness of the protagonist; they *constitute* the dilemma of the protagonist.

In many of the best *nouveaux romans* written in the 1950s and 60s one finds what might be called narrational terrorism, a kind of fiction in which the character is systematically undone by the "manner" of the text. The myopic, quasi-biological scrutiny that characterizes the work of Nathalie Sarraute, the unswerving focus on what she called, some fifty years ago, the "tropisms," are the predictable modus operandi of a body of work in which loss of identity and erosion of form are among the principal crises. The same kind of analysis is applicable to the texts of Michel Butor: his experiments with the "vous" narrative in *La Modification* are exquisitely designed to teach a lesson to his protagonist, poor man, who thought he could break free from his wife and home, little knowing that he is a pawn in a labyrinth-fiction that will lushly and mercilessly expose his lack of authority and maneuvering room. Finally, there is the fiction of Claude Simon, a writer of undeniable pathos and tragic vision, in which the power of language has *partie liéé* with the undoing of character. More even than the others, Simon reveres the sovereignty of his verbal medium, loves puns and word play, outdoes Faulkner with his endless present participles and gerund constructions, creates a heady prose that seems downright autogenerative, so enamored is it of its own fabrications, its own potency. And although he has a kind of moral seriousness and absolute honesty that are lacking in Robbe-Grillet's work, Simon's books nonetheless stage a kind of warfare, are usually devoted to some kind of defeat, most often at the hands of natural process, a frenzied, speeded-up entropic scheme in which all constructs (rational or moral or physical) collapse, are shown to be futile; it is doubtless this view of life which accounts for the odd heroics of Simon's style, his visible effort to meet chaos by capturing it within his words.

There is no seeing clear in this kind of work. You cannot *live* in these mobile settings. These remarks hardly constitute a criticism of such art, for we have learned to see the world a little bit differently, thanks to the *nouveau roman*. But it is important to give proper due to their stylistic innovations, to see how their narrative experiments impinge on the sanctity of their characters. (Taken to its logical extreme, this argument probably goes right into madness, since any narrative style could be shown to be more "active," more of a player and a determinant, in the events of the story than we had realized; consider *La Princesse de Clèves* or *The Return of the Native* or *Madame Bovary* in this light, and you will see a peculiar dialectic between character-exploitation and authorial style.) The revelatory text has little appeal to an age that no longer believes in secrets, that no longer conceives of the novel as a document for self-instruction. The *nouveau roman* certainly opens up the picture of where we keep house, but when the smoke clears, there is usually no self sufficiently intact left to live there. And perhaps that is what these books have still to teach us: that the self is a fiction, that the sky is always falling in, that both London and Paris are on the move. The scene out there is energized, can be looked at in more than thirteen ways, contains a great deal that cannot ordinarily be perceived at all. The Swedish poet Lars

Gustafsson has written a poem called "San Francisco Sailing on under the Earth," and its last lines read:

> If you keep quiet you can hear the Creoles dancing.
>
> Schooners, galleons, four-masters, barks
> whole city districts consist of sunken ships
>
> filled with sand, anchored like sisters
> close to one another.
>
> All of the Embarcadero rests on a subterranean fleet.
>
> The Pan Am Building, the Bank of America
> the skyscrapers are standing on decks far down in the depths
>
> *and that fleet sails on under the earth.*[27]

Mies van der Rohe and Le Corbusier could not have suspected that their edifices went quite so deep into our turf. In this expanded economy, the old units of measure no longer obtain. The textual scene has become multilayered, often bordering on the fantastic, going beyond the scope of any single subject. "Seeing clear" can no longer mean that there is an individual left at the far side of the text who has "educationally" ingested everything the text had to offer. The self is no longer a viable frame for the vistas that are unfurling.

For a final text that recasts the drama of seeing clear onto an altered and expanded stage, it seems fitting to examine a few passages of Italo Calvino's *Invisible Cities*. In reading Calvino, one remembers the lines of Stevens: "Natives of poverty, children of malheur / The gaiety of language is our seigneur." Language, in this text, dances and preens throughout, joyously committed at once to demonstrating and outperforming the empire of the Khan, to building a world of its own, to making visible all those invisible cities which exist in, around, above, below, in front of, and behind us. Kublai Khan, the richest and most powerful of mortals, is poor in comparison to Marco Polo, who plays out Ibsen's master builder a century later, moving beyond castles into entire metropolises in the air. Polo makes us understand that we are natives of poverty, with our eyes and ordinary systems of measurement, because we make no place for desire or memory, cannot imagine alternative worlds. Echoing Ibsen's "Gi plads!" "make space!" he closes his book of parables with the exhortation, "dargli

27. Lars Gustafsson, *Warm Rooms and Cold*, trans. Yvonne Sandstroem (Providence, R.I.: Copper Beach Press, 1975), p. 38.

spazio": "*cercare e saper riconoscere chi e cosa, in mezzo all'inferno, non è inferno, e farlo durare, e dargli spazio*" (*seek and learn to recognize who and what, in the midst of the inferno, are not inferno, then make them endure, give them space*).[28]

The space that is made and the vistas that are achieved in Calvino's book are produced by language, not by explorers or contractors or architects. But the beauty of *Invisible Cities* lies in the way its constructs of imagination intersect with our buildings of stone, how its word-world adds precious data to our everyday agenda. One of his most delightful and impudent parables has to do with the city of Sophronia, a place

> di due mezze città. In una c'e il grande ottovolante dalle ripide gobbe, la giostra con la raggiera di catene, la ruota delle gabbie girevoli, il pozzo della morte coi motociclisti a testa in giú, la cupola del circo col grappolo dei trapezi che pende in mezzo. L'altra mezza città è di pietra e marmo e cemento, con la banca, gli opifici, i palazzi, il mattatoio, la scuola e tutto il resto. Una delle mezze città è fissa, l'altra è provvisoria e quando il tempo della sua sosta è finito la schiodano, la smontano e la portano via, per trapiantarla nei terreni vaghi d'un'altra mezza città. [69]

> [made up of two half-cities. In one there is the great roller coaster with steep humps, the carousel with its chain spokes, the Ferris wheel of spinning cages, the death-ride with crouching motorcyclists, the big top with the clump of trapezes hanging in the middle. The other half-city is of stone and marble and cement, with the bank, the factories, the palaces, the slaughterhouse, the school and all the rest. One of the half-cities is permanent, the other is temporary, and when the period of its sojourn is over, they uproot it, dismantle it, and take it off, transplanting it to the vacant lots of another half-city. (63)]

Has there ever been a reader who did not second-guess the author here, who did not know that the permanent city of stone and marble

28. Italo Calvino, *Le città invisibili* (Turin: Einaudi, 1972), p. 170. Subsequent quotations will be taken from this edition and noted parenthetically in the body of the text. The English version that follows is that of William Weaver (*Invisible Cities* [New York: Harcourt, Brace & Jovanovich, 1978], p. 165); subsequent English versions will be taken from this edition and noted parenthetically in the body of the text.

and cement and factories, banks, and palaces was the Real World, whereas the temporary realm of roller coasters and carousels and trapezes stands for the frills of art, the weekend entertainment when the week's work is done? Ha. The second paragraph suavely begins:

> Cosí ogni anno arriva il giorno in cui i manovali staccano i frontoni di marmo, calano i muri di pietra, i piloni di cemento, smontano il ministero, il monumento, i docks, la raffineria di petrolio, l'ospedale, li caricano sui rimorchi, per seguire di piazza in piazza l'itinerario d'ogni anno. [69]

> [And so every year the day comes when the workmen remove the marble pediments, lower the stone walls, the cement pylons, take down the Ministry, the monument, the docks, the petroleum refinery, the hospital, load them on trailers, to follow from stand to stand their annual itinerary. (63)]

These are the kinds of reversals of which Calvino is capable, and he is saying something serious in his fun-and-games: namely that fun-and-games, the play of society, the arenas of adventure and chance, the freedom of the *carnaval*, are arguably the enduring bases of human life, the "facts of life," rather than its escapist fictions.

Calvino radically challenges our sense of propriety, of what the rules are. In a light, festive way, he undertakes to knock the props out from us no less than Sophocles tragically did in his story of incest and parricide. Seeing clear, in this sparkling text, entails opening oneself to fiction and realizing that the dreary cause-and-effect world of realism might be a limited, constrictive environment. Calvino expands our sense of the possible, and, by showing that desire and language spawn the very realms in which we live, he dramatically increases the size of our holdings, the parameters of our estate. As a way of bringing this argument to a close, I would like to return to Stevens' dictum: "The gaiety of language is our seigneur," and to insist on gaiety as the legacy with which Calvino's stories leave us. His is a vision of language-as-happiness, of the creations of language as joyous celebrations, and as such, it contrasts sharply with the darker machinations of Robbe-Grillet or the tragic dilemmas of Claude Simon. Let us consider, in this light, his treatment of the city of Raissa, a city where "life is not happy," a place where nothing goes right: crying children, smashed fingers, bad dreams, errors in your figures, quarrels and broken dishes. Calvino introduces into this world of broken connections the fiction of relationship, and he does so as pure verbal chain:

> Eppure, a Raissa, a ogni momento, c'è un bambino che da una finestra ride a un cane che è saltato su una tettoia per mordere un pezzo di polenta caduto a un muratore che dall'alto dell'impalcatura ha esclamato:—Gioia mia, lasciami intingere!— a una giovane ostessa che solleva un piatto di ragú sotto la pergola, contenta de servirlo all'ombrellaio che festeggia un buon affare, un parasole di pizzo bianco comprato da una gran dama per pavoneggiarsi alle corse, innamorata d'un ufficiale che le ha sorriso nel saltare l'ultima siepe, felice lui ma piú felice ancora il suo cavallo che volava sugli ostacoli vedendo volare in cielo un francolino, felice uccello liberato dalla gabbia da un pittore felice d'averlo dipinto piuma per piuma picchiettato di rosso e di giallo nella miniatura di quella pagina del libro in cui il filosofo dice: "Anche a Raissa, città triste, corre un filo invisibile che allaccia un essere vivente a un altro per un attimo e si disfa, poi torna a tendersi tra punti in movimento disegnando nuove rapide figure cossiché a ogni secondo la città infelice contiene una città felice che nemmeno sa d'esistere." [154–55]

> [And yet, in Raissa, at every moment there is a child in a window who laughs seeing a dog that has jumped on a shed to bite into a piece of polenta dropped by a stonemason who has shouted from the top of the scaffolding, "Darling, let me dip into it," to a young serving-maid who holds up a dish of ragout under the pergola, happy to serve it to the umbrella-maker who is celebrating a successful transaction, a white lace parasol brought to display at the races by a great lady in love with an officer who has smiled at her taking the last jump, happy man, and still happier his horse, flying over the obstacles, seeing a francolin flying in the sky, happy bird freed from its cage by a painter happy at having painted it feather by feather, speckled with red and yellow in the illumination of that page in the volume where the philosopher says, "Also in Raissa, city of sadness, there runs an invisible thread that binds one living being to another for a moment, then unravels, then is stretched again between moving points as it draws new and rapid patterns so that

> at every second the unhappy city contains a happy city unaware of its own existence." (148–49)]

This is a game every child has played, probably in a collaborative mode with others in a ring, the challenge of keeping your sentence open, finding some narrative glue that lets you continue, moving through an itinerary that has no end in sight so long as the imagination works. The passage deals with nurturance and giving, with the very dynamic of nurturance and giving, and its real theme, its underlying "thread," its "filo invisibile" is happiness. The happiness that is gradually surfacing in this sad city is the happiness of connection, the elemental joy in putting things together, and it is demonstrably a form of freedom, a way to fly, to leave one's cage; but it is equally clear that its ultimate locus is on the earth as well as in the sky, among and between people: brief, moving, possibly fictive moments of relationship where one sees and feels the invisible thread.

Many other writers—from North and South, and from East and West—might be brought into this discussion, because the older revelatory text no longer seems credible in the modernist literary climate. In the newer literature, one sees a celebration of authorial freedom, as well as the creation of a world that is strangely active and charged, and in these realms space and time no longer behave as they did in "realist" texts, and the old cause-and-effect logic has lost much of its former authority. Science-fiction and utopian writers have created their own repertories here, as have the "magic realists" and the American "fabulators," and it is probably fair to say that many more surprises are still in store for us. There will be ecological fictions which are still more drastically non-anthropocentric than the suspect work of Robbe-Grillet, fictions which somehow render the teeming life of the universe in such a way that the self and its projects finally take up no more space than is their due. There will doubtless be fictions which reflect the newer storage-and-retrieval procedures of the computers, animated by radically new notions of sequence and arrangement. There will be "piggyback" fictions that engage in time-loops, that replicate the shifting from one dimension to another, just as we already see in our computer graphics or in such films as *Tron* or *The Purple Rose of Cairo*. Such art will deeply challenge our sense of things, because it will generate its own reality-constructs, making it necessary for us to develop new models of coherence and propriety. It is possible that such art will seem disturbingly coercive (as in much of the *nouveau roman*), since design will everywhere predominate. But it is also possible that such art will challenge its readers to posit new connections on their own, to establish, affirm, and believe in linkages of their own devising, just as they do in their own lives. If so, the fiction of relationship will assume the centrality it deserves, as a process of discovery and also a process of creation.

Conclusion

Ever since Homer constructed the *Iliad*, we have known that literature did not begin at the beginning. Flaubert sounded the modern note, a good century ago, by pointing out the idiocy of conclusions. As some kind of distilled wisdom or bottom-line logic, conclusions are no longer in good odor. But endings are real nonetheless, in books and elsewhere, and no amount of sophistication or circular thinking will put this chapter anywhere else. What, then, do the preceding chapters point to?

Perhaps the more appropriate question is: Do these chapters suggest something coherent, when seen together? More than anything else, I would argue that this book is about seeing things together. So, let this be a conclusion in the horizontal rather than the vertical sense, a widening of perspective and a corraling of views, rather than a deepening of issues. Seeing things together characterizes every operation both shown in this study and lurking behind this study: *relationship* is a composite form, and the chapters all deal with the ways in which individuals are linked with other individuals and with their environment; each chapter also focuses on disparate texts, frequently texts with radically different provenances. In attempting to counterpoint these texts in such a way as to propose a composite of its own, this study has been an overt exercise in comparative criticism, in the ways that we can link artworks together and discover them anew. Finally, this book stems from a belief that art extends our private view of things, that we read novels in order to see more; and complementing that readerly principle is a personal one: we achieve love and knowledge only by stretching the self, opening it to the world of others, establishing through our energy or our love or our life some link with those others. All of these issues belong in my conclusion, and all of them involve seeing things together. Let us begin to look at them.

This book and the books it undertakes to discuss, all depend, albeit in varying ways, on a simple truth, one that accompanies us from birth to grave: we can see only with our own eyes, think with our own minds, feel with our own bodies. Life enmeshes us with one another and with the world; we are constantly part of a larger scene, either seeking or stumbling into or discovering (with hindsight) the phenomenon of linkage. It is both humbling and exhilarating to discern the lines of this larger picture, to see, through the agency of literature, how the self longs for union but is blind to the reality of the other; how the self evolves over time while remaining linked to another; how the self is involved in "breaking-and-entering" schemes, be they erotic, chemical, or ideological; how the self comes to adequate knowledge of the other only by becoming that other, and the cost of such transformation; how the self may apprehend—with joy or with misery, as heaven or as hell—the larger configuration of which it is a part; how the self goes about the world taking measure—of itself and of its world—finding what it can assimilate, what it must avoid, what it can invent. Such are the ventures central to the chapters of this study. To encounter these ventures through fiction is humbling, because one's own day-to-day grasp of such matters is so murky, so much in the middle, and because the novelist—even the meanest-spirited of them—gives us light and makes us see our darkness, offers us a model of our situational drama, makes us sense, through the resources of narrative, that figure in our carpet which must elude us as we live. I hope that something like exhilaration has been experienced in engaging these fictions, an exhilaration that is proper to art itself: namely the discovery that each of these texts is peculiarly suited to tell us something we cannot hear and show us something we cannot see. Such an attitude toward art may seem idolatrous to those who are committed to deconstruction, but it may be time to celebrate art rather than peering behind (or beneath or above or beyond) it, to experience its vision (to experience its blindness) because we are short on experience, to take what it offers (rather than seeking what it conceals), to take it as the greatest of "unnatural" resources, as a tool for widening and deepening our estate, for giving us essentially what Moll Flanders wished for her own readers: "a clearer sight into things to come, than they had here, and a dark view of their own concern in them" (225).

If we borrow a term that smacks of an earlier decade, it is possible to designate what I have been calling a "composite" or "larger view" as an *ecosystem*. This notion will effectively cover all of our bases: the characters within a text inhabit such an ecosystem, one that contains their individual perspective and their private projects within its larger constellation; literature itself is, as Eliot suggested many years ago, an ecosystem, consisting of all the works that have ever been written, so that novels published today exist in some viable continuum with works of the past, and there are hence no hard-and-fast rules as to what fits with what.[1] Following hard on that premise is the notion that literary criticism, especially comparative criticism, is in the service of these constellations or ecosystems, and that such service can be of at least two kinds: the *revelatory* kind, which illuminates the "known" interactions between texts (such as the study of periods or schools or movements or influences of any type), and the *generative* kind, which posits lines of its own between apparently dissimilar texts. This second kind of comparative criticism will then fashion some kind of meta-text, a construct that is based on the (argued) commonality of these materials. Each chapter of this study seeks to articulate such a meta-text, and it goes one step further by believing, provisionally, in the "laws" it founds, by assessing the single novels in the light of these larger, shared principles which enable the comparison in the first place. In short, the ecosystem need not be tryannically binding, a Dedalean maze that imprisons the individual text, but rather a flexible consort, a resilient construct of the mind, a putative notion of a "working" wholeness.

The liability of such creative ecosystems is that they may be arbitrary, even preposterous, misguided *idées fixes*, felt to be unconvincing "containers" of the materials in question, felt to offer little purchase on the issues under discussion. That is a risk which I have taken again and again in this study, and only the reader knows whether it was worth taking. The benefits of such a notion are several: it lifts texts out of the small home we are accustomed to giving them; it may reveal unsuspected kinships and new features of items (texts and also individuals) we thought we knew; it offers a kind of capaciousness

1. T. S. Eliot, "Tradition and the Individual Talent," reprinted in *Visions and Revisions in Modern American Literary Criticism*, eds. Bernard Oldsley and Arthur O. Lewis, Jr. (New York: Dutton, 1962), pp. 71–80. Eliot would have choked at the word, "ecosystem," but his meaning is unmistakably oriented in the same direction: "The existing monuments form an ideal order among themselves, which is modified by the introduction of the new (the really new) work of art among them. The existing order is complete before the new work arrives; for order to persist after the supervention of novelty, the *whole* existing order must be, if ever so slightly, altered; and so the relations, proportions, values of each work of art toward the whole are readjusted. Whoever has approved this idea of order, of the form of European, of English literature, will not find it preposterous that the past should be altered by the present as much as the present is directed by the past" (p. 73).

and multiple perspective that "positions" the elements of each book, is capable of honoring the individual contours while at the same time integrating it into something larger than itself, thereby approximating somewhat more closely our own position in the world. This kind of criticism makes continuously visible the tension between freedom and bondage, an "Olympian" freedom enjoyed by the observer-maker-critic and a sobering ecological "fit" for the creature inside. Those two issues, the *freedom* of interpretation and the *connectedness* of the individual text—indeed, of the individual person—have been the guiding and enabling principles of this book; they are the two reasons why it was written: to seek a freer kind of criticism, to give to the relationship theme some of the richness, pathos, and cautionary power it deserves. Ultimately, this view of literature and life as ecosystem is at once invigorating and arresting: invigorating because it surrounds us with neighbors we never knew we had, and arresting because it surrounds us with neighbors we never knew we had.

It is clear enough to any reader who has read this study up to this point that "ecosystem" is hardly a scientific or rigorous concept, and it is used to indicate a spectrum of constellations: the larger environment that a text offers its characters, the construct provided by juxtaposed texts, the wider design that art itself offers to living readers, giving them that unique "dark view" in things to come and in their own lives. The ecosystem is of especial value in studying the fortunes of the couple. Here is where the single vision is at once authoritative and painfully insufficient: the hunger of the self and the individual consciousness are the only vehicles for presenting this story, both rhetorically and essentially, if it is to be conveyed to a reader and to exist at all. As we witness the ways in which the text enmeshes, rewards, traps, coerces, liberates, and alters its protagonists, we cannot fail to see our own lives writ large, caught in that relational mesh that we inhabit and experience but do not see. The story of the couple is fabricated frequently out of individual desire—for this is the most powerful force which links people—but it takes place on a map and involves elements over which and whom personal desire has no control. If anything has emerged from these essays, it should be a more chastened sense of our "involvements" with others, involvements having nothing to do with desire or choice, but emerging simply from our status as co-players on a large stage. It is good to see the kinds of collision and interactions such a schema presents, for a number of reasons: (1) the world and the other are *real*, with a dimensionality of their own, and not merely objects of our desire; (2) in seeing how beleaguered relationship is, how problematic it is, how beset it is by alterity and time, I would like to think that we acquire a deeper, more abiding reverence and awe for it than we initially had. Given that the term itself—relationship—is such a trivialized concept in today's culture, I will be happy if this study helps to illuminate the many ways in which linkage constitutes both the fact and the fiction of our lives.

In the 1950s, Ian Watt argued that *Moll Flanders* called a particular bluff of the European novel, namely its (bogus) claim that relationship was the be-all and end-all of life; Moll's career, Watt claimed, brought one back to basics, removed the accessories from the stage, and demonstrated that the survival of the individual was the real story of the day, Defoe's day and our own. Some thirty years after Watt, I would like to suggest that the fiction of relationship addresses issues that will emerge as dominant in the latter part of our century. Relationship betokens, as we have had ample opportunity to note, an end to the blindness and hegemony of the self, a fuller recognition that the other is both real and linked to us. The massive revisions of history and culture that have been made possible by Marxist criticism, feminist studies, and minority views have underscored the myopia, lopsidedness, and complacency of much mainstream criticism, have shown that most notions of "representative" experience are demonstrably partial, often cyclopic, leaving entire populations out of their investigation. New histories are being written, new voices are heard. There is, as there should be, much stridency, indeed much "separatism" in all this.

But, as has been stated, one of the greatest enemies of political change is blindness, not malice, the blindness and complacency of the imperialist self—all too often a privileged white-male figure—who has never grasped the injustice or the poverty of his self-enclosed world view. By now it should be clear that the theme of connection is a sociopolitical theme, every bit as much as it is a psychological one. The ecological scheme that it draws from informs the major issues of our time: the geopolitical conflicts, the North/South and the East/West axes, the stewardship of the environment and of the planet. These are sweeping generalizations, patently ideological in nature, involving large sociocultural issues that have not been much talked about in this book, but they condition the world in which universities exist and literary criticism is written. There is something, therefore, to be said for the very notion of linkage. We need, in addition to the "separatist" studies that are everywhere appearing and challenging the canons and the assumptions of entire fields, "connective," comparatist studies as well, studies of a "linking" nature that move toward synthesis at every level: in their choice of materials, in their view of the subject, in their own critical strategy. Understanding of the other will be brought about only when the individualist code is challenged and altered. And, at bottom that is a perceptual matter. *The Fiction of Relationship* is about that issue: the challenging and altering of individual perception, the need to recognize that the self is part of a larger world. That lesson begins at home; it ends by redefining home.

Some final words are in order about the manner of this study. The personal, self-dramatizing narrative style is fully intended to convey the feel and the texture of the private view; it has its place in this study, and I make no apologies for it. As for the freewheeling strategy of grouping together texts from different eras and cultures, several arguments have already been made. In closing, however, I would like, once more, to invoke Borges' lovely essay "Kafka and His Precursors." There we see a brilliant kind of cubistic history: a sequence of writers, ranging from Zeno to Chesterton who *acquire* a family resemblance, a kind of intellectual or spiritual kinship by virtue of the writings of one Franz Kafka, coming after all of them, indebted to none of them. Kafka, as Borges writes, "creates his precursors." Borges' story has always seemed to me emblematic of the openness of literature and the freedom of criticism. Lines of kinship do not have to proceed linearly, over time, genealogically; they can also go backward or spiral or pirouette. Works of art are so rich, so unbounded, possessed of so much more than the historian or critic can account for, that we absolutely must be free to poach in their preserves; to take from them more than their name, rank, or serial number; to link them in new ways; to illuminate features of them that may have gone unnoticed; and to supply them ultimately with strange bedfellows if we so choose, because every liberty we can possibly take with them is still an act of homage, a way of taking them seriously. So, it follows that comparative literature is quintessentially an exercise in freedom, a way of "forging" connections between texts that are divided by history and language. Comparative literature allows us to respond fully to the world of literature by having our own shaping say; it reveres the texts it studies by linking them and creating a fiction of relationship.

WORKS CONSULTED

Arrowsmith, William. "The Criticism of Greek Tragedy." Cook 154–69.

Artaud, Antonin. *Le Théâtre et son double*. Paris: Gallimard, 1964.

Auerbach, Erich. *Mimesis: The Representation of Reality in Western Literature*. New York: Doubleday, 1957.

Barthes, Roland. "Littérature objective." *Essais critiques*. Paris: Seuil, 1964.

—— *Le Plaisir du texte*. Paris: Seuil, 1973.

—— *Sade, Fourier, Loyola*. Paris: Seuil, 1971.

Bass, Alan, trans. *Writing and Difference*, by Jacques Derrida. Chicago: University of Chicago Press, 1978.

Beaver, Harold. "Introduction." Melville 9–50.

Beckett, Samuel. *Molloy*. Paris: 10/18, 1963.

Bersani, Leo. *Balzac to Beckett: Center and Circumference in French Fiction*. New York: Oxford University Press, 1970.

—— *A Future for Astyanax*. Boston: Little, Brown, 1976.

—— *Marcel Proust: The Fictions of Life and of Art*. New York: Oxford University Press, 1965.

Blanchot, Maurice. "D'un art sans avenir." *Le Livre à venir*. Paris: Gallimard, 1959. 195–201.

Blewett, David. *Defoe's Art of Fiction*. Toronto: University of Toronto Press, 1979.

Bliss, Michael. "The Orchestration of Chaos in William Burroughs' *Naked Lunch*." *enclitic* 1, 1 (1977): 59–69.

Borges, Jorge Luis. *Borges: Narraciones*. Ed. Marcos Ricardo Barnatán. Madrid: Cátedra, 1981.

—— *Borges: Sus mejores páginas*. Ed. Miguel Enguídanos. Englewood Cliffs: Prentice-Hall, 1970.

—— *La muerte y la brújula*. Buenos Aires: Emecé, 1951.

—— *Obras completas*. Buenos Aires: Emecé, 1957–1960. 9 vols.

—— *Otras inquisiciones*. In *Obras completas*. Buenos Aires: Emecé, 1960.

Boris Vian: Colloque de Cérisy. Proceedings of *Colloque du Centre culturel international de Cérisy-La-Salle, 23 juillet au 2 août 1976*. Paris: 10/18, 1977. 2 vols.

Bradbook, M. C. *Ibsen the Norwegian: A Revaluation*. London: Chatto & Windus, 1948.

Brandell, Gunnar. *Strindberg in Inferno*. Trans. Barry Jacobs. Cambridge: Harvard University Press, 1974.

Brooks, Cleanth. *William Faulkner: The Yoknapatawpha Country*. New Haven: Yale University Press, 1963.

Brustein, Robert. *The Theater of Revolt*. Boston: Little, Brown, 1964.
Burroughs, William. *Naked Lunch*. New York: Grove Press, 1959.
Calvino, Italo. *Le città invisibili*. Turin: Einaudi, 1972.
Cameron, Alister. *The Identity of Oedipus the King*. New York: New York University Press, 1968.
Carlson, Harry G., trans. *Strindberg: Five Plays*, by August Strindberg. New York: New American Library, 1984.
Carlyle, Thomas. "Typhus Fever in Edinburgh." Dickens 912–13.
Clements, Robert J. *Comparative Literature as Academic Discipline*. New York: Modern Language Association of America, 1978.
Cohen, J. M. *Jorge Luis Borges*. New York: Harper & Row, 1974.
Cook, Albert, ed. *Oedipus Rex: A Mirror for Greek Drama*. Prospect Heights, Ill.: Waveland Press, 1982.
Costes, Alain. "Le Désir de Colin." *Boris Vian: Colloque de Cérisy 1* 169–77.
—— "L'Écume du corps." *Boris Vian: Colloque de Cérisy 1* 111–36.
Curtis, Laura. *The Elusive Daniel Defoe*. London: Vision Press, 1984.
Defoe, Daniel. *Moll Flanders*. Ed. Edward Kelly. New York: Norton, 1973.
DeJean, Joan. *Literary Fortifications: Rousseau, Laclos, Sade*. Princeton: Princeton University Press, 1984.
Deleuze, Gilles. *Proust et les signes*. Paris: P.U.F., 1970.
Derrida, Jacques. "La Parole soufflée." Bass 169–95.
—— "The Theater of Cruelty and the Closure of Representation." Bass 232–50.
Dibattista, Maria. "*To the Lighthouse*: Virginia Woolf's Winter's Tale." *Virginia Woolf: Revaluation and Continuity*. Ed. Ralph Freedman. Berkeley: University of California Press, 1980.
Dickens, Charles. *Bleak House*. Eds. George Ford and Sylvère Monod. New York: Norton, 1977.
Dillingham, William. *Melville's Short Fiction, 1853–1856*. Athens: University of Georgia Press, 1977.
Durbach, Errol. "Introduction." *Ibsen and the Theater*, by Durbach. New York: New York University Press, 1980.
Eliot, T. S. "Tradition and the Individual Talent." *Selected Essays*, by Eliot. London: Faber & Faber, 1932. (Repr. in *Visions and Revisions in Modern American Literary Criticism*. Eds. Bernard Oldsley and Arthur O. Lewis, Jr. New York: Dutton, 1962. 71–80).
Faulkner, William. *Absalom, Absalom*! New York: Modern Library, 1951.
—— *As I Lay Dying*. New York: Vintage Books, 1957.
—— *Light in August*. New York: Modern Libary, 1950.
Flaubert, Gustave. *Madame Bovary*. Paris: Garnier Flammarion, 1966.
Ford, Ford Madox. *The Good Soldier*. New York: Vintage Books, 1951.
Foucault, Michel. *Histoire de la sexualité*. Paris: Gallimard, 1976 and 1984. 2 vols.

—— *Les Mots et les choses*. Paris: Gallimard, 1966.

Free, Lloyd, ed. *Laclos: Critical Approaches to* Les Liaisons dangereuses. Madrid: Ediciones José Porrúa Turanzas, 1978.

Genette, Gérard. *Figures*. Paris: Seuil, 1966.

—— *Figures II*. Paris: Seuil, 1969.

—— *Figures III*. Paris: Seuil, 1972.

—— "Proust et le langage indirect." *Figures II* 287–91.

—— "Proust palimpseste." *Figures* 39–65.

—— "Silences de Flaubert." *Figures* 223–43.

—— "Sur Robbe-Grillet." *Tel Quel* 8 (Winter 1962): 34–44.

—— "l'Utopie littéraire." *Figures* 123–32.

—— "Vertige fixé" (*postface*). *Dans le labyrinthe*, by Robbe-Grillet. Paris: 10/18, 1964.

Girard, René. *Mensonge romantique et vérité romanesque*. Paris: Grasset, 1961.

Goethe, Johann Wolfgang. *Die Leiden des jungen Werther*. In *Gedenkausgabe der Werke, Briefe und Gespräche*. Zurich: Artemis Verlag, 1953. 24 vols.

Gray, Ronald. *Ibsen: A Dissenting View*. Cambridge, Eng.: Cambridge University Press, 1977.

Gustafsson, Lars. *Strandhugg i Svensk Poesi*. Kristianstad: F.I.B., 1977.

—— *Warm Rooms and Cold*. Trans. Yvonne Sandstroem. Providence, R.I.: Copper Beach Press, 1975.

Hynes, Samuel. "The Epistemology of *The Good Soldier*." *Ford Madox Ford: Modern Judgements*. Ed. Richard Cassell. London: Macmillan, 1972.

Ibsen, Henrik. *Ghosts*. Meyer, *Ibsen: Plays*, vol. I, 27–98.

—— *Lady from the Sea*. Meyer, *Ibsen: Plays*, vol. III, 127–209.

—— *The Master Builder*. Meyer, *Ibsen: Plays*, vol. I, 245–319.

—— *Rosmersholm*. Meyer, *Ibsen: Plays*, vol. III, 31–110.

—— *Samlede Vaerker*, vols. 4 and 5. Kristiania: Gyldendalske Boghandel, 1908. 5 vols.

Irwin, John. *Doubling and Incest, Repetition and Revenge: A Speculative Reading of Faulkner*. Baltimore: Johns Hopkins University Press, 1975.

Jaspers, Karl. *Strindberg und Van Gogh: Versuch einer pathographischen Analyse unter vergleichender Heranziehung von Swedenborg und Hölderlin*. Munich: Piper, 1950.

Johnson, J. Theodore Jr. "Against 'Saint' Proust." *The Art of the Proustian Novel Reconsidered*. Ed. Lawrence D. Joiner. Proceedings of the First Winthrop Symposium on Major Modern Writers, 1978. Rock Hill, S.C.: Winthrop College, 1979.

Joyce, James. *Ulysses*. New York: Vintage Books, 1961.

Kafka, Franz. "In der Strafkolonie." Raabe 100–123.

—— "Die Verwandlung." Raabe 56–99.

Kayser, Wolfgang. "Entstehung von Goethes *Werther*." *Deutsche*

Vierteljahrsschrift für Literaturwissenschaft und Geitesgeschichte 19 (1941): 430–51.

Kenner, Hugh. *Joyce's Voices*. Berkeley: University of California Press, 1978.

Laclos, Choderlos de. *Les Liaisons dangereuses*. Paris: Garnier Flammarion, 1964.

Lagercrantz, Olof. *August Strindberg*. Stockholm: Wahlström & Widstrand, 1979.

Lamm, Martin. *Strindberg och makterna*. Uppsala: Svenska Kyrkans Diakonistryrelses Bokförlag, 1936.

Lattimore, Richmond, "*Oedipus Tyrannus*." O'Brien 41–48.

Mann, Thomas. "Goethes *Werther*." *Goethe im XX Jahrhundert: Spiegelungen und Deutungen*. Ed. Hans Mayer. Hamburg: Christian Wegner Verlag, 1967.

Meixner, John. *Ford Madox Ford's Novels, A Critical Study*. Minneapolis: University of Minnesota Press, 1962.

Melville, Herman. *Billy Budd, Sailor and Other Stories*. Ed. Harold Beaver. Harmondsworth, Eng.: Penguin, 1967.

Meyer, Michael, trans. *Ibsen: Plays*. London: Eyre Methuen, 1980. 4 vols.

—— "Introduction." *The Ghost Sonata*, by August Strindberg. In *The Plays of Strindberg*, ed. Meyer, vol. 1. New York: Vintage Books, 1964. 419–24

—— *Strindberg: A Biography*. New York: Random House, 1985.

Moore, Fernanda. "On *Naked Lunch*." Unpublished essay, 1986.

Morrissette, Bruce. *Les Romans de Robbe-Grillet*. Paris: Editions de Minuit, 1965.

Mottram, Eric. *William Burroughs: The Algebra of Need*. London: Marion & Boyars, 1977.

Mulvey, Laura. "Visual Pleasure and Narrative Cinema." *Screen* 16 (Autumn 1975): 6–18.

"*Naked Lunch* on Trial." Excerpts from Attorney General vs. A Book Named *Naked Lunch*, Supreme Court of Massachusetts 1966 (Repr. in Burroughs vii–xxxvi).

Naremore, James. *The World without a Self*. New Haven: Yale University Press, 1973.

Nicod-Saraiva, Marguerite. "L'Ecume des jours, Un Univers stratifié." *Boris Vian: Colloque de Cérisy I* 139–48.

Novak, Maxmillian E. "Defoe's 'Indifferent Monitor': The Complexity of *Moll Flanders*." *Eighteenth-Century Studies* 3, 3 (Spring 1970): 351–59, 365 (Repr. in Defoe 414–21).

O'Brien, Michael J., ed. *Twentieth Century Interpretations of* Oedipus Rex. Englewood Cliffs: Prentice-Hall, 1968.

Palka, Keith. "Chance as a Means of Balancing a Closed Ecological System." Free 137–66.

Politzer, Heinz. *Franz Kafka: Parable and Paradox*. Ithaca: Cornell University Press, 1966.

Prévost, Abbé. *Manon Lescaut*. Paris: Garnier Frères, 1965.

Price, Martin. *To the Palace of Wisdom: Studies in Order and Energy from Dryden to Blake*. New York: Doubleday, 1964.

Proust, Marcel. *A la Recherche du temps perdu*. Paris: Edition de la Pléiade, 1963. 3 vols.

Raabe, Paul, ed. *Franz Kafka: Sämtliche Erzählungen*. Hamburg: Fischer, 1970.

Reille, J.-Francis. *Proust: Le Temps du désir*. Paris: Editeurs Français Réunis, 1979.

Reinhardt, Karl. "*Oedipus Tryannus*: Appearance and Truth." O'Brien 49–56.

Richard, Jean-Pierre. "La Création de la forme chez Flaubert." *Littérature et sensation*. Paris: Seuil, 1954.

Riquelme, John Paul, ed. *Joyce's Dislocutions: Essays on Reading as Translation*, by Fritz Senn. Baltimore: Johns Hopkins University Press, 1984.

Robbe-Grillet, Alain. *L'Année dernière à Marienbad*. Paris: Editions de Minuit, 1961.

—— *Dans le labyrinthe*. Paris: 10/18, 1964.

—— *Projet pour une révolution à New York*. Paris: Editions de Minuit, 1970.

Rodríguez Monegal, Emir. *Borges, Hacia una lectura poética*. Madrid: Ediciones Guadarrama, 1976.

Rolleston, James. *Kafka's Narrative Theater*. University Park: Pennsylvania State University Press, 1974.

Rosbottom, Ronald. "Dangerous Connections: A Communicational Approach to *Les Liaisons dangereuses*." Free 183–221.

Rougemont, Denis de. *Love in the Western World*. Trans. Montgomery Belgion. New York: Pantheon, 1956.

Rybalka, Michel. "*L'Ecume des jours*: Amour-fiction." *Boris Vian: Colloque de Cérisy I* 209–213.

Sandbach, Mary. "Introduction." Strindberg, *Strindberg: Inferno, From an Occult Diary*. 7–90.

Schorer, Mark. "An Interpretation." *The Good Soldier*, by Ford Madox Ford. Vintage, 1957.

—— "Technique as Discovery." *Forms of Modern Fiction*. Ed. William Van O'Conner. Bloomington: Indiana University Press, 1959.

Schroeter, James. "The Four Fathers: Symbolism in *Oedipus Rex*." *Criticism* 3, 3 (Summer 1961): 186–200 (Repr. in Cook 121–33).

Segal, Charles. "Time, Theater, and Knowledge in the Tragedy of Oedipus." *Edipo: Il teatro greco e la cultura europea*. Rome: Ateneo, 1986. 459–84.

Senn, Fritz. "Book of Many Turns." Riquelme 121–37.
—— "Nausicaa." Riquelme 160–87.
Seylaz, Jean-Luc. *Les Liaisons dangereuses et la création romanesque chez Laclos*. Geneva and Paris: Droz, 1958.
Simms, Ruth L. C., trans. *Other Inquisitions: 1937–1952*, by Jorge Luis Borges. New York: Simon & Schuster, 1968.
Slatoff, Walter. "The Edge of Order: The Pattern of Faulkner's Rhetoric." *William Faulkner: Three Decades of Criticism*. Eds. Daniel Hoffman and Olga Vickery. New York: Harcourt, Brace & World, 1960.
—— *Quest for Failure: A Study of William Faulkner*. Ithaca: Cornell University Press, 1960.
Snitow, Ann. *Ford Madox Ford and the Voice of Uncertainty*. Baton Rouge: Louisiana State University Press, 1984.
Sophocles. *Oedipus the King*, trans. David Grene. In *The Complete Greek Tragedies*. Eds. Grene and Richmond Lattimore. Chicago: University of Chicago Press, 1959. 11–76.
Spilka, Mark. "On Lily Briscoe's Borrowed Grief: A Psycho-Literary Speculation." *Criticism* 21 (Winter 1979): 1–33.
Spinchorn, Evert. *Strindberg as Dramatist*. New Haven: Yale University Press, 1982.
Steinberg, Erwin. "Die zwei Kommandanten in Kafkas 'In der Strafkolonie.' " *Franz Kafka*. Ed. Maria Luise Caputo-Mayr. Berlin: Agora Verlag, 1978.
Sterne, Laurence. *The Life and Opinions of Tristram Shandy, Gentleman*. Ed. Ian Watt. Boston: Houghton Mifflin, 1965.
Stevens, Wallace. *The Palm at the End of the Mind*. New York: Vintage Books, 1972.
Stockenström, Göran. *Ismael i Öknen: Strindberg som mystiker*. Uppsala: Acta Universitatis Upsaliensis, 1972.
Strindberg, August. *A Dream Play*. Carlson 209–274.
—— "Gatubilder III." *Strandhugg i Svensk Poesi*. Gustafsson 23.
—— *The Ghost Sonata*. Carlson 275–309.
—— *Strindberg: Inferno, From an Occult Diary*. Trans. Mary Sandbach. Harmondsworth, Eng.: Penguin, 1979.
Tanner, Tony. *Adultery in the Novel: Contract and Transgression*. Baltimore: Johns Hopkins University Press, 1979.
Terdiman, Richard. *The Dialectics of Isolation: Self and Society in the French Novel from the Realists to Proust*. New Haven: Yale University Press, 1976.
Thieberger, Richard. "The Botched Ending of 'In the Penal Colony.' " *The Kafka Debate*. Ed. Angel Flores. New York: Gordian Press, 1977.
Thorlby, Anthony. "From What Did Goethe Save Himself in 'Werther'?" *Versuche zu Goethe: Festschrift für Erich Heller*. Eds. Volker Dürr and Géza v. Molnár. Heidelberg: Lothar Stiehm Verlag, 1976.

Timm, Werner. *The Graphic Art of Edvard Munch*. Trans. Ruth Michaelis-Jena. London: Studio Vista, 1969.

Todorov, Tzvetan. "Les Catégories du récit littéraire." *Communications* 8 (1966): 125–51.

—— *Littérature et signification*. Paris: Larousse, 1967.

Trilling, Lionel. "James Joyce in His Letters." *Joyce: A Collection of Critical Essays*. Ed. William Chace. Englewood Cliffs: Prentice-Hall, 1974.

Van Ghent, Dorothy. *The English Novel: Form and Function*. New York: Harper & Row, 1953.

Vian, Boris. *L'Ecume des jours*. Paris: 10/18, 1963.

Vickers, Nancy J. "Diana Described: Scattered Woman and Scattered Rhyme." *Critical Inquiry* 8 (Winter 1981): 265–79.

Watt, Ian. *The Rise of the Novel*. Berkeley: University of California Press, 1957.

Weaver, William, trans. *Invisible Cities*, by Italo Calvino. New York: Harcourt, Brace & Jovanovich, 1978.

Weinstein, Arnold. *Fictions of the Self: 1550–1800*. Princeton: Princeton University Press, 1981.

—— "Fusion and Confusion in *Light in August*." *The Faulkner Journal* 2 (1986): 2–16.

—— *Vision and Response in Modern Fiction*. Ithaca: Cornell University Press, 1974.

Weinstein, Philip. "Precarious Sanctuaries: Protection and Exposure in Faulkner's Fiction." *Studies in American Fiction* 6 (1978): 173–91.

Weisstein, Ulrich. *Comparative Literature and Literary Theory*. Bloomington, Indiana University Press, 1973.

Woolf, Virginia. *To the Lighthouse*. New York: Harcourt, Brace & Co., 1927.

Yates, Donald, and James Irby, eds. *Labyrinths: Selected Stories and Other Writings*, by Jorge Luis Borges. New York: New Directions, 1964.

INDEX

PN 3352 .I56 W45 1988

Weinstein, Arnold.

The fiction of relationship